The Faith of a Heretic

WALTER KAUFMANN was born in Freiburg, Germany, in 1921, came to the United States in 1939, and graduated from Williams College in 1941. During World War II he served first with the U. S. Army Air Force and then returned to Europe with Military Intelligence. In 1947 he received his Ph.D. from Harvard and became an Instructor at Princeton University, where he is now Professor of Philosophy.

He has also been a visiting professor at Cornell, Columbia, The New School for Social Research, and the Universities of Michigan and Washington; and, on Fulbright grants, at the Universities of Heidelberg (1955–56) and Jerusalem (1962–63). In 1961 he was awarded an international Leo Baeck Prize. He has published a dozen books, including *Cain and Other Poems, Twenty German Poets, From Shakespeare to Existentialism* (Anchor 213), *Critique of Religion and Philosophy* (Anchor 252), and *Goethe's Faust: A New Translation* (Anchor 328).

THE FAITH OF A HERETIC

by Walter Kaufmann

ANCHOR BOOKS
DOUBLEDAY & COMPANY, INC.
GARDEN CITY, NEW YORK

The Faith of a Heretic was originally published in a hardbound edition by Doubleday & Company, Inc. in 1961.

Anchor Books Edition: 1963

To My Uncles

WALTER SELIGSOHN

who volunteered in 1914 and was
shot off his horse on the Russian front in 1915

JULIUS SELIGSOHN

AND

FRANZ KAUFMANN

both Oberleutnant, Iron Cross, First Class, 1914–18,

one a devout Jew,
one a devout convert to Christianity,

one killed in a Nazi concentration camp in 1942,
one shot by the Secret Police in 1944,

both for gallantly helping others
in obedience to conscience, defiant

JEREMIAH: They have healed the wound of my people lightly, saying, "Peace, peace," when there is no peace.

KANT: All the interest of my reason (speculative as well as practical) comes together in the following three questions:
1. What can I know?
2. What ought I to do?
3. What may I hope?

Critique of Pure Reason

WHITMAN: Piety and conformity to them that like,
Peace, obesity, allegiance, to them that like . . .
I am he who walks the States with a barb'd tongue,
    questioning every one I meet,
Who are you that wanted only to be told what
    you knew before?
Who are you that wanted only a book to join you
    in your nonsense?

By Blue Ontario's Shore

NIETZSCHE: Is it really so difficult simply to accept . . . what is considered truth in the circle of one's relatives and of many good men, and what, moreover, really comforts and elevates man? Is that more difficult than to strike new paths, fighting the habitual, experiencing the insecurity of independence and the frequent wavering of one's feelings and even one's conscience, proceeding often without any consolation. . . . Here the ways of men part: if you wish to strive for peace of soul and pleasure, then believe; if you wish to be a devotee of truth, then inquire.

Letter, 1865

TOLSTOY: I do not believe my faith to be the one indubitable truth for all time, but I see no other that is plainer, clearer, or answers better to all the demands of my reason and my heart; should I find such a one I shall at once accept it. . . . But I can no more return to that from which with such suffering I have escaped, than a flying bird can re-enter the egg shell from which it has emerged. "He who begins by loving Christianity better than truth, will proceed by loving his own sect or church better than Christianity, and end in loving himself (his own peace) better than all," said Coleridge.

Reply to Edict of Excommunication

WITTGENSTEIN: What is the use of studying philosophy if . . . (See § 10)

SARTRE: If a writer has chosen to be silent . . . (See § 16)

Preface

Of faith and morals, one cannot speak honestly for long without hurting feelings. Therefore, most people speak dishonestly of the most important subjects. Many recent philosophers prefer not to speak of them at all. But in some situations honesty is incompatible with silence. It is in mine right now.

This book is continuous with my previous efforts, but goes beyond them. More than before, criticism is subordinated to a constructive attempt. But affirmations that entail no negations are empty. Those who loudly say Yes, but No under their breath only, or No only to what their audience negates anyway or what it does not hurt to deny, are false prophets that cry "peace, peace," when there is no peace.

This volume wants to be read as a whole, as books, unlike magazines, are generally meant to be read. It is divided into consecutively numbered sections to facilitate cross references and indexing. It is petty to worry about whether something is still referred to on the next page, or the page after that; by having sections to refer to, that problem is solved. The sections are not meant to be read out of context. Many a theme introduced early in the book is developed and varied later, and obviously much is left unsaid in the later chapters because it has been said earlier. Many sections may make sense in isolation; but their sense in context is often more judicious. Whether it is judicious enough, there is only one way of finding out.

November 30, 1960   W. K.

Contents

The Faith of a Heretic

I

Prologue

1

Heresy is a set of opinions "at variance with established or generally received principles." In this sense, heresy is the price of all originality and innovation.

In theology, any "opinion that is contrary to the fundamental doctrine or creed of any particular church" is heretical. From the point of view of the churches to which we do not belong—and none of us can belong to the lot—we are all heretics. But more narrowly speaking, a heretic is one who deviates from the fundamental doctrine of his own church, or of the church with which he was previously connected. So understood, not everybody is a heretic.

In law, finally—still according to Webster's Universal Unabridged Dictionary—heresy is "an offense against Christianity consisting in a denial of some of its essential doctrines, publicly avowed, and obstinately maintained." What keeps most men in "Christian" countries from being heretics in this sense is that they do not publicly avow their disbelief: it is in better taste to be casual about lost beliefs, and a note of wistfulness generally ensures forgiveness. Obstinacy is rare. Millions do not even know that they deny essential Christian doctrines: they have never bothered to find out what the essential doctrines are. In extenuation they may plead that the evasiveness and the multiplicity of churches create a difficulty; but to be deterred by this when one's eternal destiny is said to be at stake bespeaks a glaring lack of seriousness. Perhaps Tennyson had this in mind when he wrote in *In Memoriam:*

> There lives more faith in honest doubt,
> Believe me, than in half the creeds.

I should rather not speak of "more faith" or "less." There are different kinds of faith, and nothing is further from my mind than appropriating the word "faith" only for what is good. Neither would I redefine heresy, as Milton did in his *Areopagitica:* "A man may be a heretic in the truth; and if he believe things only because his pastor says so, or the assembly so determines, without knowing other reason, though his belief be true, yet the very truth he holds becomes his heresy." Of the man accused by Milton I approve as little as he did, but I should not call him a heretic. Rather, his faith is that of most of the orthodox. Calvin, for example, said expressly in his *Institutes of the Christian Religion* (III 2.11) that "the knowledge of faith consists more in certainty than in comprehension." Still, such blind faith is not the only kind of faith there is.

Some writers reserve the word "faith" for what they *dislike*. Nietzsche said in *The Antichrist:* " 'Faith' means not *wanting* to know what is true" (635).[1] That fits much religious faith as well as some people's faith in their wives, husbands, or political parties. Sartre, too, has suggested that faith involves bad faith: "To believe is to know that one [merely] believes, and to know that one [merely] believes is no longer [really] to believe" (69). My parenthetical additions are meant to bring out what, I believe, he means. I know that I merely believe that this is what he means; I am not absolutely certain that my interpretation is correct; but I really believe that it is right. Thus Sartre's clever formulation, like so many clever things he says, applies to certain cases only, no less than Nietzsche's epigram, and not to all faith.

Faith means intense, usually confident, belief that is not based on evidence sufficient to command assent from every reasonable person.[2] Many people assume that an intense be-

---

[1] Numbers in parentheses refer to pages; the editions cited are listed in the Bibliography at the end of this volume.

[2] This conception of faith is defended in detail in my *Critique of Religion and Philosophy,* § 36: "Knowledge, belief, and faith." Citing one's previous work like this is admittedly an evil—but a lesser one. Lengthy repetitions would be worse; and if one refrains from both one seems utterly arbitrary, as if one considered argument beneath one's dignity.

lief must be held with a closed mind—that it necessarily involves no longer "wanting to know what is true"—and that any willingness to look with an open mind at further evidence or at objections shows that one's faith is lacking in intensity and therefore not worthy of the name. Thus many a believer plays into the hands of critics like Milton and Nietzsche.

The use of "faith" in the title of this book depends on the assumption that a man who cares intensely may have sufficient interest to concern himself with issues, facts, and arguments that have a vital bearing on what he believes. In sum, there are at least two types of faith, though possibly many more: the faith of the true believer and the faith of a heretic.

2

Why should one present the faith of a heretic in a book? This is not one of those things which "one" either should or should not do; it involves a deeply personal decision. It is fashionable to apply to experts, to ask for proofs, and to suppose that a crucial choice is either right or not, like an angle. But one cannot prove that one ought to have written a certain book, painted this picture, or written that piece of music. In some cases, it would make more sense to say: I had to.

Such constraint does not attenuate responsibility. On the contrary, the decision cannot be charged to a general rule or to anything outside oneself. Neither is it arbitrary. To be quite candid, one has to say: this is why I did it, and my reasons seem good to me; if you have any doubts, consider what you would have done in my situation. Perhaps that will lead you to reconsider your own life and decisions.

I was brought up a Lutheran. When I found that I could not believe in the Trinity, and especially not that Jesus was God, I decided to become a Jew. I was only eleven, and my parents felt that I was too young to make such a far-reaching choice. I persisted, and the matter was discussed for months. During that time, Hitler came to power; and now I was told that in view of the persecution my decision might entail I should certainly wait until I was older. I insisted that one could not change one's mind for a reason like that. I did not realize until a little later that all of my grandparents had been Jewish; and none of us knew that this, and not one's own religion, would determine the Nazis' classification.

Later I learned that my grandmother, Julie Kaufmann, had urged her sons to become Christians after her father's death. She did not believe in Judaism and persuaded herself that Christianity was the natural continuation of the Jewish religion and, in Heine's words, the entrance ticket to European civilization. She passionately wanted her children to be respectable, even at the price of conformity. But she herself remained unconverted and was a heretic's heretic who loved to ignore, lampoon, or defy convention. I loved her dearly. My father's father had died long before I was born.

My mother's father, Arnold Seligsohn, would have liked to become a professor of history. In those days, however, no Jew could become a German professor unless he submitted to baptism, as many did. He would not consider such a step, became a lawyer, and eventually an outstanding authority on patent law. After my conversion, we went to the synagogue together for many years, sitting and standing next to each other. In German "liberal" synagogues, men and women were separated, and my mother sat in a different section Friday nights and in the balcony on holidays. When I was small, she had very rarely attended services. As I learned more about Judaism, I became more and more orthodox; first my brother and then my father became Jewish, too; and eventually my brother and I often went to orthodox services.

There are heretics from resentment and iconoclasts who attack from outside what they never loved. There are also heretics from love who feel grateful to many with whom in the end they cannot agree. Need I add how beautiful Christmas Eve in our house used to be before we gave up celebrating it? The ceilings were high, the tree enormous, the candles real, the occasion full of warmth and love. We even had an Advent wreath suspended from a chandelier and lit one candle on the first Advent Sunday, two on the second, three on the third, and four on the Sunday before Christmas.

Later, when we celebrated Hanukkah, the sumptuous Christmas tables became a matter of the past, but there were presents each of the eight nights and, infinitely more important, our religious intensity increased with every year.

The editors of a popular magazine once asked me to introduce an article autobiographically. I related my conversion as briefly as possible; and it was said: he discusses the world's great religions after having tried two himself. Or: tried out. Why not: tried on?

Whether I ever knew Judaism or Christianity, or both, from the inside might possibly be relevant to this book; but if I merely said I did, you might still doubt my word or think that I deceived myself. To prove my point, I should have to cite what I wrote as a boy: letters, poems, prayers. To show something important in this way—about religion, heresy, or how a human being develops—would be worth-while. But that could not be done in passing. It would take a whole book—an autobiography. I have no wish to write that. I only want to give some idea at the outset in what spirit *The Faith of a Heretic* was written.

Ideally, that should not be necessary. The book should speak for itself. And to say that it was not written in a captious spirit would be futile. But we are all in danger of forgetting that writers with whom we disagree are human beings like ourselves and not merely authors. A writer who is sharply critical of some positions runs the risk of being more widely applauded or resented than understood.

This book was not written to comfort those who might find my views congenial, nor to shock and offend those whose ideas I question. The ideal reader would engage in a common quest with me; he would be willing to reconsider his views and some of his basic decisions in the course of this quest. To that end it might help if we had some common ground in the beginning—not a common platform but some recognition of our common humanity. It might seem that any reader would take that for granted; but when a writer touches on questions of faith, most readers would rather erect a protective barrier by labeling him as if he were the incarnation of a position.

This book is part of a quest that began before I found fault with many notions that are considered in these pages; and I criticize them not because they do not agree with my current results, but because I encountered them in the course of my quest and found them wanting. It is for that reason that I am asking the reader to go back—briefly, for a few Prologue pages—to a time when I did not yet hold my present views. None of the biographical events matters for its own sake. The point is to show how the quest for honesty might begin— how it did begin—in one man's life. Many a reader must have had similar experiences, similar qualms. The whole point here is to recall these and to establish some common ground of perplexity and concern.

I was seventeen when I entered Williams College in February 1939. I had just arrived in the United States, and my parents were still in Germany. My father had been released from a concentration camp after some hideous weeks, on condition that he leave the country; but he had no visa yet. In March Hitler took Czechoslovakia, and war seemed imminent. A month later, my parents reached London, where they were to spend the war years; but many others I loved were still in Germany, threatened with extermination.

That summer I read Stone's *Lust for Life*, a novel based on Van Gogh's life. He decided to live with the miners, to descend into the pits with them and share their miseries. Then he met Zola, who told him that all this was senseless and no help whatever to the miners. Zola had written a novel, *Germinal*, depicting their wretchedness, though he did not share it; and this book had helped them far more than Van Gogh's decision to suffer as they did. There had been strikes, the public conscience had been sensitized, and things were being done. I read *Germinal*. It might be all right to continue college if that would enable me to do some service that I could not do without an education.

This does not explain the choice of philosophy. But who could give a compelling reason for that? I have no regrets about it. If there had been a religion major, I should probably have chosen that; and I took courses in comparative religion, philosophy of religion, and psychology of religion. I had no clear notion how philosophy might enable me to contribute anything, but I loved it. Unexpectedly, I won a scholarship to do graduate work in philosophy. It was the spring of 1941. Hitler had not yet attacked Russia, and the United States had not yet entered the war. Should I try to volunteer or accept the scholarship? My teachers thought the choice was obvious. I did not, but I went to Harvard, determined to finish as quickly as possible. By the fall of 1942, I had almost all the requirements out of the way, but my attempt to finish my thesis in three months failed.

Returning from military service in Germany, in 1946, I felt little desire to go back to the classroom. But in September I returned to Harvard, and in April 1947 I submitted a dissertation on "Nietzsche's Theory of Values." It was a resented requirement, but I could not help pouring my heart into it. By the end of the month, I was appointed an instructor at Princeton. Soon I rewrote my thesis entirely and added a great deal more to make a book of it. Before long, friendly scholars urged me to follow it up with a similar book on Hegel.

Had I survived to write monographs—on Nietzsche first, then on Hegel, and perhaps eventually on Kant? A scholar's life is not necessarily dull. One can train oneself to find excitement in questions of exegesis. In fact, it is far easier to learn to love a life like that than to enjoy the kind of work most men do. Enjoyment was not the issue; conscience was. There is a haunting passage in William James, in quite a different context, that comes closer to the point, provided only it is read as a challenge not to others but to oneself:

"If the generations of mankind suffered and laid down their lives; if prophets confessed and martyrs sang in the fire . . . for no other end than that a race of creatures of such unexampled insipidity should succeed, and protract . . . their contented and inoffensive lives, why, at such a rate . . . better ring down the curtain before the last act of the play, so that a business that began so importantly may be saved from so singularly flat a winding up."

I do not mean to disparage scholarship or painstaking work of a highly technical nature. I should like to think that I myself have made some contributions of that sort, and I hope to make more. Certainly I respect some men who write monographs on other philosophers; but for me right now this would not do. This is a personal matter, and that is the reason for giving a personal account of it.

I was confronted not with a drab life but with the question whether I had become a traitor. Writing on Hegel and translating Nietzsche and Goethe did not help—unless it helped to make me a better writer and added to my armory. In 1958 I finally published a book of a different kind, *Critique of Religion and Philosophy,* and a year later another volume, on which I had been working during the same years, *From Shakespeare to Existentialism.* Critical discussion of the work of others became a point of departure for attempts to develop my own views. Criticism predominated, but scholarship had become engaged.

Soon after my *Critique* appeared, I was asked to write an article for a projected series on religion. There were to be a Protestant, a Catholic, a Jew—and I was to represent a critical, rationalist point of view. It was a ticklish assignment, and the magazine was not a scholarly journal, but one could hardly say: congratulations, gentlemen, on your decision to present this point of view along with more popular attitudes, but if you don't mind, ask someone else. I stipulated that I must be under no pressure to pull my punches, and that the editors must not rewrite my essay. They did not change a word, but thanked me for "The Faith of an Agnostic." I preferred "The Faith of an Infidel." That would not do: it would look as if, along with two Christians and a Jew, a Muslim had been included. The editors proposed "The Faith of a Pagan." I did not think I was a pagan and, after some further thought, hit on "The Faith of a Heretic."

This book is no mere expansion of that article. It is an altogether new book and deals at length with many questions not even touched in the article. But the title had struck a sensitive nerve. I had not done justice to it. Could one develop the faith of a heretic in less than seven pages in a popular magazine? Perhaps not even in a book, but it is worth a try.

3

There is another, less personal way of approaching this book. "I divide men," said Tolstoy, "into two lots. They are freethinkers, or they are not-freethinkers. I am not speaking of . . . the agnostic English Freethinkers, but I am using the word in its simplest meaning. Freethinkers are those who are willing to use their minds without prejudice and without fearing to understand things that clash with their own customs, privileges, or beliefs. This state of mind is not common, but it is essential for right thinking; where it is absent, discussion is apt to become worse than useless. A man may be a Catholic, a Frenchman, or a capitalist, and yet be a freethinker; but if he put his Catholicism, his patriotism, or his interest, above his reason, and will not give the latter free play where those subjects are touched, he is not a freethinker. His mind is in bondage" (xvi).

It is always tempting to divide men into two lots: Greeks and barbarians, Muslims and infidels, those who believe in God and those who don't. But who does *not* fear to understand things that threaten his beliefs? Of course, one is not consciously afraid; but everybody who is honest with himself finds that often he does not try very hard to understand what clashes with his deep convictions.

It is therefore popular to say something like this: we are all slaves of prejudice; this bondage is part of the human condition. Every man has his own commitment, and none of these is capable of rational proof. Man is irrational; there are no freethinkers—only shallow people who *think* they are rational.

Such rhetoric sounds profound and fits the fashions of the day. It carries overtones of existentialism and psychoanalysis, original sin and democracy: we are all equal, depraved, irrational, and committed, whether we know it or not. Modesty is so much easier than honesty because it is compatible with sloth.

None of us can say that his thinking is entirely free; therefore, it would be better not to distinguish freethinkers and not-freethinkers. But all of us sometimes make some efforts to break the bondage of the mind; only some are more obstinate than others. Too many give up too soon. Why not encourage such efforts? And what better way is there than publicly presenting a fairly obstinate attempt—not a shining example of freethinking, but the faith of a heretic?

Listing articles of faith, of course, would not do. Articles of faith are meant for groups of people: they are begotten by the need for ritual and mothered by the need for compromise. They reduce the believer to exegesis—unless he denies one of the articles and becomes a heretic. A heretic wants no articles of faith. The point of this book is not to amuse the reader by making an exhibition of my faith, but to make him feel throughout that *sua res agitur*, that *his* case is at stake.

For the same reason it would not do to present a system. As soon as it is granted that the premises are not really certain, not based on evidence sufficient to compel assent from every reasonable person, and hence merely a matter of faith, it becomes simple for the reader to avoid concern. Worse, it would give the impression that the author's mind is closed on fundamentals, and that he proposes to solve life's problems by seeing what follows from his presuppositions. Nothing could be further from the truth.

What I want to communicate is not a faith that happens to be heresy today, although tomorrow it might be acclaimed as orthodox. I naturally hope that some of my suggestions may be accepted widely in time, but I should not want to win agreement without capturing in prose the struggle against bondage.

The starting point is not a set of premises that I refuse to question. This book is based not on the all-too-widespread will to believe, but on the will to be honest. This is not a presupposition like any other; for, in Tolstoy's words, "where it is absent, discussion is apt to become worse than useless." Indeed, there is no need to say "apt to become"; where the will to be honest is lacking, discussion is wholly pointless.

This is of considerable importance. Sooner or later, when some cherished belief or position begins to appear endangered, many people ask: why is honesty so important? They suddenly talk as if somebody else were committed to honesty much as they themselves are committed to something else. But the will to honesty is no man's prerogative. It is not a starting point that you can repudiate at will. Every book and every discussion presuppose the will to be honest. The man who repudiates honesty repudiates discussion. There is no point in dialogue with a man who does not acknowledge this standard.

In effect, this is generally recognized. Nobody says that he is not at all committed to honesty. Nobody entirely lacks the will to be honest; but most people settle for rather a small share of it. They favor honesty within limits, though they do not explicate these limits or reflect on them. This question, whether we should set limits to honesty and, if so, what limits, deserves discussion. And this theme, like the other motifs sounded in this Prologue, except the autobiographical note, will be developed in the following chapters.

4

One more motif should be introduced here to avoid misunderstanding, though it, too, requires further exploration later on. It is widely held that honesty requires scrupulousness and an effort to be rational—so far so good—and that it follows that one must try to be scientific and impersonal. This popular inference deserves a name: *the pedantic fallacy.*

The ostentatious use of jargon is mistaken for objectivity; pretension is confounded with precision, and elaborate complexity with carefulness. A lack of ardor passes for a token that one is not arbitrary. Yet neither a lack of passion nor the anxious dissimulation of every personal element is either required or sufficient for intellectual honesty.

An attempt to do justice to our own experience, to the feelings and the judgments tutored by our reading and reflection and discussions—for that matter, even by despair and sleepless

nights—can be scrupulous; it need not be. But it is not pedantry that makes the difference. Rather, the single most important factor is a sustained willingness to consider informed
objections.

Some philosophic works seem closer to literature than to
science. This has been noted by a few men who depreciate
logic and favor a blend of intuition and associative thinking.
They, too, are guilty of the pedantic fallacy: they also assume
a close connection between pedantry and responsible thinking, but renounce both.

A philosopher can fight men's fear "to understand things
that clash with their own customs, privileges, or beliefs." He
can try to make men more sensitive to other points of view,
and to show how an outlook that is widely slandered and
misunderstood looks and feels from inside. To that extent, his
efforts may resemble literature. What distinguishes philosophy is the sustained attempt to explore ramifications, objections, and alternatives.

A novelist or dramatist may occasionally examine an argument, too; he does not have to; and if he does a lot of this,
the result is usually bad literature. For a philosopher, on the
other hand, an opinion should never be more than a starting
point. But the study and evaluation of ramifications and objections and alternatives need not be tedious, trivial, or pedantic.

To probe the weaknesses of many popular assumptions,
to develop alternatives, and to make one's fellow men more
thoughtful is a contribution worth attempting. Obviously, this
does not preclude specific contributions to the discussion of
such topics as morality, commitment, or theology.

The word "faith" may suggest something diametrically opposed to the spirit of philosophy. The world abounds in
strong faiths that prize conformity above honesty, and we
are often told that we can never hope to meet such faiths successfully unless we develop a comparable faith on which all
of us can enthusiastically concur. We must stop, more and
more men say, being so critical. Dissenters should at least have
the grace to keep quiet. Criticism is negative, and we need
positive thinking; heresy creates division, and we need uni-

formity; honesty is fine, of course, but within limits—rather drastic limits.

My faith is not that kind of faith. Far from viewing philosophy or heresy with suspicion, I believe that the enemies of critical reason are, whether consciously or not, foes of humanity.

For centuries heretics have been persecuted by men of strong faiths who hated non-conformity and heresy and criticism while making obeisances to honesty—within limits. In our time, millions have been murdered in cold blood by the foes of non-conformity and heresy and criticism, who paid lip service to honesty—within limits.

I have less excuse than many others for ignoring all this. If even I do not speak up, who will? And if not now, when?

II

The Quest for Honesty

5

Philosophy is commonly considered a chaos of abstruse ideas. Even authors of histories of philosophy and professors who teach the subject outline the gradual accumulation of fantastic systems. Another, very different, perspective seems much more illuminating: one may view the history of philosophy as a history of heresy.

Almost invariably, histories of philosophy begin with the so-called pre-Socratics—Greeks of the sixth and fifth centuries B.C., whose writings are lost except for occasional quotations that are found in later writers. Thales, who is said to have predicted an eclipse that occurred in 585 B.C., is generally called the first philosopher. From him an unbroken line of thinkers leads to Socrates, Plato, and Aristotle. What these men have in common, and what distinguishes them from the sages of the Upanishads in India, some of whom lived a century or more before the time of Thales, is a truly stunning lack of reverence for the past. The pre-Socratics shared the Indian sages' and the Hebrew prophets' scorn for the opinions of the common people of their day; but they did not counter these opinions by referring to the scriptures or traditions of the past. Far from reading their own views into, or out of, the inspired poetry of Homer, Hesiod, or some other ancient writer, they included the teachings of these poets in their cutting strictures.

"Homer and Hesiod ascribed to the gods whatever is infamy and reproach among men: theft and adultery and deceiving each other." "Mortals suppose that the gods are born and have clothes and voices and shapes like their own." "But if oxen, horses, and lions had hands or could paint with their hands and fashion works as men do, the horses would paint horselike images of gods, and the oxen oxlike ones, and each would fashion bodies like their own." "The Ethiopians consider the gods flat-nosed and black; the Thracians, blue-eyed and red-haired." "Not from the beginning have the gods revealed all things to mortals, but by long seeking men find what is better."

These are some quotations from the writings of Xenophanes. Heraclitus, a generation later, was no less outspoken: "The consecrations of the mysteries, as practiced among men, are unholy." "Being a polymath does not teach understanding: else Hesiod would have had it and Pythagoras; also Xenophanes and Hekataeos." "Homer deserves to be thrown out of the contests and whipped; and Archilochus, too." "The most popular teacher is Hesiod. Of him people think he knew most—he that did not even know day and night: they are one." "Corpses should be thrown away more than dung." "To God everything is beautiful and good and just; but men have posited this as unjust and this as just." "Sane thinking is the greatest perfection, and wisdom consists in saying the truth. . . ." "All men are granted what is needed for knowing oneself and sane thinking."

Clearly, these men were heretics. They not only opposed the common sense of their time and some of the most revered names of the past but they did not presume to speak in the name of the Lord or to interpret correctly a previously misunderstood tradition. They pitted their own thinking against the religion and the poetry they knew. And by breaking with the exegetic mode of thought and every other form of appeal to authority, they initiated philosophy.

One of the pre-Socratics, Anaxagoras, came to Athens. His predecessors had lived in Asia Minor and in southern Italy, and Empedocles, a contemporary philosopher, lived in Sicily. Anaxagoras arrived in Athens when the city was at the peak of her power, culturally no less than politically, during the so-called Periclean Age. Pericles became his friend; but soon Anaxagoras was tried for heresy and had to leave the city. For he taught that the sun and moon were made of earth and stone instead of being gods.

A generation later, Socrates, the first great philosopher to have been born in Athens, was tried—also in Athens—for impiety and corrupting the youth, and was put to death in 399 B.C. Moderns often think of Aristotle as a great conservative; but toward the end of his life he fled from Athens to avoid a similar trial, and himself said that he left "lest the Athenians should sin twice against philosophy."

Medieval philosophy was of a different mold, though not quite so homogeneous and conservative as many moderns think. Even St. Thomas Aquinas ventured a few propositions which the Bishop of Paris and the Archbishop of Canterbury, who was a Dominican like Aquinas himself, censured in 1277; but when Thomas was sainted, the censures were withdrawn as far as they affected him. Eckhart, the great German mystic, taught a good deal that the church found unacceptable and, after formal inquiry, condemned as heresy. But, in general, the history of medieval philosophy was not a history of heresy. Indeed, medieval philosophy was so different from both Greek and modern philosophy that it is somewhat misleading to call it by the same name. And if philosophy were defined as a search for truth that involves following arguments and evidence, without recourse to authority, wherever they may lead, frequently arriving at unforeseen conclusions, then medieval philosophy would not deserve the name at all. But the definition of philosophy that has just been suggested is partial at best.

In all ages, philosophy contains two different tendencies: one is heretical, iconoclastic, critical; the other is apologetic and conservative. The first has been illustrated from Xenophanes and Heraclitus; the second has been summed up beautifully by a nineteenth-century British philosopher, F. H. Bradley, when he said that "metaphysics is the finding of bad reasons for what we believe on instinct." It is not clear why he said "metaphysics": ethics, aesthetics, and philosophy of religion, theory of knowledge and political philosophy might well be described in the same words. The tendency to rationalize preconceived conclusions has been prominent in all fields of philosophy, and it is astounding how often the reasons really *have* been bad.

There is no reason to suppose that Xenophanes and Heraclitus were completely free of this addiction; and in the writings of the first philosopher most of whose works have survived intact, the dialogues of Plato, both tendencies are certainly prominent. If one might call him a heretic for all that, it would be because he does not appeal to authority and relies on his own thinking instead.

In keeping with this last point, the teachings of the Buddha and his contemporary, Vaddhamana the Jina, who differed from the sages of the Upanishads by not recognizing the authority of the ancient Vedas and by refusing to present their doctrines as interpretations of the ancient texts, are known in India as "great heresies." That neither of these founders of two great religions became the fountainhead of a philosophy in the Western, or Greek, sense is due to the fact that their own teachings were accepted as authoritative by their followers, as those of the pre-Socratics were not.

In medieval philosophy, apologetics triumphed over criticism. In modern philosophy, critical thinking re-emerges. Both tendencies are prominent in the great modern thinkers. But as we examine their progression we discover that their rationalizations have proved less enduring than their criticism. And instead of seeing the history of philosophy as an accumulation of fantastic systems, one may view it as the gradual analysis of, and liberation from, one illusion after another, a stripping away of fantasies, a slow destruction of once hallowed truths that are found to be errors.

Descartes is generally singled out as the first modern philosopher—not because he, like his medieval predecessors, tried to prove that God exists and that the human soul is immortal, but because he resolved to doubt everything. He made a fresh start and decided to rely solely on his reason, instead of citing Scripture to his purpose or, as Aquinas had done also, Aristotle. When Francis Bacon rather than Descartes is called the first modern philosopher—the two were contemporaries, and nothing important is at stake—the point is substantially the same: he, too, refused allegiance to ancient authorities and tried to teach men to seek truth by relying on their reason and on observation.

Spinoza was quite literally a heretic and expelled by the synagogue of Amsterdam. He expressly denied the authority of Scripture in matters of truth; he rejected the God of Judaism and Christianity, though he used the term "God" for what he believed in; and he repudiated the belief that the world is governed by a purpose. Berkeley is remembered as a great philosopher not because he was a bishop and believed in God but because he argued most ingeniously that the belief in matter is untenable and that there is no material substance. Hume, another generation later, criticized the notion of spiritual substance, too, and questioned many other commonplaces, including the axiom that every event has a cause.

Kant, yet a little later, smashed the foundations not only of so-called rational cosmology and rational psychology but also of natural theology. He showed that all proofs of God's existence are fallacious. (The neo-Thomists do not accept his demonstration and consider Descartes, and the development he initiated, a disaster.) That Kant later claimed that God's existence and the immortality of the soul were postulates of the practical reason is not considered one of his great contributions to philosophy but, at least by most philosophers, a bit of backsliding. In the next generation, Fichte lost his professorship at Jena on a charge of atheism, though he later became the first Rektor of the newly founded university of Berlin.

During the Victorian Era, John Stuart Mill declared, in his *Examination of Sir William Hamilton:* "Whatever power such a being may have over me, there is one thing which he shall not do: he shall not compel me to worship him. I will call no being good, who is not what I mean when I apply that epithet to my fellow-creatures; and if such a being can sentence me to hell for not so calling him, to hell I will go." Later, in his posthumously published *Three Essays on Religion*, Mill affirmed his belief in a benevolent god, but denied his omnipotence. A generation later, William James proclaimed his faith in "a finite god" in *A Pluralistic Universe.* Meanwhile, Nietzsche had carried heresy to new heights. During World War

II, Bertrand Russell was declared by an American court to be unfit to teach at the City College of New York because of his heretical views. A little later, he became a member of the House of Lords in England, though a British court had sent him to prison during World War I; and yet a little later he received the Nobel Prize for literature.

All these men also rationalized many preconceived opinions, but generally it was the critical part of their work that proved to have lasting importance. Philosophers have rarely given *good* reasons for what was believed previously. Much more often, their denials, their heresies, their exposures of long unquestioned doctrines continue to be taught.

6

It may be objected that if this is true it is terrible; that if so much philosophy is heresy it ought not to be taught. But what is the point of a liberal education?

If the point were simply to give information, we should not require universities. There would be no need for faculties and classrooms. Lectures for the whole United States, if not for the English-speaking world, could be mimeographed once and for all and sold for a minute fraction of the price of a college education. To provide a touch of drama, some lectures could be tape-recorded—no doubt, often more effectively by actors rather than the scholars who prepared them. Occasionally, a good student could recite and record a lecture much more clearly and quickly than a professor who might have a strong accent, a speech defect, or simply be old or tired. And the exceptional blend of ham and egghead might appear on television. No physical plant would be needed for the humanities and social sciences. Even the devices mentioned so far might well be dispensable: libraries might prove sufficient if they featured reading lists.

In sum: if universities and colleges were meant primarily to furnish information, they would be dated by the printing press and some more recent technical advances. Professors and students who, often at considerable inconvenience to themselves and to each other, come together in the classroom would be wasting time. Surely, most students and professors do waste an enormous quantity of time and effort; but at his best a teacher transmits something more than information: the student discovers the techniques and joys of critical thinking.

To this end, narrow specialization must be discouraged, and students have to be prevented from attaching themselves closely to a single teacher, in the manner still traditional at German universities, in spite of Mephisto's forthright mockery in Goethe's *Faust*:

> Here, too, it would be best you heard
> One only and staked all upon your master's word.
> Yes, stick to words at any rate;
> There never was a surer gate
> Into the temple, Certainty.

It would, of course, be silly for a teacher to lean over backward to make sure that no information leaks out to his students. But he might do well to ask himself what could be got as well, if not much better, by consulting books, and what is better learned through personal encounter with a teacher.

The classroom situation lends itself much better than most books to stimulating and maintaining real interest in a variety of different views. Most people tend to restrict their reading to congenial views and like to be confirmed in what they believe anyway. Exposure to different teachers, encountered in the flesh, and to other students, preferably from different backgrounds, can compel the student to consider many different views, taking them seriously. This should wean him from bigotry and blind naïveté. He should also learn that no man has authority, except provisionally: all opinions are subject to critical examination, though some may prevail even after acid tests.

Is such pervasive mistrust of authorities arrogant? On the contrary: through the painful discovery that even very great men have been guilty of egregious errors, we learn that the chances are that we ourselves, even when very confident that we are right, may overestimate our case. Constant contact with minds greater than our own is humbling; constant reminders of their shortcomings, doubly so. Moreover, it is difficult to recognize one's own mistakes. They are much more easily recognized when one encounters them in someone else's prose. Dissatisfied with oneself, one becomes a seeker. Difficulty becomes a challenge and delight; critical thinking, a way of life.

In an education so conceived, philosophy should play a central role. The fragmentary epigrams of Heraclitus and Xenophanes may sound arrogant, and it is not likely that either of them excelled in humility. But exposure to both of them and to other thinkers besides may help to develop qualities which these men lacked. In the generation after these two men, the Greek philosophers began to back up their views with sustained attempts at argument; and soon apodictic criticism, in itself a wholesome departure from obsequious respect for reputations and traditions, gave way to dialogue and the attempt to progress together.

The social importance of the kind of education here described should not be underestimated. The aim of a liberal education is not to turn out ideal dinner guests who can talk with assurance about practically everything, but people who will not be taken in by men who speak about all things with an air of finality. The goal is not to train future authorities, but men who are not cowed by those who claim to be authorities. The alternative to gullibility, is not lack of respect for competence but the ability to find out who is competent and who is not.

Attitudes toward authority carry over into politics, and a people who suspect political authoritarianism and who cherish their own freedom can ill afford to tolerate authoritarianism in their education. Nor is the only alternative to indiscriminate docility a no less undiscriminating relativism. A liberal education should teach men to turn a variety of information and opinion to advantage instead of either picking one view arbitrarily or choosing resignation in the face of an embarrassment of riches.

Ever since the days of ancient Athens, there have been a multitude of men who have looked askance upon philosophy because it is not pious, positive, and patriotic. Socrates and Plato compared the philosopher to a physician. One might add that one of the functions of philosophy is to inoculate men against bigotry, inhumanity, and propaganda by teaching them to think carefully, conscientiously, and critically.

Commonly, people think of philosophy as a quest, however ill advised, for truth. John Dewey called it the quest for certainty. But it is more illuminating to say that, at its best, philosophy is the quest for honesty.

7

What is honesty?

Some men readily persuade themselves that they have said what in fact they did not say, or that they never made a statement that in fact they made, or that you said something you never said. Such lack of scruple is extremely widespread and easy to cultivate. Many children and politicians are masters of the art of telling falsehoods with sincerity.

There are cases when it is doubtful whether we should call a man honest. This epithet, like most interesting words, does not have sharp edges. It is possible to be mistaken yet honest. But when we clearly ought to know better, when ordinary care would have led us to discover that our belief was wrong, then we certainly did not come up to any high standard of honesty.

There are degrees of honesty no less than of courage or humility. As one speaks of greater courage and more humility, one might well speak of greater, or more, honesty. There is a sense in which it is an insult to question any man's honesty; there is another sense in which calling Lincoln "Honest Abe" is a supreme compliment.

The man who, charged with some falsehood, retorts imperiously, "Are you calling me a liar?" shows gross insensitivity to elementary distinctions. One who knowingly and maliciously tells a falsehood is a liar. The man who knowingly tells a falsehood, motivated by kindness, however ill advised, would not usually be called a liar. Nor would a man who utters a falsehood unthinkingly, absent-mindedly. Certainly not a man who thinks he is telling the truth, though he is in a position to know that it is not the truth: he is irresponsible and shows little regard for honesty, but we should not call him a liar. It is a vicious but common fallacy to suppose that all who are not liars are honest.

The quest for honesty is not like a search for a jewel that may end happily with the sudden attainment of what is wanted. It is rather like the quest for excellence, a prolonged struggle.

One need not hesitate to say that Shakespeare was an excellent poet, far more excellent than Joyce Kilmer, although it makes no sense to say that he was perfectly, completely, or fully excellent. Elijah was a courageous man, much more courageous than St. Peter, although it makes no sense to say that he was perfectly, completely, or fully courageous. And it makes sense to say that Lincoln was an honest man, and that Joe McCarthy was not, without claiming that anyone ought to be called perfectly, completely, or fully honest. There are enormous differences of degree, and these merit emphasis.

Judged by extremely high standards, perhaps every historian is lacking in objectivity. It does not follow that honesty is a chimera, not worth striving for. There are staggering differences between historians: some are thoroughly biased and lack any profound respect for evidence, while others fight steadfastly against any bias they may have. The difference in attitude is easily illustrated by divergent reactions to criticism: some men are impervious to criticism while others welcome it.

Some speakers welcome criticism but are impervious to it; after lectures, they ask for questions, but never answer any, offering irrelevant homilies instead. Those who welcome queries but are unable to understand them, or who ask for criticism but never get the point of any objection, lack the kind of imagination that is an indispensable ingredient of any high degree of honesty. The unusually honest man is his own severest critic. He has the imagination to see his own ideas from many different points of view.

Instead of asking whether you are honest or a liar, ask how

you might become more honest. The answer: by raising your standards and by cultivating the habits of honesty—developing a keen intellectual conscience. And what does that involve? Intellectual imagination, carefulness, conscientiousness, scrupulousness—making one's beliefs and statements matters of conscience. The man who lacks such habits may be honest —but not very. He has low standards of honesty.

It is useful to distinguish physical and moral courage. Old-fashioned German education emphasized the latter insufficiently: one was trained to risk one's life in battle, but not to buck authority, pitting integrity against power. One might similarly distinguish physical and moral honesty, though these terms do not matter: the former concerns audible or visible statements only; the latter, a triumph over self-deception. Again, there are people who possess the physical variety but lack the moral: they make no false statements, but they are not honest with themselves.

The man who lacks courage, even if "only" moral courage, is afraid of getting hurt. His friends may prefer to call him prudent. A man who does not want to know the truth and deceives himself may also be called prudent by some, but he lacks honesty, even if "only" moral honesty. He probably also lacks courage and is afraid of being hurt. And the man who lacks moral courage is usually deficient in honesty, subordinating his regard for truth to his interest in popularity. Moral courage and moral honesty are twins, but they are not inseparable, and the trained eye can tell them apart. One may be wonderfully honest with oneself and know that one lacks the moral courage to speak out boldly. And another man may have moral courage but may yet be lax in matters of beliefs. Moral honesty is even rarer than moral courage.

8

There are few things about which people are less honest than their attitude toward honesty. Everybody claims to favor it and to consider it important, and an open accusation of dishonesty is a heinous, actionable insult. Yet our public life is permeated by a staggering tolerance for quite deliberate dishonesty.

In advertising, people put up with constant, willful, scientifically studied misrepresentations, without objecting seriously to being duped systematically. At most, sophisticated people joke about it.

In politics, an avowal of agnosticism would ruin a man's career, at least in the United States, while a record of repeated and premeditated falsehoods about facts, calumny about rival candidates, and broken promises is not considered any bar to the highest offices the people can bestow. Nor is it only during a political campaign that candidates are, as it were, allowed to lie. After election, too, both President and legislators are expected every now and then to deny quite calmly, in cold blood, reports that shortly after are found and acknowledged to be true. This, too, is considered a sort of family joke. But when the Russians question the good faith of American statesmen and assume that they are apt to be flagrantly dishonest, most Americans refuse to credit that such doubts could be ingenuous. To be sure, the Western statesmen often mean precisely what they say at points where Soviet statesmen question their sincerity; but can the Russians tell when our statesmen do and do not tell the truth?

Russian suspicion is, no doubt, increased by the awareness of the Soviet statesmen that they themselves would not hesitate, and do not hesitate, and have not hesitated in the past, to lie. Compared to the manners of some other countries, even American advertising and politics are relatively innocent. The cultivated virtuosity of bland deceitfulness that flourishes in Cairo's bazaars and propaganda broadcasts, and in its daily news reports as well, has no real parallel in most Western countries. But even here the lack of standards in the West is striking: the lies of the bazaars are shrugged off as a laughing matter, and the mendaciousness of Cairo's radio and press is widely ignored as unimportant. When the reports from Egypt differ from those issued by another government whose standards, though not lily white, are still as different from Cairo's as day is from night, one supposes simply that the truth lies somewhere in-between. One does not get excited about truthfulness; and even the brazen dishonesty of dictators agitates exceedingly few people, unless animosity has first been aroused by other matters which are considered more important. Honesty is not something one makes a point of: a gentleman treats others as if they were honest, even when he knows enough to realize that they are not.

Religion is as privileged a field as politics and advertising. It is widely held to call for tact, not truthfulness. It is considered perfectly all right for men of the cloth to make a business of pretending they believe what really they do not believe; to give the impression, speaking from the pulpit, that they are convinced of things that, talking to philosophers, they are quick to disown; and to feign complete assurance about matters that, in private, trouble them and cause them endless doubts. One does not even demand that a preacher should at least be honest with himself and know precisely what he does believe and what he does not, what he means and what he does not mean, what he knows for certain and what he considers probable or merely possible. One does not make such strict demands on him—or on oneself.

Advertisers, politicians, and men of the cloth have no monopoly on laxity regarding honesty; they are merely favored groups. Occasionally, a philosopher and a historian are granted the same special privileges. Extreme cases come to our notice but are really mere symptoms of our laxity with ourselves.

Perhaps the single best example of the common lack of high standards in questions of honesty is our tendency to think in labels. Terms like existentialism, pragmatism, and empiricism, liberalism and conservatism are, more often than not, so many excuses for not considering individual ideas on their merits and for not exposing oneself to the bite of thought. For less educated people, words like Jew and Catholic, Democrat, Republican, and Communist do much the same job. These labels have some uses that are perfectly legitimate, but frequently they function as an aid to thoughtlessness and permit people to appear to *think* when they are merely talking.

9

The practice of seizing on a label instead of considering a man's ideas is common, if often unconscious. The labels, theist, atheist, and agnostic, provide an especially important example. One supposes that the theist believes God exists, while the atheist denies that God exists, and the agnostic, in the absence of sufficient evidence, suspends judgment. It is further supposed that theists agree about the facts of the matter. One rarely stops to think about what these facts are supposed to be, except, of course, to say that theists think that God exists. But what does this assertion mean?

To many millions it means that there is someone high up in the sky who looks like an old man with a long beard; but millions of other theists are quite sure that this is not a fact at all but a crude superstition, though a harmless one. They believe that God has no body at all and is a spirit. Asked whether they believe in spirits, most of them would probably say: No, but God is an exception. Some people have a pretty clear conception of God, but all such clear conceptions, provided only they amount to more than the mere substitution of an equally vague synonym for God, are invariably rejected by the vast majority of other theists. And millions of theists have no clear idea whatsoever about what it means to say that God exists, but feel very sure that it is impious and terrible to say that he does not exist.

Late in 1960, the U. S. Supreme Court agreed to rule on the constitutionality of a requirement in Maryland that officeholders profess belief in God. The Maryland Court of Appeals had ruled against a professed atheist who wanted to be commissioned as a notary public, for, the court had said, a person who does not believe in God is "incompetent to hold office, to give testimony, or serve as a juror."[1] In 1958, the Gallup

[1] *U. S. News and World Report*, November 21, 1960, p. 16. Bishop James A. Pike says in "The Right to be an Atheist" (*Coronet*, April 1961): "In Maryland, Pennsylvania, Tennessee and Arkansas, in order to hold public office a man must believe in the being of God.

Poll asked a sample of the American electorate: "If your party nominated a generally well-qualified person for President, and he happened to be a Catholic [or a Jew, Negro, atheist, or woman], would you vote for him [or her]?" Result: 25% said that they would vote against a Catholic; 28% against a Jew; 43% against a woman; 53% against a Negro; and 75% against an atheist.[2]

This horror of atheism is related to the notion that morality depends on religion. This idea will be considered later (Chapters VIII–X). What concerns us here is the contrast of "theism" and "atheism." On examination, it turns out that what theists agree on is a formulation, not a state of affairs; and this formulation, to cite the admirably candid words of St. Paul about himself, means "all things to all men."

Seeing how some philosophers and theologians have employed the word "God," it is evident that no man, believe he ever so little, would be unable to say in all sincerity that he believes that God exists: all he would require would be the addition, if he should be pressed, which is exceedingly unlikely, that he has his own conception of God. He need not fear that anybody would be at all likely to press him further; but if anybody did, the public would side with the man who refused to discuss such a personal matter.

The doubter, in other words, need not fear public censure if only he is agreeable to using the word "God" for something that he does believe; and he need not even specify what that might be. What matters is agreement to such formulas as "God exists" or "I believe in God." But the man who refuses to employ such formulations, or who, worse, insists on saying that he does not believe God exists, appalls his fellow citizens although he may merely reject beliefs that they, too, regard as superstitions. To be scrupulously honest in such matters, to go out of one's way to avoid misunderstanding, and to refuse to use ancient terms in novel and surprising ways is widely held to be a dreadful thing.

In many places, testimony of a witness in court may be impeached if it can be shown that he is an atheist."

[2] S. M. Lipset, "Some Statistics on Bigotry in Voting," *Commentary*, October 1960.

To be an agnostic is considered more nearly respectable, or at least not quite so bad. But agnosticism is really a confused position. The agnostic is supposed to be the man who finds that there is not sufficient evidence to be sure either that God does or that God does not exist; so he suspends judgment. But for what is there not sufficient evidence? About what precisely does he suspend judgment? Like most people, he, too, overlooks the staggering ambiguity of that strange formulation, "God exists." Without determining first what is meant by that, one cannot say in candor whether one believes that it is true, that it is false, or that there is lack of evidence both ways. To say that whatever could be meant by it is false is militant, but shows vast ignorance of the attenuated and innocuous beliefs theologians and philosophers, preachers and laymen have been reading into this hallowed phrase for centuries.

A man who prizes honesty above the good opinion of his fellow men might say this: I cannot believe what most people in ancient times believed when they affirmed their faith in God; nor can I believe what most medieval people meant when they said "God exists." The point is not that there is insufficient evidence which keeps me from making up my mind, but that I very plainly do not believe what these men believed. My disbelief is based on an analysis of what they meant, of the evidence they credited, and of the arguments they used to back up their beliefs. The same goes for millions of modern theists. But there are men who use ancient formulations of belief in order to express their own lack of belief, or at least beliefs very different from those of, say, the evangelists—men who use old terms in new ways. Aquinas already did this when he defined God as the pure act of being. Tillich does it today when he defines God as being-itself. Spinoza, who was frank enough about his many heresies, spoke of "God or Nature"; John Dewey, who did not pretend to be a theist, said, not without irony, that if God were defined as the active relationship between the ideal and the actual, he, too, could say that he believed in God. Clearly, there is ample precedent for redefining ancient terms and then affirming one's belief that God exists. I prefer not to use the ancient labels. I should rather find out just what I can believe and what is not believable—find it out in detail—instead of glossing over some of life's most crucial issues by escaping into hallowed formulas.

This position may seem evasive to those who are used to the customary labels. They are apt to feel that the question "Does God exist?" calls for a clear-cut answer: either "Yes" or "No" or "I don't know." Two examples may help them to see the question in a different light.

Suppose you were asked, "Does Aphrodite exist?" Presumably, you would say "No." Surely, you would not say, "I don't know." The unqualified "No" would probably be based on the assumption that Aphrodite must be conceived anthropomorphically—more or less the way she appears in Homer's epics—say, as a beautiful, eternally young woman who lives on Mount Olympus. But in Hellenistic times and in the first centuries of our era, pagan theologians interpreted the ancient myths allegorically. They did not believe in an anthropomorphic Aphrodite any more than you do, but they professed belief in Aphrodite, meaning that the ancient stories could be given profound interpretations, and that love is beautiful and deserves reverence. When a modern theologian says that he does not believe in Aphrodite, he does not necessarily disagree with these ancient theologians about any matters of fact. Rather, he declines to use their language, their formulations. And some modern theologians say outright that they prefer a different set of myths. What is at issue, then, is not a question of the existence or non-existence of some entity, as the agnostic, too, supposes when he suspends judgment, pleading insufficient evidence. The issue is rather whether one feels committed to certain formulations; and, assuming that this commitment is not dictated by considerations of social advantage, what is at stake is loyalty to a tradition—not a question of fact.

Other examples may be taken from the Christian tradition. "Does Satan exist?" Or: "Do angels exist?" The Catholic scientist who would answer both questions in the affirmative does not necessarily believe that there are entities in which the Protestant scientist does not believe. And the self-styled agnostic who suspends judgment about the existence of God while asserting without hesitation that, of course, Satan does not exist, and there are no angels, is confused: he takes it for granted that Satan and angels have to be conceived anthropomorphically, while God must not be considered that way. And his reason for treating the formula "God exists" differently is presumably that it is central in his religious tradition, while Satan and angels are not. But the man who believes in the devil and in angels is not necessarily superstitious; he may merely be loyal to another religious tradition.

One need not conclude that all religious beliefs are on a par—not only with each other but also with atheism. Disagreements about loyalties are no less serious than disagreements about facts, and not all loyalties are on a par. "Religion and loyalty" and "Loyalty and truth" are discussed at length in Sections 78–80 of my *Critique*, and there is no need here to duplicate that discussion. What matters in the present context, in connection with the quest for honesty, is how easy it is to be deceived about the nature of religious beliefs and disbeliefs, and how labels help us to avoid any honest account of what we believe and what we do not believe.

Anybody can reiterate ancient creeds and reinterpret them till they no longer mean what non-believers think they mean, or what millions of the faithful, past and present, who believed much more than he can credit, found in them. At that point, the creed becomes a way of saying what the infidel next door believes, too: the avowed believer, who disdains outspoken unbelievers, often really agrees with them, while disagreeing with the vast majority of his fellow believers. When this happens, it does not necessarily involve any mental acrobatics. What one is conscious of is not a strenuous intellectual effort but rather a wealth of childhood associations that evoke a sense of fellowship with others, past and present, and the reassurance that we are far from alone. It feels fine, but is it honest? And if one has a highly sensitive intellectual conscience, does it still feel fine?

In his splendid book on *The Greeks and the Irrational*, E. R. Dodds, Regius Professor of Greek at Oxford University, remarked that "when the archaic Greek poured liquids down a feeding-tube into the livid jaws of a mouldering corpse," he wisely refrained, like a little girl feeding her doll, from thinking about what he was doing (136). Surely the same consideration applies to most religious practices: ritual, prayer, and religious affirmations generally involve a suspension of one's critical faculties—a refusal to be completely honest with oneself.

The situation cannot be assimilated either to beholding or acting in a play or to participation in a game. In all these cases one is willing to admit, even if unfeeling interruptions are resented, that there is some make-believe. In the case of religion, hardly anyone would be prepared to admit this even to himself.

There are at least three ways of transcending the naïveté with which most men perform religious rites, say prayers, and reiterate religious affirmations without ever stopping to reflect what they are doing. One can recognize the element of make-believe and give up doing all of these things. Or, having recognized the make-believe involved, one may nevertheless continue, from a sense of reverence for tradition, loyalty, and emotional satisfaction, to do what one began to do as a child. Or, finally, the theologian may step in and furnish systematic reasons for the cult and for the central affirmations of his own denomination. He may be prompted by the desire for honesty, but he mistakes articulateness and assurance, which are easy, for honesty, which is far more difficult.

10

Religion is merely one area in which words often lure us from the path of honesty. As mentioned before, labels quite generally threaten to derail attempts at honest thinking.

No philosopher has done more to make us aware of this than Ludwig Wittgenstein (1889–1951). His writings bear the stamp of his tormented personality and are not transparent at a glance. One is apt to come away with the impression that because he wrote philosophy mainly for philosophers his contributions are of no concern to others. He once described philosophy as a fight against "the bewitchment of our intelligence by language," and some of his academic followers inferred that only philosophic language constitutes a menace, while those who adhere to ordinary usage are quite safe. But this is surely wrong, unless we broaden "philosophic usage" to include a vast amount of ordinary talk about God and what is good and beautiful, about freedom and equality, and about liberals and conservatives.

Wittgenstein's thought was subtle, and it would be folly to attempt to summarize it in a paragraph or two. But part of his contribution can be stated very simply: he did more than any philosopher before him to wean us from our common tendency of thinking in terms of labels, or rather of seizing on labels as an excuse for terminating thought.

One of the most illuminating passages occurs in his posthumously published *Philosophical Investigations,* in a discussion of games: "Do not say: 'They *must* have something in common; else they would not be called "games" '—but *look* whether all of them have something in common." If we do not seize upon the label as a welcome opportunity to stop thinking, we are likely to discover "a complicated net of similarities which overlap and intersect"; and for this Wittgenstein suggests the name "family resemblances" (§§ 66 f.).

The great philosopher with whom he differs most obviously at this point is Plato, who taught that all beautiful things are beautiful by virtue of their participation in the Idea, or Form, of Beauty; that beds are beds by virtue of their participation in the Idea, or Form, of Bed; and, by implication, that all games participate in the Idea, or Form, of Game. Under Plato's influence, the young philosopher tries hard to rise beyond particulars and hopes eventually to behold the universal. Studying religion, he looks for the common essence of the individual religions known to him—or rather those *of* which he knows. Following in Plato's footsteps, he looks for the essence of equality and justice, of democracy and knowledge, perhaps also of theism. Wide individual differences between particular instances are charged to imperfect participation: there is never any doubt that there is a pure essence or

Form, albeit not in this world but beyond, in the realm of Forms.

Still it would be a grave error to suppose that only Plato and philosophers who follow, or have followed, his example are the butt of Wittgenstein's critique. Non-philosophers, too, talk constantly in the same manner, and scores of protracted, futile arguments can be illuminated and henceforth avoided by considering Wittgenstein's conception of family resemblances and by heeding his imperatives, which have been quoted.

People argue, for example, about whether Camus or Pascal were existentialists. They talk as if this were a question of fact. They assume that the so-called existentialists *"must have something in common; else they would not be called"* by the same name, and that we only have to see whether Pascal or Camus share this common quality: if they do, they are plainly existentialists. As a matter of fact, however, there is no clearly defined set of qualities that all the existentialists have in common. Heidegger, like Kierkegaard, but unlike Sartre, disparages reason; but like Sartre, and unlike Kierkegaard, he is no Christian and does not avow belief in God. Sartre once ventured to give a definition of existentialism—as the doctrine that existence precedes essence—but Heidegger and Jaspers promptly pointed out that in that sense they were not existentialists. In sum, there is "a complicated net of similarities which overlap and intersect." It is pointless to insist that Camus was, or was not, an existentialist. But it may well be worth while to point out what he had in common with some other so-called existentialists, and what set him apart.

Is communism a religion? Is Ethical Culture? Follow the same procedure, listing traits shared with various members of the family as well as traits distinguishing the doubtful relative. All this does not involve any Wittgensteinian orthodoxy. All it involves is an analytic mind or, to use a much less fancy term, a bit of carefulness.

Is Freudianism true? We have to ask, what is Freudianism? Does it include Freud's later attempts to revise his early views? Or is it rather the selection that some self-styled Freudians have made from the master's works?

When did the Renaissance, or the Middle Ages, or "Modern Times" begin? Again, it is not the nature of history—its alleged subjectivity—that precludes a precise and definitive answer, but rather the nature of such labels.

Ever so many arguments revolve around some undefined, vague, or ambiguous term. Goethe's Mephistopheles said very neatly:

> Just where no ideas are
> The proper word is never far.

This remark, like the other quotation from *Faust*, earlier in this chapter, is aimed at theology. So is Mephisto's comment in another scene:

> Men usually believe, if only they hear words,
> That there must also be some sort of meaning.

Often, however, the trouble is that there is an excess of ideas and meanings that people have not taken the trouble to sort out; and men talk past each other because they have in mind, if only very vaguely, different meanings. Either way, those who "stick to words" are likely to purchase "certainty" at the price of honesty.

To bring out the connection with honesty, let us return to Wittgenstein. His writings are extremely technical, designed largely for philosophers and mathematicians. But in his very interesting and moving little book, *Ludwig Wittgenstein: A Memoir*, Norman Malcolm tells us how a casual remark he once made in a conversation in the fall of 1939 about the British "national character" vexed Wittgenstein; and he quotes a letter Wittgenstein wrote him five years later: "Whenever I thought of you I couldn't help thinking of a particular incident which seemed to me very important. You & I were walking along the river towards the railway bridge & we had a heated discussion in which you made a remark about 'national character' that shocked me by its primitiveness. I then thought: what is the use of studying philosophy if all that it does for you is to enable you to talk with some plausibility about some abstruse questions of logic, etc., & if it does not improve your thinking about the important questions of everyday life, if it does not make you more conscientious. . . . You see, I know that it's difficult to think *well* about 'certainty,' 'probability,' 'perception,' etc. But it is, if possible, still more difficult to think, or *try* to think, really honestly about your life & other people's lives. And the trouble is that thinking about these things is *not thrilling*, but often downright nasty. And when it's nasty then it's *most* important" (39).

Taken in its original context, Wittgenstein's annoyance with Malcolm's remark is likely to seem excessive. Malcolm's point was merely that the British would not hire a man to assassinate Hitler. But one may surmise that in his childhood and youth Wittgenstein had been subjected to a lot of silly and not altogether innocuous chatter about what German men are like, and Austrian women, and Poles, and Czechs, and Jews, and Russians, and Italians, and that he had slowly come to loathe these thoughtless generalizations with their air of dogmatism and omniscience. If this guess is right, one can understand how a fairly innocent remark might have wounded him deeply: how he was startled and shocked to find a man who apparently had learned a great deal from him evidencing the same thoughtlessness—as if all of Wittgenstein's instruction had been in vain.

As a general statement, Wittgenstein's remarks about "studying philosophy" are magnificent. If they have any fault, it is that the kind of thinking to which Wittgenstein refers *is* thrilling. Indeed, few things are more exciting. But Wittgenstein is right that it is "often downright nasty. And when it's nasty then it's *most* important." Socrates would have agreed wholeheartedly. But scarcely any of Wittgenstein's followers do.

Georg Christoph Lichtenberg (1742–99), a satirical writer whom Wittgenstein greatly admired, once wrote a nasty aphorism: "When a certain worthy died, one man copied his way of wearing his hat, another his way of carrying his sword, a third the cut of his beard, and a fourth his walk; but not one tried to be the honest man he was." What happened after

Wittgenstein's death is somewhat different. Many of his followers, including even pupils of his pupils, copy the very same gestures and mannerisms; and presumably they try to emulate his honesty, too. Some of them even say that this constitutes a "revolution in philosophy": in the twentieth century, philosophers have learned at long last to examine language critically.

There is some justice in this claim. More than ever before, philosophers are exerting themselves "to think *well* about 'certainty,' 'probability,' 'perception,' etc. But it is, if possible, still more difficult to think, or *try* to think, really honestly about your life & other people's lives." And few of Wittgenstein's followers try to do that. This failure is actually connected with the revolution in twentieth-century philosophy: this revolution, though often referred to, is generally misunderstood. We shall examine it in the next chapter.

III

Philosophy and Revolution

11

When philosophers speak, as they often do, of a revolution in philosophy, they generally refer to what is variously called analytic, linguistic, or ordinary language philosophy. They mean the kind of philosophy that developed at the universities of Oxford and Cambridge on the eve of the Second World War. Since the war, it has spread to the United States and become far more influential among professional philosophers than any other single philosophic movement, emphatically including pragmatism and existentialism. This new philosophy owes a great deal to Wittgenstein's later teaching and his posthumously published books. It is also indebted to the work of G. E. Moore (1873–1958), to whose chair at Cambridge Wittgenstein succeeded. But the place where this kind of philosophy flourishes more than anywhere else is Oxford.

Few, if any, philosophers of this type see the history of philosophy in the way proposed in the previous chapter, and an alternative view that is widely shared by competent philosophers deserves our consideration. Moreover, some profound changes really have taken place in twentieth-century philosophy—changes that I have not taken into account so far, although they pose special problems for the enterprise attempted in this book.

Let us begin with the so-called revolution and then go on to consider some of these changes. Throughout, the point will be not to run down what others are doing; but, in Lincoln's celebrated words, "if we could first know where we are, and whither we are tending, we could better judge what to do, and how to do it."

This undertaking is hazardous. Our best literary and philosophic criticism tends toward the microscopic, and reflections on entire movements or on "whither we are tending" are often animadversions. Hence, such attempts are suspect and prone to be misunderstood.

There are two unhelpful precedents. First, one can hide behind statistics, à la mode. That way one can have one's critical analysis and eat one's popular acclaim, too. If the prophets came back and used this procedure, they would be received gladly and dent no one. Happily, this dodge is not available in philosophy.

Second: there are the examples of two ancient philosophers. Heraclitus singled out for criticism men of the first rank, but made a point of speaking of them disrespectfully, even abusively. Socrates, in the *Apology*, insisted that he had concentrated on the greatest reputations of his time; and apparently he did his best to ridicule these men in public, catching them in verbal snares, not always fairly, to deflate them and to let the audience that had gathered laugh at them. Far more than Whistler, who coined the delightful phrase, both philosophers were masters of "the gentle art of making enemies." Such techniques had a point when anti-authoritarianism took its first steps against overwhelming odds. But to illustrate the difficulty of the quest for honesty, it will be best to concentrate throughout this book on men whom I admire and respect.

When names are mentioned, there ought not to be the least presumption that their choice is prompted by resentment or hostility. It is widely believed that strong affection precludes basic disagreements, but this popular conceit is incompatible with high standards of honesty.

As far as the present chapter is concerned, there may not be many basic disagreements with the major figures. I may be at odds more with their influence than with them; and in philosophy one should not blame men too much for their influence, which is usually in large measure unfortunate.

12

It is a little book of B.B.C. lectures that bears the title, and has popularized the notion, of *The Revolution in Philosophy*. In his introduction to that volume, Professor Gilbert Ryle of Oxford University makes no claim that there has been a revolution and insists with plausible modesty that it is much too early to judge the achievements of the movement with which he is associated. But many others have been less reticent than Ryle. And nobody could quarrel with one of his younger Oxford colleagues, Geoffrey Warnock, when he begins the last chapter of his account of *English Philosophy Since 1900* by saying: "Philosophy in the last fifty years has often been said, both by its friends and its enemies, to have undergone a 'revolution.'" The question remains whether what has often been said is also true.

At the very least, there has been a revolution in *Oxford* philosophy since Ryle succeeded R. G. Collingwood as Waynflete Professor of Metaphysical Philosophy. Collingwood was a highly individualistic idealist, much closer to Croce and Hegel, though not to the popular misconceptions about Hegel, than to Bradley and Bosanquet and other British idealists. Now any form of philosophic idealism, in the technical sense of that word, is practically extinct at Oxford, and most of the dons, and almost all who have influence, work in the tradition of Moore and Wittgenstein, not in that of Hegel and Bradley.

Such labels as "linguistic" or "analytic" philosophy are sometimes resented because, for the reasons given above, good philosophers generally do not care for labels. Still, it is useful sometimes to be able to lump many men together to stress that they have something in common, without denying that they are thoughtful individuals, not members of a party. Some of these philosophers are touchy on this point and disclaim emphatically that they belong to any school of thought; but, for all that, their publications generally leave no doubt, any more than their conversation, as to who belongs and who does not, who "does philosophy" the way "one does philosophy" and who does not. And when there is talk of a revolution in philosophy, the whole point is that now "we do philosophy" quite differently from the way it was done formerly.

Nor is this change confined to Oxford. There has been a radical shift in the tone and temper of "English philosophy since 1900," allowing for a few outsiders and survivals from earlier times, and not judging merits for the moment. This change has not greatly affected continental European or South American philosophy, but it is very notable in most of the leading colleges and universities in the United States.

How should one describe the change? One could emphasize the frequent appeal to ordinary language and the popularity of such locutions as "wouldn't it be very odd to say . . . ?" and "doesn't this sound rather queer?" To evaluate this strategy, one would have to consider how it works in the hands of competent practitioners—and we should be led away from our primary concerns. But another aspect of the so-called revolution in twentieth-century philosophy takes us straight back to some of the central themes sounded in the previous chapter, especially in Wittgenstein's wonderful letter.

Warnock says: "It is at any rate certain that questions of 'belief'—questions of religious, moral, political, or generally 'cosmic' variety—are seldom if at all directly dealt with in contemporary philosophy. Why is this so? The first part of an answer to this question can easily be given: There is a very large number of questions, not of that variety, which philosophers find themselves more interested in discussing."

One might doubt whether a mere shift of interest deserves to be called a revolution, until one realizes what most of these philosophers are prepared to relinquish: they no longer "*try* to think really honestly about your life & other people's lives." And they do not only abdicate one of the noblest functions of philosophy as a matter of individual choice but they hail this surrender as a major advance and discourage others from carrying the quest for honesty into less academic questions. Since so many highly intelligent and deeply humane people take this view, it will be well to consider their reasons, if only briefly.

"Religious, moral, political, or generally 'cosmic'" questions are not considered the business of philosophers because philosophers do not seem to possess any special qualifications for dealing with them; and if one holds a post in a university, along with natural and social scientists, one ought to have some specialized professional competence, else one is an impostor.

What, then, *is* the proper function of philosophy? In an early essay on "Systematically Misleading Expressions," Ryle argued that the analysis of such expressions "is what philosophical analysis is, and this is the sole and whole function of philosophy." Oddly, this statement itself is seriously "misleading": it is a recommendation disguised as a description. And taken at face value, as a description, the statement is plainly false. If you look up what any good dictionary says about philosophy, or if you read any good history of philosophy, you find that the analysis of systematically misleading expressions has plainly not been "the sole and whole function of philosophy"; nor is it today, unless you refuse to call philosophy what those philosophers are doing who do not confine themselves to such analysis.

Such analyses can be of great importance, and I have nothing against them. The analysis of theism, atheism, and agnosticism in Section 9 could be easily assimilated to this genre, and at the end of the next chapter I shall deal with some misleading expressions concerning commitment. But the claim that the analysis of systematically misleading expressions is, or ought to be, "the sole and whole function of philosophy" remains arbitrary and implausible. One can try to remove its sting by pointing out how much traditional philosophy could be presented in this form; and one could even empty the claim of all meaning by arguing that, with some ingenuity, everything that a philosopher might wish to do could be forced into this mold. In his later books, *The Concept of Mind* and *Dilemmas,* Ryle showed sufficient scope, without repudiating his early dictum, to have led some admirers to adopt one or the other of these two views. In that case, however, no revolution in philosophy has ever been attempted. But this seems false.

Surely, Ryle's point—and the point of the attempted revolution—was that philosophers should cease to occupy themselves with empirical data because they lack any special competence to deal with these: such data should be left to scientists or historians, while philosophers should stick to analysis—for example, of systematically misleading expressions. But while they oppose any trespasses into the domains of colleagues in other fields, the linguistic philosophers themselves trespass into linguistics. If they should plead that there is still a dearth of professional linguists, two very damning answers are possible and mutually compatible.

First, there may be a dearth of professionals in other fields. If philosophers are justified in trespassing on vacant lots, or vacant regions of other men's fields, this description does not fit linguistics only. Second: even as various other sciences have gradually broken away from philosophy and gained autonomy—psychology and sociology quite recently—linguistics is a field in which academic chairs and departments are being created even now. What, then, is to become of philosophy in another few years? Should philosophers close up shop? Or should not philosophers rather resist the growing trend toward specialization and trespass freely?

The best linguistic philosophers have noted things that linguists without thorough philosophic training did not see. The moral is obvious: philosophy of religion and political philosophy need not be abandoned any more than philosophy of science or of language; but the man who ventures into other fields should have some extraphilosophic competence. If he does, he stands a fair chance of making contributions that political scientists and politicians, theologians and preachers, physicists and philologists would be much less likely to make.

Some philosophers feel that if a philosopher has such a dual competence it may be all right for him to put it to use, though they doubt that any resulting essay could be classified as philosophy. Moreover, they see no special reason why philosophers should master the techniques of other subjects and labor in other fields. Men in physics and psychology, political science and theology, might just as well study philosophy.

So they might; but the primary question is whether the job is important and worth doing. If it is, there is not much point in insisting that somebody else could do it just as well, though admittedly no more easily. Moreover, if such efforts are needed, philosophers have less excuse for not undertaking them than anybody else; for in philosophy attempts of this sort are traditional, and shying away from them involves a deliberate abandonment of this tradition.

Some of the pre-Socratics were no mean scientists. The Sophists were pioneering students of grammar. Aristotle was a polymath. Descartes and Leibniz were topflight mathematicians. Spinoza's *Theological-Political Treatise* made first-rate contributions to the critical study of the Bible. Hobbes kept up with the science of his day and also translated Thucydides and Homer. Hume was a historian. Kant formulated the so-called Kant-Laplace theory of the origin of the solar system and also wrote an essay to demonstrate the need for a "League of Nations." Hegel was an outstanding historian. Nietzsche, according to Freud, "had a more penetrating knowledge of himself than any other man who ever lived or was ever likely to live," and his "insights often agree in the most amazing manner with the laborious results of psychoanalysis."

Perhaps Hobbes's translation of Thucydides was a mere side line, almost a hobby? This is admittedly an extreme case, but even here it is likely that not only Hobbes's superb prose style profited from this effort but also his political philosophy. Such a translation is not on a par with Spinoza's making a living by grinding lenses; it is much closer to Spinoza's Biblical studies which were closely related to *his* political philosophy. Similarly, Kant's great *Idea for a Universal History with Cosmopolitan Intent* (1784) contains his philosophy of history and introduces the "League of Nations" in that context. Confining philosophers to linguistic analyses and discouraging them from dealing with the empirical data of other fields would lead to an unfortunate impoverishment of philosophy, also of humanity.

13

What at first glance may seem to be no more than a shift of interest is in fact a symptom of a much more basic change. Philosophy has become academic because almost all twentieth-century philosophers write in academics, as Descartes and Spinoza, Leibniz and Locke, Bacon and Berkeley, Hobbes and Hume did not. What is new is that philosophy has become a profession—a job rather than a vocation.

If this should seem an impressionistic distinction, the point can be quantified, too: the most fundamental change in philosophy is that formerly there were perhaps a dozen men engaged in it at any one time, give or take a few, while today there are thousands.

Near the end of his book, Warnock rightly calls attention to the philosophic journals. Indeed, until some time after 1950, most Oxford philosophers considered it definitely not "U" to publish books: "one" wrote for the journals and let German and American philosophers write books. In the fifties there was a sudden change and it became quite fashionable to write *little* books, like Warnock's. He does not mention this, but he notes with entire justice: "This new professional practice of submitting problems and arguments to the expert criticism of fellow craftsmen led to a growing concern with questions of technique." More controversially, he charges the public with "a vague feeling that the total amateur ought not to be disqualified from engaging in what was, so recently, an amateurish pursuit."

Such remarks about amateurs are often heard. Sometimes people in armchairs are introduced as an elegant variation. But such ploys are easily turned round. It is surely one reason for the popularity of the new philosophy that any bright young man can play; he needs no special knowledge, only a command of "U" English. Even a bad paper on this kind of philosophy is likely to elicit an intense discussion: it breaks the ice better than two martinis. It is all good fun once you get the hang of it, and there is room for some to show a special flair and to excel. All this is very well; but it is ironical when the participants look down on traditional philosophy as "an amateurish pursuit."

There have always been amateurs, and there are more than ever now. But the great philosophers accepted some responsibilities that most analytic philosophers decline. They were interested in "questions of 'belief'—questions of religious, moral, political, or generally 'cosmic' variety"; and they tried to think "honestly about your life and other people's lives." If Kant, Hume, and Spinoza had written only for "fellow craftsmen," there would not have been any need to print their works: circulating the manuscript would have done the trick. It does not follow that their practice of addressing non-philosophers, too, made their work less important—on the contrary.

The main reason for our many philosophic journals is, of course, that suddenly there are thousands of men professionally engaged in the subject—thousands who have to publish now and then to gain some recognition, to win raises and promotions, and to show themselves and fellow members of their "association" that they are both physically and mentally alive. Quotation from a letter of recommendation in 1960: "During the last year he has published three times."

What used to be a rare vocation for uncommon individuals who took a bold stand has become an industry involving legions. Naturally, the whole tone and level of discussion had to change. When there are over a thousand colleges in one country, and most of them have departments of philosophy, many of them with a dozen or more members, it would be ridiculous if every professional tried to emulate Spinoza's *Ethics;* or if they urged millions of students in their courses to write something like Hume's *Treatise of Human Nature, being an Attempt to Introduce the Experimental Method of Reasoning into Moral Subjects.* But the reason why it would be absurd is not that these books were written by amateurs, perhaps in armchairs; nor even that the *Treatise,* like some other philosophic classics, was the work of a young man in his twenties. It would be bizarre only because these books are so great and so bold.

The new, professional philosopher does not vie with the great philosophers of former ages but with other men in his own age group in the other departments of his college. He may well be older than Berkeley and Hume were when they wrote their masterpieces, but he would be likely to make a fool of himself if he stuck out his neck as they did. It is far safer and much more prudent to insist on being a professional. One publishes papers in learned journals, often employs symbols even when they are dispensable, and uses a jargon that stumps everybody but fellow professionals. Perhaps the average paper now is better than the average paper fifty years ago: that would hardly be a great compliment; and, to be sure about it, one would have to compare thousands of papers. Life is too short for that.

No doubt, philosophers, like their colleagues, should have their own journals. What is appalling is not the quality of most papers but the suggestion that we should look down condescendingly on the great "amateurs" of former times and do our best to prevent any recurrence.

In a fine passage in *Beyond Good and Evil* (§ 212), Nietzsche says that, traditionally, the great philosopher has always stood "in opposition to his today." Philosophers have been "the bad conscience of their time." They knew "of a *new* greatness of man, of a new untrodden way to his enhancement. . . . Confronted with a world of 'modern ideas,' which would banish everybody into a corner and a 'specialty,' a philosopher—if there could be any philosophers today—would be forced to define the greatness of man, the concept of 'greatness,' in terms precisely of man's comprehensiveness and multiplicity, his wholeness in manifoldness." After some illustrations from the sixteenth century and some remarks about Socrates, Nietzsche continues: "Today, conversely, when only the herd animal is honored and dispenses honors in Europe, and when 'equality of rights' could all too easily be converted into an equality in violating rights—by that I mean, into a common war on all that is rare, strange, or privileged, on the higher man, the higher soul, the higher duty, the higher responsibility, and on the wealth of creative power and mastery—today the concept of 'greatness' entails being noble, wanting to be by oneself, being capable of being different, standing alone, and having to live independently. . . ." Thus, in 1886. Wittgenstein would have fully understood.

In some ways the so-called revolution in philosophy is counterrevolutionary: its influence leads men away from trying to stand alone; it would banish philosophers "into a corner and a specialty." It teaches young philosophers not to become heretics or revolutionaries because they lack any special qualifications for that. Yet it might be part of a philosopher's task to acquire the necessary qualifications. Of course, not everybody can do that; but to say that what not all can do, none should even try to do, is a recipe for mediocrity— "a common war on all that is rare, strange, and privileged."

14

Instead of speaking of a revolution in philosophy, it might be more accurate to speak of a great crisis in philosophy. In some ways it is comparable to the crisis in modern religion. The great progress in the sciences has made many traditional beliefs, tenets, and assumptions highly problematic, if not untenable. As a result, some theologians have reinterpreted many old beliefs—to the point where some thoughtful people have begun to wonder what, if any, meaning remains. The old beliefs were clear but are now given up as false; the reinterpreted beliefs, which are said to be immune to all scientific advances, are often highly elusive and perhaps in some instances mere formulas devoid of any clear content.

For once, the philosophers excel the theologians in oneupmanship. Instead of conceding that the progress of science has produced a major crisis in philosophy because so many doctrines of traditional philosophy have now come to appear naïve or false, many philosophers speak cheerfully and proudly of a revolution in philosophy. Yet a great heritage has been called into question, in philosophy as well as in religion; the great names of over twenty centuries are suddenly in danger; and it is no longer clear whether the great classics should be taught.

The story goes that a famous contemporary philosopher was offered a position at a leading university, but refused it when told that among other things he should have to teach Plato. Allegedly he replied: "I shall teach only the truth." The story is probably apocryphal: one would hardly insist that a celebrated man teach a course he would rather not teach. But this legend illustrates the crisis. It also raises the question whether, instead of charging modern philosophers with one-upmanship, one ought not rather to congratulate them on their honesty because they openly break with tradition. But scarcely any contemporary philosophers go so far as the positivist in this story, and the story itself is considered grotesque and something of a joke among philosophers.

One might liken the situation in philosophy to that in the sciences rather than to that in religion, if most philosophers did break with tradition as much as the man in our story; if recent philosophers towered above Plato and Aristotle, Kant and Spinoza; and if contemporary philosophy were as manifestly superior to previous philosophy as modern science is to previous science. But while in the sciences there are giants who need not fear comparison with the greatest innovators of the past, and there are literally scores of topflight scientists who have made revolutionary discoveries and propounded far-reaching theories, the whole atmosphere in English-speaking philosophy is marked by a pervasive mistrust of giants and of far-reaching theories. Not only is scope sacrificed for frequently unsuccessful attempts at rigor but theory, once almost synonymous with philosophy, is widely abandoned in order to obtain agreement about facts. If one stopped teaching Plato and the other traditional philosophers, so little would be left that the contrast with the sciences would stare us in the face. Hence, one has recourse to a double standard.

One continues to teach Plato and, occasional jibes at amateurs notwithstanding, generally looks up to the giants of the past. Indeed, in the English-speaking world a reputation in philosophy can still be built by writing *about* Plato or the pre-Socratics, Hegel or Nietzsche, but it cannot be built by writing as they did. The situation parallels that in religion, not that in the sciences. In our seminaries and in college Departments of Religion, it is respectable to write and dote on Kierkegaard or other, greater figures of the more remote past; but woe unto the man who emulates them!

In philosophy it is respectable to give elaborate accounts of bygone theories on matters on which it would not be respectable to theorize oneself. Similarly, an exposition of Kant's, Hegel's, or Nietzsche's criticisms of Christianity is considered a worth-while and useful contribution which deserves an honored place in philosophic journals, even if the criticisms summarized should be unsound. But the very same people who are grateful for a documented exposition of past criticisms are far from grateful for contemporary criticisms of Christianity, even if some of the strictures should be more judicious. To report other men's unsound criticisms is considered worthy of a philosopher; to offer sound criticisms of Christianity on one's own is not considered part of a philosopher's job.

Fleetingly, one might wonder whether the situation in philosophy might not resemble that in history: a historian is expected to write about Napoleon, not to emulate him. But this analogy is utterly misleading. Napoleon himself was not a historian, and the historian who writes about him does not suppose he was. Philosophers, on the other hand, write about past philosophers who are considered sufficiently great and important as philosophers to render competent discussions of their work deserving of a place in philosophic journals, while essays in the vein in which these past philosophers themselves wrote are conspicuously absent from the journals.

No doubt, many factors are at work here, but the most important is the vast prestige of science. The advice which members of the American Philosophical Association received in the mail in 1960 is profoundly symptomatic: ". . . many research applications from philosophers compare unfavorably with applications from scholars in other fields. We believe this impression is due, in part, to the fact that Foundation and University Research Committees have become accustomed to the appearance of precision and definiteness in scientific projects. Philosophical investigations, in many instances, do not have precise and narrow limits. In order to overcome this handicap, our Committee makes a few suggestions: *Design:* Specify a proposition to be verified or a well-defined area to be explored, Or give as much definiteness to your proposal as possible by: A. Stating the problem or group of problems on which you propose to work; B. Outlining a plan of work; C. If you wish to collaborate with other scholars, indicate the nature and extent of the collaboration. . . ."

Philosophers have no preference for the history of philosophy as such. On the contrary, owing in part to the insufficient emphasis on languages in the American secondary school system, most American philosophers are handicapped in this field. What they want is agreement about facts, progress in the accumulation of knowledge, a clear-cut contribution. The history of philosophy is merely one area in which such agreement may be obtainable. Reading the advice on research applications, one sees at a glance that research on Spinoza's *Ethics* or Plato's *Republic* is respectable, particularly if the applicant should stress the "precise and narrow limits" of his project and confine himself to certain aspects of the masterpiece on which he wants to write. But suppose that Plato or Spinoza had applied!

"I should like to write a book of medium length, dealing with God, man, and the world. I envisage five short parts, the first dealing with God, the second with the nature and the origin of mind, the third with the nature and the origin of the emotions. I contemplate no laboratory work and no collaboration—in fact, strictly speaking, no research. I propose to sit in my armchair and think. At home. No travel contemplated. No need to go to libraries or seek out fellow scholars. If time permits, I shall deal in the last two parts with human bondage and the power of the emotions, and with the power of the intellect and human liberty. I find it difficult to state the problem or the group of problems on which I propose to work because, frankly, there are few problems with which I don't propose to deal. Expected result: one short book. Sincerely, B. Spinoza."

"I want to write a dialogue, somewhat under 300 printed pages in length. It will begin with a discussion of justice, but later on I hope to deal with *all* the virtues and with other problems of importance for moral philosophy. Actually, the major topic will be political philosophy, and I am planning to develop at some length my own conception of an ideal state. More briefly, near the end, I shall criticize all the major forms of government now in existence. I have done some traveling in the past and have had some contact with philosophers and statesmen; there is no need for further travel or consultations now. Nor do I need the resources of any library. All I require is an armchair and some peace and quiet. In any case, the criticism of the various forms of government will be quite brief. I hope to devote far more space to metaphysics, theory of knowledge, my ideas about education, literary criticism, and theology. I do not mean to preclude the possibility that, as I write, some other subjects may swim into view and cry out to be brought in, too. What I want to write is a well organized book—indeed, a beautifully organized book—but at this stage I am not quite ready to tell you in what way some of these topics will be introduced: that will become clear to me only as I write—perhaps only as I rewrite, and continue to rewrite, my book. If it should turn out in the end that I have omitted any important problems or group of problems, I propose to make up for that by shortly dealing with such problems in other dialogues. Collaboration is out of the question. As for the title, I have not decided yet; but I think I shall choose a single word, probably some comprehensive label. Perhaps I should add that I am not at all sure whether my philosophy admits of verbal formulation. I rather think that it does not. What really matters is not to arrive at assured results that can be assimilated by reading my book but rather to strike some sparks, and probably the book will not be fully understood by anyone except those who have spent a few years working closely with me. Even they might not get what matters most to me. But such is philosophy. The greatest philosopher that ever lived—my master, Socrates—never even tried to teach results. Some people say he taught a method; but there is no agreement among those who knew him best just what this method was. Anyway, my master was put to death for his teachings. Hoping for your support, Yours, Plato."

Such applications would "compare unfavorably with applications from scholars in other fields," and "Research Committees have become accustomed to the appearance of precision and definiteness in scientific projects." They would not be likely to act favorably on such projects, while a secondary, historical study, with "precise and narrow limits," might well be supported. The irony of the contemporary situation in philosophy is best brought out by adding that the advice to America's philosophers that has been quoted came from the "Committee to Advance Original [!] Work in Philosophy."

The situation being what it is, the Research Committees are not to be blamed. As chairman of a major one, I can vouch that no promising young man would submit a project like the two proposed here; and if a project did look like this, there would be every presumption that the applicant *was* muddleheaded, and that any number of others were more deserving. The point of this chapter is not to accuse committees, dons, or any alleged conspiracy of sinister powers; it is rather to see how philosophy has changed, and how the present situation differs from that in former ages.

Some of the most brilliant and original minds now go into physics and other sciences where boldness and disciplined imagination may achieve great triumphs. A remark attributed to David Hilbert, the great mathematician, sounds less paradoxical now than a few decades ago. When a student abandoned mathematics to write novels, Hilbert commented: "It was just as well; he did not have enough imagination to become a first-rate mathematician."

Of those who do become philosophers, many of the brightest go into symbolic logic—the one branch of philosophy that resembles mathematics. Here precision is at home; one can compel the agreement of fellow scholars, make genuine contributions, and score advances. A large number of the best minds also go into analytic philosophy. If one follows the lead of the young Ryle and analyzes misleading expressions, there is hope that one can reach agreement and make clear-cut contributions. Others take their cue from Professor J. L. Austin (1911–60), also of Oxford, whose skill at linguistic analysis was blended with a rare sense of humor and a still more exceptional moral authority that issued from the force of his personality and his high standards of honesty. In his classical account of his method, in "A Plea for Excuses," he declared: "Our common stock of words embodies all the distinctions men have found worth drawing, and the connexions they have found worth marking, in the lifetimes of many generations: these surely are likely to be more . . . sound, since they have stood up to the long test of the survival of the fittest, . . . than any you or I are likely to think up in our armchairs of an afternoon—the most favoured alternative method" (8). Fine distinctions in ordinary language may help to call our attention to important differences, and Austin excelled at noting small discrepancies between apparent synonyms. In fact, he so immersed himself in work of this kind that he rarely deigned to point out philosophic implications; and occasionally he said pointedly, perhaps with just a touch of irony, that we are not ready for "philosophical" questions.

The trouble with "religious, moral, political, or generally 'cosmic'" questions is that one despairs of reaching agreement and is therefore unsure what might constitute a worth-while contribution. If one does deal with ethics, one goes into "meta-ethics." Urmson's *Concise Encyclopedia of Western Philosophy and Philosophers* distinguishes "(1) *Moral questions:* for example, 'Ought I to do that?'; 'Is polygamy wrong?' . . . (2) *Questions of fact about people's moral opinions:* for example, 'What did Mohammed (or . . . what do I myself) in fact think (or say) about the rightness or wrongness of polygamy?' (3) *Questions about the meaning of moral words (for example, 'ought,' 'right,' 'good,' 'duty'); or about the nature of the concepts or the 'things' to which these words 'refer':* for example, 'When Mohammed said that polygamy is not wrong, what was he saying?' These three sorts of questions being quite distinct, the use of the word 'ethics' to embrace attempts to answer all three is confusing, and is avoided by the more careful modern writers. . . . We shall distinguish between (1) morals, (2) descriptive ethics and (3) ethics, corresponding to the three sorts of questions listed above." Most analytic philosophers favor "confining the word 'ethics' (used without qualification) to the third sort of question," though some students prefer "the more guarded terms 'the logic of ethics,' 'metaethics,'" or various other locutions.

The same distinctions apply to the philosophy of religion, political philosophy, and other fields. The few analytic philosophers who have gone into these fields have dealt with *The Vocabulary of Politics,* to cite the title of a book, or with "religious language." Here again there is some hope of reaching agreement and making a definite contribution.

The threefold distinction is certainly helpful, and the clarification of the meaning of moral or religious words is important. The wish to make a clear-cut contribution is legitimate and reasonable, and there is nothing wrong with turning to these fields.

Still, it is notable that traditional philosophy did not stop with "meta" questions. It somehow stood between the sciences and literature. Plato required the study of mathematics as a prerequisite for the study of philosophy, and he was immensely interested in significant terms; but, for all that, it is doubtful that he aimed at making a "contribution" any more than Sophocles, Shakespeare, or Goethe did. And we still look upon the books of great philosophers of former ages more the way we look at Sophocles', Shakespeare's, or Goethe's works than the way a scientist looks at the classics in his field. The writings of Plato, Aristotle, Spinoza, and Kant *are* philosophy in a sense in which we should not think of saying that the works of Archimedes or Copernicus *are* science. The great philosophers did make contributions, as was acknowledged in Chapter II; but the primary reason for reading Plato or Kant is not to absorb these contributions or to gain historical knowledge, though these are, of course, perfectly legitimate secondary reasons. In philosophy, as in literature but not in science, objectionable views and arguments are no sufficient reason for not studying the works of a great writer.

The best British analytic philosophers have retained literary quality far more than their American cousins. It is not just that Ryle writes superb English, or that Austin had a highly individual style—perhaps his essay on "Pretending" is the most hilarious piece of philosophy ever written—or that Professor John Wisdom of Cambridge also has a manner all his own. The point is rather that one learns easily as much from their highly personal way of looking and going at things as from any results they contribute.

One of the most important parts of any education is to learn to understand views different from one's own and to outgrow the narrow-mindedness and lack of intellectual imagination that cling to us from our childhood. Dostoevsky does not condone murder, but *Crime and Punishment* and his other major novels change most readers' attitudes toward criminals, toward other human beings, and, not least, toward themselves. Reading Plato and Spinoza also affects our attitudes toward men whose values and beliefs are different from our own and makes us see ourselves in a new light.

The great philosophers were for the most part heirs of Socrates, who claimed in the *Apology* that he was his city's greatest benefactor. He prided himself on having fulfilled "the philosopher's mission of searching into myself and other men"; on having shown that men who were considered wise both by themselves and by their fellow men were really not wise; and on having made his fellow citizens "ashamed of heaping up the greatest amount of money and honor and reputation, and caring so little about wisdom and truth." He likened himself to a gadfly that did not permit the conscience of his fellow citizens to fall asleep.

Toward the end of Plato's *Symposium*, Alcibiades says of Socrates: "I have heard Pericles and other great orators, and I thought that they spoke well, but I never had any similar feeling; my soul was not stirred by them, nor was I angry at the thought of my own slavish state. But this Marsyas has often brought me to such a path, that I have felt as if I could hardly endure the life which I was leading. . . . He makes me confess that I ought not to live as I do."

Spinoza and Nietzsche have a comparable impact; and while few other great philosophers approximate the eloquence of Socrates' *Apology*, almost all of them issue a similar challenge. This challenge is not quite the same as that we encounter in great plays and novels: the philosophers make us ashamed of our lack of thoughtfulness, our slovenly habits of mind, our slothful intellects. This is also true of Wittgenstein and Wisdom, Ryle and Austin, even if they seem at times to lean over backward to hide that unprofessional challenge— and it therefore escapes some of their students and followers.

Almost all outstanding philosophers echo Socrates' great dictum that "the unexamined life is not worth living." Of course, the philosophers are often wrong themselves; but some of their errors only serve to reinforce their challenge. The program of a Descartes or a Kant may set a student's mind afire, while their shortcomings may reassure him that not everything worth doing has been done.

To deal well with problems that are crucial for "your life and other people's lives" is extremely difficult; and in the light of the best work of the analytic philosophers, much traditional philosophy appears sadly inadequate. If most philosophers want to confine themselves to less dramatic and more manageable problems, that is surely sensible.

Spinoza concluded his *Ethics* by saying: "Everything excellent is as difficult as it is rare." That is no reason why *everybody* should renounce the quest for excellence. And even those who discount Socrates' proud claim that "no greater good has ever happened in the state than my service" might well admit that the Socratic gadfly makes a contribution, too; and if that is not philosophy, what is it?

15

In a sense, every truly great philosopher has revolutionized philosophy: that is one of the criteria of greatness in philosophy. In our histories of philosophy we concentrate on those who left some lasting mark, who somehow changed the course of subsequent philosophy, as Plato did, or Aristotle, or Descartes, or Kant. After Hegel, during the nineteenth century, the European philosophic community ceased to exist. Toward the end of that century, Nietzsche still exerted an enormous influence on French and German thought, but not on the English-speaking world. There is then a sense in which there has not been a revolution in philosophy in general since Kant or Hegel. At most, there have been local revolutions: possibly pragmatism in the United States, though it is very doubtful whether Peirce, James, or Dewey really effected any basic and enduring change; perhaps existentialism on the European continent; and analytic philosophy in England and in the United States. But even insofar as analytic philosophy involves a local revolution, it has had a counterrevolutionary aspect. It would be tempting to conclude: what matters is not to revolutionize philosophy, but to make philosophy once again revolutionary.

Yet it would be folly to suggest that all philosophers ought to be doing the same thing. It is no cause for regret that not every philosopher is a self-appointed critic of the age. But it would be a shame if *everybody* waited to criticize until appointed, as if one became a gadfly by appointment.

There is no single central tradition in philosophy, and men with different interests and inclinations have no difficulty in appealing to divergent precedents. A critic who protests his fellow philosophers' growing preoccupation with agreement need not conclude that all philosophers ought to agree. On the contrary, he should protest against the many pressures brought to bear on young philosophers to ensure that almost all of them are in agreement that "doing philosophy" precludes being a gadfly.

That philosophers disagree is no cause for shame and no objection to philosophy. To the most important questions, several answers are defensible; and most answers are reprehensible. Most answers are thoughtless, conflict with relevant evidence, or involve confusions, inconsistencies, and fallacies.

Scylla, the rock, thinks her own position the only one that is respectable. Charybdis, the whirlpool, considers all outlooks equally tenable. A virtuoso can triumphantly defend alternative positions. Charybdis, her mind reeling, concludes giddily that all religions and philosophies, all moral codes and

works of art are on a par. Scylla, with a mind of stone, resists all reasoning and insists that she alone is right.

Petrified dogmatism and the eddies of relativism are equally
unworthy of philosophers. They should sift the tenable from
the untenable, criticize what is false, especially when it is
popular, and develop with care plausible alternatives to what
is long familiar. Let one man champion one alternative, and
his fellow another: fear of disagreement is for a philosopher
what fear of getting hurt is for a soldier—cowardice. And delight in a revolution that has brought an end to widespread
disagreement on important questions would be uncomfortably
close to rejoicing that philosophy "is in his grave; after life's
fitful fever he sleeps well."

Let some philosophers analyze misleading expressions while
others note discrepancies between synonyms; let some study
the meaning of moral terms while others become logicians
and still others write on Plato; and let a few continue to reflect
on "moral questions," in the hope that those who have given
some thought to metaethics and to the literature on both
"morals" and metaethics might be able to say something
worth while about "morals." And let some philosophers deal
with religious questions, in the hope that those who have
thought about the meaning of religious terms and studied the
literature on religious terms, on diverse religious views, and on
religious questions might be able to contribute something to
the discussion of religious questions. Even if such hopes should
not be realized in the individual case, they are surely reasonable, and the tradition is therefore worth continuing: if we
fail, others may learn from our mistakes and do better.

Similar considerations apply to form. Let some philosophers
favor the monograph, and others more artistic forms. Clearly,
the scholarly monograph is the best way of making some
kinds of contributions; but it would be a pity if the monographic mind monopolized the field. Let us remember
that most of the finest philosophic classics were not monographs; for example, Plato's *Symposium* and Plato's *Republic*,
Hobbes's *Leviathan* and Spinoza's *Ethics*, Hume's *Treatise*
and Hume's *Dialogues Concerning Natural Religion*, Hegel's

Phenomenology of the Spirit, and the whole lot of Nietzsche's books.

Each form has its dangers. They are too numerous to catalogue. One obvious danger of the monograph is pedantry (see § 4). But pedantry will always be with us. The prophets scorned it, but some of the Talmudic rabbis carried it to new heights. Jesus opposed it, but at the church councils it reached unprecedented triumphs. It is not the shadow of science, but found in all ages: the misguided aping of the natural sciences is merely one form of pedantry—to which Schiller's verse applies:

> How he coughs and how he spits
> Is quickly aped by lesser wits.

Pedantry is the mode in which the relatively uncreative can be endlessly creative. Since creativity flags even in creative geniuses, some of the very greatest, too, have sometimes sought security on the crutches of pedantry—including, for example, Thomas, Kant, and Hegel.

Obviously, an aversion to pedantry is no guarantee of any worth; and no philosopher has ever supposed that it was. Pretentious non-pedants of little or no substance are legion.

Artistic modes of expression are likely to be merely suggestive and needlessly inconclusive. One is apt to be treated to a brilliant display of epigrammatic fireworks, but sometimes the writer does not stick long enough with any point to show us what might be said for it and what against it. Everything remains at the level of a suggestion, and little is done to help us decide whether the suggestions are good or bad. It is at this point that the monograph may seem to have its strength; but actually many articles of the best analytic philosophers are strangely inconclusive, too. No form is a panacea.

Some philosophers want to get across their experience of philosophy, too—that way of life in which the particular problems they treat are merely episodes. They recall, and take seriously, Plato's disdain, in his Seventh Letter, for "those who are not genuine philosophers but painted over with opinions" and his insistence that there neither was nor ever would be any written work of his containing his own philosophy: "for this cannot be formulated like other doctrines; but through continued application to the subject itself and living with it, a spark is suddenly struck in the soul as by leaping fire, and then grows by itself" (340 f.).

A philosopher may try to communicate what, as he knows, cannot be communicated to everybody. He may exert himself to strike a spark here and there in a mind that is ready. He may hope that, though some readers will merely browse, whether to take offense or pleasure, others may, as it were, live with his book until the spark leaps over.

Nor is there only one way of sticking with a point—the monographic way. One may want to show how one point is related to others, how a judgment derives part of its meaning from its relation to other judgments, how a view that is seemingly clear appears in a different light when seen in a wider context. Microscopic work can be of the greatest importance; but it has no monopoly on importance, and not everything macroscopic is necessarily popular in the bad sense—or popular at all. The gadfly's function is hardly a paradigm of popularity.

One can take up a single point and worry it as a dog worries a bone, though occasionally with more fruitful results. One can also ask oneself about the significance of a whole trend in philosophy, and be carried hence into reflection about commitment, and then theology, and then a non-theological approach to a theological problem, and a non-theological appraisal of our religious heritage, and the nature of organized religion, and morality. Such an attempt to spell out a comprehensive position does not have to be uncritical, merely inspirational, and unworthy of a philosopher. To be sure, the effort is more hazardous than a painstaking and detailed analysis of a single problem, and it is more likely to fail. But as Whitehead remarked in *Modes of Thought*, "Panic of error is the death of progress" (22). As long as one is aware of the dangers and warns one's readers, instead of wearing the mantle of omniscience, the risk is hardly excessive: if the prose is clear, errors can be corrected.

Too many philosophers resemble Graham Greene—or,

rather, try to: they strive for a competence that is always at its best—professional, craftsmanlike, even slick. Compared with Greene's fiction, some of Camus's seems amateurish: his fiction has flaws and sometimes does not quite achieve what it seems to aim for; it is not slick but approximate greatness.

This point received its classic statement from a somewhat amateurish poet who is in eclipse in our current period of professionalism—in poetry, too: it is the theme of Robert Browning's long poem, *Andrea del Sarto (Called "The Fault-less Painter")*. A few lines at least may conclude this argument:

> Ah, but a man's reach should exceed his grasp,
> Or what's a Heaven for? all is silver-grey,
> Placid and perfect with my art—the worse!

Then, looking at a work by Rafael (a curious choice—Browning's, not mine):

> That arm is wrongly put—and there again—
> A fault to pardon in the drawing's lines,
> Its body, so to speak: its soul is right,
> He means right—that, a child may understand.
> Still, what an arm! and I could alter it. . . .
> I hardly dare—yet, only you to see,
> Give the chalk here—quick, thus the line should go!
> Ay, but the soul! he's Rafael! rub it out!

16

The intellectual conscience of Socrates was superbly embodied by J. L. Austin, who also had a keen wit and a wonderful sense of humor. G. E. Moore, whose writings are lacking in humor, stood for the same heritage. And honesty that tries to live up to high standards is so rare that such men as these deserve ungrudging admiration. Still, it would be wrong to leave the case for Socrates' other legacy, best symbolized by his own image of the gadfly, on an unduly defensive note. It would be wrong, as well as deeply un-Socratic, to ask merely that the gadfly, too, ought to be tolerated.

The anti-academic conception of philosophers as "the bad conscience of their time"—to cite Nietzsche's phrase once more—was taken up to some extent by Sartre and Camus, though their philosophic works compare unfavorably with the writings of the best British philosophers in intellectual conscientiousness and carefulness, as will be shown later in this book.

In a lecture at the Sorbonne, in 1946, at the first general meeting of UNESCO, Sartre spoke on "The Responsibility of the Writer." Like most of his non-fiction, the lecture is curiously uneven; and in the next chapter, on "Commitment," I shall argue that it is a central weakness of existentialism that it does not adequately understand the nature of responsibility.

Sartre's reach often exceeds his grasp; but his best is magnificent, and the following passage says powerfully what badly needs to be said. (The curious "if" will be discussed later, in Section 92.)

"If a writer has chosen to be silent on one aspect of the world, we have the right to ask him: Why have you spoken of this rather than that? And since you speak in order to make a change, since there is no other way you can speak, why do you want to change this rather than that? Why do you want to alter the way in which postage stamps are made rather than the way in which Jews are treated in an anti-Semitic country? And the other way around. He must therefore always answer the following questions: What do you want to change? Why this rather than that?"

IV

Commitment

17

Until recently, "being committed" meant being insane and having been found out. But today it is widely felt that something must be wrong with you if you are *not* committed to an institution. Indeed, you are not supposed to wait for others to commit you; you are expected to commit *yourself*.

One used to "commit" murder and armed robbery, adultery and suicide, which were considered heinous crimes; one did not "commit" good deeds and scarcely misdemeanors. "Commit" was a vicious word until it was emancipated by Jean-Paul Sartre. To be more precise, "commitment" was rescued by those who sought an English equivalent for Sartre's *engagement*. First they tried "engaging oneself" and "engagement"; then they switched to "committing oneself" and "commitment." Immediately, the theologians, preachers, and evangelists took over. Always on the lookout for the newest wine to replenish their dry old skins, they took enthusiastically to existentialism and commitment.

In their eminently understandable concern lest what they have to offer us might be considered dated and anachronistic, those who grace our pulpits often try to balance the imposing archaism of most of their utterances with some of the latest jargon. The holy tone of many sermons, with its air of omniscience, conveys a mixture of ancient and modern notions, some wise and some foolish; and most preachers lack the scholarship and thoughtfulness required for a real grasp of either the new or the old.

The reasons for this lack of scholarship and thoughtfulness

are manifold. Some of them are plainly connected with the kind of training offered in theological seminaries, which will be considered in the next chapter. Others are peculiar to the United States, where a genuine reading knowledge of foreign languages has become a rarity, and the seminaries, like even the best graduate schools, are unable to remedy defects which should have been taken care of early in the student's education.

As it is, "most clergymen . . . undertake to expound or defend the scriptures without understanding the languages in which they are written"—to cite a profoundly thoughtful and scholarly clergyman, Frederick C. Grant, whose *Ancient Judaism and the New Testament* represents an admirable effort to fight the ignorance, the "prejudices," and the "misinterpretations" that are shared by "the vast majority of the clergy in most churches"—and, of course, by their flocks.

"Unable to read their own sacred books," they are even less able to keep up with the latest scholarship in history, philology, philosophy, and other subjects that are relevant to their sermons. Many, no doubt, lack the scholar's conscience; but even those who keenly suffer from their lack of knowledge are generally in no position to do much about it: the pressures of their office leave them little time for study, and their income is for the most part inadequate for buying many books. But unfortunately scholarship is not irrelevant to the majority of sermons.

Even so, it is widely supposed that those who spurn the Pablum of the pulpits are of necessity an uncommitted lot. Surely, there are many forms of commitment, and men of the cloth have no monopoly on a term that they have appropriated from an avowedly atheistic philosopher. Since "commitment" owes it current vogue to a philosopher, it seems reasonable for a philosopher to take a critical look at it and to call attention to some common errors.

This is doubly appropriate, considering that the previous chapter dealt critically with analytic philosophy and ended with an eloquent quotation from Sartre. It was suggested that too many English-speaking philosophers were too exclusively academic. The idea of commitment is close to the heart of existentialism; but it is surrounded by confusions, not all of which are contributed by theologians. It will not do to spurn the academicians and espouse commitment. A detailed consideration of commitment is needed. I propose to take up several important pitfalls, one by one.

18

The first can be summed up in any one of three epigrams. With apologies to Socrates, it might be phrased thus: the uncommitted life is not worth living. Worse, it has been said that the only sin is indifference—a claim that indicates a staggering innocence of the imagination. Most of us can think of other sins. Third, and worst of all, any commitment is better than none.

All three formulations call attention to the shortcomings of lukewarmness, timidity, and ceaseless hesitation. We are reminded of the joys of courage and intensity. We recall Elijah risking his life to say to his people, defying the king and his queen: "How long will you go on limping on both legs? If the Lord is God, follow him; but if Baal, then follow him." And the New Testament: "You are neither cold nor hot. Would that you were cold or hot! So, because you are lukewarm, and neither cold nor hot, I will spew you out of my mouth." And Nietzsche: "The secret of the greatest fruitfulness and the greatest enjoyment of existence is: *to live dangerously!*"

Among the finest writers of the twentieth century some have used their best persuasive powers to make us feel the poverty of any uncommitted life. Martin Buber tells of a Hasidic rabbi who said—and Buber agrees: "Everybody should see which way his heart draws him, and then he should choose this way with all his heart." And Hermann Hesse, in his *Journey to the East* (*Morgenlandfahrt*), created a short novel in which a number of people who are dissatisfied with the emptiness of modern life—men, as it happens, who come out of his previous novels—decide to go on a curious crusade. They are not at all clear about the aim and object of their journey: what matters to them is the break with their futile, prosy lives and the commitment—not to anything specific. We are led to feel that the hero of the story, who loses faith, questions the journey, and withdraws, has sinned; that unquestioning and blind obedience is a price that must be paid for an intense commitment; and that, apart from this, life cannot be worth-while.

Hesse left Germany before the First World War and then did not return because he strongly disapproved of all those tendencies that not long after culminated in the horrors of the Nazi regime. Like Buber, he is deeply sensitive. It is from men like these that the rest of us learn, if we ever do, the meaning of humanity. Their personalities qualify their ideas. But if the same ideas are considered apart from the men proposing them and accepted by men of a different character, we realize that these ideas badly need qualification and without it are untenable.

Hesse's novel appeared just before the Nazis came to power and in retrospect helps to explain Hitler's success. To be sure, Hesse did not influence events: he was not an author cherished by the brown shirts—on the contrary. But Hesse's *Journey to the East* reflects a state of mind, a mood, a yearning that was widespread at that time; and millions of young men who shared it, without also sharing Hesse's other qualities, found the commitment they required by becoming Nazis.

When a man like Buber stops to "see which way his heart draws him" before he decides to "choose this way with all his heart," the question is presumably whether to write this book or that, whether he should continue work on his German version of the Hebrew Bible or give some lectures. But another man might find that *his* heart draws him to the Nazi party and might choose that way with all his heart, becoming a fanatical Elite Guard. The rabbi whom Buber quotes was thinking of different ways of serving God, but many a heart has been drawn to serve God in strange ways.

In *Europe and the Jews*, Malcolm Hay, a Catholic historian, reminds us that "the First Crusade (1096) . . . began and ended with a massacre. 'The men who took the cross,' wrote [Lord] Acton [another great Catholic historian], 'after receiving communion, heartily devoted the day to the extermination of the Jews.' They killed about ten thousand of them. When Godfrey of Bouillon, in the summer of 1099, succeeded after a heroic assault in capturing Jerusalem, he spent the first week slaughtering the inhabitants. The Jews were shut up in their synagogue, which was then set on fire. 'If you want to know what has been done with the enemy found in Jerusalem,' wrote Godfrey to the Pope, 'learn that in the Porch and in the Temple of Solomon, our people had the vile blood of the Saracens up to the knees of their horses'" (37).

Clearly, the Crusaders were a committed lot and followed the way toward which their hearts had drawn them with uncompromising and devout intensity. Hay's book shows that the Crusaders were emphatically no exception any more than the Inquisitors. In this profound lack of humanity, some of the greatest saints, Luther, and Calvin were at one.

The generation born just before and during the Second World War has been called unsilent and beat; but on reflection these labels do not fit, or at least do not set these young men apart. It is more illuminating to speak of an *uncommitted generation*. Few indeed are beat, and the young people after the Second World War are not more vocal than the young men after the first. What distinguishes them is that they are not committed to any cause. This may possibly be regrettable, but one would have to be blind indeed to claim that any commitment is better than none: blind to the atrocities committed by committed Christians, Communists, Nazis, and other fanatics.

If it should be held that "bad" commitments are not really commitments, we should still need criteria for telling the good from the bad, or the commitment that is a commitment from one that is not. What is untenable is the indiscriminate claim that any commitment is better than none. With the qualified assertion that a good commitment is better than none, one need not quarrel; but it raises the question how we are to tell a good commitment from a bad one, regardless of the name we reserve for the latter.

19

The second great pitfall is to pit commitment against reason. If, again, we want a representative who deserves our respect and in many ways our admiration, too, the best man to consider may well be Kierkegaard. In his *Journals* he confided: "The point is to find the truth which is truth for me, to find that idea for which I am ready to live and die" (§ 22). With single-minded passion and sincerity he looked for a commitment and found that neither reason nor philosophy could furnish him with the idea that he needed. He concluded that at least reason and philosophy should "take nothing away and least of all should fool people out of something as if it were nothing" (*Fear and Trembling*, 44). Yet precisely this is the function of a training in philosophy: to fool people out of something as if it were nothing.

Most teachers of philosophy, to be sure, do not have any list of notions that they want to fool their students out of; nor are they insidious. But any training in philosophy will fool people out of many of their childhood beliefs—incidentally, by training their critical powers and by leading them to think more carefully and more conscientiously. Beliefs common in the child's environment and never questioned previously fall victim to a newly learned demand for clarity, consistency, and evidence. Racial and other prejudices, superstitions, and the parents' firm religious and political convictions are often outgrown.

There are many who simply ignore this. Others, who are alarmed, may take heart from the fact that the average college graduate does not require more than ten or twenty years to revert to many of the notions of his childhood. Having accomplished this feat, he is likely to condemn all that reminds him of his brief, faint-hearted glimmerings of wisdom as an adolescent folly. He mistakes his own adolescent intimations of the outlook of the Buddha, Socrates, or Nietzsche for the views of these men; his own short-lived and shallow atheism for the one alternative to Christian faith as he now understands it; and the notions of his immaturity for the quintessence of philosophy, liberalism, rationalism, radicalism, or whatever else he now disdains and thinks he knows first hand.

Though the majority of those who during their student days have been exposed briefly to philosophy have never felt its bite and therefore do not take it very seriously, Kierkegaard was not one of those. To him, philosophy appeared as a great threat, critical thinking as insubordination, and reason as the enemy. Objections to Christianity, he says, do not issue from doubt, as many people think. "Objections against Christianity come from insubordination, unwillingness to obey, rebellion against all authority" (*Journals* § 630). What is wanted is blind obedience, acceptance of what seems absurd to our reason, and belief without any chance of comprehension. "The misfortune of our age—in the political as well as in the religious sphere, and in all things—is disobedience, unwillingness to obey. And one deceives oneself and others by wishing to make us imagine that it is doubt. No, it is insubordination."

These sentences, written shortly before the revolutions of 1848, Kierkegaard reaffirms a year later in another preface for the same book, *On Authority and Revelation*. And in that book he argues quite specifically that it is blasphemy to base obedience to words that are presented to us as the words of God on their profundity or beauty, or even to base our belief that they are truly words of God on an examination of their contents. Whether the words are the words of Scripture, the words of a contemporary apostle, or words that are directly revealed to us, those who say, "Let us see whether the content of the doctrine is divine, for in that case we will accept it along with the claim that it was revealed," are mocking God. Nor should a son obey his father because the father has greater wisdom and experience than the boy, "which is entirely beside the point." He should obey simply because his father is his father; and the words of God should be obeyed because they are presented to us as the words of God. Those who doubt whether they truly come from God are guilty of insubordination.

Kierkegaard was not blind to the dangers of his doctrine,

and with that wholehearted radicalism which distinguished him he faced these dangers squarely in a little book which he himself esteemed one of the very best of all the more than twenty books he published in a dozen years—not counting several he did not himself publish and the many volumes of his *Journals*. In *Fear and Trembling*, Kierkegaard confronts the possibility that God's word might be absurd not merely by coming into conflict with our reason but by contradicting morals. And instead of pussyfooting by considering white lies or some really not very serious matters, Kierkegaard has us reflect on murder—not assassination of a tyrant but premeditated murder of one's own son. We have no right whatever to admire Abraham as the great paragon of faith, as Christians have done ever since St. Paul and as Kierkegaard himself does plainly with awe-struck enthusiasm, unless we are prepared, he says, to look up with an equal reverence to a man who in our time is prepared to murder because God commands him to—or rather because he *believes* that God commands this sacrifice.

Out of the complacency of the Victorian Era, irritated beyond measure by the stuffy smugness of the little capital of Denmark, Copenhagen, Kierkegaard longed for the strong faith of those distant ages when men did not shrink from translating religion into action and did things that would have shocked Victorian Denmark. Sadly, he described himself as a mere "knight of resignation" whom his critical intelligence had rendered quite incapable of ever acting with the confident assurance of the "knight of faith" who never doubts that all the suffering he must inflict on others will be for the best.

When Johannes Hus, the Bohemian reformer and forerunner of Luther, was burned as a heretic at the Council of Constance in 1415, he described the qualities Kierkegaard so wistfully extolled in just two words. Tied to the stake, with the flames already licking at his body, Hus beheld an ardent peasant stepping forward to contribute a small piece of wood to the burning pile; and Hus expired with the exclamation: *sancta simplicitas*—holy simplicity!

After the Second World War, it is obvious that the world is beset by not a lack but a frightening excess of such simplicity. There are only too many who are quite prepared to kill for their faith's sake, quite confident that all the suffering they spread will prove somehow to be worth while, even if at the moment that should seem absurd.

Kierkegaard, of course, was thinking of a sacrifice that was at least as painful for the agent as it might be for the victim. In fact, he improved on the motto "it hurts me more than it hurts you" by refusing altogether to consider any suffering but the agent's. Neither the feelings of the boy about to be sacrificed nor the probable reaction of his mother when she hears of what has happened are considered relevant. The agent simply does what, but for the express command, he never should have done and even now should hate to do, were it not for his utter confidence that all will somehow turn out well. He does not question how; he has no doubts; he is not insubordinate. Little does Kierkegaard realize that of such are the kingdoms of darkness!

What Kierkegaard sanctions in effect is fanaticism: the attitude of those who willingly suffer everything for their unquestioned faith, and who obediently commit atrocities for it, too. What he had in mind, however, is not the fanatic as the popular mind pictures him, brandishing fire and sword. In ordinary life, says Kierkegaard, we could not tell the knight of faith from any simple tax collector. A frightening insight! It applies not only to the peasant who evoked Hus's final words, or to the businesslike, unsentimental, unsadistic men whom Rubens pictured driving nails through St. Peter's hands and feet, completely unaware of what the man might feel whom they are crucifying upside down; it also applies to millions in Hitler's Germany, Soviet Russia, and elsewhere. As Oscar Wilde said: "Ordinary cruelty is simply stupidity. It is the entire want of imagination."

Kierkegaard saw that reason and philosophy were unable to tell him what idea he should choose to live and die by. Hence, he despised philosophy and reason. What he, like millions of others, overlooked is a very simple but important point: reason and philosophy may well safeguard a man against ideas for which he might better not live or die. Indeed, if reason and philosophy had no other function what-

soever, this alone would make them overwhelmingly important. But Kierkegaard, and by no means only he, defiantly
abandons reason in his eager search for a commitment, and
sanctions atrocities beyond his own imagination.

"What our age lacks is not reflection but passion," says
the author of *Fear and Trembling*. By reminding ourselves
of his Victorian setting and recalling that the issue for himself was at the moment nothing more than breaking his engagement in the firm belief that marriage would not be
compatible with his true calling, we can sympathize. For all
that, it is clear that he was wrong in 1843; and a hundred
years later, if not before that, his sentence reads like a poor
joke. There is no longer any excuse for this pitfall.

Kierkegaard and the later existentialists and theologians
who have followed in his steps direct our attention to the limits of reason. But they overlook the crucial difference between
responsible and irresponsible decisions. There are situations
in our lives when all the reasoning of the world cannot tell
us what to do. We reason one way and another, and we
weigh the interests of all the people who are likely to be
affected by this decision or that, and we still do not know
what to do. Should we conclude then that all deliberation is
a waste of time, and always beside the point, and that it
would be just as well to throw a coin, to count our buttons,
or to act on impulse? The person who does that acts irresponsibly, even if by sheer luck he should do something that
turns out well. The person, on the other hand, who does reflect on the probable effects of his decisions on the people
who are likely to be affected, who relies on reason and on
evidence, if only to eliminate some choices, acts responsibly
even if he later finds that he has done the wrong thing. (Cf.
§§ 22 and 85.)

The whole point of an education, and not only of philosophy, is to make people more responsible. One cannot teach
one's students, nor even oneself, always to do what is best;
but one can try to teach oneself and others to become a
little less impulsive and irrational and more conscientious and
responsible. Nobody favors always acting with an utter disregard for evidence and reason; but some people admonish

us to throw both to the winds when it comes to the most important choices—which is rather like being very careful when walking, but shutting both eyes firmly when one drives at high speeds; or like choosing one's dinner guests carefully, while picking the name of one's bride-to-be out of a hat; or like playing cards with great care but also being addicted to playing Chinese roulette—a new game that consists of pointing a revolver now in this direction and now in that, spinning the chamber and pulling the trigger, knowing that there is one dud in the chamber and hoping for the best.

The idea that a man must crucify his reason before he commits himself is not original with Kierkegaard. There is a long Christian tradition behind it, and Luther expressed it even more powerfully than Kierkegaard. He called reason "the devil's bride," a "beautiful whore," and "God's worst enemy," and said: "There is on earth among all dangers no more dangerous thing than a richly endowed and adroit reason." Again: "Reason must be deluded, blinded, and destroyed," and "faith must trample under foot all reason, sense, and understanding" (XII, 1530; VIII, 2048; V, 1312; and III, 215).

If we discard our reason, mortify our understanding, and take leave of our senses, how can we be sure that what we accept is the word of God? The mere fact that something is presented to us as the word of God is clearly insufficient. One has only to write an article on matters of religion in a popular magazine to be swamped with letters, little pamphlets, and big books that claim to offer nothing less than God's own truth; but, alas, they are far from agreeing with each other. Which one, then, should we accept? Perhaps one of those that claim to have been written by celestial beings? Pray, some people counsel, and God will reveal himself to you. The Crusaders, after praying and receiving communion, "heartily devoted the day to the extermination of the Jews." Luther, who prayed with uncommon passion and intensity, counseled the Germans to "set fire to their synagogues," to "break down and destroy their houses," and to "drive them out of the country" (XX, 2478 ff.). But perhaps it is a mistake to pray to the God of Christendom; perhaps we should rather pray to Allah, or to Shiva, or possibly to some Australian god, or to some idol? How are we to choose if evidence and reason are thrown out of court?

This, then, is the second pitfall concerning commitment: to pit commitment against reason and to claim that reason, because it has its limitations, must be trampled underfoot.

20

The third common error about commitment is less radical and dangerous than either of the first two: it does not consider just any commitment better than none, nor does it oppose reason altogether; but it pits commitment against philosophy, scholarship, and the academic life.

This, too, may be illustrated from the writings of a man who deserves respect and admiration: the Jewish existentialist, Franz Rosenzweig. On the basis of his two-volume study of *Hegel und der Staat,* the great German historian, Friedrich Meinecke, offered him a university lectureship, which Rosenzweig declined. Explaining his decision in an interesting letter (August 30, 1920), Rosenzweig refers to his more recent religious book, *Der Stern der Erlösung (The Star of Redemption),* which had ended with the words "into life," and to his work as the founder of an institute of Jewish studies in Frankfurt:

"My new book is only—a book. . . . The . . . demands of the day which are made on me in my position . . . I mean, the nerve-wracking, picayune, and at the same time very necessary struggles with people and conditions, have now become the real core of my existence. . . . The search for knowledge no longer seems to me an end in itself. . . . It is here that my heresy against the unwritten law of the university originates. Not every question seems to me worth asking. . . . Now I only inquire when I find myself *inquired of.* Inquired of, that is, by *men* rather than by scholars. . . . You will now be able to understand what keeps me away from the university and forces me to follow the path I have chosen. . . ."

As a personal statement, explaining his own decision, Rosenzweig's letter is hardly debatable, though one may note that most professors, too, do not consider every question worth asking, and that it does not follow from that alone that one should inquire only when presented with questions by other people. To arrive at that conclusion, one requires an additional presupposition: that no problems at all are left that bother us ourselves—or, to approximate Rosenzweig's formulation, that no question whatsoever seems to me worth asking as long as I am left to myself. Having finished his book, Rosenzweig appears to have reached a state of intellectual satiety—a state most other people reach without writing a book first.

This analysis is borne out by another letter, written eight years later (September 2, 1928), not long before his death: "With my philosophic writings my experience resembles Schopenhauer's: after the 'main work' everything else turns into parerga, paralipomena, and a Second Part that is a commentary on the first. Or rather—since Schopenhauer's pompous and bombastic self-importance isn't at all my style . . . everything that still comes in my case comes as verse for special occasions."

There are personal circumstances that are not relevant to the issue here but still worth mentioning. Shortly after the first letter, Rosenzweig was attacked by a very rare disease and gradually became paralyzed. Soon he could neither speak nor write. A special device was constructed for him, so he could look at one letter at a time, and his wife, following his eyes, as nobody else was able to, would take dictation. In this state he undertook a new translation of the Hebrew Bible, together with his close friend, Martin Buber, and kept writing ceaselessly, essays as well as letters, without ever letting the enormous pains involved in every single word keep him from sprinkling everything he wrote—and his conversation, too—with his abundant wit. Never satisfied with mere approximations and all but incapable of compromise in matters of this sort, he considered every word and every phrase an issue of conscience in translating the Bible, and he retained enough vitality in conversation and dictation to refuse, to the very last day, to deny himself a jocular remark or a nice phrase. The epic of his illness is one of the really imposing tales of heroism in the modern world.

What is germane in the present context, however, is Rosenzweig's implication that those who lecture at a university and write are necessarily uncommitted, unlike politicians and administrators, preachers and journalists. This is a popular and false idea.

If committing oneself means not being noncommittal; if it means taking a stand, sticking one's neck out, and refusing to remain aloof and lukewarm; then many a writer, scholar, and teacher commits himself far more courageously and unmistakably than most theologians and administrators.

There is a wonderful sentence in Simone de Beauvoir's *Les Mandarins:* "He contemplated the world from the height of an unwritten book." To publish any book at all involves some commitment, doubly so if the volume is, as it were, a piece of the writer and not a piece of history or sure of the acclaim of some group.

A philosopher or playwright need not renounce his vocation and become a journalist or politician to commit himself; and if he has it in him to write an outstanding play or essay he would be a fool to bury his talent, or to exchange it for what Nietzsche once called "the wretched ephemeral babble of politics" and the papers. Conversely, one may hazard the guess that the man who does give up philosophy, plays, or the novel to commit himself to journalism or administration is in all probability unsure that he can write another good book.

Those committed to an institution generally claim that all those who prefer fresh air and freedom lack the courage to commit themselves. In fact, the shoe is on the other foot. More often than not, commitment to an institution issues from a want of courage to stand up alone. Typically, it is an escape, a search for togetherness, for safety in numbers. Whether one joins the Communist party or the Catholic church, the Nazis or one of the Protestant denominations, the point may be, though it need not be, that one avoids the risk henceforth of sticking out one's neck, except in company; one no longer needs to take a stand from day to day, from issue to issue, from question to question. From now on, answers need no longer be sought; they can be looked up in the catechism or sidestepped with a firm reminder of one's institutional identity.

Of course, there are institutions to which one can commit oneself without compromising freedom, integrity, and honesty. And one can compromise all three without joining any institution.

Commitment to a doctrinaire position is usually a form of escape. The classical analysis of this was furnished by Sartre in his "Portrait of the Anti-Semite." This essay does not by any means deal with racial prejudice only.

"The rational man seeks the truth gropingly, he knows that his reasoning is only probable, that other considerations will arise to make it doubtful; . . . he is 'open,' he may even appear hesitant. But there are people who are attracted by the durability of stone. They want to be massive and impenetrable, they do not want to change: where would change lead them? This is an original fear of oneself and a fear of truth. And what frightens them is not the content of truth which they do not even suspect, but the very form of the true—that thing of indefinite approximation. . . . They want to exist all at once and right away. They do not want acquired opinions, they want them to be innate; since they are afraid of reasoning, they want to adopt a mode of life in which reasoning and research play but a subordinate role, in which one never seeks but that which one has already found. . . . Only passion can produce this. Nothing but a strong emotional bias can give instant certitude, it alone can hold reasoning within limits, it alone can remain impervious to experience. . . . If out of courtesy he consents momentarily to defend his point of view, he lends himself without giving himself; he simply tries to project his intuitive certainty onto the field of speech. . . . If you insist too much they close up, they point out with one superb word that the time to argue has passed. . . . This man is afraid of any kind of solitude. . . . If he has become an anti-Semite, it is because one cannot be anti-Semitic alone. This sentence: 'I hate the

Jews,' is a sentence which is said in chorus; by saying it
one connects oneself with a tradition and a community. . . ."
(274 ff.).

Similar needs may be satisfied by joining a church or the
Communist party or—with almost, if not entirely, equal success—by adopting some definitive position (saying, for
example, "As for me, I am an atheist") or by seeking an
identity by means of certain mannerisms or a jargon. One
may escape into a jargon that allies one with a school and
shows at one blow where one stands—sometimes a style will
do as well—or, more rarely, a man may seek refuge in a
jargon of his own. What matters is that, once this step is
taken, no more really disturbing questions can arise. The
fundamentals are settled once and for all, and henceforth
all problems are solved by extrapolation. And one conceals
one's fear of freedom, novelty, and future choices by imputing
to all those who have not similarly sought security a lack of
courage to commit themselves.

This is one of the most striking instances of those peculiar
linguistic habits that George Orwell ridiculed in *Nineteen
Eighty-Four*. Just as most of Sartre's readers assume thoughtlessly that he is criticizing anti-Semites only, Orwell's think
for the most part that he is writing only about communism
or, at most, about totalitarianism. Few realize how similar
the conclusion of Orwell's novel is to ever so much preaching.
In the end the hero is converted and renounces heresy:

"He was back in the Ministry of Love, with everything
forgiven, his soul white as snow. He was in the public dock,
confessing everything, implicating everybody. . . . He gazed
up at the enormous face. Forty years it had taken him to
learn what kind of smile was hidden beneath the dark mus-
tache. O cruel, needless misunderstanding! O stubborn, self-
willed exile from the loving breast! Two gin-scented tears
trickled down the sides of his nose. But it was all right, everything was all right, the struggle was finished. He had won
the victory over himself. He loved Big Brother.

21

Some who love Big Brother claim that, deep down, everybody loves Big Brother; only some of us fail to realize it. To be more precise: some modern theologians argue that everybody is committed, whether he knows it or not. Some put the point this way: the question is merely who our gods are, for everybody has some gods. Others claim that all men have some ultimate concern or something that is holy to them, and the question is only whether the object of this concern is really ultimate or rather idolatrous. Some admit that most men have many ultimate concerns and are really "polytheists"; others insist that true ultimacy involves monotheism, and that as long as we are dealing with many concerns none can be really ultimate.

All these ways of speaking are metaphorical, evocative, and exceedingly unclear. Not only frivolous people lack any ultimate concern and are in an important sense uncommitted but the same is true of millions of very serious college students who wonder what they should do with themselves after graduation. There is nothing to which they greatly desire to give themselves, nothing that matters deeply to them. They are not shallow; they are not playboys; they enjoyed many of their courses and appreciate the opportunity to discuss their problems with sympathetic professors. They do not say: nothing matters to me. What they do say is: no one or two things matter more to me than anything else. These young men and women constitute the uncommitted generation; and it seems better to recognize this difference than to gloss it over by claiming that everybody has his own ultimate concern.

In any case, what is an "ultimate concern"? What is mine? What is my "God"—if these theologians are right and everybody ultimately has his "God"? I am not non-committal, not adrift, not hard put to find some project to devote myself to. I feel no inclination to pose as a cynic, saying: nothing is holy to *me*. But what, specifically, *is* holy to me?

The fashionable assumption that what is holy to a man is what he is ultimately concerned with is extremely dubious. When we say that something is holy to a person, we often mean that he won't stand for any humorous remarks about it, that the object is taboo for him in some sense. But such a taboo does not necessarily indicate any ultimate concern, perhaps only an underdeveloped sense of humor.

The dedications of at least some of my books, including this one, point to deep concerns, but hardly to "gods" or to any one "ultimate" concern. Some sense of responsibility to the six million Jews killed in my lifetime, especially to some whom I loved and who loved me, and to millions of others, Jew and Gentile, killed in our time and in past centuries, is certainly among my deepest feelings. Still, that is hardly my ultimate concern. Neither is this book, though I am deeply involved in that. Nor is it at all plausible to say that these are symbols for something more ultimate.

Perhaps I come closest to discovering my ultimate concerns when I ask what I consider the cardinal virtues. I shall try to answer that question in the "Morality" chapter of this book. But here, too, it is exceedingly difficult to know just what virtues one considers most important. And if one selects several, does that make one a polytheist?

The point at stake here is not autobiographical. I merely want to bring out how unhelpful and misleading many fashionable statements about commitment are. And instead of confining myself to semantic considerations, I have tried to take these statements as seriously as possible, seeing what they might mean if one applied them to oneself.

Much of the talk in this vein that one hears from theologians can hardly be taken seriously. It is said that man must have a god, or that man always worships either God or an idol, and that man cannot find true existence in the worship of an idol. One asks oneself whether Shakespeare, Goethe, or Van Gogh worshiped God or—hateful thought—unlike our theologians, never did find "true existence." Surely, some great artists are believers, and some are not; there is no party line among great artists in this matter; and it is futile to argue who did, and who did not, achieve "true existence."

One question, however, is worth pressing. Who really has a single ultimate concern? If that phrase has any definite meaning, it would seem to imply a willingness to sacrifice all other concerns to one's sole ultimate concern. Having only one ultimate concern might well be the recipe for fanaticism. It is the mark of a humane person that he has several ultimate concerns that check and balance each other.

To have many commitments might seem to be the formula of an arid and scattered life, spread thin, lacking depth; but it is hard to generalize about that. Goethe had a staggering number of commitments—and a singularly rich and fruitful life, with no lack of passion or profundity. But one can safely generalize that those who, spurning more than one concern, insist on a single commitment either abandon humanity for fanaticism or, more often, engage in loose talk.

22

Others confound commitment with faith, trust, and loyalty, as if, of these terms, the first two and the last two were the same. Faith and commitment are not the same. I can have faith in a person without feeling committed to that person; and I can feel committed to a person without expecting much of him. Similarly, one can be loyal to a man although one does not trust him entirely; and one can trust him but not be loyal to him.

Faith, including faith *in* a person, always involves belief *that* some propositions are true; for example, that he will do this and not that. Faith in God, too, cannot be wholly divorced from beliefs. That everybody has beliefs is surely true; but the difference that matters is not, as some theologians suppose, between belief *in* and belief *that,* but between beliefs held rationally and responsibly, and beliefs held irrationally and irresponsibly.

The distinction between responsible and irresponsible decisions has already been explained earlier in this chapter, in connection with Kierkegaard. Nor would it matter greatly if someone insisted that all beliefs are irrational to some extent: as was pointed out in the course of our contrast of honesty and sincerity (§ 7), one does not speak of perfect courage or humility, and it is not necessary to speak of perfect honesty or rationality either to make sense of all-important differences of degree. Some beliefs are far more irrational than others.

Commitments do not necessarily involve beliefs that anything is the case; but they can still be more or less rational and responsible. They are more so, if we have conscientiously considered any relevant evidence and what can be said against them. They are irrational and irresponsible if they are made blindly and maintained with closed minds.

It is widely supposed that one simply has to have firm beliefs and close one's mind to be able to act, at least in matters of importance. This is surely false.

As children, many of us had doctors who seemed omniscient, though in retrospect it turns out that some of our physicians knew very little. They made a great show of taking our temperature once or twice a day when we had chicken pox or measles, and they wisely predicted that after so many days we should probably be well again. We gained the impression that they had cured us. A little later in life we began to encounter doctors who frequently admitted that they did not know what was the matter, doctors who frankly conceded their ignorance and acted without the benefit of firm beliefs—and sometimes, though not always, did effect cures. They might say something like this:

There are several possibilities. I should like to run a series of tests which will probably not be conclusive, but which should eliminate some possibilities. Then we can try such and such a treatment; and if that does not work, another.

In a more drastic case, a doctor might say: the chances are that you do not have a malignancy; but if I wait till I can be sure of that, it might be too late if I discovered after a while that there was a cancer, so I suggest an operation.

It may be more comforting to have a doctor who pretends to know what in fact he does not know; but it is part of growing up to realize that, lacking knowledge, men must constantly act on uncertainties. The doctor who operates need not believe firmly that he is removing a cancer. If he is responsible he will try to act on the best guess that the time and circumstances permit, remembering all the while that his best guess might prove to be wrong. And when evidence turns up to show that he was wrong, or even that his guess was not the best one possible under the circumstances, he will face the facts. Remembering that one might be wrong, and being willing to admit one's errors even in important matters, may be difficult; it is certainly not impossible. It constitutes a large part of honesty and rationality.

Some commitments may have to be honored even if one comes to see in time that it was a mistake to undertake them in the first place. Even in such cases, it does not follow that, being committed, one has to believe firmly that one did the right thing. One can do what is honorable, and be honest, too.

23

It is hazardous to generalize about existentialism because the denotation of this label is a matter of debate. But it seems safe to say that most of the so-called existentialists, as well as most, if not all, of the theologians who like to call themselves existentialist, have occupied themselves with commitment without ever seeing or saying clearly what distinguishes a responsible commitment from an irresponsible one. (In Sartre's case, I hope to show this at the end of the "Morality" chapter, at least as far as his celebrated lecture "Existentialism Is a Humanism" is concerned.) While most analytic philosophers do not philosophically examine life's most important decisions because they think that philosophers have no special competence for that, the spokesmen of commitment generally refrain from such scrutiny because they commit one or more of the errors analyzed here.

Let us look back once more at the pitfalls considered in this chapter: if committing oneself means taking a stand instead of being non-committal, few indeed will say after reflection, though many have said thoughtlessly, sometimes in understandable exasperation, that any commitment at all, no matter how horrible, is still better than none. And if committing oneself is taken more narrowly to mean joining a group of people dedicated to some cause, it is doubtful whether anybody would maintain that joining any group, however horrible, is to be preferred to going it alone.

Those who pit commitment against reason and advise us to blind and destroy our reason before making the most crucial choice of our life are apologists for one specific set of doctrines which, to use Paul's word, are "foolishness" to those who have not taken leave of reason. They say their doctrine is infallible and true, but ignore the fact that there is no dearth whatsoever of pretenders to infallibility and truth. They may think they chose their doctrine because it is offered to us as infallible and true, but this is plainly no sufficient reason: scores of other doctrines, scriptures, and apostles, sects and parties, cranks and sages make the same claim. Those who claim to know which of the lot is justified in making such a bold claim, those who tell us that this faith or that is *really* infallible and true are presupposing in effect, whether they realize this or not, that they themselves happen to be infallible. Those who have no such exalted notion of themselves have no way of deciding between dozens of pretenders if reason is proscribed. Those who are asking us to spurn reason are in effect counseling us to trust to luck. But luck in such cases is unusual.

Those who pit commitment against writing and philosophy, as if only politicians and administrators ever took a stand or stuck their necks out, are plainly wrong about the facts. Indeed, joining an organization often, though not always, serves the function of escaping from the threat of ever again having to make up one's own mind about matters of importance. What is most often spoken of as commitment par excellence is really a studied refuge from commitments.

Those who say that everybody is committed, or that everybody has some ultimate concern, or that man must have a god, engage in needlessly vague and elusive talk that blurs significant distinctions. The fashionable juxtaposition of belief *in* and belief *that* generally overlooks that belief *in* involves beliefs *that;* and it, too, distracts attention from the crucial difference between responsible and irresponsible commitments.

The point of this chapter is not to attack commitment, but to attack some widespread confusions that surround the concept of commitment and vitiate not only most discussions of the subject but also the commitments which some people actually make. I am far from opposing all forms of commitment: this book invites the reader to commit himself to the quest for honesty. It does not follow that the philosopher and the theologian are two birds of a feather, and that one commitment is as good as another; nor even that all commitments have the same structure and, at least basically, the same effects. Far from it. To show this clearly, we must consider theology at some length.

V

Against Theology

24

What is theology? Certainly not what Webster's New International Dictionary says it is when giving one of its meanings as the "critical, historical, and psychological study of religion." This definition is introduced with the words, "More loosely"; but any definition which would make Gibbon's *Decline and Fall of the Roman Empire*, Nietzsche's *Antichrist*, and Freud's *Future of an Illusion* exercises in theology is not only loose but absurd.

The same dictionary, which is known as "the supreme authority," defines a theologian as "a person well versed in theology" or a "writer on theology." This would not only turn Gibbon, Freud, and Nietzsche into theologians; any *critic* of theology, being a "writer on theology," would himself be a theologian.

This usage has no basis in the etymology of the word nor in judiciously spoken English, though such thoughtlessness occasionally finds expression in the language. The Unabridged furnishes a motive for this misuse of "theology" by immediately following it up with a quotation from the *Encyclopaedia Britannica:* "Many speak of *theology* as a science of religion [instead of "science of *God*"] because they disbelieve that there is any knowledge of God to be attained." In other words: some people, believing that theology involves deception and that such great theologians as Aquinas and Calvin were impostors, prefer not to say so outright and instead appropriate such words as "theologian" and "theology" for something else which is respectable.

Some of those who say that every man has an ultimate concern, and that man must have a god, also say that every scientist is a hidden theologian because he is a human being. Since the Second World War, theologians have amassed a whole arsenal of such ploys. To use an ancient name, the stratagem is a form of *tu quoque*—you are doing it, too. To do justice to its kindly intent, one can call it instead conversion by definition. And to call attention to its occasionally crushing effect on unsuspecting victims, one may christen it the bear's hug.

All these comfortable ambiguities forestall a critical appraisal of theology, though this is badly needed. To be sure, the early positivists rejected theology as meaningless; but they rejected so much else as no less meaningless that theology was in good company: it was not singled out for criticism and examined closely.

Soon, moreover, it was noted that the early positivists had used "meaningless" in a rather unusual sense: what was "meaningless," as they employed that term, was really quite "meaningful" in the usual sense of that word, so one cared even less. When it was widely recognized that some of the positivists' prose was meaningless by their own standards, their initial repudiation of theology came to be considered an amusing episode, no more.

Wittgenstein himself had taken this insight in his stride. In his *Tractatus*, he had said: "Most of the propositions and questions that have been written about philosophical matters are not false but nonsensical" (62); also, "My propositions elucidate by leading him that understands me to recognize them in the end as nonsensical, after he has climbed through them—on them—beyond them" (188).

After the Second World War some of the heirs of the later Wittgenstein reversed the line of his early followers and tried to rehabilitate theology. Wittgenstein had talked of language games and urged his students to discover the meaning of words by considering how they are actually used in various contexts; so one began to discuss the language of theology in an attempt to see how this or that phrase functions in the discourse of the theologians. Ineffectual criticism gave way to appreciation, and philosophers came to confirm the common notion that theology is eminently respectable. But is it really?

Much depends, of course, on how we define theology. Webster's main definition is all right, but takes up fifteen lines and then is followed by the loose one that has been discussed. The most complete dictionary of the English language, the twelve-volume Oxford English Dictionary, is brief and to the point when it defines theology as "the study or science which treats of God, His nature & attributes, & His relations with man & the universe." Further, it defines: "*Dogmatic theology,* theology as authoritatively held & taught by the church; a scientific statement of Christian dogma. *Natural theology,* theology based upon reasoning from natural facts apart from revelation." It also allows that "theology" sometimes means "a particular theological system or theory" and that it may be "applied to pagan or non-Christian systems." Finally, it lists two obsolete meanings: "Rarely used for Holy Scriptures" and "Metaphysics."

25

There are, then, two types of theology: natural and dogmatic. Natural theology purports to tell us about God, his nature and attributes, and his relations with man and the universe, on the basis of reasoning from facts of nature, without relying on revelation. But from the facts of nature one cannot even infer God's existence, much less his attributes and his relations with man and the universe, still less the qualities which theologians, as we generally use the term, ascribe to him: omniscience and omnipotence, justice and love, perfection and infinity.

From the facts of nature one can infer further facts of nature, but one cannot with any certainty infer anything beyond nature, not even with any probability. At most, one can say that there are some events one is not able to explain by means of any hitherto known facts; and at such points one may possibly elect to postulate some occult entities or forces, pending further research. Past experience indicates that all such invocations are extremely likely to be dated by a new advance in science. Indeed, even as one writer postulates some unknown entity outside of nature, some scientist elsewhere may be able to dispense with it. Moreover, even if it were permissible to infer something supra-scientific from the facts of nature, it is never really the facts of nature that determine what precisely is invoked at that point, but some preconceived ideas mediated by religion. *At the crucial point, natural theology falls back on dogmatic theology.* It is the teachings of the theologian's religion, not the facts of nature, that decide whether, where other explanations fail, he should invoke one god or two, or more; a god of love, a god of wrath, or one of each, or several of each, or one who loves some and hates others, or perhaps a god of perfect love who permits, or insists upon, eternal torment.

To be sure, there are those who believe that God's existence can be proved from facts of nature, notwithstanding Kant's classical refutations of what he considered the only three basic types of alleged proofs. I shall not discuss these proofs here, having dealt in detail with the five proofs of Aquinas and with Plato's argument, Kant's "postulate," and Pascal's "wager," as well as the question whether God's existence can be proved, in Chapter V of my *Critique of Religion and Philosophy.*

Most Protestant theologians admit that God's existence cannot be inferred from facts of nature and that knowledge of "his attributes and his relations with man and the universe" has to be based on faith and revelation. In sum, they repudiate natural theology. Most Catholic theologians believe that God's existence can be inferred from facts of nature; but they, too, base most of their alleged knowledge of "his attributes and his relations with man and the universe" on faith and revelation.

What people in the twentieth century generally mean when speaking of theology, whether they are Catholics, Protestants, Jews, or agnostics, is what the Oxford English Dictionary calls *dogmatic theology* and defines as "theology as authoritatively held & taught by the church." But this definition overlooks that there are *many* churches, and that each has its own theology—or rather *many* theologies.

26

The first point to note about theology, as the term is generally understood, is that it is denominational. Moreover, a theologian does not merely *expound* the beliefs, particularly those about God, held by his denomination; he also offers a sympathetic exegesis and, in fact if not expressly, a defense. Neither Presbyterian missionaries nor agnostic anthropologists who offer careful expositions of the beliefs of the Navahos would be called Navaho theologians. To be called a theologian, one must be committed to the beliefs about God, or gods, of which one offers an account. By betraying a lack of sympathy, or by evincing hostility, a writer makes clear beyond a doubt that he is not a Navaho theologian or a Christian theologian, even if he should be very "well versed" in Navaho or Christian theology. A man may be well versed in theology without being a theologian; and he may be a theologian without being well versed in theology.

To understand theology, one has to understand commitment to an institution. As a first example of a very educated and intelligent writer whose books cannot be well understood unless we keep in mind that he has committed himself to an institution, consider not a theologian but a Communist: Georg Lukacs. Many Western writers, including Thomas Mann and Herbert Read, have hailed him as the most intelligent Marxist critic and historian of ideas, and his erudition is amazing.

In *From Shakespeare to Existentialism,* I attempted a quick sketch of Lukacs. In the present context only three points matter.

First: no dead writer who has not specifically been condemned by the party is safe from being enlisted as a comrade who all but took the final step. Second: Lukacs adopts a peculiar language which shows at a glance that one is reading a committed Communist. Third: he continually cites authority to back up what he says. Points are proved by quoting Marx, Engels, Lenin, and, depending on the party line around the time of publication, sometimes, but not always, Stalin.

Confronted with all this, two reactions are possible. One may say: How perceptive and erudite this writer is! How liberal, really! He almost agrees with me! Of course, he puts all his points in rather odd ways; but, being a Communist, he is doing the best he can. Or one can say: If he is so liberal, why does he not draw the consequences? Why does he not come out in the open and say what he thinks? For years he did not have to be a Communist; why, then, did he write as he did? The answer is clear: because of his commitment.

The parallel with many Catholic intellectuals is obvious. They, too, assimilate to Catholic doctrine the most divergent materials and enlist all kinds of writers as searching souls who all but took the final step. They, too, adopt a peculiar language. And they, too, back up their views by constantly quoting authority. And here, too, one may exclaim: How erudite! How liberal! The man almost agrees with me! Of course, he puts his points a little oddly; but, being a Catholic, or a Thomist, he is doing the best he can. Or one can ask why such writers do not draw the consequences and say freely what they think without encumbering every utterance with such an involved ritual.

Instead of laboring this point, let us begin with Protestant theology. For the point suggested here is easier to see, and has been noted much more often, in connection with Catholicism, and millions of English-speaking people would readily grant that Catholic writers are vulnerable to such charges; but very few have noticed that Protestant theology is in the same boat.

The choice of a peculiar language and the quoting of authority stare us in the face; and the leading Protestant theologian in the United States, Paul Tillich, counts the Hebrew prophets among the greatest Protestants of all time, assures us that Marx, Freud, and Nietzsche were the most outstanding Protestants of the last hundred years, and considers Picasso's art deeply Protestant, too.

The point here is not merely that the same three points

we have noted among Communists and Catholic intellectuals are found among the Protestants as well. But to prepare for our central criticism, let us explore a few examples in more depth.

27

Toward the middle of the twentieth century, no Protestant theologian in Germany attracted more attention than Rudolf Bultmann. Long known as an outstanding New Testament scholar, he published an article in 1941 in which he urged that the New Testament must be "demythologized" in order that its central message might reach modern man, unencumbered by the myths of the first century. His article was widely debated, outside Germany, too; more and more of Bultmann's books were translated into English; and eventually he was invited to give the Gifford Lectures in Scotland and various other lectures in the United States.

Of the many criticisms of his call to demythologize, few, if any, annoyed Bultmann as much as an essay by Karl Jaspers, widely known as one of the two leading German existentialists although he, like Martin Heidegger, repudiates this label. Jaspers' critique of Bultmann is open to many objections, but it has the great merit of having stung Bultmann into making a staggering admission. (The two essays, together with Jaspers' reply to Bultmann's reply and Bultmann's laconic response to Jaspers' second essay, are available in English in a paperback, *Myth and Christianity*.) In his initial reply, Bultmann says of Jaspers: "He is as convinced as I am that a corpse cannot come back to life and rise from his tomb. . . . What, then, am I to do when as a pastor, preaching or teaching, I must explain texts . . . ? Or when, as a scientific theologian, I must give guidance to pastors with my interpretation?"

Up to this point, Bultmann had generally referred to "the Easter event," and students had debated just what, according to Bultmann, had happened at the first Easter. Now Bultmann let the cat out of the bag, not only about one particular belief but about the nature of theology. Here we have an excellent formulation of the dilemma Bultmann shares with Catholic as well as Protestant theologians, and with men like Lukacs, too.

The retort to his rhetorical questions need not be the answer he intends. Again one might well say: If you consider false the beliefs in terms of which the institution to which you are committed defines itself, why don't you draw the consequences and renounce your allegiance to the church, the party, or St. Thomas, as the case may be?

The matter of the Easter event is no isolated instance. Here is another illustration. In the wake of Bultmann's challenge, there was a great deal of discussion about demythologizing hell. At the German universities the debate raged around such questions as whether the fire in Luke 16 is a physical fire. Surely, this is a relatively trivial question. Even the Nazis were able to devise subtler torments and, for example, made a woman's hair turn white overnight by falsely telling her that the screams she heard from the next room were those of her son under torture. If there were an omnipotent god, intent on inflicting piteous sufferings on some of his creatures, he could certainly improve on physical fire. The serious question which one would expect the theologians to discuss is how they propose to reconcile eternal torment, no matter how "spiritual," with divine perfection. Most American Protestant theologians refuse to consider this question: they prefer to talk about the kingdom of God. And German theologians prefer to discuss whether the fire is physical fire. Even when asked outright about the other problem, most theologians manage somehow to change the subject quickly.

Bultmann, asked about eternal torture in a conversation, said that on that subject he agreed with Lessing. He had every right to expect that a younger colleague, no less than a student, would proceed to the nearest library and begin reading through a set of Lessing's works, in search of the crucial passage. After the first ten volumes, he could safely be expected to give up. Encouraged by my American training, however, I asked: "And what did Lessing say?" The great theologian hesitated, then allowed that Lessing had once said somewhere that if even a single soul were in eternal torment he would certainly refuse to go to heaven. It would seem, then, that Bultmann disbelieves in *any* form of eternal torment, but he does not make a point of this. In his huge *Theology of the New Testament,* hell and eternal damnation are simply ignored.

This refusal to let one's No be a No is one of the central characteristics of theologians no less than of committed Communists. One does not emphasize one's points of disagreement with tradition or the scriptures; instead, one emphasizes points of agreement and sidesteps embarrassing issues by raising questions of exegesis. As a consequence, the agreement among committed believers is, to a surprisingly large extent, apparent only: they proclaim their allegiance to the same scriptures and traditions, but the very passages that are to one man the superlative expression of his faith are to another a source of embarrassment and an unexampled challenge to his exegetic skill. And two men who love the same sentence are likely to interpret it quite differently.

One need not even run the full gamut of Christian views from the first century to the twentieth, from Presbyterianism to Catholicism and the Greek Orthodox church, from the Armenian church to Christian Science, from superstitious peasants to scholarly professors, to see how little agreement there is among Christians who profess the same beliefs. Billy Graham, Paul Tillich, and Reinhold Niebuhr are all twentieth-century American Protestants; indeed, there are few, if any, other spokesmen of mid-century American Protestantism who are so well known and so influential. Yet Tillich, like Niebuhr, shares few of Graham's religious beliefs. Now compare what men like Tillich and Niebuhr actually believe and disbelieve with the beliefs of avowed fundamentalists, or of Martin Luther and John Calvin, or of St. Augustine and St. Athanasius, or of St. Paul and St. John the Evangelist: surely, the beliefs and disbeliefs of our two most celebrated Protestant theologians are much closer to mine than they are to those of millions of their fellow Christians, past and present. But, like Bultmann, they say No in ways that sound like Yes.

28

Catholic theology may seem to be more forthright, but certainly not as forthright as most people suppose. An involuntarily amusing editorial in the Chicago diocesan newspaper, entitled "Yes, Professor, There Is A Hell," is not unrepresentative. Taking issue with an article that a professor had contributed to "a well-known magazine," the editorial made a great point of the fact that it "is by no means the position of the Catholic Church" either "that 'the great mass of mankind' will be tormented for all eternity" or that "only those who are a part of the Christian communion will find salvation, whereas 'the rest of mankind [will] suffer eternal torment.'" As it happened, the professor had not said that this *was* "the position of the Catholic Church." But be that as it may, the editorial ends: "There is a hell, professor, and the easiest way to find out is by not believing in it, or in God."

This is a mere editorial, full of misrepresentations, and it would be foolish to saddle the church with it. What is typical about the editorial is the alternation of protestations of liberality with threats. One does not usually find both so close together; but the two strains are almost omnipresent contemporary Catholicism.

On the one hand, scholarship insists that "though a few individual teachers of the Church may have held this, it has never been regarded as a matter of the Church's teaching"; on the other hand, preaching requires threats and promises. As we listen to the preacher or the missionary, everything appears to be as clear as could be; but under the scholar's or the critic's questioning, this surface clarity gives way to endless complications and uncertainties.

St. Thomas Aquinas, who will be considered in due course, was on the whole exceptionally clear; but the Catholic Church is not committed to his views. In his encyclical *Aeterni Patris*, Pope Leo XIII, in 1879, said: "As far as man is concerned, reason can now hardly rise higher than she rose, borne up in the flight of Thomas; and Faith can hardly gain more helps

from reason than those which Thomas gave her." He cited
many previous popes who had spoken similarly of the saint:
"Pius V acknowledged that heresies are confounded and exposed and scattered by his doctrine, and that by it the whole
world is daily freed from pestilent errors." And, "The words
of Blessed Urban V to the University of Toulouse seem to be
most worthy of mention: 'It is our will, and by the authority
of these letters we enjoin you, that you follow the doctrine of
Blessed Thomas as true. . . .'" And the encyclical cites "as
a crown, the testimony of Innocent VI: 'His doctrine above
all other doctrine, with the one exception of the Holy Scriptures, has . . . such a truth of opinions, that no one who holds
it will ever be found to have strayed from the path of
truth. . . .'"

From all this, one might conclude that the pope, speaking
ex cathedra on matters of faith and morals, and therefore
infallibly, had taught us that we shall not stray from truth if
we accept St. Thomas' view that the blessed in heaven will
see the punishments of the damned so that their bliss will be
that much greater. Or that one angel can speak to another
without letting other angels know what he is saying. One
might even suppose that his views on scientific matters are
invariably true. But Leo XIII also says, in the same long
encyclical: "We, therefore, while we declare that everything
wisely said should be received with willing and glad mind,
. . . exhort all of you, Venerable Brothers, with the greatest
earnestness to restore the golden wisdom of St. Thomas, and
to spend it as far as you can. . . . We say the wisdom of St.
Thomas; for it is not by any means in our mind to set
before this age, as a standard, those things which have been
inquired into by Scholastic Doctors with too great subtlety;
or anything taught by them with too little consideration,
not agreeing with the investigations of a later age; or, lastly,
anything that is not probable."

In a similar spirit, Etienne Gilson, one of the most outstanding Thomists of the twentieth century, says at the outset of *The Christian Philosophy of St. Thomas Aquinas*:
"Personally, I do not say of Thomas that he was right, but
that he *is* right." But this does not prevent him from admitting

now and then in passing, without emphasis, that Thomas was *not* right.

Moreover, many Catholic scholars have argued at length that papal encyclicals are not necessarily infallible. Father Thomas Peguès, for example, has tried to show in an article in *Revue Thomiste,* which is quoted in Anne Fremantle's edition of *The Papal Encyclicals in Their Historical Context,* that their authority is not infallible but "in a sense, sovereign." While "the solemn definitions *ex cathedra . . .* demand an assent without reservation and make a formal act of faith obligatory," in the case of the encyclicals only "an internal mental assent is demanded."

There is never a lack of surface clarity; but if one is genuinely perplexed, the apparently neat conceptual distinctions are not always very helpful; and having accused Protestant theologians of a failure to let their No be a No, I see no reason for not bringing the same charge against Catholic theologians.

In an essay on "How to Read the Encyclicals," in *The Church Speaks to the Modern World: The Social Teachings of Leo XIII,* Gilson says: "When one of us objects to the pretension avowed by the Popes to state, with full authority, what is true and what is false, or what is right and what is wrong, he is pitting his own personal judgment, not against the personal judgment of another man, but against the whole ordinary teaching of the Catholic Church. . . . The Church alone represents the point of view of a moral and spiritual authority free from all prejudices." Clearly, we are being discouraged from saying No to authoritative pronouncements. That, however, does not necessarily mean that everybody has to agree. *Where the heretic would say No, the theologian interprets.*

"When it seems to us that an encyclical cannot possibly say what it says, the first thing to do is to make a new effort to understand what it does actually say," says Gilson. And what texts "actually" say is often very different from what they seem to say.

In the first of the three volumes of *Five Centuries of Religion,* G. G. Coulton, the great historian, relates how "the *Catechism of the Council of Trent,* drawn up by a papal commission as an unerring guide to priests and their flocks lays it down that unbaptized infants, 'be their parents Christian or infidel, are born to eternal misery and perdition' (authorized translation by Professor Donovan, Manchester, 1855, p. 167; *Of Baptism,* quest. XXX). For the arguments by which the Roman Church of today has persuaded itself that these words mean 'they will eternally enjoy a state of perfect natural happiness,' I must refer my readers to my 16th *Medieval Study* [i.e., *Infant Perdition in the Middle Ages*], or to the *Catholic Encyclopedia,* s.v. *Limbo*" (443). The original Latin words of the *Catechism* are: *sempiternam miseriam et interitum.*

In his monograph on *Infant Perdition,* Coulton, who concerns himself only with Roman Catholic theology and not with theology in general, offers this comment: "It is strange that theologians who juggle thus with language should never suspect the double-edged nature of the tools they are using. The anonymous champion of the Catholic Truth Society thinks that, if I had been more familiar with Catholic ways of thought, I should have seen at once that the 'eternal misery and destruction' of the Council of Trent means eternal and perfect natural happiness. But what is to prevent a later and more learned generation of Catholics from discovering that the 'perfect natural happiness' of the *Catholic Encyclopedia* really means eternal misery and destruction? Even in theology, it is fatal when we can no longer trust a man's word. . . ." (29).

What Coulton takes for a special vice of the Roman Catholic church is really of the essence of theology, as the many illustrations from Protestant theologians in this chapter should show. If I concentrate more than is usually done on the Christian conception of hell, this is because no other aspect of God's "relations with man and the universe" is anywhere near so important for us. If there is a possibility, perhaps even a probability, that God may consign us or some of our fellow men to eternal misery, it is certainly the very height of irresponsibility to sweep the relevant doctrines under the rug. By seeing, on the other hand, how theologians deal with this most crucial question, we stand an excellent chance of finding out just how much knowledge is available concerning

God's "relations with man and the universe," and what methods theologians use to obtain such knowledge.

At the end of *This Is Catholicism* (1959), John Walsh, S.J., reprints an important document which he introduces thus: "All the principal beliefs of Catholicism are summed up in the Profession of Faith which is made by converts on their entrance into the Catholic Church and by all candidates for the priesthood before ordination. It is a fitting conclusion for this book." Here a great many beliefs are summarized succinctly in less than three pages. The final paragraph begins: "This true Catholic faith, outside of which no one can be saved. . . ." A few pages earlier, in the body of the book, we are also told that "membership in the Catholic Church, the mystical body of Christ, is the solitary means of salvation. Apart from the Church, exclusive of it, independently of it, there exists absolutely no possibility of attaining heaven." This is the kind of forthright, unequivocal doctrine that at first glance seems to make it utterly unfair to claim that Catholic theologians, like Protestant theologians, disregard Jesus' commandment, in the Sermon on the Mount, that we should let our Yes be Yes, and our No, No; "anything more than this comes from evil."

Immediately, however, Father Walsh asks: "Does this signify that all who are not actually members of the Catholic Church will be lost?" and in comformity with contemporary Catholic doctrine he replies: "Certainly not." This is explained as follows: "When a person . . . makes an act of perfect contrition, he must simultaneously determine, as we saw, to accomplish everything which he judges necessary to attain salvation. Now since the Catholic Church is, in fact, the sole means of salvation, a non-Catholic's resolve to do everything needful to gain heaven is, objectively considered, exactly equivalent to a resolve to belong to the Catholic Church. The two resolves automatically merge; one coincides with the other. A non-Catholic is unaware, certainly, of the identity of the two. . . . He may never have heard of the Catholic Church. Or he may . . . be quite indifferent to it. Or . . . he may be quite hostile to it and consequently would indignantly deny that his desire to please God coalesced in any way, shape, or fashion with a desire to join Catholicism. Such subjective misapprehensions on his part would not alter the objective fact, however. A sincere desire for salvation coincides necessarily with a desire to belong to the Catholic Church. . . . Strange as it may seem, therefore, a non-Catholic who sincerely yearns to do everything necessary for salvation (even when he believes that one of the requisites for salvation is to condemn Catholicism!) (John 16:2) is, all unconsciously, longing to be a Catholic. Now this unconscious longing God recognizes as a substitute for belonging . . . as the equivalent of real membership." So the doctrine "still stands: outside the Catholic Church there is no salvation."

29

The most crucial criticism of theology ought now to be apparent: theology depends on a double standard. One set of standards is employed for reading and interpreting one's own tradition and its texts; another, for the texts and traditions of all other. Here, one is committed not only to make sense of everything but to make everything come out superior, profound, and beautiful; there, one is not averse to finding fault and even emphasizing all that is inferior to one's own tradition.

Protestants are perceptive regarding the faults of Catholicism and not inclined to make allowances for them the way they do for Luther's faults or Calvin's, or for those of their own articles of faith—those of the Westminster Confession, for example. Catholics can see plainly what was wrong with all of these, but approach their saints with a very different attitude. Pressed about eternal damnation, Protestant theologians point out that this doctrine impresses on us how important our choices in this life are; asked about the latest Catholic dogma, they do not exert themselves to find a profound meaning in it, but are quick indeed to disown it as sheer superstition. Christians stress the references to divine wrath in the Old Testament while ignoring or interpreting away the references to wrath, relentless judgment, and eternal torment in the New

Testament; they point to the references to love in the New Testament, less to those in the Old; and they conclude, as if they had not presupposed it, that the God of the Old Testament is a God of justice, wrath, and vengeance, while the God of the New Testament is a God of love, forgiveness, and mercy. Moreover, one contrasts the realities and mediocre representatives of other traditions with the ideals and the saints of one's own.

Theology is a comprehensive, rigorous, and systematic attempt to conceal the beam in the scriptures and traditions of one's own denomination while minutely measuring the mote in the heritages of one's brothers. Of course, that is not all there is to theology. Theology is also a comprehensive, rigorous, and systematic avoidance, by means of exegesis, of letting one's Yes be Yes, and one's No, No: instead of saying No, one discusses other matters, and in a pinch one "interprets" and converts beams into slivers, and slivers into gold. Theology is also a continual attempt to force new wine into old skins. The new wine is not always the best available, and perhaps the old skins aren't either; but the whole point is to avoid a fair comparison of skins: into one's own, one stuffs whatever looks good, while one associates the skins of others with an inferior vintage, going back, if necessary, a few centuries to find a really bad year.

Theology is antithetic not only to the Sermon on the Mount but to the most elementary standards of fairness. It involves a deliberate blindness to most points of view other than one's own, a refusal to see others as they see themselves and to see oneself as one appears to others—a radical insistence on applying different standards to oneself and others.

It is, no doubt, exceedingly difficult to be completely fair, but theology is founded on a comprehensive, rigorous, and systematic refusal to as much as attempt to be fair. It does not merely occasionally lapse into acceptance of a double standard: theology is based on a devout commitment to a double standard.

This central flaw permeates theology and takes many forms. Let us concentrate on two of the most important.

30

One word that sums up a great deal of theology is *gerrymandering*. As I pointed out in my *Critique* (§ 56), "politicians have no monopoly on dividing districts in an unnatural and unfair way to give one party an advantage over its opponent. Many theologians are masters of this art."

Instead of giving many brief illustrations from a lot of theologians, let us begin by considering the method of the man who was probably the greatest theologian of all time, St. Thomas Aquinas. That Aquinas carved up Aristotle, citing to his purpose what he could make fit, meets the eye. But it is scarcely less obvious that he also gerrymandered Scripture. The basic method of his imposing *Summa Theologica* is simple enough, though the amount of Gothic detail is staggering.

A question is asked and first of all answered in a manner that Aquinas considers false. This false answer is then buttressed with a few quotations that would seem to support it. Then a quotation is introduced which apparently conflicts with everything said so far. A tension is created but immediately resolved by Aquinas' concise *Respondeo,* or "I reply." He takes his stand with the immediately preceding quotation, gives his reasons, and then replies, one by one, to the objections raised before he stated his position.

In this manner, every question is answered: Whether God reprobates any man? Whether God can do what he does not? Whether God can do better than what he does? Whether several angels can be at the same time in the same place? Whether the semen in man is produced from surplus food? There is never any hesitation, any slight lack of self-confidence, any suspense of judgment. Thomas knows it all and proves it all—proves it in his own fashion, which amounts to quite the boldest and the most extensive feat of gerrymandering ever undertaken. Proof involves, and frequently consists in, the adducing of quotations—usually from the Old or New Testament, from Aristotle, or from pseudo-Dionysius (a fifth-century Neoplatonist whom Aquinas and his contemporaries mistook for a contemporary of St. Paul and the Blessed Virgin). One of the few things all of these authoritative proof texts have in common is that Thomas was unable to read any of them in the original. But even if he had been a still greater scholar than he was, even if he had been able to read Greek and Hebrew instead of occasionally misconceiving Biblical and Aristotelian passages, and even if he had known that the pseudo-Dionysius had not been converted by St. Paul himself, his method would for all that have been thoroughly unsound.

Unlike historical and philological scholarship in the employ of conscientious efforts at interpretation, the theologian's method is not designed to uncover the original intent and meaning of the quoted passages. Rather, Thomas chooses what fits, and ignores or reinterprets what does not fit. Some readers fail to realize this because at the beginning of every question he sets up a few straw men whom he can knock down a page later with the aid of rival quotes—if necessary, from the pseudo-Dionysius. This was the greatest theologian of them all.

To be sure, Thomas has to be seen in the context of his time if one wants to arrive at a fair judgment of the man. What appears monstrous in the perspective of a later age is always apt to have been commonplace when it occurred. But the whole point of the present discussion is that Thomas' method is by no means *exceptionally* unsound. On the contrary, he is a splendid representative not only of his time but of theology in general. What distinguishes him is not that he was arbitrary. What is exceptional is rather his unflagging patience, his attempt at comprehensive coverage, and his clarity, which shows us at a glance what he is doing. Faithful throughout to the same simple method, he takes up question after question, stamping out his treatment with a stencil, as it were—or, metaphors apart, dictating relentlessly, only stopping occasionally, we are told, to pray.

On major points, the conclusions are predetermined, and Thomas himself makes a point of this. In the Second Part of the Second Part of the *Summa Theologica,* he insists that we "ought to believe matters of faith, not because of human reasoning, but because of the divine authority." But he writes theology because "when a man has a will ready to believe, he loves the truth he believes, he thinks out and takes to heart whatever reasons he can find in support thereof." Only when faith is primary and seeking understanding, only when we are finding reasons for what we already believe, instead of basing our faith on reason, "human reasoning does not exclude the merit of faith, but is a sign of greater merit" (Article 10).

On lesser points, of course, the conclusion is not always predetermined by tradition or authority, and Thomas has some freedom to develop a position of his own. Like most theologians, however, he blurs this distinction, backs up controversial stands, too, with citations of authority, and thus gives the appearance that his system is not only singularly comprehensive and consistent but the gospel truth. In fact, the tightly woven structure is a doubtful asset: if a few key concepts are based on confusions, or if a few basic suppositions are no longer plausible or tenable in view of some advance in knowledge, the whole edifice may topple.

Such criticisms are not heard gladly in the twentieth century, although far more radical estimates of scholasticism were quite common in the nineteenth. F. W. Farrar, D.D., F.R.S., late Fellow of Trinity College, Cambridge, Archdeacon and Canon of Westminster, and Chaplain in Ordinary to the Queen, said of the Scholastics in his beautifully documented *History of Interpretation: Eight Lectures Preached Before the University of Oxford in the Year MDCCCLXXXV:*
"Their theology is a science . . . in which a congeries of doubts is met by a concatenation of baseless assumptions. The result is a dull mythology in which abstractions are defined, not in the gracious atmosphere of Poetry, but in the sterile desert of logical discussion. They were enabled to unite obedience with rationalism, and the Hierarchy successfully disguised intense intolerance under an apparent permission to philosophise at will" (266). "The historic feeling and the critical faculty are entirely in abeyance in their writings. . . . The neglect of Philology by the Schoolmen was equally fatal. Only one or two of them possessed even a smattering

of Hebrew, and the vast majority of them were no less ignorant of Greek. They philosophised and theologised over what they assumed to be the supernatural accuracy of largely vitiated manuscripts of a very imperfect translation; and often with no better aid than heterogeneous glosses from the Fathers, and those not infrequently from poor versions and spurious writings. And as they 'rack the text and so to speak drag it along by the hair,' they constantly rely on the most grotesque etymologies. If, as Luther said, 'the science of theology is nothing else than grammar applied to the words of the Holy Spirit,' the Schoolmen were indeed ill-prepared" (285 ff.).

Farrar specifically includes Thomas in his strictures. Plainly, some of these faults are much less glaring in *modern* theology, though they are far from being entirely a matter of the past. For that matter, Thomas' vast erudition, straightforward clarity, and noble simplicity have rarely been matched. What *is* encountered again and again in subsequent theologians is his bold air of omniscience and his gerrymandering. In twentieth-century Protestant theology, men like Heidegger have taken the place of Aristotle (hardly an improvement), and Marx (in the thirties) and Freud (in the forties) that of the pseudo-Dionysius. The Bible, however, is gerrymandered as artfully as ever.

Our concern here is not with Scholasticism but with theology. Farrar warms up to Luther as he does not to the Schoolmen, but Luther, too, gerrymandered. How many of those who cheer Luther's celebrated declaration that he would not recant unless refuted from the Holy Scriptures are aware of what he wrote just a little later in discussing his new translation of the Bible? "You have to judge correctly among all the books and discriminate which are the best. For the Gospel of John and the Epistles of Paul, especially that to the Romans, and the First Epistle of Peter are the real core and marrow of all the books. . . . The Gospel of John is the sole fine and right main Gospel, far to be preferred and elevated above the other three. The Epistles of Peter and Paul are also far more eminent than the three Gospels of Matthew, Mark, and Luke. . . . The Epistle of St. James is an epistle of straw, for it has no evangelic manner" (XIV, 105). Luther also said of John that "one might even call him alone an evangelist" (XI, 1462), and he argued that all the moral commandments of the Bible were "ordained solely that man might thus realize his incapacity for good and learn to despair of himself" (XIX, 992*).

Such forthrightness is not characteristic of theology and led Luther into open disagreement with the leading theologian of Lutheranism: "Many have labored and toiled and sweated over the Epistle of St. James when they compared it with St. Paul. Thus Philip Melanchton treats of it, too, in his *Apologia*, but not with real seriousness; for it is a flat contradiction, faith justifies, and faith does not justify. If any man can rhyme that together, I will give him my cap, and he may call me a fool" (XXII, 2077).

The reason theologians gerrymander should be obvious. They set themselves an impossible task that cannot be solved with sound methods: to present to us "the message" of the New Testament, indeed of the whole Bible. But the books of the Christian Bible were written over a period of approximately thirteen centuries by men who did not always agree with each other. Characteristically, Luther, without the benefit of Bible criticism, called a spade a spade and, in effect, admitted openly that he was gerrymandering the Bible and that a Christian teacher could not do otherwise.

Luke introduced his Gospel by remarking that others had written lives of Jesus, but that it seemed good to him to write another version, "that you may know the truth." Scholars agree that he knew, and used extensively as one of his sources, the Gospel according to Mark. Where he differs with Mark, which is often, he evidently differs deliberately, "that you may know the truth."

Matthew, too, knew and used Mark's Gospel, and his disagreements with Mark are also manifold and obviously deliberate. In *Christian Beginnings*, an exemplary study of the New Testament in the light of modern criticism, head and shoulders above most similar efforts, Morton Scott Enslin argues very plausibly, though this is still a minority view, that Luke also knew and used the Gospel according to Matthew. If so, the disagreements between these two evangelists would also be deliberate.

In any case, the striking disagreements of the fourth Gospel with the first three are not only a commonplace of modern scholarship but were noted by Luther already. And that James and Paul did not agree need not be gathered either from a careful comparison of both writers or from our Luther quotation: the Book of Acts in the New Testament gives a detailed account of some of these disagreements.

If Thomas gerrymandered the Bible, this was not his innovation, nor merely a personal shortcoming. Some of the evangelists as well as Paul had treated the Old Testament in similar fashion, and the rabbis had preceded them.

As Farrar says, discussing the approach to Scripture which was formalized by Hillel, the Pharisee: "It means the isolation of phrases, the misapplication of parallel passages, the false emphasizing of accidental words, the total neglect of the context. . . . It is just as prominent, and quite as mischievous, in Hilary and Augustine, in Albert and Aquinas, in Gerhard and Calovius, as in Hillel or Ishmael" (22). Thomas, of course, lacked whatever feeling for the Hebrew Scriptures Hillel had, and "a large part of his method consists in the ingenious juxtaposition of passages of which the verbal similarity depends only upon the Vulgate [the Latin Bible]. From these imaginary identities of expression, by a method which seems to have survived from the days of Hillel, he deduces systems extremely ingenious but utterly without foundation" (271). "But while the scriptural exegesis of the Schoolmen was injured by all these causes, the worst plague-spot of it was the assumption that every part of Scripture admitted of a *multiplex intelligentia*. . . . A favourite illustration of this supposed fourfold sense was the word 'Jerusalem,' which might stand for a city, for a faithful soul, for the Church militant, or for the Church triumphant. Another was the word 'water,' which literally means an element; tropologically may stand for sorrow, or wisdom, or heresies, or prosperity; allegorically may refer to baptism, nations, or grace; anagogically to eternal happiness. Thomas Aquinas tells us that *'Let there be light'* may mean historically an act of creation; allegorically, 'Let Christ be love'; anagogically, 'May we be led by Christ to glory'; and, tropologically, 'May we be mentally illumined by Christ'" (294 f.).

From the rabbis I should like to give an example not found in Farrar. In New Testament times, the Pharisees believed in the resurrection of the dead, while the Sadducees did not. Far from admitting, as almost all modern scholars do, that this belief had developed in Judaism only after the Babylonian exile, the Pharisees claimed that it had been taught by Moses and could also be deduced from all sorts of Scriptural verses in which the untrained eye would never find any such implication. According to the Babylonian Talmud (Sanhedrin 90b), "The Sadducees asked Rabban Gamaliel: How can you prove that God will bring the dead back to life? He replied: From the Torah, the Prophets, and the Scriptures [i.e., the third division of the Hebrew Bible, comprising, e.g., Psalms, Job, Song of Songs]. But they did not accept this. From the Torah: The Lord said to Moses: Behold you are about to sleep with your fathers and will rise [Deuteronomy 31:16]. They replied to him: But perhaps we should read [as the Revised Standard Version does and any ordinary reader would: Behold you are about to sleep with your fathers;] then this people will rise and play the harlot after the strange gods of the land." From the Song of Songs he cited: "Like the best of wine that goes down smoothly for my lover and makes the lips of the sleepers [here interpreted as the dead] murmur" (7:9).

According to Sifre on Deuteronomy (132a), "Rabbi Simai said: There is no passage [in the Hebrew Bible] in which the resurrection of the dead is not hinted; only we lack the power to interpret."

According to all three Synoptic Gospels, Jesus offered a comparable proof to the Sadducees who questioned him: "As for the dead being raised, have you not read in the book of Moses, in the passage about the bush, how God said to him: I am the God of Abraham, and the God of Isaac, and the God of Jacob [Exodus 3:6]. He is not God of the dead but of the living; you are quite wrong" (Mark 12:26 f.; cf. Matthew 22:31 f. and Luke 20:37 f.).

31

When the Catholic church "interprets" the meaning of "eternal misery and perdition," or when Father Walsh explains how the church does not contradict itself when it claims on the one hand that "outside the Catholic Church there is no salvation," and on the other hand that this certainly does not mean that "all who are not actually members of the Catholic Church will be lost," or when Thomas uses Scripture to prove his doctrines, or when Bultmann tells us about "the message of the New Testament"—they are all far closer in spirit and method to the rabbis of the first centuries A.D. than they are to modern philosophy since Bacon and Descartes, to modern science, or to the spirit of a liberal arts education. But while hardly anybody today would think of holding up the ancient rabbis as examples of sound method, many intellectuals since the Second World War consider theology once again the queen of sciences, and Thomas the prince of theologians. With the last claim I have no quarrel, but the assumption that theology closely resembles philosophy, or that liberal education can be revitalized by bringing theologians into a great university, is based on insufficient reflection on the nature of theology and its methods.

It was unfortunate that Paul referred to the Torah, the Five Books of Moses, as "the Law," seeing how much there is in those five books that is not "law"; and it is doubly unfortunate that so many readers of the New Testament have come to think of Judaism as the religion of "the Law." For the same reason it is misleading that occasionally a rabbi is called "a lawyer" in the Gospels. In the context of our present discussion, however, this last misnomer points to an important insight. The rabbis and St. Thomas, Bultmann and Father Walsh, and legions of other theologians are really closer to lawyers than they are to either philosophers or scientists.

Indeed, they resemble lawyers in two ways. In the first place, they accept books and traditions as data that it is not up to them to criticize. They can only hope to make the best of these books and traditions by selecting the most propitious passages and precedents; and where the law seems to them harsh, inhuman, or dated, all they can do is have recourse to exegesis.

Secondly, many theologians accept the morality that in many countries governs the conduct of the counsel for the defense. Ingenuity and skillful appeals to the emotions are considered perfectly legitimate; so are attempts to ignore all inconvenient evidence, as long as one can get away with it, and the refusal to engage in inquiries that are at all likely to discredit the predetermined conclusion: that the client is innocent. If all else fails, one tries to saddle one's opponent with the burden of disproof; and as a last resort one is content with a reasonable doubt that after all the doctrines that one has defended *might* be true.

With this second model—that of the counsel for the defense —I have dealt critically in the section on "Religion at the Bar" (§ 34) in my *Critique*. At bottom, the objection to both models is the same. In the law, special conditions obtain that are not duplicated in theology; and it is only these special conditions that can justify such behavior. In the case of the first model, some of these special conditions were still present to some extent in the first centuries, and even in the time of St. Thomas: one constantly had to pit one's skill and ingenuity, one's proof texts and interpretations, against keen competitors. If there was not quite a war of all against all, there were at the very least the schools of Hillel and Shammai, or the Dominicans and the Franciscans; and it was understood that, to prevail in argument, one had to develop a supreme forensic skill. There was almost constant debate and a war of interpretations and reputations.

With some exaggeration, one might liken the milieu of those days to the jungle, and the seminaries of today to a zoo. The theological animals are still addicted to some of the ancient procedures; but they do not have to fight any more, and one is not even supposed to tease them. They are contemplated with respect, even awe; but they live in a world by themselves in which their ancient habits are no longer functional but mere curiosities.

To bring out the arbitrariness of theological method, consider how a group of students might be given the following exercise: construct on the basis of the same body of scriptures half a dozen different theologies—Catholic, Lutheran, Presbyterian, Anglican, Greek Orthodox, and Unitarian, for example. The task could be made still more complex and fill a whole year's course: for each of these six denominations, construct two different theologies by using any two of the following interpretations—Neoplatonic, Aristotelian, Kantian, romantic, liberal, or existentialist. This might make some people aware of the utter arbitrariness of the procedures used by theologians, for the most part without any self-consciousness. It might also keep pious men from writing and talking as if the sole alternative to what they had to offer was some sort of crude, insensitive materialism. It would thus deprive theology of one of its foundations: the loaded alternative.

Emphatically, theology does not closely resemble either a science or philosophy. The model of the law is far more illuminating. So is another model that may well be more than merely a model: literary criticism. Outsiders often assume that theologians either have, or claim to have, some special direct insight into the nature and attributes of God. In fact, the theologians deal with problems that are posed by texts. The texts may differ with the denomination. Typically, they comprise either the Bible alone, or the Bible together with certain formulations devised at church councils, or the Bible along with some creeds. Other traditional statements may be included, too. But generally the secondary material, including even the texts hammered out at the church councils, represents attempts to meet problems created by the primary texts, those of the Bible.

In Genesis it is said, "Is anything too hard for the Lord?" (18:14); and Jesus says more than once that "all things are possible with God" (e.g., Mark 10:27). He also says that not a sparrow "will fall to the ground without your Father's will" (Matthew 10:29). Verses like these lead to discussions of divine omniscience and omnipotence, predestination and free will. The literature on damnation, original sin, and grace took shape in the same way—as the interpretation of texts.

Traditional theology resembles the so-called "new" criticism: it treats the text as an autonomous world, illuminating a word or a passage from other words and passages in the same book. "Modern" theology prides itself on imitating nineteenth-century literary criticism, which heavily stressed history and the authors' biographies. Not knowing who the authors were, one *postulated* authors not only for the various books of the Bible but even for their alleged sources and then tried to reconstruct the mentalities of these supposed authors —something good literary critics did not do, say, in the case of Homer. "Post-modern" theologians follow the lead of the new critics, who, in turn, closely resemble the old theologians.

It may seem that theologians differ sharply from literary critics because they do not write as critics of the texts but, on the contrary, accept the texts as true in some important sense. Clearly, theologians are not like those literary critics who are out to get the author. Rather, they resemble that majority of good literary critics who are not really critics at all but rather interpreters. They are not like men writing on controversial modern authors but like "critics" dealing reverently with a poet who inspires awe—the *Dantisti*, for example. Here we have a universe of discourse in which "true" and "false" no longer have a place—unless they should be applied to interpretations. But even interpretations are not usually called true or false—rather, traditional or novel, profound or daring, and perhaps heretical.

It may be objected that the theologian, unlike the writer on Dante, believes that his statements about God and hell *are* true; that they are not only good interpretations of the texts but also accurate descriptions of reality. Surely, that *is* an important difference; but even when this additional assumption is made explicitly, it does not necessarily change the procedure or even the atmosphere. Whether you said at an international congress of *Dantisti*, "But I think Dante is despicable," or whether you said at a meeting of theologians, "I think the Bible is a terrible book," the reaction would probably be very similar in both cases: "Go to hell!" Only some—not all—of the theologians would mean this literally.

The additional assumption that the text is true in some im-

portant sense remains in the background and is rarely clarified
very much. The typical theologian believes in the truth of
Scripture, but not that everything Scripture says plainly (or
seems to say plainly) is true. His respect for, and love of, the
text are clearer than his conception of its truth; and when he
does theology, the problems posed by the text are in the fore-
ground, while the question of reference beyond the text, to
"reality," is more often than not out of focus and just a little
dim.

There is, however, one crucial difference between theology
and literary criticism. It is often exceedingly difficult to give
a responsible account of Homer's or Sophocles' views, or of
Plato's or Heraclitus'. But the task most theologians set themselves is more nearly comparable to an effort to interpret "the
message of the Greeks" in a single treatise: if they must offer
a single message, they simply have to gerrymander; and it
stands to reason that different theologians will come up with
different messages. If they were determined to be fair and to
employ the methods used by conscientious historians and philologists, they would have to admit that there is no single
message; that there are many different views; and that an
honest and careful interpreter must often be unsure even about
the views of Paul, Matthew, or Luke—not to speak of Jesus. So
much for gerrymandering.

32

The other major fault of theology is also understandable
as the result of a quixotic task. The theologians have a way
of redefining terms in rather odd ways and then engaging in
something best called *double-speak:* their utterances are designed to communicate contradictory views to different listeners and readers.

In spite of the similarity of the terms, no insinuation is intended that double-speak is a sort of double talk. There is
some double talk in theology, too—and, for that matter, in
philosophy and literary criticism—but the two are recogniza-
bly different. To show this, let us begin with Kafka's parody

of theological double talk, which he entitled, "Of Parables [*Von den Gleichnissen*]":

"Many complain that the words of the sages are always also mere parables, inapplicable in daily life, which is all we have got. When the sage says, 'Go beyond!' he does not mean that one should proceed to the other side, which one might be able to bring off if only the result were worth the effort; he means some legendary beyond, something we do not know, something he himself cannot designate more closely, something, then, that cannot be of any help to us here. All these parables really only want to say that the Incomprehensible is incomprehensible; and that we knew. But the objects of our daily exertions are quite a different matter.

"Then someone said: 'Why do you resist? If only you followed the parables, you yourselves would have become parables by now, and then you would be rid of your daily exertions.'

"Another said: 'I bet that this, too, is a parable.'

"The first said: 'You have won.'

"The second said: 'But unfortunately only in the parable.'

"The first said: 'No, in reality; in the parable you have lost.'"

This wonderful sketch deals with one aspect of the theologians' recourse to "analogy" and "symbol." With this aspect I have tried to deal in Chapter VI of my *Critique*. Poetic parables are not necessarily in the least objectionable, but discourse that is ostensibly designed to elucidate them scientifically, while in fact its clarity is of the surface only, and on analysis it turns out to approximate double talk, is quite a different matter.

In double talk, the question is whether any meaning remains; the epithet is justified when a passage lacks any coherent meaning. In double-speak, there is a clear meaning; but there is also a second meaning that contradicts the first. This epithet applies when a passage is designed to communicate one message to one group and a contradictory message to another group.

Some instances of this have already been noted, but the rationale of this procedure has probably been stated best by Tillich in his *Dynamics of Faith*. In a little over one hundred pages, he redefines such terms as faith and heresy, atheism and revelation. It turns out that the man who accepts the ancient beliefs of Christendom, the Apostles' Creed, or Luther's articles of faith may well be lacking faith, while the man who doubts all these beliefs but is sufficiently concerned to lie awake nights worrying about it is a paragon of faith. "Atheism, consequently, can only mean the attempt to remove any ultimate concern—to remain unconcerned about the meaning of one's existence. Indifference toward the ultimate question is the only imaginable form of atheism" (45 f.). Other forms of atheism, not at all hard to imagine, are defined out of existence; and it turns out that millions of theists may really be atheists, while such avowed atheists as Freud and Nietzsche aren't atheists at all.

It becomes clear that when Tillich preaches, writes, or lectures, he is not saying what those who don't know his definitions think he says. If a large percentage of his audience is misled and thinks he means what he in fact does not mean, is this unintentional on Tillich's part? Apparently not. Taken literally, Tillich considers the Christian myths untenable; but "the natural stage of literalism is that in which the mythical and the literal are indistinguishable," and this is characteristic of "the primitive period of individuals and groups. . . . This stage has a full right of its own and should not be disturbed, either in individuals or in groups, up to the moment when man's questioning mind breaks the natural acceptance of the mythological versions as literal." When that point is reached, one can "replace the unbroken by the broken myth," saying frankly that what was so far believed literally is, so understood, absurd—but capable of reinterpretation. Yet many people "prefer the repression of their questions to the uncertainty which appears with the breaking of the myth. They are forced into the second stage of literalism, the conscious one, which is aware of the questions but represses them, half consciously, half unconsciously. . . . This stage is still justifiable, if the questioning power is very weak and can easily be answered. It is unjustifiable if a mature mind is broken in its personal center by political or psychological methods, split in his unity, and hurt in his integrity" (52 f.).

It is clear that Tillich stands unalterably opposed not only to the Inquisition and to any physical coercion but also to authoritarian methods that harm people's mental health without touching their bodies. No man must be forced to believe. But Tillich considers it all right to let people believe things that are plainly false—things they would not believe unless the churches made them believe at an early age, before "man's questioning mind" discovers difficulties. And even when that point is reached, it is all right, according to the passage cited, to put the believer's mind at ease by reconfirming him in his false literal beliefs, "if the questioning power is very weak and can easily be answered."

One can picture the theologian's problem as he is confronted with a doubter: should the young man be initiated into the inner circle of the broken myth, or is his questioning power weak and does he belong in the second stage of literalism? It all depends on whether he "can easily be answered." If the theologian were a bit crude, he would throw an argument for God's existence at his questioner, or possibly the wager of Pascal, or an appeal to miracles. If the questioner accepted that, this would be proof that his questioning power was weak and that the second stage of literalism was just right for him. But if the young man saw through the answer given him, then one might pat him on the back, congratulate him on his acumen, and let him graduate into the inner circle.

Tillich, however, does not favor the crude method of confronting men with arguments that he himself considers bad. Instead he redefines the crucial terms and cultivates a kind of double-speak. Literalists thus feel reconfirmed in their beliefs and are pleased that so erudite a man should share their faith, while the initiated realize that Tillich finds the beliefs shared by most of the famous Christians of the past and by millions of Christians in the present utterly untenable; and some unbelievers conclude that unbelief is no reason for renouncing Christianity. The central point was most perfectly stated by St. Paul when he concluded his attempt to explain his method to the Corinthians by saying succinctly: "I have become all things to all men, that I might by all means save some" (I.9:22).

The theological virtuoso far transcends double-speak and triple-speak to speak to each man's need. But double-speak at least is required: to seem to agree with tradition while also being up-to-date, or, as suggested previously, to say No in such a way that those who would resent No, or be troubled by it, hear Yes.

A rare reader will remark that any such account of Tillich is misleading because Tillich says publicly—in his *Dynamics of Faith*, for example—that he considers the central Christian articles of faith untenable, if they are taken literally: clearly, then, if anybody is deceived, that is not Tillich's fault. But the reader arguing that way is almost certainly one of the initiated. Bright students studying religion and philosophy at leading universities are generally quite unsure where Tillich stands, and they rarely find unaided that Tillich says what those defending him occasionally claim he says so plainly.

The point is not that some theologians, like Shakespeare and many others, offer more to the discerning reader than to the less thoughtful. Rather, they say A to the one, and not-A to the other, confirming one in his childhood beliefs while informing the other that, of course, no thoughtful person can share such primitive fancies. But unlike politicians who make statements in Harlem that they contradict in Virginia, theologians cultivate the art of double-speak.

What is unusual about Tillich's little book is that it is so short and relatively simple and explains the rationale of methods used by other theologians, too. Here is a brief work of some stature that exemplifies some of the central problems theologians face and some of the devices they employ to cope with them.

33

Some of the other charges made here can be illustrated from this book, too; for example, gerrymandering one's own religion to make it attractive while presenting other religions in a less favorable light. "Every type of faith has the tendency to elevate its concrete symbols to absolute validity. The criterion of the truth of faith, therefore, is that it implies an element of self-negation. That symbol is most adequate which expresses not only the ultimate but also its own lack of ultimacy. Christianity expresses itself in such a symbol in contrast to all other religions, namely, in the Cross of Christ" (97). Jesus' death on the cross is apparently to Tillich a reminder that Jesus was not really God—if he had been, he would not have died—but a symbol of God. The crucifix "expresses not only the ultimate but also its own lack of ultimacy." But instead of conceding that Christianity went further than many another religion, and especially Judaism, in mistaking a symbol for the ultimate and a human being for God, Tillich gives Christianity the benefit of his daring reinterpretation; and instead of admitting that Calvin no less than Aquinas would have favored burning him for so heretical a piece of exegesis, he proclaims that Christianity (with the benefit of his interpretation) is superior "to all other religions."

Two questions present themselves. First, could Tillich be unaware of the vast difference between his own views and those of the Reformers, not to speak of Catholics? At times, he frankly admits fundamental disagreements, but at other times regard for history and facts simply evaporates, and on the next page (98) we are told: "Doctrinal formulations did not divide the churches in the Reformation period." As if Luther did not dispute over doctrines first with papal representatives later with Zwingli; and as if the splintering of Protestantism had not been precipitated by doctrinal differences over the sacraments.

The second question is whether other religions, given the

benefit of equally daring exegeses, not to speak of such a thoroughgoing disregard for inconvenient facts, might not be formidable rivals for the faith the theologian champions. But other religions are gerrymandered in opposite fashion. And even Tillich, who has more feeling for the Hebrew Bible and for Judaism than most Christian theologians, suggests that in Judaism God "can be approached only by those who obey the law" (65). One thinks of the Book of Jonah, of ever so much of the Old Testament, and of dozens of famous quotations from rabbinic literature—and would be stunned if one had never read theology before.

The last two quotations—about Judaism and the churches in the Reformation period—are passing remarks, and it might seem captious to attach much weight to them. In fact, however, the point at stake here undermines a crucial portion of *Dynamics of Faith* and, indeed, Tillich's—and not only his—theology.

If one rejects the traditional beliefs of Christianity and claims that "man's ultimate concern must be expressed symbolically, because symbolic language alone is able to express the ultimate" (41), the question arises whether one is still a Christian. When we interpret Christianity symbolically, we should recall that other religions can be interpreted symbolically, too. As we saw in the chapter on "The Quest for Honesty," the pagan theologians of the Hellenistic and the early Christian Era were profuse in their symbolic exegeses of their own traditions. There would then seem to be no need to reject—possibly even no excuse for rejecting—any religion as untrue: truth might well be out of the picture.

If so, Christian theology would have finally reached the position which in antiquity it attacked: that an educated man should not be exclusive and intolerant in matters of religious truth; that he should not consider his religion right and other religions wrong; and that he should consider different religions mutually compatible. But at that point our modern Christian theologians pull back from the consequences of their own position to insist that, after all, Christianity is superior to "all other religions."

Tillich's attempt to substantiate this last point fails for the reasons already indicated. But to see precisely how it fails, we must consider his three short pages on "The Truth of Faith and its Criteria," from which we have already quoted. Tillich answers his own question how one can "speak of the truth of faith" by claiming that there are two criteria, one subjective and one objective. "From the subjective side one must say that faith is true if it adequately expresses an ultimate concern."

The subjective criterion alone would lead to relativism, as Tillich realizes. Indeed, judged "from the subjective side," the faith of Communists would seem to be truer than the faith of most Lutherans and other Protestants: "'Adequacy' of expression means the power of expressing an ultimate concern in such a way that it creates reply, action, communication. Symbols which are able to do this are alive." During the Second World War, though not since the end of the war, the Nazi faith, too, would have been truer than the Protestant faith. "Symbols which for a certain period, or in a certain place, expressed truth of faith for a certain group . . . have lost their truth, and it is an open question whether dead symbols can be revived." Subjectively, "the criterion of the truth of faith is whether or not it is alive."

Tillich loathed Nazism from the beginning, and did not consider it true even when it was very much alive and created "reply, action, communication." But to *show* that it was not true, or that communism is not true, or that Christianity is superior to other religions, Tillich depends entirely on his second, objective criterion. His initial formulation—"faith is true if its content is the really ultimate"—is not as clear as one might wish; but as soon as Tillich discusses this criterion he makes it clear that he wants to rule out "idolatrous" faith, and that Protestant Christianity, too, "is open to idolatrous distortions. . . . Every type of faith has the tendency to elevate its concrete symbols to absolute validity." Then the three sentences cited at the beginning of this section follow.

By the second, objective criterion, too, communism and Nazism might well be truer than Protestantism and Catholicism. German, Russian, and Chinese soldiers who died eagerly for their faith did not, for the most part, mistake the swastika, or hammer and sickle, or Hitler, or Stalin, or Mao, for "the ultimate." They did not elevate such symbols "to absolute validity"; they realized their "lack of ultimacy"; and they probably would have been hard put to say what, ultimately, they were killing and dying for. Tillich's criteria do not allow him to find even Nazism and communism untrue; much less do they permit him to find Christianity superior to other religions.

The Hebrew prophets, the Buddha, and Lao-tze resisted "the tendency to elevate . . . symbols to absolute validity" much more successfully than the New Testament writers, the church fathers, or Luther. Indeed, Luther insisted against Zwingli that the sacramental bread and wine were not symbols of Christ's flesh and blood but really Christ's flesh and blood; and this doctrine became one of the distinctive marks of Lutheranism.

Tillich does not merely gerrymander incidentally; he depends utterly on gerrymandering and the double standard to escape from a pervasive relativism that would relegate Christianity to being nothing more than one of many faiths that are patently false as usually understood but capable of impressive interpretations, if only one has a little ingenuity. This would scarcely be worth mentioning if it were merely Tillich's personal predicament. It is part of the point of this chapter that it is not.

34

Millions of Christians today believe, in effect, that in the first-century controversy between the Jews and the early Christians the Jews were right. Like the Jews, they believe that the early Christians were wrong when they claimed that on the third day Jesus rose from the dead, supped with some of his disciples at Emmaus, and said: "See my hands and my feet, that it is I myself; handle me, and see; for a spirit has not flesh and bones as you see that I have" (Luke 24:39). They flatly disagree, though they do not make a point of this, with Paul's emphatic dictum, which follows upon Paul's elaborate recital of the evidence for Jesus' resurrection: "If Christ has not been raised, then our preaching is in vain and your faith is in vain. We are even found to be misrepresenting God, because we testified of God that he raised Christ. . . . If Christ has not been raised, your faith is futile" (I Corinthians 15).

The Christian who believes, in Bultmann's words, that Jesus did not "come back to life and rise from his tomb" rejects the very belief in terms of which Christianity defined itself vis-à-vis Judaism. If he holds that this false belief is nevertheless a particularly edifying symbol, and thus tries to shift religious controversies to the plain of literary criticism, he goes against the grain of his religion and takes the side of those whom the authors of his Scriptures and the architects of all the major Christian churches, from the Greek and Latin fathers down to the Reformers, fought with all their might.

This is not the only objection to this post-Christian stratagem. To an even moderately sophisticated and well-read person it should come as no surprise that any religion at all has its hidden as well as its obvious beauties, and that a resourceful interpreter can come up with sapphires where there seemed to be nothing but mud. The trouble with most such interpreters is that they overlook, and that they lead their audiences to overlook, that other religions and denominations can play the same game. And they allow the believer to say Yes while evading any No.

While these faults are deeply ingrained in theology, it is by no means impossible for a religious person to avoid them. When the Hebrew prophets interpreted their religious heritage, they were not conformists who discovered subtle ways in which they could agree, or seem to agree, with the religion of their day. Nor did they show how the cult was justifiable with a little dexterity. Far from it.

Let those who like inspiring interpretations be no less forthright in telling us precisely where they stand on immortality, the sacraments, and hell; on the virgin birth and resurrection; on the incarnation and the miracles; on John's theology, and Paul's, and James'; on Augustine and Aquinas, Luther, Calvin, and the various creeds. And on: "Resist not evil." And: "Let him who would sue you in court for your coat have your cloak, too." And: "No one comes to the Father but through Me."

That would clearly be the end of theology. The theologians pay a price for perpetuating a mass movement; they are not content, as the prophets were, with a small remnant. If each spoke out boldly and unequivocally, no mass movement would be left. It would become apparent that there are almost as many different views as preachers, that such phrases as "the message of the New Testament" and "the Biblical view" and "the Christian answer" are hollow, and that the temporal and spatial continuity of Christendom depends on ambiguity.

The preacher who insists on being forthright loses at least half his audience: at best, he has the choice which portion he would like to keep. If he wants to have a congregation that does not consist solely of intellectuals, he has to speak in a manner that makes sense at what Tillich calls "the natural stage of literalism . . . in which the mythical and the literal are indistinguishable"; and he must also keep the confidence of those who have reached "the second stage of literalism, the conscious one, which is aware of the questions but represses them"; nor must he antagonize those who despise literalism.

To understand theology, one has to recognize that pastors and priests, as well as the theologians who train them, work in an environment that is quite different from the universities in which philosophers and scientists pursue their work. The preacher has dissimilar responsibilities and is subjected to different pressures. To put it crudely, he lacks tenure and academic freedom: if he alienates half of his congregation, he is likely to be out of a job.

Suppose he spurns economic considerations and gives little or no thought to his own welfare; suppose he either has no family or utterly subordinates their future and security to his conception of his duties: he still has a responsibility to the congregation as a whole and not just to those who share his ideas. He is not like a lecturer who speaks once a week in an adult education program to those who happen to be interested in his subject. Nor is it his job to disseminate information and to promote critical thinking. His audience, unlike that of a philosophy or science professor, expects to be fortified against the inroads of new information and critical thinking. Those who are most traditional in their beliefs would withdraw their confidence if he said clearly that he disbelieves what they believe, but they need him most. The highly educated are more likely to turn elsewhere when they are in trouble, especially if their religion is extremely liberal or altogether non-theistic: they may go to doctors, psychoanalysts, or social workers, for example. Those, on the other hand, who take many ancient beliefs literally need their pastor.

One only has to put oneself in the preacher's place to understand how his predicament quite naturally leads him to resort to the devices we have discussed. There, but for the lack of God's grace, go I.

35

Theology, of course, is not religion; and a great deal of religion is emphatically anti-theological. At the very least, large *parts* of the Sermon on the Mount are anti-theological, not only those alluded to earlier in this chapter. Parts of the New Testament seem to say that what ultimately matters is our conduct and not our beliefs, and least of all theology. But the claim that this is *the* message of the New Testament, however dear to many liberals, can be backed up only by gerrymandering.

If only implicitly, the teachings of the Hebrew prophets are much more consistently and radically anti-theological. "I hate, I despise your feasts, and I take no delight in your solemn assemblies. . . . But let justice roll down like waters, and righteousness like an everflowing stream." These words of Amos state one of the central themes of the prophetic books. Isaiah says similarly: "When you come to appear before me, who requires of you this trampling of my courts? Bring no more vain offerings; incense is an abomination to me. Cease to do evil, learn to do good; seek justice, correct oppression; defend the fatherless; plead for the widow." And

Micah: "What does the Lord require of you but to do justice and to love mercy and to walk humbly with your God."

In the Prophets and in parts of the New Testament—though certainly only in parts—love, justice, and humility appear to be all that is asked of man, and questions of belief entirely peripheral, while precise formulations about God, "his attributes, and his relations with man and the universe" are altogether out of the picture. Perhaps the Book of Jonah goes furthest: here the wicked men of Nineveh are forgiven everything because they are sincerely sorry; they are pagans and they need not even be converted or acknowledge any new beliefs whatever.

The Buddha brushed aside all theological and metaphysical queries as "questions that tend not toward edification" and proclaimed that all we need to know to live good lives and find salvation are four simple truths about suffering; its cause in human ignorance, desire, and attachment; its cessation when detachment is achieved; and the kind of life that leads to the cessation of desire. Around the same time, about 500 B.C., Confucius, in China, disparaged questions about the supernatural and taught men to concentrate on this life and their relations to other human beings.

In the Confucian Analects we are told that "the Master would not discuss . . . supernatural beings" (VII:20) and discouraged concern with men's "duty to the spirits" (XI:11). The other great sage of China, Lao-tze, went even further in disparaging speculations, doctrines, and pretensions to knowledge. With a whimsical humor he extolled the virtues of a simple life.

An attack on theology, therefore, should not be taken as necessarily involving an attack on religion. Religion can be, and often has been, untheological or even anti-theological.

36

Whether Christianity can ever dispense with theology is another matter. Christianity has always emphasized beliefs that must seem foolish to the uninitiated—a point already made in the oldest part of the New Testament, the Epistles of Paul. Shorn of these beliefs, Christianity ceases to be Christianity and becomes some kind of Reform Judaism or Unitarianism. Christianity defined itself less as a way of life than as a faith which, right from the beginning, involved assent to various propositions. Disputes over these beliefs and their correct interpretation led to the establishment of different churches and denominations. Confronted with so many theologies, a Christian faces a variety of possibilities.

First, he can try to ignore this abundance, refuse to give himself any account of the meaning of his beliefs, and repeat the hallowed articles of faith without caring how they are interpreted. This leaves open the question to which church he belongs and goes. If he goes to the nearest one, or to the one that other people of his social status generally attend, while turning a deaf ear to his minister's interpretations of Christian belief, he is likely to be a pillar of society; but he could hardly be said to take his Christianity seriously. It was against nominal Christians of this sort that Kierkegaard wrote his life long. Though Kierkegaard is popular today, he is enlisted, much against his express will, as an apologist, and people overlook the fact that the kind of Christianity Kierkegaard attacked is precisely the kind of "religion" whose revival in the middle of the twentieth century we are asked to note with hope.

Secondly, a Christian can acquaint himself with more than one theology and then choose a denomination that makes sense to him, that he finds congenial, that says more or less in Christian terms what he believes in any case. And if the theologians of this church do not carve exactly what he wants out of the Gospels and Epistles, he may attempt some small adjustments of his own.

One might suppose that this is what most Christians do; but in fact the vast majority even of educated Christians fall into the first class and not into this one. Few Presbyterian college students or college graduates know what the Westminster Confession is; fewer have read it; hardly any have compared it with the basic documents of other denominations.

The present critique of theology would be grossly misleading if it gave the reader the impression that theology is generally very much more than window dressing. Theology moves no mountains; it rarely moves people: it is something most people put up with, something they do not take seriously, something good manners require one to respect—and not to think about.

How little people think about theology, how much it is a mere epiphenomenon of organized religion, has been shown in some detail by Richard Niebuhr in *The Social Sources of Denominationalism*. As long as Protestant denominations have existed, social status rather than theology seems to have decided in most cases to what church a family belonged—and "doctrines and practice change with the mutations of social structure, not vice versa" (21) . This analysis by a man who is often called a theologian is influenced by Marxism—the book first appeared in 1929—and gives a picture that is just a little too extreme in emphasizing economic factors while reducing ideologies to ineffective superstructures. But what matters in the present context is not the precise percentage of unthinking Christians who, while they resent all critical reflections on theology, cannot be bothered to inform themselves about beliefs that they claim to think may seriously affect our posthumous careers. Statistics offer a welcome escape from self-reflection.

In the end, a Christian may choose to reject theology—for some of the reasons given here, and for others besides. But in that case he gives up Christianity, though in some laudatory senses of the word he may be a better Christian than some theologians. In that way, many Buddhists, Jews, Confucianists, and atheists are also better Christians than most Christians.

After all, Christianity is inescapably a theological religion, and those who give up the ancient formulations of alleged knowledge about "God, his nature and attributes, and his relations with man and the universe" break with Christianity. They may still admire Jesus, as some Jews and Hindus do, too; but they are no longer Christians. But could one remain a Christian and retain the ancient formulations without employing any double standard, without gerrymandering or double-speak?

One can avoid all this by the simple expedient of refusing to think about one's religion. But if one does that, is one a Christian? Or one can say: I accept everything, though on the face of it a lot of what I am accepting appears mutually contradictory—which only shows that reason is, as Luther said, "the Devil's bride" and "God's worst enemy" (XII, 1530; VIII, 2048). Again, one refuses to think about one's religion. But if one insists on thinking about it without gerrymandering and double-speak, one has to say: this I accept, this not; this I believe, this not; this I admire, this not. And if one employs no double-standard, one will have to add: in other scriptures and religions, too, I find things I accept, believe, and admire, including much that compares very favorably with much in my own tradition. Still, one may conceivably conclude, it is my own tradition that I love best, though I really agree with no more than a fraction of it. And if that is what one does, one may wish to be a Christian, but one is, literally, a heretic.

37

To show what is wrong with theology in the ordinary sense of that word (dogmatic theology), one does not require a positivistic, Kantian, or Humean theory of knowledge. The faults of theology can be seen with the naked eye. To show that these charges against theology can be sustained against the best theologians, one must consider some of these men. If I had named no names, I should be open to the allegation that nobody, or at least no one of any stature, had actually done what I accused theologians of doing. I have therefore singled out a few men of acknowledged stature.

Profound disagreements are compatible with profound, albeit only partial, admiration. But anyone with high standards of honesty will have more than partial admiration for exceedingly few people.

Those who wish that I might have dealt at greater length with Bultmann, Tillich, or Aquinas will find that I have dealt with some of their other writings in my *Critique*, Chapters V–VIII; and that there I have also considered some other theologians. Here I have confined myself to what seemed necessary to support my criticisms. So the two books should supplement each other.

The rejection of natural and dogmatic theology does not involve any repudiation of the critical, historical, and psychological study of religion. On the contrary, such inquiries are most valuable. Those who want to improve their thinking about the important questions of life and become more conscientious should surely consider the divergent answers given by some of the great religions.

One need not ignore the theologians; but instead of studying theology one should study theologies—as part of the history of religions. The committed study of a single theology —or a single philosophic system, or the views of a single scientist whose theory differs from the theories of many other scientists—is a training in unsound method, partiality, and special pleading. Instead of being taught how some one theory can be patched up indefinitely if only we allow it privileges that we carefully deny to its competitors, students should be exposed to a variety of views and led to discover what can be said for and against each.

Moreover, theological approaches, being denominational, are not at all propitious for determining what answers were actually given by the great religious figures of the past, or even what questions they asked. In few areas is it so hard to read honestly and responsibly, instead of reading one's own prior convictions into the texts; and in theology the latter tendency is institutionalized.

This is not to say that theologians have a monopoly on reading religious texts badly. It is exceedingly difficult to read them. Tolstoy wrote an essay *How to Read the Gospels and What is Essential in Them* and argued: "To understand any book one must choose out the parts that are quite clear, dividing them from what is obscure or confused. And from what is clear we must form our idea of the drift and spirit of the whole work. Then, on the basis of what we have understood, we may proceed to make out what is confused or not quite intelligible. . . . That was how I read the Gospels, and the meaning of Christ's teaching became so clear to me that it was impossible to have any doubts about it. . . . What is comprehensible to one may seem obscure to another. But all will certainly agree in what is most important. . . ." *Sancta simplicitas!* That is what Luther thought, too. But Luther considered Paul and John most important, and especially the doctrine of justification by faith alone; Tolstoy, the Sermon on the Mount, and especially the commandment, "Resist not evil."

Such divergent responses of great human beings to texts, such total responses to verses that set languishing hearts afire, have a more unsettling effect on us than the neat systems of theologians. Luther and Tolstoy openly based their religion on a few key passages; the unsoundness of their procedure is obvious; but as we read them, and others like them, we experience the challenge of religion: we are put on trial and stand some chance of becoming more thoughtful and sensitive, less slothful and complacent. Theological systems, on the other hand, lack what Luther, depreciating Melanchthon's system, called "real seriousness." They mute the challenge and, albeit unwittingly, facilitate complacency.

Some people who are misleadingly called theologians might well agree with all this. This critique is directed, as was made plain at the beginning of this chapter, against what the Oxford English Dictionary calls "dogmatic theology," not against everybody who happens to be teaching at a theological seminary or against so-called theologians who are really philologists or historians. Ernst Troeltsch's *Social Teachings of the Christian Churches* is a monument of impartial and fair-minded scholarship and not in any proper sense of the word a theological work, although he was still a professor of theology when he wrote it and did not formally abandon theology to become a professor of philosophy until a little later (1915). Hermann L. Strack was a professor of theology at the University of Berlin, and Paul Billerbeck was a pastor, but their fascinating five-volume *Kommentar zum Neuen Testament aus Talmud und Midrasch* is not a work of theology either. The same consideration applies to Richard Niebuhr's *Social Sources of Denominationalism* and Morton Scott

Enslin's *Christian Beginnings*. It would be easy and pointless to lengthen this list.

From the claim that dogmatic theologians use unsound methods and are unfair to rival points of view when they do theology, it does not follow that they are unsound or unfair when they do other things, or that they have a monopoly on the faults charged against them. Some philosophers, past and present, are open to the same charges. A philosopher who criticizes theology is surely under no compulsion to defend all philosophers; and I certainly have never come close to doing that.

If a philosopher takes the attitude that Plato and Kant must be defended at all costs, if necessary by the most far-fetched interpretations, and that their works must be read as we should not read those of any other philosopher, this would be a personal defect; it is certainly not of the essence of philosophy. On the contrary, his approach would be patently unphilosophical. In theology, on the other hand, such partiality, such special pleading, such a double standard is institutionalized.

One practical conclusion remains to be drawn. Theological seminaries create many of the problems that their products are expected to resolve. For years the students at the seminaries are trained to see their own denomination as they see no other one; then they are supposed to go out as spiritual leaders, teaching people how to love their neighbors as themselves, sitting down with representatives of other faiths in mutual respect and understanding. Having been trained to see Catholicism as the Catholics do not see it, Judaism as the Jews do not experience it, and other Protestant denominations as they do not look to their own members, the young clergyman is expected to collaborate with priests and rabbis and to busy himself in the ecumenical movement, doing his best throughout his professional career to heal breaches which, but for the training which he and the other ministers, rabbis, and priests received, would long have disappeared.

These criticisms of theology leave open the question how, in detail, I should deal with such an ancient theological problem as that of suffering; or how I should read the Old Testament, or the New Testament. In the next three chapters I propose to take up these problems in turn.

My point of view is not that of a disciple. But if a man were a true disciple of the Buddha, of the prophets, or of Jesus, could he fail to be against theology? Could he help becoming a heretic?

VI

Suffering and the Bible

38

No other problem of theology or the philosophy of religion has excited so sustained and wide an interest as the problem of suffering. In spite of that, people keep saying, as if it were a well-known truth, that you cannot prove or disprove God's existence. This cliché is as true as the assertion that you cannot prove or disprove the existence of y. Of course, it is easy to construct a formally valid proof that y, or God, exists—or, for that matter, that they do not exist: x said that y exists; x always spoke the truth (in fact, he said: I am the truth); hence, y exists. Or: y is a z; no z exists; hence, y does not exist. But whether the existence or non-existence of y, or God, can be proved from plausible premises depends on the meaning we assign to y, or to God. And the term "God," as we have seen, is almost, though not quite, as elastic as the symbol "y."

One's strategy in trying to defend or to attack the claim that God exists obviously depends on what is meant by "God." It may be objected that it is not so difficult to isolate what might be called the popular conception of God. *The problem of suffering is of crucial importance because it shows that the God of popular theism does not exist.*

The problem of suffering is: why is there the suffering we know? Dogmatic theology, criticized in the preceding chapter, has no monopoly on dealing with this problem. Let us see how a philosopher might deal with it, after repudiating dogmatic theology and endorsing the importance of the "critical, historical, and psychological study of religion." My approach will be part philosophical, part historical—only partially philosophic because the problem can be illuminated greatly by being placed in historical perspective. What matters here is not to display philosophic acumen but really to remove some of the deeply felt perplexity that surrounds this problem; and toward that end, we shall have to draw on history as well as philosophy.

There are at least three easy ways of disposing of the problem why there is suffering. If we adopt the position that everything in the universe, or at least a great deal, is due to chance, the problem is answered in effect. Indeed, as we reflect on this solution, it becomes clear that the "why" of the problem of suffering asks for a purpose; a mere cause will not do. Immediately a second solution comes to mind: if we say that the universe, far from being governed by chance, is subject to iron laws but not to any purpose, the problem of suffering is again taken care of. Thirdly, even if we assume that the world is governed by purpose, we need only add that this purpose—or, if there are several, at least one of them—is not especially intent on preventing suffering, whether it is indifferent to suffering or actually rejoices in it.

All three solutions are actually encountered in well-known religions. Although the two great native religions of China, Confucianism and Taoism, are far from dogmatic or even doctrinaire, and neither of them commands assent to any set of theories, both approximate the first solution which accepts events simply as happening, without seeking either laws or purposes behind them.

The second solution, which postulates a lawful world order but no purpose, is encountered in the two great religions which originated in India: Hinduism and Buddhism. Here an attempt is made to explain suffering: the outcaste of traditional Hinduism is held to deserve his wretched fate; it is a punishment for the wrongs he did in a previous life. We are all reborn after death in accordance with the way we behaved during our lives: we receive reward and punishment as our souls migrate from one existence to the next. The transmigration of souls proceeds in accordance with a fixed moral order, but there is no purpose behind it. The scientific world view also disposes of the problem of suffering by denying that the laws of nature are governed by any purpose.

The third solution is familiar from polytheistic religions—for example, the *Iliad* and the *Odyssey*—but present also in the Persian religion of Zarathustra (or Zoroaster), who taught that there were two gods, a god of light and goodness (Ormazd or Ahura-Mazda) and a god of darkness and evil (Ahriman). Here, and in many so-called primitive religions, too, suffering is charged to some evil purpose.

In all three cases, and for most human beings, the problem of suffering poses no difficult problem at all: one has a world picture in which suffering has its place, a world picture that takes suffering into account. To make the problem of suffering a perplexing problem, one requires very specific presuppositions, and once those are accepted the problem becomes not only puzzling but insoluble.

For atheism and polytheism there is no special problem of suffering, nor need there be for every kind of monotheism. The problem arises when monotheism is enriched with—or impoverished by—two assumptions: that God is omnipotent and that God is just. In fact, popular theism goes beyond merely asserting God's justice and claims that God is "good," that he is morally perfect, that he hates suffering, that he loves man, and that he is infinitely merciful, far transcending all human mercy, love, and perfection. Once these assumptions are granted, the problem arises: why, then, is there all the suffering we know? And as long as these assumptions are granted, this question cannot be answered. For if these assumptions were true, it would follow that there could not be all of this suffering. Conversely: since it is a fact that there is all this suffering, it is plain that at least one of these assumptions must be false. Popular theism is refuted by the existence of so much suffering. The theism preached from thousands of pulpits and credited by millions of believers is disproved by Auschwitz and a billion lesser evils.

The use of "God" as a synonym for being-itself, or for the "pure act of being," or for nature, or for scores of other things for which other terms are readily available, cannot be disproved but only questioned as pettifoggery. The assertion that

God exists, if only God is taken in some such Pickwickian sense, is false, too: not false in the sense of being incorrect, but false in the sense of being misleading and to that extent deceptive.

It is widely assumed, contrary to fact, that theism necessarily involves the two assumptions which cannot be squared with the existence of so much suffering, and that therefore, *per impossibile,* they simply have to be squared with the existence of all this suffering, somehow. And a great deal of theology as well as a little of philosophy—the rationalizing kind of philosophy which seeks ingenious reasons for what is believed to begin with—has consisted in attempts to reconcile the popular image of God with the abundance of suffering.

39

In this perspective, much of the Old Testament appears in a new light. In most of the Hebrew Scriptures it is simply axiomatic that suffering comes from God. "Is a trumpet blown in a city, and the people are not afraid? Does evil befall a city, and the Lord has not done it?" asked Amos (3:6). About 150 years later, after the fall of Jerusalem in 586, Jeremiah exclaimed in his Lamentations: "Is it not from the mouth of the Most High that good and evil come?" (3:38). And not quite fifty years later, as the Persians, who believed in two great gods, one good and one evil, were approaching Babylonia, the so-called Second Isaiah repudiated any such dualism: "I am the Lord, and there is no other; besides me there is no god. . . . I form light and create darkness, I make peace and create evil; I am the Lord who do all these things" (45:5 ff.). Evil and suffering do not come from an evil god, Ahriman, but from the one and only God. In the same spirit, Job asks his wife: "Shall we receive good at the hand of God, and shall we not receive evil?" (2:10).

It also seems to have been accepted as a fact—and it surely is a fact—that children often suffer for their parents' deeds. This evidently offended Jeremiah's moral sensibility, but he was less prone than most men to retouch reality. Nothing ever kept him from telling his contemporaries how grim he considered both the present and the imminent future. But looking into the very distant future, he gave voice to his hopes: "And it shall come to pass that as I have watched over them to pluck up and break down, to overthrow, destroy, and bring evil, so I will watch over them to build and to plant, says the Lord. In those days they shall no longer say: 'The fathers have eaten sour grapes, and the children's teeth are set on edge.' But every one shall die for his own sin; each man who eats sour grapes, his teeth shall be set on edge" (31:28 ff.). With his grim realism, Jeremiah did not question the plain fact that those who suffer frequently do not deserve their suffering; but he felt that this was unjust, and he proclaimed that a time shall come when it will not be that way any more. As for the present, he did not question the patent injustice of history: "Our fathers sinned, and are no more; and we bear their iniquities" (Lamentations 5:7).

Only a few years later, possibly even at the very same time, another prophet arose in the Babylonian captivity and took a further step: Ezekiel. He marks a new point of departure.

One ought to divide the Hebrew prophets into three groups instead of distinguishing the "major" from the "minor" prophets, using the mere size of their books as the sole criterion. Nor is it sufficient to separate the pre-exilic from the later prophets: in a crucial way, the so-called Second Isaiah is closer to the pre-exilic Isaiah than he is to Ezekiel, his own contemporary.

Three types of Hebrew prophets might be distinguished as follows. First, there are those who did not write books or compose magnificent speeches. Among these, the most memorable is Elijah in the ninth century; and the Bible also devotes a good deal of space to his follower, Elisha. Both stand in a tradition that is easily traced back at least another 200 years to the time of Saul and David; and from the time of David a notable parable, told by the prophet Nathan, has been preserved. The Books of Samuel and Kings are full of similar prophets, though not all were of equal stature.

The two first representatives of the second type were Amos and Hosea, in the eighth century. They were soon followed by Micah and Isaiah, a century later by Jeremiah, and still later by the Second Isaiah. There were others, more or less similar though not quite so impressive. What sets the men of the second type apart is that they spontaneously composed great poetic speeches, generally in the name of the Lord. They did not, like some of the prophets of the first type, induce ecstatic trances by dancing, nor did they wait to be consulted, nor did they claim to perform miracles, nor did they merely tell the king after special provocation what they thought of him, with the whole emphasis falling on the contents of their remarks and little or none on the precise words. Whether the prophets of this second type recorded their own words in writing or left it to others to do, they were great literary artists as well as moralists. The gist of their messages was generally that their people were acting immorally, that such conduct was bound to lead to hideous consequences, and that the people should mend their ways, the consequences being inevitable unless the people should repent and return from their wicked ways.

The first great representative of the third type is Ezekiel who, during the Exile, turned away from reality and had visions. When Isaiah described the Lord's call, in Chapter 6, he gave us the bare bones of a vision, providing no more than the setting in which he found himself addressed. Everything leads up to the words he heard: what really mattered could not be seen. God's "train filled the temple," and Isaiah saw some amazing creatures whom he called seraphim; but all this merely underlines the exceptional nature of his experience. The climax is not reached until Isaiah is addressed: "Whom shall I send, and who will go for us? Then I said: Here I am, send me! And he said: Go and say to this people: . . ." Isaiah, Micah, Jeremiah, Hosea, and Amos were not visionaries. Their experiences were primarily auditory: they heard God's voice, they were inspired to say things. Only very occasionally are their messages underscored by visual detail; but even then they do not lose themselves lovingly in elaborations; what matters is the spoken word and not a vision. All this is different in Ezekiel who, as it were, founded a new genre.

In the Old Testament, the next two major representatives of this genre are Zechariah and Daniel. Outside the Old Testament, a whole vast apocalyptic literature developed in which various authors spun out their visions in minute detail, showing the influence of Ezekiel and Daniel in a great variety of ways, not least by taking over many of their images. While this literature was not accepted as canonical by the Jews and deliberately excluded from the Hebrew Bible, one apocalypse, known variously either as The Revelation of St. John the Divine or as *The* Apocalypse, was included in the New Testament; and the influence of apocalyptic literature is plain in the Gospels and in other parts of the New Testament, too.

It is a commonplace that Jesus stands in "the prophetic tradition." Our distinction between three types of prophets allows a certain refinement of this cliché. Jesus does not go as far as Amos and Hosea, Micah and Isaiah, and Jeremiah did in their radical criticism of the cult of their religion and their exclusive insistence on justice, mercy, and humility, though it is plain that the general tenor of his preaching was closer to this tradition than it was to ritualism or theology. Still, seeing that others before him had gone so far, it is noteworthy that he went so much less far. Although Bultmann, in his *Theology of the New Testament*, ascribes to Jesus "a great protest against Jewish legalism" (10), he has to admit that "there is not the slightest trace in Jesus' words of any polemic against the temple cult" (16). The great prophets of the second type had outdone each other in such polemics. And in his early book on the Synoptic Gospels, Bultmann points out that it is highly significant that various minor violations of the ritual law are "related of the disciples only and not of Jesus himself"; and he gives reasons for believing that "the 'disciples' who have broken with these customs are the primitive Christian community" (23; cf. my *Critique*, § 57).

To be sure, the New Testament relates that Jesus healed a man on the Sabbath, but the Pharisees would have considered this permissible if there had been an emergency. Since the man had been lame all his life, most of them felt, no doubt, that Jesus might have waited a few hours until the Sabbath was over, though a minority might have been as liberal as he was. Clearly, this was a borderline case which involved the interpretation of the law: the whole atmosphere is that of first-century Judaism, not that of the great prophets of the second type. Like many, though by no means all, of his contemporaries, Jesus and the evangelists were evidently much more deeply influenced by the Biblical stories of Elijah's miracles and ascent to heaven and by the apocalyptic tradition than by Amos and his successors. It is not merely such a phrase as "Son of Man" which recalls Daniel and Ezekiel but, more importantly, Jesus' whole attitude toward *this* world and his concern with another world: *this* world ceases to be the center of attention, as it was in the tradition that led from Amos to the Second Isaiah; *this* world is about to come to an end; and even now it behooves us to concentrate much less on *this* world than on another—indeed, if possible, to have no thought of this world at all and to subordinate everything to preparing for the other.

Ezekiel was the grandfather of the apocalyptic tradition—a new point of departure—but not himself preoccupied either with the end of the world or, strictly speaking, with another world. He was a man who, literally, had visions. Some doctors have speculated that he may have been an epileptic, and Karl Jaspers has written a paper on this question. If Ezekiel had told his people that they would one day return from their Babylonian exile and rebuild their temple, they might well have laughed at him. No other people had ever returned from this kind of exile, and the memory of the destruction of the northern kingdom, Israel, was still fresh: Samaria had been razed by the Assyrians, the people had been exiled, and the ten tribes had been lost forever. But Ezekiel *saw* the rebuilt temple—saw it in such minute detail that he could go on and on describing it and giving measurements. He could see even now what was to be, and many people believed him; and later on, no doubt, some insisted on rebuilding the temple just as he had described it.

With Ezekiel, the Ought took precedence over the Is, even to the extent of a flat defiance of everyday realities. Expressly going beyond Jeremiah, Ezekiel said: "What do you mean by using this proverb about the land of Israel, 'The fathers have eaten sour grapes, and the children's teeth are set on edge'? As I live, says the Lord God, this proverb shall no more be used by you in Israel" (18:2 f.).

It takes only one further step, and we are assured that, appearances notwithstanding, God is just—not merely that "in those days," in some distant future, things will change and God will become just, but that even now he is just. The New Testament assures us, climaxing a development that began in exilic Judaism: God is perfect. He is not unjust. As the German poet, Christian Morgenstern, said in a very different context, in one of his many delightfully funny poems:

> For, he argues razor-witted,
> That *can't* be which is not permitted.

40

It is at this point that the perplexing problem of suffering is created and at the same time rendered insoluble—unless either the traditional belief in God's boundless power or the belief in his perfect justice and mercy is abandoned. Short of that, only pseudo-solutions are possible. Three such pseudo-solutions were offered in short order and later, in Christian times, a fourth as well.

The first was inspired by the religion of Zarathustra, with which the Jews came into contact a generation after Ezekiel. The Second Isaiah had met the dualism of the Persians, and their belief in an evil deity, with a firm denial that there is more than one God and with an equally unequivocal assertion that the one and only God creates evil as well as good. But soon a new conception arose in Israel: that of Satan.

Literally, Satan means accuser or slanderer, and he was evidently originally conceived as a functionary at the Lord's court, the way the prologue to the Book of Job pictures him—or, to use the language of a later age, as one of the angels. Satan never gained any great importance in Judaism, least of all in the Hebrew Bible, but some of the lesser minds invoked him to solve the problem of suffering.

In the Second Book of Samuel (24), it is said that "the anger of the Lord was kindled against Israel, and he incited David against them, saying, Go, number Israel and Judah." David then gave orders to number the people "that I may know the number of the people"; and this order prevailed over the warning of Joab, his general. "But David's heart smote him after he had numbered his people. And David said to the Lord: I have sinned greatly in what I have done. . . ." Even so, "the Lord sent a pestilence upon Israel . . . and there died of the people from Dan to Beer-sheba seventy thousand men." To understand the mind of the historian, one needs only to recall the words of Amos: "Does evil befall a city, and the Lord has not done it?" If a pestilence struck down seventy thousand people, surely the Lord had sent it; and if shortly before that David numbered the people, though he knew that this was a great sin, surely "the anger of the Lord was kindled against Israel, and he incited David."

After the Babylonian exile, when it was widely believed that God was perfect and just, the historian of the First Book of Chronicles, who retold this story, leaning heavily on the Second Book of Samuel, could no longer accept this naïve, pre-moralistic, non-utopian conception of God. Why, then, did David number the people? The later historian has recourse to a pseudo-solution of the problem of suffering. He begins his account (21): "Satan stood up against Israel and incited David to number Israel."

That this is no solution appears as soon as we ask why God allowed Satan to do such a thing. The problem has merely been pushed back, not solved.

The second pseudo-solution invokes the immortality of the soul or an eventual resurrection of the dead. These are two very different ideas, though most people do not bother to distinguish them. According to one conception, the soul lives on after death, without a body, and retains some sort of consciousness. According to the other notion, we do not survive death; but some time in the future, possibly thousands of years hence, our bodies will be resurrected from the dust, and we shall come back to life to be judged. It is interesting that religious people who disdain all disbelief in an afterlife have for the most part thought so little about this whole question that they do not even know which of these two claims they themselves believe. But as far as the problem of suffering is concerned, there is no important difference between the two.

We are assured that although there is patently little or no justice in this life and the wicked flourish more often than the just, the day of reward and retribution will come. This idea, too, seems to have been suggested to the Jews by the Persians, and later it was powerfully supported by Greek influence. By the time of Jesus, most, but not all, of the Jews took it for granted. As was mentioned in the last chapter, the Pharisees accepted it, while the Sadducees did not. But in the Old Testament this idea is mainly notable for its absence, and only a few traces of it are found in occasional verses which, scholars almost unanimously agree, are of very late origin, even later than the few references to Satan. The dominant Old Testament view finds expression in the 6th Psalm: "Turn, O Lord, save my life; deliver me for the sake of thy steadfast love. For in death there is no remembrance of thee; in Sheol who can give thee praise?" King Hezekiah's prayer in Isaiah 38 is very similar. In this matter, Ecclesiastes is no exception at all: "Whatever your hand finds to do, do it with your might; for there is no work or thought or knowledge or wisdom in Sheol, where you are going" (9:10). It is Isaiah 26:19, parts of Isaiah 66, and Daniel 12:2 that are exceptional.

What matters in the present context is that no doctrine of immortality or resurrection can solve the problem of suffering. Suppose that Anne Frank enjoys eternal bliss in heaven: should an omnipotent god have found it impossible to let her have eternal bliss without first making her a victim of the Nazis and without having her die in a concentration camp? If you treat a child unfairly, it may possibly forget about it if you afterward give it a lollipop, but injustice remains injustice. Faith in immortality, like belief in Satan, leaves unanswered the ancient questions: is God unable to prevent suffering and thus not omnipotent? or is he able but not willing to prevent it and thus not merciful? And is he just?

The question remains why such conceptions as immortality, resurrection, and Satan were accepted from other religions after the Exile, seeing that the Jews had much earlier encountered similar beliefs among the Egyptians and rejected them rigorously. Indeed, the Egyptians' preoccupation with the life after death exceeded that of the Persians and Greeks. Apparently there were mainly two reasons.

The first, not sufficient in itself, is that the Exile marks a turning point in Jewish history. After the Jews left Egypt, in the days of Moses, Joshua, the judges, and the kings, the people assumed responsibility for their own affairs, took a healthy interest in this world, and never quite lost the initiative for more than a short spell of time. When their enemies got the better of them, they soon rallied around a new leader who, before long, succeeded in liberating them. There was always hope, never long deferred. The Babylonian exile was an utterly new and thoroughly traumatic experience: here was a disaster from which their own power could not possibly deliver them, not even with the aid of God. It took another great power, the Persians, to end Babylonian dominance and restore Jewish freedom. But post-exilic freedom was not what freedom used to be. Persia might have been an instrument of God's plan; but henceforth Israel did not recover complete control over its own affairs. One was dependent on Persia, later on Alexander and his successors, still later on Rome. This loss of initiative was accompanied by some loss of interest in this world and by the growth of speculations about another, better world, a world to come—after death or at the end of history. The people of Moses, Joshua, and the judges had no reason to hope for the end of history; the nations of the Hellenistic and the Roman world had every reason, and the growth of otherworldliness is not a phenomenon confined to Israel but characteristic of the Near East following Alexander's conquests.

For all that, it is much more astonishing than most people realize that the *ancient* Hebrews should have developed a religion that was so free from the most central concerns of the religion of Egypt. Even if not all of the people had spent some centuries in Egypt, as the Bible claims, Egyptian influence in Palestine was powerful, and contacts with Egypt were manifold. The reasons suggested so far are utterly insufficient to account for the complete rejection of any belief in a life after death. There must have been a will as grand and granitic as the death-intoxicated art of Egypt—an uncompromising will that hammered an unprecedented ethos of resistance into heart and mind, creating a new conscience. There is no prodigy of which the Hebrew Bible gives a more elaborate, grateful, and loving account than this: Moses. That Israel, after the Babylonian exile, succumbed to some extent to the syncretism of that time was due in part to the lack of another Moses. But that it succumbed so little and, on the whole, withstood the tidal wave of syncretism as a rock of non-conformity was largely due to the enduring force of Moses' heritage and the labors of his heirs, the prophets. The Second Isaiah, for example, may deserve much of the credit for the fact that Satan never could gain much importance in Judaism; but it would have taken another Moses to keep Satan, immortality, and resurrection altogether out of Judaism.

Besides Satan and immortality, a third pseudo-solution remains. It consists in asserting, in flat defiance of experience, that everybody gets precisely what he deserves—no better and no worse: if Anne Frank suffered more than Heinrich Himmler, that proves that she was much more wicked.

41

The one book of the Old Testament that is given over to an extended consideration of the problem of suffering, the Book of Job, rejects the first of these pseudo-solutions out of hand, refuses to take up the second, and repudiates the third emphatically.

The frame story, unlike the core of the book, is in prose. Here Satan appears, and the few words put into his mouth show a master's touch. As Heyman Steinthal, one of the founders of *Völkerpsychologie,* remarked in the first essay of *Zu Bibel und Religionsphilosophie* (1890): probably nowhere in world literature before Goethe's Mephistopheles, who was deliberately modeled in the image of the prologue to Job, can we find words that are equally "Mephistophelic." After Satan has remarked that he has been walking up and down on the earth, the Lord asks him whether he has noticed "my servant Job, that there is none like him on the earth, a blameless and upright man who fears God and turns away from evil. Then Satan answered the Lord: Does Job fear God for nothing? Have you not put a hedge around him and his house and all that he has, on every side? You have blessed the work of his hands, and his possessions have increased in the land. But put forth your hand now and touch all that he has, and he will curse you to your face. And the Lord said to Satan: Behold, all that he has is in your power; only on him do not put forth your hand."

Job loses everything but does not curse God. The Lord asks Satan what he thinks of Job now, and Satan replies: "Skin for skin. All that a man has he will give for his life. But put forth your hand now and touch his bone and his flesh, and he will curse you to your face. And the Lord said to Satan: Behold, he is in your power, only spare his life." Now Job is afflicted "with loathsome sores from the sole of his foot to the crown of his head"; he sits down in ashes, and three friends come to comfort him. At first they cannot recognize him, then they sit on the ground with him seven days and nights, "and no one spoke a word, for they saw that his suffering was very great. After this Job opened his mouth and cursed the day of his birth"—in magnificent poetry.

From this point, at the beginning of the third chapter, through the first half of the last chapter (42), great poetic speeches alternate. First, Job's alternate with those of his three friends, several times over; then a fourth friend joins in—a later interpolation, according to the scholars—and then God himself delivers his reply to Job, speaking out of the whirlwind. In the last half of the last chapter, the prose narrative is resumed.

Throughout, it does not occur to anybody even to try to

solve the problem of suffering by pointing to Satan. God's omnipotence is never questioned, and all concerned apparently realize that no reference to Satan can explain Job's suffering without in effect denying either God's justice or his omnipotence. Job's friends refuse to question either of these. All four of them take the same stand: it being certain that God is both almighty and just, the only conclusion possible is that Job deserves his suffering. Since he is suffering, he must have sinned.

Job refuses to accept their reasoning. He never questions either God's existence or his omnipotence; but God's justice, mercy, and goodness he not only questions but denies outright. This is a highly unusual approach to the problem: almost all Christian theologians and philosophers who have dealt with the problem of suffering have clung to God's moral perfection while in effect, though hardly ever admittedly, they have denied his omnipotence.

In the Old Testament there is no exact equivalent of "omnipotence," though *shadday* is generally translated as Almighty. It is a numinous term which stresses mysterious and unbounded power, not a cerebral concept. The play on words in Isaiah 13:6 and Joel 1:15 shows that in Biblical times the word was associated with *shod*, devastation. Nowhere else in the Bible does *shadday* appear so constantly as the name of God as in the Book of Job. But the claim that God's omnipotence is not questioned in the book does not rest merely on the use of a word. Rather, the point is that it does not occur to anybody that God might simply be unable to prevent Job's suffering.

Job's denial of God's goodness takes many forms. In Chapter 3, in powerful verse, he curses the day when he was born; then the first friend replies; and Job's response surpasses even his previous speech, reaching a climax in Chapter 7: "I will not restrain my mouth; I will speak in the anguish of my spirit; I will complain in the bitterness of my soul. . . . When I say, 'My bed will comfort me, my couch will ease my complaint,' then thou dost scare me with dreams and terrify me with visions, so that I would choose strangling and death rather than my bones. I loathe my life; I would not live for

ever. . . . If I sin, what do I do to thee, watcher of men?
Why hast thou made me thy mark? . . . Why dost thou
not pardon my transgression and take away my iniquity?"
Job does not say that he has done evil but insists that, even if
he had, this would not justify God's treatment of him. If a
child has done wrong, a loving father has no excuse for tor-
menting him cruelly without respite. Centuries in advance,
Job replies to generations of philosophers and theologians.

The second friend speaks, and Job in his reply says: "I am
blameless; I regard not myself; I loathe my life. It is all one;
therefore I say, he destroys both the blameless and the
wicked. When disaster brings sudden death, he mocks at
the calamity of the innocent. The earth is given into the hand
of the wicked; he covers the faces of its judges—if it is not he,
who then is it?" (9:21 ff.). Job, like the early prophets, has
no patience with the utopian religion that divorces God from
reality and uses the name of God as a synonym for moral
perfection. He echoes Amos' "Does evil befall a city, and the
Lord has not done it?" The innocent suffer and the wicked
flourish, and Job insists that God is responsible: "If it is not
he, who then is it?"

To be sure, occasionally one may detect something of poetic
justice in history, but Job asks (21:17): "How often is it?"
And two verses later: "You say, 'God stores up their iniquity
for their sons.' . . . What do they care for their houses after
them?"

Later (29), Job gives an account of his righteousness: "I
was eyes to the blind, and feet to the lame"; and two chapters later he offers a famous "negative confession" in which
he lists the things he did not do; and in both cases we may
well marvel at the exalted standards that find expression here.
To take offense at Job's conviction of his own righteousness
and to suppose that for that he after all deserved his af-
flictions is surely to miss the point of the book and to side
with his friends: Job is not presented to us as a historic figure
but as a character who is, as we are assured at the outset
in the words of the Lord, "blameless"; and the Lord adds that
"there is none like him on the earth." Nor does the Lord, when

he finally speaks from the whirlwind, accuse Job of any sin. The point is clearly that even if there were a human being who had never done any wrong at all and who was "eyes to the blind and feet to the lame," there would not be any reason at all to suppose that he would be less likely than others to come down with some dreadful disease or to suffer unspeakable torments.

Indeed, that is the point of the Lord's great speech. Far from insisting that there is some hidden justice in the world after all, or from claiming that everything is really rational if only we look at it intelligently, God goes out of his way to point out how utterly weird ever so many things are. He says in effect: the problem of suffering is no isolated problem; it fits a pattern; the world is not so rational as Job's comforters suppose; it is uncanny. God does not claim to be good and Job in his final reply does not change his mind on this point: he reaffirms that God can do all things. And then the Lord says in the prose conclusion that Job's friends have aroused his anger, "for you have not spoken of me what is right, as my servant Job has; . . . and my servant Job shall pray for you, for I will accept his prayer not to deal with you according to your folly; for you have not spoken of me what is right as my servant Job has."

The last words of the book seem offensive at first. "The Lord restored the fortunes of Job when he had prayed for his friends; and the Lord gave Job twice as much as he had before." Also, Job again had seven sons and three daughters, even as he had had seven sons and three daughters at the beginning, before all ten had been killed early in the book. But, after all, the book does not say or imply that this vindicates God's mercy or justice, or that Job felt that his second set of ten children was fair compensation for the first. There is no need to charge this strange conclusion either to an insensitive editor who had missed the point of all that went before or to an old folk tale. Probably it did come from a folk tale, but the author knew what he was doing in retaining this conclusion. It underlines the weirdness of the ways of this world, which is nothing less than grotesque.

42

Nietzsche remarked in *The Dawn* (§ 84) how Christian scholars and preachers had spread "the art of reading badly." The usual treatment of the Book of Job furnishes a fine example of that. Again and again one reads and hears that in the end Job is given twice as many children as he had in the beginning, and his forthright denial of the justice of God, which the Lord himself accepts as "right" in the end, is simply ignored. Worst of all, it is accepted as a commonplace that the ethic of the Old Testament is an ethic of prudence and rewards, as if the point were that it pays to be good. Clearly, it is the whole point of the Book of Job that this is not so, but Protestant scholars and preachers have often claimed that Job's friends represent the ethic of the Old Testament. This is rather like claiming that the sinners in Dante's *Inferno* represent the Christian virtues. If it should be countered that large numbers of Jews in Old Testament times were probably like the friends of Job rather than like Job himself or the author of the book, it is equally probable that most Christians in the age of faith resembled the sinners in Dante's hell rather than the poet or the saints in his heaven.

Still, it might be objected that the authors of most of the other books of the Old Testament are closer to Job's friends than to the author of the Book of Job. But this is simply not so. This common claim involves a thorough misunderstanding of the ethic of the Old Testament. Not even the moralistic historians who considered it essential to grade the behavior of the kings of Israel and Judah inferred, like the friends of Job, that success proved virtue; failure, sin. Omri, one of the most powerful kings, who would certainly have been glorified in the annals of any other nation, and who died in splendor and peace, was said to have done "more evil than all who were before him" (I Kings 16); but of Josiah, who suffered a diasastrous defeat at Megiddo and was slain in battle, it was said that "he did what was right in the eyes of the Lord, and walked in all the way of David" (II Kings 22).

To be sure, we encounter perennial appeals to the consequences of moral and immoral conduct, but in the overwhelming majority of cases it is the nation that stands to profit or to suffer, not the individual. The dominant ethic of the Old Testament does not invite comparison with the ethic of the Roman church but rather with the ethic of ancient republican Rome: the individual is expected to subordinate his own pleasure and profit to the interests of the commonwealth; it is presupposed that ethical conduct involves such unselfishness. Even as the ancient Roman did his stint and risked his life when called upon, and then, if he survived, returned to the anonymity of private life without even expecting fame, the ancient Hebrew, too, is called upon to do what will benefit the people as a whole, if only in the long run, and to refrain from doing what will hurt the people, even if only after his death.

In this respect, too, Jesus does *not* stand in the prophetic tradition: in the Gospels this ancient appeal to selflessness is no longer encountered; it is presupposed that every soul is concerned with how *he* may enter the kingdom of heaven; and prudence has come to mean enlightened selfishness.

This is not the way the New Testament is usually read; and such an important matter cannot be settled in passing. We shall return to this question in Chapter VIII.

Between the age of the prophets and the time of Jesus, the whole climate of thought had changed about as much as it had in Rome between the time of the first Brutus and the age of Caesar Augustus. Concern with oneself and the other world was common indeed, though by no means universal— and Jesus and the evangelists were not as independent of their age as Moses and some of the prophets had been of theirs. The author of the Book of Job had been more independent, too.

The author of Job had been at one with the prophetic ethic in his radical opposition to the vulgar ethic of his day, and of all times, and in his radical opposition to syncretism. In an age in which the ancient sense of solidarity was crumbling and the individual experienced his sufferings in that utter solitude which is now once again the mark of modernity,

the author of Job refused all the comforts that go with the
assurance that God is perfectly merciful and just—the promises that being moral pays either in this life or the next—and,
with a radicalism that has parallels in Amos and the other
prophets of his type, but scarcely in the Gospels, claimed
that God was neither just nor the embodiment of mercy or
perfection.

43

Later theological attempts to solve the problem never
advanced beyond the Book of Job. The theologians always
insisted on God's justice, goodness, and perfection, like Job's
friends, and generally had recourse to one or another of the
three pseudo-solutions which we have considered—or to a
fourth.

The fourth spurious solution, which is one of the prime
glories of Christian theology, claims in effect that suffering
is a necessary adjunct of free will. God created man with
free will, which was part of God's goodness since a creature
with free will is better than one without it. (Why, in that
case, he first made so many creatures without it, we are not
usually told.) Man then misused his free will, disobeyed God,
as God knew he would do, and ate of the fruit of the one tree
in Paradise whose fruit he was not supposed to eat. This
made suffering inevitable. (We are not told why.) The uncanny lack of logic in this supposed solution is generally covered up with a phrase: original sin.

How old this doctrine is is arguable. Some of the motifs
are encountered in pre-Christian times, not only in Judaism
but also in Greek thought. But in its familiar form it is a
specifically Christian dogma. Augustine thought that he
found it in Paul's Epistle to the Romans 5:12: "Therefore,
as sin came into the world through one man and death
through sin, and so death spread to all men—*eph ho pantes
hamarton*." What was the meaning of these four Greek
words? The last two clearly mean "all have sinned"; but what
does *eph ho* mean? Augustine did not read Greek but Latin,

and wrote Latin, too, and took it to mean "in whom" (*in quo*), while the King James Bible and the Revised Standard Version translate "in that" or "because" (*eo quod*). As George Foot Moore puts it: "For . . . 'for that all have sinned,' the Latin version has *in quo omnes peccaverunt* 'in whom (*sc.* Adam) all sinned.' If the translator had rendered *eo quod,* it is possible that the Western church might have been as little afflicted with original sin as the Greeks or the Orientals" (II, 198).

The doctrine of original sin claims that all men sinned in Adam; but whether they did or whether it is merely a fact that all men sin does not basically affect the problem of suffering. In either case, the following questions must be pressed.

First: if God knew that man would abuse his free will and that this would entail cancer and Auschwitz, why then did he give man free will? Second—and this question, though surely obvious, scarcely ever gets asked—is there really any connection at all between ever so much suffering and free will? Isn't the introduction of free will at this point a red herring? To show this, it will be best to give a vivid example. Here is one from the beginning of Nathanael West's short novel, *Miss Lonelyhearts:*

"Dear Miss Lonelyhearts

"I am 16 years old now and I don't know what to do and would appreciate it if you could tell me what to do. When I was a little girl it was not so bad because I got used to the kids on the block makeing fun of me, but now I would like to have boy friends like the other girls and go out on Saturday nites, but no boy will take me because I was born without a nose—although I am a good dancer and have a nice shape and my father buys me pretty clothes.

"I sit and look at myself all day and cry. I have a big hole in the middle of my face that scares people even myself so I cant blame the boys for not wanting to take me out. My mother loves me, but she crys terrible when she looks at me.

"What did I do to deserve such a terrible bad fate? Even if I did do some bad things I didnt do any before I was a year old and I was born this way. I asked Papa and he says he doesnt know, but that maybe I did something in the other world before I was born or that maybe I was being punished for his sins. I dont believe that because he is a very nice man. Ought I commit suicide?

> "Sincerely yours,
> "Desparate."

Far from solving the problem by invoking original sin, Augustine and most of the Christian theologians who came after him merely aggravated the problem. If such suffering as is described in this letter and the New York *Times'* annual pre-Christmas survey of "The Hundred Neediest Cases," and in any number of other easily accessible places, is the inevitable consequence of Adam's sin—or if this is the price God had to pay for endowing man with free will—then it makes no sense to call him omnipotent. And if he was willing to pay this price for his own greater glory, as some Christian theologians have suggested, or for the greater beauty of the cosmos, because shadows are needed to set off highlights, as some Christian philosophers have argued, what sense does it make to attribute moral perfection to him?

At this point, those who press this fourth pseudo-solution invariably begin to use words irresponsibly. Sooner or later we are told that when such attributes as omnipotence, mercy, justice, and love are ascribed to God they do not mean what they mean applied to men. John Stuart Mill's fine response to this has been cited in Chapter II (§ 5). In a less rhetorical vein, it may be said that at this point the theologians and philosophers simply repeat ancient formulas in defiance of all sense. One might as well claim that God is purple with yellow dots, or circular, or every inch a woman—provided only that these terms are not used in their customary senses. These, of course, are not ancient formulas; hence, it is not likely that anybody in his right mind would seriously say such things. But the point is that when anybody has recourse to such means, argument fails. It is as if you pointed out to someone that eleven times eleven were not equal to one hundred and he said: it is, too—though of course not if you use the terms the way one usually does.

To be sure, one need not remain speechless. One can ask for the admission that, as long as we use the terms in the only way in which they have ever been given any precise meaning, God is either not omnipotent or not perfectly just, loving, and merciful. Some people, when it comes to that, retort: How do you know that we use the words right? Perhaps the way in which we ordinarily use these terms is wrong. This might be called psuedo-solution number five.

To this, two replies are possible. The first is philosophically interesting but may not persuade many who are sincerely perplexed. When we use English, or Greek, or Hebrew words in conformity with their generally accepted meanings and fully obeying the genius and the rules of the language, it makes no sense to say that perhaps their "real" meaning is quite different. It does make sense to suggest that a particular term has an additional technical sense; but, if that is the case, one should admit that, as long as it is used in its ordinary, non-technical sense, God is, say, unjust, or cruel, or lacking in power.

The second reply interprets the question differently. What the questioner means may well be that our ordinary conceptions of love, justice, and mercy stand in need of revision; that our ideals are perverted. If so, we should presumably model ourselves on God's "justice" and "love." But this is precisely what former ages did. Children who disobeyed and adults who broke some minor law or regulation were punished in ways that strike us as inhumanly cruel. Those who do not like reading history will find examples enough in Charles Dickens and Victor Hugo.

This last point, which is surely of very great importance, can be put differently by recalling once more Job's wonderful words: "If I sin, . . . why dost thou not pardon my transgression and take away my iniquity?" *The attempt to solve the problem of suffering by postulating original sin depends on the belief that cruelty is justified when it is retributive; indeed, that morality demands retribution.* Although Job denied this, most theologians have clung to it tenaciously; and to this day the majority of Christian theologians champion the retributive function of punishment and the death penalty. At this point, some liberal Protestants who invoke the fifth psuedo-solution are less consistent than more traditional theologians and ministers: they fight as unjust and unloving what they consider compatible with perfect justice and love. But, as we have seen, the traditional theologians did not solve the problem either, and their conceptions of love and justice are inhuman—especially if one considers that Job and Jonah were part of their Bible.

Indeed, Augustine and his successors aggravated the problem of suffering in yet another way, instead of approaching a solution: by accepting as true Jesus' references in the Gospels to hell and eternal torment, and by bettering the instruction. According to Augustine and many of his successors, all men deserve eternal torture, but God in his infinite mercy saves a very few. Nobody is treated worse than he deserves, but a few are treated better than they deserve, salvation being due not to merit but solely to grace. In the face of these beliefs, Augustine and legions after him assert God's perfect justice, mercy, and goodness. And to save men from eternal torment, it came to be considered just and merciful to torture heretics, or those suspected of some heresy, for a few days.

44

The major modern philosophers who have tackled the problem of suffering have contributed little indeed. Generally they have implicitly, but not admittedly, denied God's omnipotence. Three may be considered very briefly.

Pierre Bayle (1647–1706) claimed that reason was strong in discovering fallacies but weak in attempting to reach positive knowledge; and even his critics grant that this was true of his own reason. He excelled in pointing up all kinds of contradictions in the Christian faith; he insisted that Christian doctrine goes against reason; and he said that only for that reason was it meritorious to accept it on faith.

The German philosopher Leibniz (1646–1716) sought to

answer the Frenchman in a book he dedicated to the first Queen of Prussia. He called it *Theodicy* (a justification of God, or a vindication of God's justice) and composed it in French. He wrote philosophy either in French or in Latin, never in German. Ernst Cassirer, a famous twentieth-century philosopher and historian of ideas, says in his work on *Leibniz* —and he is surely right—that the book might just as well have been called "Logodicy" (a vindication of reason). Leibniz denies that reason contradicts faith, and to that extent he rehabilitates reason. God's will, he says, is subject to his wisdom, and his wisdom knows the eternal verities. God did not make the eternal verities; he did not decide that things should be subject to certain unalterable rules; he could not help evil. Evil is not something positive but a lack, a privation, a deficiency, an aspect of finitude. But forces are necessarily finite, and a world without evil would be a world without forces—and hence nothing at all, which would be the greatest of evils. Our world, on the contrary, is the best of all possible worlds. A world must consist of things finite, and perfect finite things would be like square circles, a contradiction in terms.

On the popular level, Voltaire answered Leibniz when writing *Candide*. On the philosophic level, one may reply that, whatever else is odd about Leibniz' solution, he certainly denies God's omnipotence; for if God is unable to prevent the suffering of girls born without noses, of childbed fever, cancer, and millions of specific instances of suffering, without every time incurring a still greater evil, then he is clearly not omnipotent.

The claim that suffering is somehow logically necessary poses a special problem for the Christian conception of heaven, assuming that in heaven there is no suffering. If God could create a heaven without suffering, why not an earth without suffering—or why not just heaven and no earth at all? Or would a heaven without any earth, and without any hell or purgatory, really be inferior to the world we have? Would the blessed in heaven be unable to appreciate their bliss if they could not observe the torments of the damned? If so, they do not deserve their bliss. But if they could, why then is suffering necessary?

Even if we do not enter into speculations about a world without any suffering at all, no adequate theological or metaphysical justification can be offered for the presence in the world of as much suffering as there is. Let us say, for example, that Dostoevsky's suffering bore fruit in his great novels which, in turn, make many readers more humane and better. An omnipotent God could have presented us with Dostoevsky's novels simply by saying "Let there be *The Brothers Karamazov, Crime and Punishment, The Idiot, The Possessed*"; or, for that matter, he might have created us more humane and better.

Two separate points are involved. First, having to use means to achieve ends is one of the features that distinguishes limited power from omnipotence. The original model of omnipotence is surely found in Genesis I: "God said: Let there be light. And there was light." Plato's demiurge, in the *Timaeus*, not being omnipotent, made the world by imposing Forms, as eternal as he was himself, on an equally eternal receptacle: he made the best world he was able to make under the circumstances; but his power was limited, and what imperfections there are in the world must be charged to the material with which he had to work. Clearly, Leibniz' God is closer to Plato's demiurge than to the God of Genesis.

Second: the uneconomic use of unpleasant means to achieve doubtful ends with frequent failures clearly points to limited power rather than omnipotence. Whatever results can be shown to have been attained with the aid of suffering generally seem to have been obtainable with less suffering; and more often than not, what suffering there is does not appear to be instrumental in the achievement of any good.

If it should be objected that nothing could prevent an omnipotent God from choosing not to avail himself of his omnipotence, from using means to achieve ends though he did not have to, and even using these means uneconomically and often unsuccessfully, this would amount to an indictment of God's mercy and justice. In any case, this is not Leibniz's view; for Leibniz insists that this is the best of all possible worlds.

45

Among recent treatments of the problem of suffering, Josiah Royce's essay on "The Problem of Job" is of special interest. Royce, William James's younger colleague at Harvard around 1900, was the chief exponent of American philosophical idealism and tried to blend religion and philosophy. He clearly saw the faults of many previous solutions. He admitted that one could bypass the whole problem by declining to believe that the world is governed by a purpose. He rejected the suggestion that evil is an insignificant and inevitable incident of a plan that subjects men to some law; that suffering is a kind of discipline, a needful warning, or "the dirt of the natural order, whose value is that, when you wash it off, you thereby learn the charm of the bath of evolution. . . . This explanation of one evil presupposes another, and a still unexplained and greater evil"; namely, "why I was created so far from my goal."

What must be shown, Royce says, is "not a physical but a logical necessity." Those who assert that free will requires the possibility of evil claim a logical necessity; but it is empirically false that men are always responsible for their own suffering. And if we revise the position and say that "the innocent may suffer for the guilty," then it appears that God does not "protect the innocent"; and so "Job's cry is once more in place." If the position is revised again to say that men do suffer only for their own sins, but often for sins committed in a previous life, Royce counters, perhaps under James's influence, with a pragmatic argument: this suggestion would discourage men's impulse to help their fellows; the claim that "no harm can come to the righteous" implies "this cynical consequence."

After these inadequate solutions have been shown up, there remains idealism. "Job's problem is, upon Job's presuppositions, simply and absolutely insoluble." Like practically every-body else, Royce, conditioned by centuries of utopian piety, does not see Job's emphatic denial of God's justice and, in flat defiance of the text, assumes that Job presupposes God's moral perfection. Royce would deny another presupposition of the problem, namely, "that God is a being other than this world." In other words, he rejects theism for some form of pantheism. But with the typical assurance of an idealist phi-losopher, not one whit less bold than Hegel and legions of theologians, he assures us that his doctrine is nothing less than "the immortal soul of the doctrine of the divine atonement." He exhorts us: "Your sufferings are God's sufferings." That is the real meaning of incarnation and crucifixion: God did not remain a being apart from the world. This is, after all, as Leibniz already said, "the best possible world": if God could do any better, there would not be any suffering. (After all, it hurts him as much as, if not more than, you.) "We ourselves exist as fragments of the absolute life," and whatever any man suffers anywhere is part of God's sufferings.

False idealism sees evil as a mere illusion, "a mirage of the human point of view," due merely to our limited per-spective; but "if the evil were but the error, the error would still be the evil." True idealism asserts that God really suffers, too; that this suffering is necessary because the good which consists in the overcoming of evil is greater than that which consists in the absence of evil. "The existence of evil, then, is not only consistent with the perfection of the universe, but is necessary for the very existence of that perfection."

Royce does not only deny God's omnipotence, nor does he merely reject traditional Christianity while boldly claiming that he gives the most truthful and faithful interpretation of what it really means. He also claims that the suffering of the girl born without a nose is justified because the discovery by some future doctors of some way to avert such mishaps makes for a better world than we should have had if there never had been any such mishaps in the first place. That is what the girl should have been told; also, that it hurt God as much as her.

46

"What," to quote Ecclesiastes, is "the conclusion of the whole matter"? There is, first of all, a Biblical notion not yet mentioned—that of vicarious suffering, beautifully expressed in Isaiah 53: "He is despised and rejected by men; a man of sorrows, and acquainted with grief. . . . Surely he has borne our griefs and carried our sorrows. . . . He was wounded for our transgressions, he was bruised for our iniquities. . . . The Lord has laid on him the iniquity of us all." Christians have seen in these words a prophecy of Christ; Jews have applied the words to their own people, in an effort to give their own perennial sufferings some meaning. The search for a purpose behind suffering is not a mere matter of metaphysical speculation, nor a frivolous pastime of theologians. Man can stand superhuman suffering if only he does not lack the conviction that it serves some purpose. Even less severe pain, on the other hand, may seem unbearable, or simply not worth enduring, if it is not redeemed by any meaning.

It does not follow that the meaning must be given from above; that life and suffering must come neatly labeled; that nothing is worth while if the world is not governed by a purpose. On the contrary, the lack of any cosmic purpose may be experienced as liberating, as if a great weight had been lifted from us. Life ceases to be so oppressive: we are free to give our own lives meaning and purpose, free to redeem our suffering by making something of it. The great artist is the man who most obviously succeeds in turning his pains to advantage, in letting suffering deepen his understanding and sensibility, in growing through his pains. The same is true of some religious figures and of men like Lincoln and Freud. It is small comfort to tell the girl born without a nose: make the most of that! She may lack the strength, the talent, the vitality. But the plain fact is that not all suffering serves a purpose; that most of it remains utterly senseless; and that if there is to be any meaning to it, it is we who must give it.

The sufferer who cannot give any meaning to his suffering may inspire someone else, possibly without even knowing it, perhaps after death. But most suffering remains unredeemed by any purpose, albeit a challenge to humanity.

There is one more verse in Job that should be quoted. At the end of the first chapter, when he has lost all his possessions and then his children as well, he says: "Naked I came from my mother's womb, and naked shall I return; the Lord gave, and the Lord has taken away; blessed be the name of the Lord." Without claiming that the following remarks represent or distill "the immortal soul" of his words, one can find more meaning in them, or find them more suggestive, than meets the eye at first glance.

Job's forthright indictment of the injustice of this world is surely right. The ways of the world are weird and much more unpredictable than either scientists or theologians generally make things look. Job personifies the inscrutable, merciless, uncanny in a god who is all-powerful but not just. One may question whether, at least today, this use of the name of God is justified—whether it does not invite needless misunderstanding. Of course, the author of the book no less than its hero is intent on the continuity of this conception with the God of the prophets; and the God of the Book of Job is addressed and replies. What is said to him and by him amounts to a radical repudiation of popular theism; but when the book was written, another, older tradition was still available, could still be appealed to, was still understood. Today this older tradition seems buried. One can no longer count on its being remembered when one speaks of God. One can at most try to dig it up again like an archaeologist or, speaking without metaphors, like an historian. This chapter represents an attempt in this direction; so does the next.

In the chapter on "The Quest for Honesty," reasons were given for not using the name of God. Soon after the Book of Job was written, the Jews stopped using what was then considered God's name and said "Lord" instead. But their piety still permitted them to speak of "God" and the "Lord."

Our new piety no longer permits that. As I have explained elsewhere,[1] "honesty is the new piety."

The reason for speaking of piety in this context is that there is something impious about the arrogance of Job's friends and their many successors who talk as if they knew what in fact they do not know. In a sense, Job is more pious; and so are those who admit, in Rilke's words, "that we are not very reliably at home in the interpreted world"; those who are open to new experiences without insisting on fitting them into some preconceived scheme. But perhaps it would be clearer and better to say that Job and his friends stand for two different kinds of impiety. Instead of speaking of "infidel piety," as I did in my *Critique* (§ 66), it might be better to say: Honesty is the new impiety.

It is not important that some heretics and infidels should be called pious. What needs to be said is rather that heresy may be prompted by humility and honesty, as it was in Job's case.

Job's cry is possible in the mouth of an unbeliever; and what Job hears out of the whirlwind could be heard by an infidel, too. The infidel's attitude would hardly be identical with that of the Biblical Job; but it might well be closer to Job's attitude than the piety of Augustine and Aquinas, Bayle and Leibniz, Royce and most believers.

Those who believe in God because their experience of life and the facts of nature prove his existence must have led sheltered lives and closed their hearts to the voice of their brothers' blood. "Behold the tears of the oppressed, and they had no one to comfort them! On the side of the oppressors there was power, and there was no one to comfort them. And I thought the dead who are already dead more fortunate than the living who are still alive; but better than both is he who has not yet been, and has not seen the evil deeds done under the sun." Whether Ecclesiastes, who "saw all the oppressions that are practiced under the sun," retained any faith in God is a moot point, but Jeremiah and Job and the

---

[1] *From Shakespeare to Existentialism*, 226 ff., 232, 243.

psalmists who speak in a similar vein did. Pagan piety rose
to similar heights of despair and created tragedies.

The deepest difference between religions is not that between polytheism and monotheism. To which camp would
one assign Sophocles? Even the difference between theism
and atheism is not nearly so profound as that between those
who feel and those who do not feel their brothers' torments.
The Buddha, like the prophets and the Greek tragedians,
did, though he did not believe in any deity. There is no
inkling of such piety in the callous religiousness of those
who note the regularities of nature, find some proof in that
of the existence of a God or gods, and practice magic, rites,
or pray to ensure rain, success, or speedy passage into
heaven.

Natural theology is a form of heathenism, represented in
the Bible by the friends of Job. The only theism worthy of
our respect believes in God not because of the way the world
is made but in spite of that. The only theism that is no less
profound than the Buddha's atheism is that represented in
the Bible by Job and Jeremiah.

Their piety is a cry in the night, born of suffering so intense
that they cannot contain it and must shriek, speak, accuse,
and argue with God—not about him—for there is no other
human being who would understand, and the prose of dialogue could not be faithful to the poetry of anguish. In time,
theologians come to wrench some useful phrases out of Latin
versions of a Hebrew outcry, blind with tears, and try to win
some argument about a point of dogma. Scribes, who preceded them, carved phrases out of context, too, and used
them in their arguments about the law. But for all that,
Jewish piety has been a ceaseless cry in the night, rarely
unaware of "all the oppressions that are practiced under the
sun," a faith in spite of, not a heathenish, complacent faith
because.

The profound detachment of Job's words at the end of
the first chapter is certainly possible for an infidel: not being
wedded to the things of this world, being able to let them
go—and yet not repudiating them in the first place like the
great Christian ascetics and the Buddha and his followers.

In the form of an anthropomorphic faith, these words express one of the most admirable attitudes possible for man: to be able to give up what life takes away, without being unable to enjoy what life gives us in the first place; to remember that we came naked from the womb and shall return naked; to accept what life gives us as if it were God's own gift, full of wonders beyond price; and to be able to part with everything. To try to fashion something from suffering, to relish our triumphs, and to endure defeats without resentment: all that is compatible with the faith of a heretic.

VII

The Old Testament

47

Until the nineteenth century, it was customary to consider the Old Testament as if it did not have any historical or literary background: it was studied as the revelation of God, as an absolute beginning, completely self-sufficient. In the eighteenth century, the sustained criticism of the Enlightenment led to a gradual decrease in respect for the Hebrew Scriptures, and interest in them diminished, too. But it was only after the publication of Darwin's *Origin of Species*, in 1859, that an altogether new approach to the Old Testament was widely accepted: an evolutionary approach that first broke down the unquestioned barrier between the Bible and its background, and eventually all but drowned the Bible in its background until no distinctive feature at all was perceived any more.

A hundred years after the concept of evolution first gained wide currency, it has become easy to recognize the foolishness of some of the excesses perpetrated in its name. Some of these excesses actually antedate Darwin, but spread like wildfire as soon as they could feed on his ideas.

As far as any background is concerned, the crucial point that should never be forgotten in the history of ideas can be put into a single sentence: one may have been influenced profoundly by others and yet be strikingly original and even revolutionary.

What makes the study of history fascinating is, among other things, the perception of discontinuity in the context of continuity. The historically ignorant believe in absolute

novelty; those with a smattering of history are apt to believe
in no novelty at all: they are blinded by the discovery of
similarities. Beyond that, however, lies the discovery of small,
but sometimes crucial, differences.

Ancient Israel was deeply influenced by two older civilizations—probably the two oldest civilizations on the earth,
excepting that of the so-called Cro-Magnon men who perished 20,000 years ago, leaving superb drawings of animals
on the walls of some caves in southern France and northern
Spain. The first two civilizations that seem to be continuous
with subsequent cultures are probably those of Egypt and
Mesopotamia, which can be traced back approximately to
4000 B.C.

The Old Testament emphasizes the relation of Israel to
both cultures. It places the Garden of Eden near, if not in,
Mesopotamia; it speaks of the Tower of Babel; and it relates
that Abraham, the ancestor of Israel, was born and brought
up in Ur of the Chaldeans. After leaving his native Mesopotamia, Abraham is said to have traveled widely in what later
became the land of Israel, and he is also said to have visited
Egypt. His grandson, Jacob, who was named Israel after his
nocturnal struggle with an angel whom he defied, saying, "I
will not let you go unless you bless me," is said to have
migrated to Egypt with his children and his children's children. And the Bible relates that the children of Israel remained in Egypt for several generations before Moses, a Hebrew versed in the wisdom of Egypt, led them out of the land
of slavery into the desert of Sinai where he gave them laws
and precepts that set them apart from all the nations of the
world. That was probably in the thirteenth century B.C., and
the name of Israel is encountered—for the first time, as far
as present records go—in an Egyptian inscription of the
thirteenth century in which Merneptah, who was probably
the Pharaoh of the Exodus, boasts of having destroyed Israel
forever.

In the next generation the Hebrews began their conquest
of the promised land where they were to live almost 700
years, midway between Egypt and Mesopotamia. After that
period of time, Nebuchadnezzar, king of Babylonia, sacked

Jerusalem and led a large portion of the Jews into the so-called Babylonian exile, from which they were liberated by the Persians in 538 B.C. At that time, many of them returned to Israel and rebuilt their temple in Jerusalem—which was eventually destroyed by the Romans in A.D. 70.

That ancient Israel was deeply influenced by Egypt and the various Mesopotamian cultures, from the Sumerians down to the Babylonians and Assyrians, should therefore have been taken for granted long before archaeological discoveries and detailed comparisons left no doubt about it. But in fact it had not been taken for granted during the many centuries in which the approach to Scripture was theological and supernaturalistic rather than naturalistic and historical. The discovery of the historical background of ancient Israel was therefore accompanied by a militant sense of opposition to what had previously been believed, and—as often happens in such cases—it was pushed to utterly absurd extremes: it became the fashion to deny all originality to the Old Testament. This view is easily as fantastic as the assumption of earlier times that there was no connection at all between the Hebrew Scriptures and the cultures of Egypt and Mesopotamia.

48

The civilization of ancient Egypt is not only as old but also easily as remarkable as any the world has seen. If we date its approximate beginning around 4000 B.C., we find that it endured for about 4000 years. The gigantic step pyramid at Saqqara, the world's first large stone structure, whose originality, verve, and power are still fascinating to behold, and the slightly later, still vaster pyramids at Giza were as old when the Parthenon and the other temples on the Acropolis in Athens were built as the Parthenon is today; but in Egypt magnificent temples were still built centuries after the completion of the Parthenon. Admirable paintings and sculptures were produced in Egypt over a period of more than 3000 years.

If we compare Egypt with Israel, what strikes us first of

all is the great difference: in many ways, ancient Israel might well be understood as the diametric opposite of ancient Egypt. In Egypt, sculpture and painting flourished; in Israel, both were expressly prohibited—according to tradition, by Moses himself. In Egypt, man's concern with the life after death was as intense as it ever was anywhere: the pyramids were tombs; the finest paintings and many of the most remarkable sculptures were found in the tombs in the Valley of the Kings, across the Nile from Luxor and Karnak, hundreds of miles upstream from Giza and Saqqara; and the treasures found in the tomb of Tutankhamen, a relatively insignificant king, give us some idea of the contents of other tombs which were robbed thousands of years ago. In ancient Israel, we find no concern with the afterlife whatsoever: for Moses, death is the end; and it is only in the very latest passages of the Old Testament, in Hellenistic times, that we find a few intimations of immortality. In Egypt, we find a profusion of gods, many of them half human, half animal; in Israel, we find none of all that: Moses expressly repudiates all belief in many gods.

These three differences are not only obvious: they far outweigh any similarities. For all that, there are continuities. First, we find in Egypt, albeit restricted to a special class, a love of learning and respect for wisdom. Here the difference in similarity was expressed in a single imperative by Moses: "You shall be unto me a kingdom of priests." And again: "You shall be holy." Not one class but all. Every man is called upon to make something of himself. Perhaps this was the most revolutionary idea of world history. In the countries to which the Old Testament has spoken either directly or by way of Luther's revival of the call for "the priesthood of all believers," this idea may appear to be a commonplace; elsewhere—for example, in Egypt, not only in Moses' time but also in Luther's and ours—one can appreciate the revolutionary impact of these words.

Secondly, we find in Egyptian architecture and sculpture an embodiment of the sublime that has never been surpassed. In parts of the Old Testament this sublimity has been transmuted into prose and poetry. This point does not depend on any ambiguity of "sublime." The similarity is genuine and deep and could be circumscribed in other words. Perhaps nowhere else in the ancient world, and nowhere at all except under the influence of the Hebrew Bible, do we encounter such a fusion of austere simplicity and overwhelming power. (The King James Bible and the Douay Version, with their more ornate and baroque flair for magnificence and rhetoric, are misleading in this respect.)

There remains one similarity which, since its relatively recent discovery, has attracted far more attention than any other: in the fourteenth century B.C., perhaps a hundred years before the Exodus, there was a monotheistic Pharaoh in the eighteenth dynasty in Egypt, Ikhnaton. After ascending to the throne as Amenophis IV, he renounced and forbade the worship of Amon and the other gods, changed his name to Ikhnaton, insisted that only Aton should be worshiped, and moved the capital to what today is known as Tel-el-Amarna— the place where some remarkable sculptures and reliefs and a fine hymn to Aton were unearthed by Ludwig Borchardt around 1900, almost 3300 years later. The notion that the Hebrews might have acquired their monotheism from the heretical Pharaoh was too intriguing not to have been taken up by at least a few writers, of whom Freud, the founder of psychoanalysis and himself a Jew, is by far the best known. He was not deterred by the established fact that Ikhnaton's innovations barely survived his early death and were ruthlessly suppressed long before the end of the fourteenth century: indeed, the very name of Aton was scratched out on all accessible works of the period. Freud speculated that, for this very reason, a surviving adherent of the Aton cult might have found himself forced to leave Egypt and, if he wanted adherents, to turn to another people. Freud himself thought of his work on this subject, *Moses and Monotheism*, as perhaps no more than "a historical novel"; and the details of his argument do not stand up. But the possibility of an influence certainly remains.

There is also the possibility that Ikhnaton derived his monotheism from the Hebrews whose presence in Egypt at that time is claimed by the Bible and admitted by Freud and most scholars. But no such influence, one way or the other, is demonstrable.

Again the difference in similarity should not be overlooked. Ikhnaton's monotheism consists of a quantitative reduction of traditional polytheism: of the many traditional gods he recognizes only one, Aton, the sun. It is the sun that awakens all life and that alone deserves worship. In the Five Books of Moses, any worship of the sun is scorned. The word used for the sun, *shemesh*, is written just like the word for servant, *shamash* (the vowels not being written); and in the creation story in Genesis the sun is created together with the moon to serve man as an instrument that makes possible the calculation of days, months, and years.

Hebrew monotheism cannot be understood as a quantitative reduction of any traditional polytheism or as an exclusive declaration of loyalty to one of the established gods: all the established gods of the nations are set aside, and the whole lot of them is considered beneath comparison with God, who not only does not happen to be identified with the sun but who is not at all an object in this world. No object in this world deserves worship: not the sun and moon and stars, which Plato, many centuries later, still considered divine; not the Pharaoh nor any other human being; nor any animal. Only God who is utterly unlike anything in the world. Man alone, according to the First Book of Moses, is made in God's image and breathes his spirit. And that means every man and every woman, not just some king, emperor, or hero, or one family or people only.

On reflection, all this appears so different from the religion of Ikhnaton that no likelihood at all remains that Hebrew monotheism was derived from the worship of Aton. Moreover, it is "debatable"—as Professor John Wilson has noted in his preface to Ikhnaton's famous hymn to Aton in *Ancient Near Eastern Texts Relating to the Old Testament*—whether the Amarna religion can really be "called monotheistic." For only the Pharaoh and his family worshiped Aton, while the courtiers worshiped Ikhnaton himself. Incidentally, "the great majority of Egyptians was ignorant of or hostile to the new faith" (369).

Finally, few Pharaohs, if any, were so possessed with the desire to make images of the things in this world, from reliefs of the disk of the sun to the beautiful birds and flowers found on the floor of the Pharaoh's palace and the magnificent sculptured likenesses of the Pharaoh and his family and the men at his court, which now grace the museums of Cairo and Berlin.

Our archaeological discoveries in Egypt leave the originality of the religion of Moses as stunning as it ever seemed. The experience of Egypt may have awakened the Hebrews to a haunting sense of the sublime, to dissatisfaction with the ephemeral, to respect for learning—and to a lasting revulsion against any concern with the afterlife, against polytheism, and against idolatry and any form at all of sculpture.

We must leave open the possibility that faith in the God of Abraham antedated the sojourn in Egypt. What the Bible claims, and what we have no good reason to doubt, is that the Hebrew religion was hammered out in response to the experience of Egypt—not by way of accepting the religion of Egypt but rather as an enduring reply to it.

49

Several generations before the Hebrews went to Egypt, Abraham is said to have come from Mesopotamia, and around 1900 it was fashionable in some quarters to juxtapose *Bibel and Babel*—to cite the title of an essay of that time—and to deny the originality of the Bible. One of the motifs in the birth story of Moses is encountered earlier in a story about a Mesopotamian king, Sargon; and the story of Noah and the flood bears some marked similarities to the far earlier Mesopotamian epic of Gilgamesh. Such literary influences are undeniable, but, if one stops to think about them, of rather limited importance. Nobody would think of denying the originality of Shakespeare, Goethe, or Sophocles on similar grounds. What matters is how such motifs are utilized.

Far more interesting is the question whether the so-called Law of Moses was significantly influenced by the Code of

Hammurabi. Hammurabi was a king of Babylonia, probably from 1728–1686 B.C. He may be the man referred to in Genesis 14 as "Amraphel, king of Shinar." His law code was discovered in the winter of 1901–2 in the course of excavations at Susa (the Shushan of Esther and Daniel) in southern Persia, where an Elamite raider had taken the diorite stela about the twelfth century B.C. The stela, topped by a bas-relief showing Hammurabi with the sun god Shamash, was found by French archaeologists who took it to the Louvre in Paris.

The code is not the earliest code of laws known to us, but in its preservation and comprehensiveness it has no equal of comparable antiquity, save only the Law of Moses, which is younger. Hammurabi's laws are framed by a poetic prologue and epilogue and deal with the following matters: accusations, witnesses, and judges; theft and robbery; a military feudal system; field, garden, and house; tradesmen and female wine sellers; articles left with another person for safekeeping; family relationships; injuries; ships; rents; and slaves. In this central portion there are no digressions, and the arrangement is far more systematic than in the comparable sections of the Five Books of Moses. This, added to the many parallels in detail, led early scholars to underestimate the striking originality of the Mosaic legislation. Confronted with such an unusually significant and unexpected discovery, these scholars could scarcely have been expected to react differently; and the tremendous influence of the Code of Hammurabi on the Law of Moses cannot be doubted. Indeed, Hammurabi and his successors succeeded in extending the influence of Babylonia as far as Palestine, and the cultural hegemony of Babylonia outlasted its political dominion. It would therefore be tedious to catalogue parallels or, for that matter, minor differences. Are there any *major* differences? Do we find any radically new point of departure in the Mosaic legislation?

The two central principles of Hammurabi's code are, first, *ius talionis* (the conception that justice in criminal cases consists in precise retaliation) and, secondly, that the law *is* a respecter of persons and that different standards must be applied to people of different social status. Both of these principles are anathema to most contemporary penologists, and retaliation is widely considered all but synonymous with the Law of Moses. The arguments of T. H. Green, Bernard Bosanquet, and other apologists for *ius talionis* notwithstanding, both of these principles have a common presupposition: they distinguish insufficiently between human beings and material objects. And the crucial difference between the Code of Hammurabi and the Law of Moses is that in the latter the unique worth of man as such is proclaimed and implicit—for the first time in human history.

The Code of Hammurabi recognizes three classes of people: an aristocracy, commoners, and slaves. Accordingly, it generally provides three kinds of punishment, depending, for example, on whether an injury has been inflicted on a member of the aristocracy, a commoner, or a slave. The slave is considered less as a human being than as a piece of property; and so are the sons and daughters even of a noble. The way in which the principle of retaliation is applied suggests that the body of the noble himself, too, is considered as essentially a material object.

Here are a few illustrations, accompanied in each case by a contrast with the Law of Moses. The man who has destroyed an eye or broken a bone of another man's slave has to pay one half his value: he merely has to compensate the owner for the damage done to his property. In the same vein, there is no penalty whatsoever for destroying an eye or breaking a bone of one's own slave. This should be compared with Exodus 21:20 and 21:26 ff., here the man who as much as breaks a tooth of his own slave must let him go free for his tooth. In the Law of Moses, the slave is first of all a human being and has to be treated as such.

According to the Code of Hammurabi, if a man either helps a fugitive slave "escape through the city gate" or harbors him in his house "and has not brought him forth at the summons of the police, that householder shall be put to death" (15 ff.). Compare this with Deuteronomy 23:15 f.: "You shall not give up to his master a slave who has escaped from his master to you; he shall dwell with you, in your midst, in the place which he shall choose within one of your towns, where it pleases him best; you shall not oppress him."

In the Law of Moses, being a slave is an accidental condition. This is further emphasized by constant reminders that the children of Israel had been slaves in Egypt themselves and should therefore know how it feels to be a slave. On the Sabbath the slave, too, should rest, and every Sabbath thus becomes a celebration of the brotherhood and equality of men.

The contrast in this respect between Hammurabi and Moses is most neatly illustrated by Hammurabi's last law (282): "If a male slave has said to his master, 'You are not my master,' his master shall prove him to be his slave and cut off his ear." In Exodus 21 we find a faint but, no doubt, deliberate echo of this law—an echo that seems designed to bring out the deep difference between the two legislations: "When you buy a Hebrew servant, he shall serve six years, and in the seventh he shall go out free, for nothing. . . . But if the servant plainly says, '. . . . I will not go out free' . . . his master shall bore his ear through with an awl; and he shall serve him for life."

Hammurabi considers a man's children, too, not as human beings in their own right but as his property. If a man strikes the daughter of another man, "if that woman has died, they shall put his daughter to death" (210). A man's daughter may thus be put to death merely to impose a severe fine on the father. The fine becomes less severe if the woman killed in the first instance was the daughter of a commoner (one-half mina of silver); and if she was a slave, the fine is still lower (one-third mina).

Similarly, if a man builds a house for another man, and he builds it badly and the house collapses—if it causes the death of the owner, the builder is to be put to death; but "if it has caused the death of a son of the owner of the house, they shall put the son of that builder to death" (229 ff.).

To such provisions there is no parallel in the Law of Moses, which insists, with striking originality, that there is only one God and that all men alike are made in his image and therefore altogether incommensurable with things or money.

The law of talion, to be sure, appears in the Law of Moses, too, but in an almost polemical manner. The Mosaic phrase, "an eye for an eye," might be said to conceal a revaluation of Hammurabi's values. Consider the three Old Testament passages in which the phrase occurs, and the first two will make plain the new spirit, while the third brings out an interesting continuity.

The first occurrence of "life for life, eye for eye, tooth for tooth" is in Exodus 21, where it is immediately followed by the provision already cited: "If he knocks out his servant's or his maid's tooth, he shall let them go free for the tooth's sake." This provision shows immediately what is amply borne out by the entire Law of Moses, that the principle of retaliation was never applied mechanically and in accordance with the letter of the phrase. Rather, the emphasis was on the spirit; to wit, that an injury is an injury and that the law is *no* respecter of persons. Or, to put it positively, the words of the ancient, pre-Mosaic law of talion are employed to announce the new principle of equality before the law.

This interpretation is corroborated by the second Biblical passage in which the phrase occurs, in Leviticus 24, where the ancient formula is followed by this declaration: "You shall have one law for the stranger and for the native; for I am the Lord your God."

The third passage, finally, in Deuteronomy 19, echoes and expands a similar law in the Code of Hammurabi: "If a malicious witness rises against any man to speak evil of him . . . the judges shall inquire diligently, and if the witness . . . has accused his brother falsely, then you shall do to him as he had meant to do to his brother; so you shall purge the evil from your midst. And the rest shall hear, and fear, and shall never again commit any such evil in your midst. Your eye shall not pity: it shall be life for life, eye for eye, tooth for tooth, hand for hand, foot for foot." In Hammurabi's similar law, there is no reference to the intention of the witness: the man who accuses another of murder and then cannot prove his charge is put to death.

It is customary today to decry "an eye for an eye" as the epitome of legal barbarism. But to arrive at a judicious evaluation one should compare this last application of the ancient principle with, say, public morality in the United States of America during the decade after the Second World War: does it manifest higher moral standards when a United States senator who advised one of his colleagues to accuse as many people as possible to increase his chances of making at least some of his accusations stick was widely admired for his exemplary honesty and integrity?[1]

It is a popular myth that the principle of talion was, as it were, left behind by Jesus' counsel that one should love one's enemies. In fact, the passage in which Jesus repudiates the ancient maxim, "an eye for an eye, and a tooth for a tooth" is the one in which he proceeds: "But I say to you, resist not evil: . . . and if any one would sue you and take your coat, let him have your cloak as well." Where he rejects

---

[1] So serious a charge should not be left at the level of insinuation. In his "Letter from Washington" in *The New Yorker* of April 22, 1950, Richard Rovere wrote, in part: "These things have been accompanied by a sophisticated callousness and mischief-making that is probably most strikingly symbolized by Senator Robert A. Taft's advice to Senator McCarthy, given several weeks ago, to go on making his accusations, in the hope that 'if one case doesn't work out, another one may.' The temper of the period can be gauged not only by the fact that this remark has received almost no censure in the press and none at all in Congress but also by the fact that Senator Taft, who has always enjoyed a formidable and by no means undeserved reputation for fairness and probity, found it possible to make it in the first place."

A fuller treatment may be found in William S. White's *The Taft Story*, in the chapter on "The Sad, Worst Period." White's political orientation is very different from Rovere's, and his biography is informed by an enormous sympathy for Taft. His evaluation of Taft's attitude toward McCarthy, however, is well summed up by the chapter heading. (See especially 84–86, 193, and 219 f.)

Since Taft is the only senator in American history to have been honored with a huge public monument in Washington, D.C., comparable to those erected in honor of Washington, Jefferson, and Lincoln, this little footnote memorial seems appropriate—not as a posthumous indictment but as an invitation to reflect on different standards of public morality. For the monument does not honor his very dubious judgment—his isolationism during the early part of the Second World War or his assurance right after the war that, if only the OPA were abolished, prices would come down—but his supposedly exemplary integrity.

talion, he rejects the courts altogether; but where he speaks of the divine judgment, he returns to talion again and again; for example, to cite the Sermon on the Mount once more: "For with the judgment you judge, you will be judged; and the measure you give will be the measure you get" (Matthew 5 and 7). Elsewhere the New Testament goes far beyond both Moses and Hammurabi by holding out *eternal* punishment for calling a man a fool or for not accepting the teachings of Jesus' apostles.

Until quite recently, the idea of retaliation was all but inseparable from the Western sense of justice. Jesus' counsel to love one's enemies is on an entirely different plane: it is a maxim for personal relations, on a level with the Mosaic injunction, "If you meet your enemy's ox or his ass going astray, you shall bring it back to him" (Exodus 23:4; cf. also verse 5 and many similar passages). In personal relations Hammurabi did not advocate retaliation either; and in their law courts Christian countries have not distinguished themselves from non-Christian countries by renouncing the principle, "life for life," or the underlying conception of retaliation.

It is only in recent times that modern penologists have moved away from the whole conception of retaliation to advocate a penal system based on the primacy of reform. And it is instructive that so many Christian writers have opposed this recent development, which is associated mainly with stubbornly un-Christian thinkers like Jeremy Bentham and George Bernard Shaw, who emphasized the inefficiency of retaliation; with Friedrich Nietzsche, whose Zarathustra says, in his discourse "On the Tarantulas," "*that man be delivered from revenge,* that is for me the bridge to the highest hopes"; and with Albert Camus, who tried to show in his "Reflections on the Guillotine" that "capital punishment . . . has always been a religious punishment" and is irreconcilable with humanism. A generation earlier, Shaw had pointed out in his Preface to *Major Barbara* that "the only editor in England who renounces punishment as radically wrong, also repudiates Christianity."

Pope Pius XII put the matter very clearly in 1953, in a manner that also shows its relevance to the discussion of ret-

ribution in Section 43. He took issue with those "modern
theories" which "fail to consider expiation of the crime committed . . . as the most important function of the punishment." Against them he cited Matthew 16:27 and Romans
2:6 and 13:4, concluding: "The function of protection disap-
pears completely in the after-life. The Omnipotent and All-
Knowing Creator can always prevent the repetition of a
crime by the interior moral conversion of the delinquent. But
the supreme Judge, in His last Judgment, applies uniquely
the principal of retribution. This, then, must be of great importance" (117 f.).

To return to Hammurabi, the most striking parallel to the
Law of Moses is not to be found in his legislation but in the
prologue and epilogue where Hammurabi declares that he is
giving his laws "in order that the strong might not oppress the
weak, and that justice might be dealt the orphan and the
widow."

50

The conceptions of God and of man in the Old Testament
differ sharply from those current in Egypt and Mesopotamia:
they are distinctive, novel, and original, and they have exerted
a decisive influence on Western thought.

What distinguishes the God of the Old Testament from the
gods of Egypt and Mesopotamia, the *Rigveda*, the *Iliad*, and
the *Edda* is not by any means adequately suggested by the
one word "monotheism." The difference is not merely quantitative: the gods of Homer are far more similar to human beings than they are to the God of the Old Testament. Unlike the
gods of polytheism, and unlike the god Aton of Pharaoh Ikhnaton, the God of ancient Israel is altogether separate from
the world which he made, and he did not make it in human
fashion, either after a fight with rival gods, demons, or drag-
ons, or after a struggle with recalcitrant material, but in a
manner as unique as he is himself—by saying, "Let there be."
He is not an object among objects but the sovereign subject
who engages in the pure unimpeded activity of speech.

He cannot be seen—he cannot be made the passive object of vision—but he speaks to man, actively. It is not possible to make an image of him: one cannot make an image of one who is essentially not an object. Nor does anything in nature represent or resemble him, unless it were man who is made in his image and who breathes his spirit.

This relation of God to man is of the essence of the religion of the Old Testament. This religion is not metaphysical, not speculative, not mythical: it does not concern itself with the nature of God as he may be, as it were, in himself; it does not speculate about his activities before the creation of the world or, quite generally, insofar as they do not affect man; it does not relate myths about his private life. The religion of the Old Testament is concerned with God only as a Thou, only as related to man, only as addressing man and as addressable by man. His deeds are a subject of concern and related only insofar as they constitute an address to man. Of other deeds, nothing is said: God is not an object of interest, study, or entertainment.

The conception of this God and his relation to man leads to a revolutionary new conception of man. Neither man in general nor any kind or race of men is a brother or cousin of the apes that so closely resemble him, or of any other animal or object in nature: having been created in the image of a God who transcends nature, and breathing his spirit, man is raised out of nature and endowed with a supra-natural dignity.

This dignity is not restricted to one man, one family, or one people, but a quality of man as such: for all men are descended from a single couple—from Adam and Eve and, again, after the flood, from Noah and his wife. Thus all men are brothers.

Two of the three great ideas of the French Revolution are readily traced back to the Old Testament: equality and fraternity. What of the third idea: liberty? At least implicitly, this idea, too, is central in the Old Testament. Having been created in the image of God, no man is merely an object or should be treated merely as an object; every man has a supra-natural dignity; all men are brothers. It would seem to follow that no man should treat another man as a slave and deprive him of his liberty.

Logic is the weak side of history, and it sometimes takes centuries before apparently obvious implications are realized. American history furnishes a ready example with its noble declaration, in 1776: "We hold these truths to be self-evident, that all men are created equal, that they are endowed by their creator with certain unalienable rights, that among these are life, liberty, and the pursuit of happiness." When these words were proclaimed to the world—and their Biblical inspiration meets the eye—their author was a slaveholder, and the country on whose behalf he was speaking was one of the few civilized countries left in which slavery was still legal. It is a long and arduous road indeed that leads from pride in such a principle to its full realization, effectively guaranteed by law.

That the implications of the Biblical conception of man regarding slavery were grasped at least to some extent even in Old Testament times is plain from the passages cited by way of contrast with the Code of Hammurabi. Since there is no Hebrew word for "slave" other than *ewed*, which means "servant," it is not an easy thing to say whether some form of slavery persisted through most of the time covered by the Old Testament or not. In theory at least, the institution of the Sabbath, on which the slave, or servant, was to rest, too, and the Sabbath year, in which any Hebrew slave was to go free (unless he wanted so badly to remain a slave that he subjected himself to the previously mentioned ceremony of having one ear pierced), and the institution of the Jubilee, every fiftieth year, in which non-Hebrew slaves, too, may have been meant to go free, would seem to have gone far toward abolishing slavery. That inhumanity nevertheless found frequent expression is obvious, but no other sacred scripture contains books that speak out against social injustice as eloquently, unequivocally, and sensitively as the books of Moses and some of the prophets.

In the religion of the Old Testament a keen social conscience is central. This is one of the distinctive features that set the Old Testament apart, quite radically, from the New

Testament and the Koran, from the Upanishads and the Bhagavadgita, from the Tao-Teh-Ching and the Dhammapada. And in the Old Testament this social conscience is by no means unrelated to the belief in God: rather, it is the most significant implication of this belief.

In the third Book of Moses, Chapter 19, we read: "You shall not hate your brother in your heart, but you shall reason with your neighbor, lest you bear sin because of him. You shall not take vengeance or bear any grudge against the sons of your people, but you shall love your neighbor as yourself: I am the Lord." And again: "When a stranger sojourns with you in your land, you shall not do him wrong. The stranger who sojourns with you shall be to you as the native among you, and you shall love him as yourself; for you were strangers in the land of Egypt: I am the Lord your God."

Malachi, the prophet, cries out: "Have we not all one father? Has not one God created us? Why then are we faithless to one another?" (2:10). And Job says: "If I have rejected the right of my manservant or my maidservant, when they contended with me; what then shall I do when God rises up? When he makes inquiry, what shall I answer him? Did not he who made me in the womb make him? And did not one fashion us in the womb?" (31:13–15).

51

One of the most important points about God and man in the Old Testament involves the person of Moses. The so-called "higher critics" of the Old Testament, who dominated the field for almost a century, beginning in the early second half of the nineteenth century, claimed that monotheism had developed very slowly and that it did not attain full purity until the time of the prophets.

This whole question is very involved, and one cannot do justice to it in passing. What needs to be shown is that the presuppositions of the "higher criticism" are untenable, that it contains a crucial self-contradiction, and that its methods are extremely unsound. Having tried to show this in detail in Chapter X of my *Critique*, I can refer interested readers to that book, and come to the point at issue in the present context.

There is ample evidence in the Old Testament—and its authors actually make a point of the fact—that the superstitions and even the idols of neighboring nations often gained a foothold in ancient Israel. No claim whatever is made that all the people from the time of Moses on were pure and dedicated monotheists or that their behavior came up to the highest moral standards. On the contrary, the Old Testament records Moses' epic struggle with his stiff-necked people; and Judges, Kings, and the books of the prophets relate the sequel, which is essentially similar. It took time before the whole people rose, even in theory, to the height of Moses' vision; and, of course, the people never became a nation of Moseses.

Two things, however, are extremely striking. First, in spite of occasional appearances of idolatry, beginning with the golden calf, the theory that objects in this world are gods and merit worship never seems to have gained ground. One gets the impression that some of the people sometimes fell into the habits of the nations among whom they lived and thoughtlessly adopted their practices. What the prophets attack is this unthinking, stupid inconsistency, never a rival creed, and least of all any belief that the traditional religion of Israel either contains or is indifferent to such ideas as, say, that the sun and moon are gods. This fact suggests most strongly that the monotheism of Israel was not derived from that of Ikhnaton, and that it was not arrived at gradually by way of a slow process of exclusion.

The second point is even more striking. In India, the Jina and the Buddha, founders of two new religions in the sixth century B.C., came to be worshiped later by their followers. In China, Confucius and Lao-tze came to be deified. To the non-Christian, Jesus seems to represent a parallel case. In Greece, the heroes of the past were held to have been sired by a god or to have been born of goddesses, and the dividing line between gods and men became fluid. In Egypt, the Pharaoh was considered divine.

In Israel, no man was ever worshiped or accorded even

semidivine status. This is one of the most extraordinary facts about the religion of the Old Testament and by far the most important reason for the Jews' refusal to accept Christianity and the New Testament.

It is extraordinary that the prophets never had to raise their voices against any cult of Moses or the patriarchs. One explanation, theoretically possible but incompatible with the evidence, would be that Moses never lived and was merely the fiction of a later age. But not one of the prophets makes the slightest claim to be an innovator: all remind the people of what they have long known and rebuke them for unthinkingly betraying standards and ideas long accepted. And there is no first prophet: before Amos came Elisha and Elijah and Micaiah and whole groups of prophets—Kings is full of them —and, before them, Nathan; and, before him, Samuel; and so forth. Yet there is not the slightest evidence that any one of them was the creator of the religion of ancient Israel or even a man who radically changed it. Everything points back at least to the time of Moses.

Why, then, was Moses never deified or worshiped—unlike Lao-tze, Confucius, and the Buddha and the Jina, and the Pharaohs of Egypt? The most obvious explanation is that he himself impressed his people with the firm idea that no human being is divine in any sense in which the rest of mankind isn't.

Being a stiff-necked and critical people, they may have been quite willing to believe that he was not a god, that no Jew is a god, and certainly no Gentile. But it seems clear that Moses himself was unequivocal on this point—as, indeed, the Buddha was, too—and that Moses, unlike the Buddha, succeeded in imprinting it forever in the minds of his followers.

It could not have been hard for a man in his position to suggest to at least some of his most ardent followers that he himself was in some sense divine and without flaw. On the contrary, the image he created of himself was that of a human being, wearing himself out in the service of God and Israel, trying against all odds to wed his people to his God, modest, patient, hard to anger, magnificent in his wrath, but completely unresentful, capable of the deepest suffering, the quintessence of devotion—human to the core.

He went away to die alone, lest any man should know his grave to worship there or attach any value to his mortal body. Having seen Egypt, he knew better than the Buddha how prone men are to such superstitions. Going off to die alone, he might have left his people with the image of a mystery, with the idea of some supernatural transfiguration, with the thought that he did not die but went up to heaven—with the notion that he was immortal and divine. He might have created the suspicion that, when his mission was accomplished, he returned to heaven. Instead he created an enduring image of humanity: he left his people with the thought that, being human and imperfect, he was not allowed to enter the promised land, but that he went up on the mountain to see it before he died.

The Jews have been so faithful to his spirit that they have not only never worshiped him but, alas, have never pitted him against the other great men of the world by way of asking who compared with Moses. To be sure, after relating the story of his death, they added: "There has not arisen a prophet since in Israel like Moses." But they have not confronted the world with this man to stake out a claim for him. One speaks of Jesus, the Buddha, and Socrates, perhaps also of Francis of Assisi, but one does not ask: Does not Moses belong with them? Was he perhaps, man for man, simply as a human being, more attractive, greater, more humane?

What the Jews have presented to the world has not been Moses or any individual, but their ideas about God and man. It is a measure of Moses' greatness that one cannot but imagine that he would have approved wholeheartedly. It would have broken his heart if he had thought that his followers would build temples to him, make images of him, or elevate him into heaven. That he has never been deified is one of the most significant facts about the ideas of God and man in the Old Testament.

The troublesome question remains how the elaborate ritual law of the last four Books of Moses is related to Moses. Traditional Judaism has assumed, as have Jesus, Paul, and traditional Christianity, that these laws were given by Moses. Goethe even suggested that the Ten Commandments did not derive from Moses, while a more ritualistic set of ten commandments, which he found in Exodus 34, did. Many of the "higher critics" agreed with Goethe: the admission that a sublime morality was taught by Moses in the thirteenth century B.C. would have been fatal to their evolutionary construction of the Old Testament. The morality they admired they ascribed to the great pre-exilic prophets, whom we shall consider shortly. The detailed ritual law they assigned to the post-exilic period; for, in brief, it does not seem at all plausible to assign it to the years in the desert, long before there was any real state, not to speak of a settled agricultural community, which seems to be presupposed by these laws. Moreover, neither the historical nor the prophetic books of the Old Testament seem to presuppose all of this legislation.

The reasons for dissociating Moses from the highly intricate ritual law are to my mind almost conclusive and establish an overwhelming probability. The reasons, on the other hand, for not ascribing to him the Ten Commandments or the moral principles traditionally associated with him strike me as utterly implausible; indeed, one is generally not confronted with any reasons at all, but merely with the presupposition that sublime moral ideas *must* be late. This assumption is surely false. Quite typically, we encounter a supreme moral challenge at the beginning of a new religion; and, more often than not, this is later subjected to compromise and dilution rather than improvement. Confucius and Lao-tze, the Buddha and Jesus furnish examples in this vein. If it should be objected that none of them stand at the beginning of a new civilization and that all four of them draw on past developments, the same consideration applies to Moses.

For all that, the problem remains whether Moses really tried to impress a high morality on his people. So far, it has merely been suggested that he well might have; that this cannot be ruled out *a priori;* and that, if he did, there would be many parallels in the history of religion. The question we must ask now can be expressed in Job's words: "If it is not he, who then is it?" Somebody must have originated this morality. The Bible critics answer: the prophets.

We are asked in effect to believe that, in the eighth century, Amos and Hosea, independent of each other and without the least awareness of their originality—in fact, emphatically disclaiming any originality—came up all at once with the same moral demands. These were echoed almost immediately by Isaiah and Micah who, rather oddly, also seemed to think that their people had long been told what they were reminding them of, and that it was truly shameful and inexcusable that Israel should have forgotten, or rather failed to live up to, these ancient standards.

The point here is not merely that the prophets must have known better whether their moral standards were original with them than any "higher critic" could. After the Exile, the practice of ascribing books to ancient authors to heighten the prestige of the works became common; and there are excellent reasons for considering Proverbs, Song of Songs, Ecclesiastes, and Daniel cases in point. It might therefore be asked whether the prophets might not have employed the same ruse, pretending that ideas original with them were ancient. There are at least two good answers to this.

The first of these may sound subjective and intuitive to anyone who has not read the great pre-exilic prophets, but it may well be conclusive for anyone who has: the indignation of these men is inseparable from their unquestioning conviction that Israel has betrayed, violated, broken the faith with norms known since the Exodus from Egypt. The second answer has already been given: the whole phenomenon of pre-exilic prophecy, of the almost simultaneous appearance, independently of each other, of men appealing to the same standards of morality, can hardly be explained if we are to suppose that these standards were original with them. It can be explained by considering Moses one of humanity's greatest teachers. That this does not deprive the prophets of their glory will be seen as soon as we come to consider them in detail. (Cf. also my *Critique*, § 90: "Religion and Progress.")

At this point it will suffice to cite a single passage from Jeremiah:

"I did not speak to your fathers, and I did not command them on the day that I led them out of the land of Egypt, about burnt offerings and sacrifices. But this is what I commanded them: Listen to my voice, and I shall be God for you, and you shall be a people for me; and walk in all the way that I command you, that it may be well with you. . . . From the day that your fathers came out of the land of Egypt to this day, I sent to you all my servants the prophets, day upon day; yet they did not listen to me, or incline their ear, but stiffened their neck" (7:22 ff.).

52

It is widely supposed that the conception of the chosen people is diametrically at odds with the humanistic strain in the Old Testament, and what has so far been pointed out is often altogether ignored or at the very least held to represent a relatively minor motif. It has become fashionable to ignore whatever in the New Testament may seem unedifying, especially the many passages on hell and eternal torment, while emphasizing out of all proportion whatever in the Old Testament is questionable from a moral point of view.

Plainly, the Old Testament, written over a period of a thousand years and containing history and poetry as well as proverbs and laws and stories, is not in its entirety a book of moral instruction. It contains, for example the Book of Joshua, which relates the conquest of Palestine and ascribes to God the command to slaughter "both men and women, young and old, oxen, sheep, and asses, with the edge of the sword." But to find the spirit of the religion of the Old Testament in Joshua is like finding the distinctive genius of America in the men who slaughtered the Indians. Many nations have their Joshuas, and the chance to make a unique contribution to humanity has often been bought with the sword: the genius of a people shows itself in what is done later to realize this costly opportunity. Survival in this wicked world may be a crime that has to be redeemed by subsequent achievements.

In the Old Testament itself, the idea of the chosen people

is not offered by way of justifying lower moral standards, as if it were claimed that, being chosen, one need not live up to standards intended only for the mass of men. On the contrary, the conception of the chosen people is inseparably linked with the twin ideas of a task and of an especially demanding law.

In two definitive passages, Amos, the first prophet to compose poetic speeches that were committed to writing, proclaims: "You only have I known of all the families of the earth; therefore I will punish you for all your iniquities" (3:2). And: "Are you not like the Ethiopians to me, O people of Israel? says the Lord. Did I not bring up Israel from the land of Egypt, and the Philistines from Crete, and the Syrians from Kir? Behold, the eyes of the Lord God are upon the sinful kingdom, and I will destroy it from the surface of the ground; except that I will not utterly destroy the house of Jacob, says the Lord" (9:7–8). Not utterly; for, as Isaiah puts it a little later when he names his son Shear-jashub: a remnant shall return—that is the meaning of the name. What matters is not the glory of the people: most of them, almost generation after generation, shall be destroyed. What matters is the task: maintaining and spreading what has been revealed to them, namely, the belief in God and the morality that goes with it. And that is why a remnant shall return, lest the flame be extinguished entirely.

This theme runs through the books of the ancient Hebrew prophets—and, beyond that, through most of the Old Testament. The original structure of the Hebrew Bible has been deliberately changed in the Christian version of it, which ends with the prophets. The Hebrew Bible has three parts. The first consists of the Five Books of Moses. The second part is the Prophets, divided, in turn, into two parts: the first part is historical and comprises the books of Joshua, Judges, Samuel, and Kings; the second and central part consists of the prophets proper—that is, of Isaiah, Jeremiah, Ezekiel, and the Twelve. Some of the Twelve are easily as impressive as Ezekiel, but their books are far shorter than those of the Big Three. The last part comprises the so-called Scriptures: Psalms, Proverbs, Job, Song of Songs, Ruth, Lamentations,

Ecclesiastes, Esther, Daniel, Ezra, Nehemiah, and Chronicles. The Hebrew Bible ends with the end of the Babylonian exile, when a remnant returned to Jerusalem; and the last words are the words of Cyrus, King of Persia: "The Lord, the God of heaven, has given me all the kingdoms of the earth, and he has charged me to build him a house at Jerusalem, which is in Judah. Whoever is among you of all his people, may the Lord his God be with him. Let him go up."

Christianity had no use for this conclusion when it put together its canon, over a hundred years after the destruction of the second temple in A.D. 70—a destruction it had come to view as a definitive punishment for the Jews' alleged rejection of Jesus. So they defied chronology and put the prophets at the end of the Old Testament. In this manner, the prophets ceased to appear as the central portion of the Hebrew Scriptures and became the transition from the Old to the New; and instead of the last sentence of the Hebrew Bible, which pronounced a blessing and a promise, one got this conclusion: "Lest I come and smite the land with a curse."

The supra-nationalistic, cosmopolitan, humanistic motif runs through the Hebrew Bible from the creation to the words of the King of Persia who, in the Hebrew view, is an instrument of God. The culmination of this motif may be found in the vision of the messianic kingdom, which will be considered shortly. But it is also noteworthy that two whole books of the Old Testament are given over all but completely to this motif: Ruth and Jonah.

The point of the Book of Ruth cannot be fully grasped if it is forgotten that she is a Moabitess, and that the feeling of ancient Israel about Moab is epitomized in the story in Genesis which relates that Moab was born to one of Lot's daughters after she had made her father drunk and spent the night with him. The point of the Book of Ruth is that Ruth, the Moabitess, became the great-grandmother of King David, the national hero. If there were any racist-minded jingoists in ancient Israel, this book must have shocked them rather more than the claim that George Washington or Robert E. Lee had a Negro great-grandmother would shock a D.A.R. in Georgia. Immediately, the question arises what special merits and resulting dispensation made it possible for Ruth to become a member of the chosen people. But the answer is that the conception of the chosen people is not racial but spiritual. No dispensation was needed, no ritual, no baptism. Ruth simply said to the mother of her deceased Hebrew husband: "Where you go, I will go, and where you lodge I will lodge; your people shall be my people, and your God my God; where you die, I will die, and there will I be buried. May the Lord do so to me and more also if even death parts me from you." These unprompted words were sufficient. No more is said. No further problem is even acknowledged.

In the Book of Jonah we are confronted not with a woman from Moab but with Nineveh, the capital of the Assyrians, who destroyed Samaria and the kingdom of Israel, who led the ten northern tribes into an exile from which they were never to return, and who came within a hair's breadth of capturing Jerusalem and destroying the southern kingdom, too. How the design of the Assyrian king was frustrated unexpectedly is the theme of one of Byron's *Hebrew Melodies*, "The Destruction of Sennacherib."

In the Bible, Jonah is sent to Nineveh to prophesy its imminent destruction as a punishment for its wickedness. He refuses, flees on a ship, is brought back in the belly of a great fish, and finally goes and utters his prophecy. Then the people of Nineveh repent, and God forgives them. They do not become Jews. They are not circumcised or baptized. They simply repent. That is enough. God decides not to destroy Nineveh. Jonah, displeased, protests that this is what he foresaw in the first place: "I knew that thou art a gracious God and merciful." That is why Jonah fled. Why now must he bear the humiliation of having been forced to make a prophecy and then to see it refuted by the event? "It is better for me to die than to live." But God replies, after a short humorous episode: "Should not I pity Nineveh, that great city, in which there are more than a hundred and twenty thousand persons who do not know their right hand from their left, and also much cattle?" Joshua is not unique: the lore of the nations abounds in men more or less like him. But in what other book of sacred scriptures do we find a book like Jonah?

It might be supposed that, if the foregoing analysis is right, the Jews would surely have endeavored to make proselytes, converting others to their own religion. And they did. An odd reference to this well-established fact is found in one of Jesus' most extreme denunciations of the Pharisees, in the Gospel according to Matthew: "You traverse sea and land to make a single proselyte" (23:15). Soon after Jesus' time, the Romans, provoked by the Jews' refusal to accept their pagan rule, first destroyed Jerusalem and then, when the Jews rebelled rather than accept the presence of an image of the emperor as god in the place of their former temple, the Romans, among other things, put an end to any further missionary activities by the Jews. Later the Christian church of Rome continued this ban, and again and again surpassed in ferocity anything the Romans had done by way of persecuting the remnant of Jewry. Still later, Luther urged the German princes to burn all synagogues and to drive all Jews out of the country. Gradually, the Jews became resigned, as Christians came to be under Hitler, to the ethos of standing fast, clinging to their religion without surrendering on any point of substance and, of course, without making proselytes.

This ethos was beautifully formulated by the Lutheran pastor Niemöller in a sermon delivered less than two weeks before the Nazis arrested him. He chose as his text the words of Jesus: "You are the salt of the earth." And he told his listeners, who, defying all threats by the government, crowded his church to hear him, that it was their task to keep themselves pure, lest the salt lose its savor: in their present situation this advice made no sense whatsoever; but that should not concern them; that was God's concern. Their task was to hold out, and someday God might find some use for his salt.

To reproach the Jews for not making more proselytes is like reproaching Niemöller for not making more proselytes in those days before his arrest. When it was feasible, the Jews made proselytes—in the Roman empire, among the Cazars in the Crimea, and elsewhere. But it is harder to persuade men to submit to circumcision than it is to baptize them; it is harder to convert to the law than to trust in grace; and those who demand works will always make fewer converts than those who stress faith and the remission of sins.

53

The influence of Old Testament ideas concerning the state has been second only to that of the ancient Hebrew conceptions of God and man. The three main points can be made briefly. They concern the origin of the state, the value of the state, and the vision of an ideal society.

Regarding the origin of the state, the first thing to note is that, according to the Old Testament, the state has an origin within history and is not the natural condition of man. The Hebrew Bible believes in the priority of the individual. This point is made twice: first, in Genesis where we find man in Paradise, without any state; then again in the Book of Judges in which we encounter this refrain, which also concludes the book: "In those days there was no king in Israel; every man did what was right in his own eyes."

The condition portrayed in the doubtless very early Book of Judges is one of attenuated anarchy. Only under foreign attack, or when foreign oppression becomes too severe, do the tribes rally now and then under a charismatic leader who, after his military triumphs, enjoys such prestige that the people come to him to arbitrate what differences may arise between them. Such men, and occasionally also women, like Deborah, are called judges and fill the otherwise vacant spot of a ruler until they die. Then the people relapse into their former state, approximating anarchy, until their enemies get the better of them and another leader rises and eventually becomes their judge.

Against this background, we find highly explicit doubts about the value of the state in the Old Testament. In the Book of Judges itself we encounter a fable whose prime intent is clearly antimonarchical, and this point was not lost on such close students of the Old Testament as Cromwell and Milton. But in the twelfth century B.C., to which this fable takes us back, there were no republics, and the issue revolves around the people's desire to form a state "like all the nations."

Abimelech, one of the sons of Jerubbaal, one of the judges, went out after his father's death and said to the people of Shechem: "Which is better for you, that all seventy of the sons of Jerubbaal rule over you, or that one rule over you?" And eventually "he slew his brothers the sons of Jerubbaal, seventy men, upon one stone; but Jotham, the youngest son of Jerubbaal, was left; for he hid himself."

Jerubbaal had not confined himself to a single wife, any more than Jacob, or David, or Moses, who married a second, Ethiopian wife—and his brother and sister, Aaron and Miriam, were severely punished by God for reproaching him. But that aspect of the Old Testament has had scarcely any influence on the history of Europe and America—except, of course, for the early Mormons—while the following fable has had more influence.

Jotham came out of hiding and told the people of Shechem his memorable fable: "The trees once went forth to anoint a king over them; and they said to the olive tree, 'Reign over us.' But the olive tree said to them, 'Shall I leave my fatness, by which God and men are honored, and go to sway over the trees?' And the trees said to the fig tree, 'Come you, and reign over us.' But the fig tree said to them, 'Shall I leave my sweetness and my good fruit, and go to sway over the trees?' And the trees said to the vine, 'Come you, and reign over us.' But the vine said to them, 'Shall I leave my wine which cheers God and men, and go to sway over the trees?' Then all the trees said to the bramble, 'Come you, and reign over us.' And the bramble said to the trees, 'If in good faith you are anointing me king over you, then come and take refuge in my shade; but if not, let fire come out of the bramble and devour the cedars of Lebanon.'"

Jotham ran away and was heard from no more, but his fable, in Judges 9, has reverberated through history. (Abimelech was killed in a battle, three years later, when he tried to take a tower "and a certain woman threw an upper millstone upon Abimelech's head, and crushed his skull. Then he called hastily to the young man his armor-bearer, and said to him: Draw your sword and kill me, lest men say of me,

'A woman killed him.' And his young man thrust him through, and he died.")

The point of the fable is clearly that nobody but an unproductive parasite would wish to be king in the first place, and that any people is better off without a king than with such a tyrant. This view is almost as far removed as possible from any belief in the divine right of kings. But the First Book of Samuel goes even further.

Samuel was a judge for a long time, and when he became old he made his sons judges. But his sons accepted bribes and perverted justice. Then the elders of Israel assembled and said to Samuel: "Behold, you are old, and your sons do not walk in your ways; now appoint for us a king to govern us like all the nations." In its context, this request seems understandable enough, though it is hardly surprising that it displeased Samuel, and that "Samuel prayed to the Lord." It is the following lines that go beyond even Jotham's fable: "And the Lord said to Samuel, 'Listen to the voice of the people in all that they say to you; for they have not rejected you, but they have rejected me from being king over them.'"

Here—and not only in this passage—the earlier, pre-monarchic condition of Israel is idealized: it was not anarchy but the kingship of God. The institution of human kings, on the other hand, and the establishment of a state after the model of "all the nations," is considered as a betrayal of God.

God's answer to Samuel continues: "According to all the deeds which they have done from the day I brought them up out of Egypt even to this day, forsaking me and serving other gods, so they are also doing to you. Now then, listen to their voice; only, you shall solemnly warn them, and show them the ways of the king who shall reign over them." The Bible relates further that Samuel told the people what God had told him, and that he offered them this picture of human kingship:

"These will be the ways of the king who will reign over you: he will take your sons and appoint them to his chariots, and to be his horsemen, and to run before his chariots; and he will appoint for himself commanders of thousands and commanders of fifties, and some to plow his ground and to reap his harvest, and to make his implements of war and the equipment of his chariots. He will take your daughters to be perfumers and cooks and bakers. He will take the best of your fields and vineyards and olive orchards and give them to his servants. He will take the tenth of your grain and of your vineyards and give it to his officers and to his servants. He will take your menservants and maidservants, and the best of your young men, and your asses, and put them to his work. He will take the tenth of your flocks, and you your-selves will be his servants."

The fable of Jotham and Chapter 8 of First Samuel are extreme, and the rest of the Old Testament does not deny all value whatsoever to the state or to kingship. But the Old Testament consistently denies any claim of the supremacy of the state in human affairs or of the superiority of kings as such. Above the state and king and any government there is a higher moral law by which states, kings, governments, and any laws that they enact are to be judged. The influence of this idea can hardly be overestimated.

54

The quintessence of this higher law was condensed into a classical sentence by the prophet Micah, in the eighth century B.C.: "He has told you, man, what is good and what the Lord requires of you: only to do justice, to love mercy, and to walk humbly with your God." (6:8). Amos and Hosea had made much the same points, insisting passionately on their social implications.

Unlike most representatives of religion in other civilizations, the prophets were not concerned about religious ritual. Their demands and their social criticism were moral. Indeed, the concern about ritual was one of the things they persistently denounced in the name of the overriding importance of social justice. Micah introduces his bold summary of what God demands with four rhetorical questions: "With what shall I come before the Lord, and bow myself before God on high? Shall I come before him with burnt offerings, with calves a year old? Will the Lord be pleased with thousands of rams, with ten thousands of rivers of oil? Shall I give my first-born for my transgression, the fruit of my body for the sin of my soul?" And then, as a bold antithesis, he proclaims the words cited above. What is wanted is not any ritual at all, but justice, mercy, and humility.

Amos, a little earlier, had been, if possible, still more explicit: "I hate, I despise your feasts, and I take no delight in your solemn assemblies. Even though you offer me your burnt offerings and cereal offerings, I will not accept them, and the peace offerings of your fatted beasts I will not look upon. Take away from me the noise of your songs; to the melody of your harps I will not listen. But let justice roll down like waters, and righteousness like an everflowing stream" (5:21 ff.).

In the name of him "who made the Pleiades and Orion, and turns deep darkness into the morning, and darkens the day into night, who calls for the waters of the sea and pours them out upon the surface of the earth, the Lord is his name," Amos denounces those who "trample upon the poor and take from him exactions of wheat" and those "who afflict the righteous, who take a bribe, and turn aside the needy" (5:8 ff.).

Isaiah, Micah's great contemporary, cries out:

"What to me is the multitude of your sacrifices?
says the Lord;
I have had enough of burnt offerings of rams
and the fat of fed beasts;
I do not delight in the blood of bulls,
or of lambs, or of he-goats.
When you come to appear before me,
who requires of you this trampling of my courts?
Bring no more vain offerings;
incense is an abomination to me. . . .
Wash yourselves; make yourselves clean;
remove the evil of your doings from before my eyes;
cease to do evil,
learn to do good;

seek justice,
abolish oppression;
defend the orphan,
plead for the widow" (Chapter 1).

The kings, too, are judged by the same standards, and no man, however admired, is exempt from judgment by the standards of this higher law. Indeed, the Old Testament goes out of its way to emphasize that the greatest national heroes had their faults. Jacob, who was renamed Israel and, according to tradition, gave his name to his children and children's children, is no exception; nor is Moses; nor David; nor Solomon. The Hebrew Bible excells in its unforgettable portrayals of human greatness, but it never fails to stop this side of idolatry.

A hundred years before Amos, Elijah applied the same standards to King Ahab, and about 1000 B.C. the prophet Nathan applied them to David, after the king had asked Joab, his general, to place Uriah, the Hittite, in an exposed place where he might get killed, so the king would be free to marry Uriah's beautiful wife, Bathsheba.

The law that asserted against the norms current in the ancient world, "You shall have one law for the stranger and for the native; for I am the Lord your God" (Leviticus 24:22), would not brook any exception on behalf of kings or nobles. And it tells us a great deal about ancient Israel that the Law of Moses should include the injunction: "You shall not be partial to the poor or defer to the great" (Leviticus 19:15; cf. Exodus 23:3). The first part of that law would not have occurred to many legislators.

55

We are ready for the Old Testament conception of an ideal society. Much of what should be said about this has by now been said: both in the Five Books of Moses and in the Prophets we constantly encounter the vision of a society in which the poor, the orphan, the widow, and the stranger are treated with special consideration; a society in which justice rolls down like water, and righteousness like an ever-flowing stream; a society based on justice, mercy, and humility. It is perhaps more often recognized that this ideal permeates the prophetic books than it is admitted, as it ought to be, that the Five Books of Moses are inspired by the same vision and seek to implement it with a wealth of detailed legislation.

What the prophets add is the great vision of the messianic kingdom which is found in both Isaiah 2 and Micah 4:

> "It shall come to pass in the latter days
> that the mountain of the house of the Lord
> shall be established as the highest of the mountains,
> and shall be raised up above the hills;
> and all the nations shall flow to it,
> and many peoples shall come, and say:
> Come, let us go up to the mountain of the Lord,
> to the house of the God of Jacob;
> that he may teach us his ways
> and we may walk in his paths.
> For out of Zion shall go forth the Torah,
> and the word of the Lord from Jerusalem.
> He shall judge between the nations
> and shall decide for many peoples;
> and they shall beat their swords into plowshares,
> and their spears into pruning hooks;
> nation shall not lift up sword against nation,
> neither shall they learn war any more."

In Micah, two further verses follow:

> "But they shall sit every man
> under his vine and under his fig tree,
> and none shall make them afraid;
> for the mouth of the Lord of hosts has spoken.
> For all the peoples walk
> each in the name of its god,
> but we will walk in the name of the Lord our God
> for ever and ever."

What distinguishes this conception from myths of a golden age among the Greeks and among other people is that the prophets stress the abolition of war and the establishment of a peaceful international community—and that they envisage this in the future and not, as other nations who spoke of golden ages, in the distant past. On paper these differences may seem small, the more so because the vision of the prophets has become a commonplace in the twentieth century. It is hard to do justice to the originality of men who, in the eighth century B.C., untutored by the horrors of two world wars with poison gas and atom bombs, and without the frightening prospect of still more fearful weapons of destruction, insisted that war is evil and must some day be abolished, and that all peoples must learn to dwell together in peace.

In retrospect we may say that they merely spelled out explicitly what was implicit in the Old Testament conception of God and man. There is nothing wrong with putting it that way, provided we remember how long it has taken the mass of men to perceive the very same implication.

56

One implication of almost everything that has been quoted here from the Old Testament, and quite especially of the commandments, "You shall be holy" (Leviticus 19:2) and "You shall be to me a kingdom of priests" (Exodus 19:6), is that man is called upon to raise his stature; that no man is a mere machine or instrument. We are called upon to be more than animals; we are summoned to freedom—whether it makes us happy or not.

Aldous Huxley created a deliberately nightmarish utopia in *Brave New World* (1932). His point was that we are on the best way toward creating a society of happy imbeciles, and that we might yet achieve a society in which everybody would be happy at a slightly subhuman level. Would anything be wrong with that? Many of us hope and think that, human nature being what it is, freedom and the fullest possible development of man's creative powers, in a society based on justice, mercy, and humility, would promote the greatest possible happiness. This faith is obviously influenced by the Old Testament. But suppose that it were possible to ensure the greatest possible happiness of the greatest possible number either by having recourse to a few injustices or by reducing man's creative powers, whether by drugs that reduced men to blissful imbecility or by operations that reduced their intelligence. What then?

Those of us who feel that happiness, however important, is not the ultimate consideration and that it would be an impermissible betrayal to sell our birthright for a mess of bliss are probably haunted by the challenge of the Hebrew Bible. Here a voice was raised that has aroused a large portion of mankind, albeit a distinct minority, from their pre-Israelitic slumber.

VIII

Jesus vis-à-vis Paul, Luther, and Schweitzer

57

The problem of happiness is scarcely considered in the Old Testament. Man is destined to be free. Whether liberty will make him happy is somehow beside the point. What matters is God's will, God's challenge.

In the New Testament, each man's overruling concern with his eternal happiness—his salvation—is central and defines the whole milieu. A similar concern had earlier found expression in Buddhism, also in the Orphic religion that probably influenced Plato's later thought. The change in the climate of opinion in the Near East between the age of the prophets and the time of Jesus has been noted above (§§ 39–40). Nation upon nation had lost its independence and its cultural initiative. Otherworldliness had spread, and millions had come to accept this world with resignation, hoping for the next. The era that, reeling from climax to climax, had witnessed Genesis and Deuteronomy, Hebrew prophecy and Attic tragedy, Greek temples and Thucydides, was long since drowned in Alexander's conquests and unprecedented syncretism. All kinds of mystery religions merged their dreams of supernatural salvation. Large masses of people felt that in this world nothing was left to live for.

Jesus did not have to persuade his listeners that they ought to be concerned about salvation, any more than the Buddha did. They came to hear him because he was offering a way. Conversely, when most men do not worry about salvation, Jesus' message is not easily made relevant to them.

According to the Gospels, Jesus' conception of salvation

was radically otherworldly, and opposed to any this-worldly messianic hopes—not only to chauvinistic dream of glory but also to swords beaten into plowshares and liberty and justice for all. The "kingdom is not of this world" (John 18:36). The perspective of the prophets is reversed. They, too, had taught humility and love, but not this preoccupation with oneself. The accent had been on the neighbor and the stranger, the orphan, the widow, and the poor. Social injustice cried out to be rectified and was no less real because it meant a lack of love and a corruption of the heart. Man was told to love others and to treat them justly—for their sake, not for his own, to escape damnation. To the Jesus of the Gospels, social injustice as such is of no concern. Heaven and hell-fire have been moved into the center.

But does not Jesus give a central place to the commandment "Love your neighbor as yourself"? It has often been said that this is the essential difference between the New Testament and the Old. Yet this commandment is taken from the Law of Moses, and the New Testament itself designates this as the ground that Jesus and the Pharisees had in common. Consider what may well be the most famous parable in the Gospels—the Good Samaritan (Luke 10). "Behold a lawyer stood up to put him to the test, saying: Teacher, what shall I do to inherit eternal life? He said to him: What is written in the Law? How do you read? And he answered: You shall love the Lord your God with all your heart, and with all your soul, and with all your strength, and with all your mind; and your neighbor as yourself. And he said to him: You have answered right; do this, and you will live." Nor is there any disagreement about the point of the parable. Having related the different conduct of priest, Levite, and Samaritan, Jesus asks his interrogator: "Which of these three, do you think, proved neighbor to the man who fell among the robbers? He said: The one who showed mercy on him."

One may doubt the authenticity of this parable. If Jesus had really told it, why should three of the evangelists have omitted it entirely? But if Jesus never told it, it would be easy to understand why, in time, it should have been attributed to him. This consideration is certainly not conclusive;

and what matters here is that, in telling the story, the third Gospel underlines the fact that, in questions of this sort, Jesus did not differ with the Pharisees; certainly they did not uphold the conduct of the priest and the Levite in the parable.

"Teacher, what shall I do to inherit eternal life?" The concern with the life to come was by then characteristic of much Jewish thinking. But the Jesus of the Gospels went much further in his otherworldliness than the Pharisees did, not to speak of the Sadducees. Salvation became with him the central motive for loving one's neighbor.

Consider the rich man who, according to Luke (18:18 ff.), asked Jesus the identical question. To him, Jesus cites five of the Ten Commandments before adding: "One thing you still lack. Sell all you have and distribute it to the poor, and you will have treasure in heaven; and come, follow me." It is no longer the poor that require love and justice; it is the giver who is to accumulate treasure in heaven. The social order, with which Moses and the prophets were centrally concerned, counts for nothing; the life to come is everything. If what truly matters is treasure in heaven, what do the poor gain from what they are given?

If, to gain salvation, we must give up all property and follow Jesus, then either salvation requires the complete disintegration of the social order, or salvation is denied to the vast majority of men and restricted to a few. The Jesus of the Gospels was clearly prepared to accept both consequences: he was willing to countenance the disappearance of any social framework and resigned to see only a few saved.

To begin with the last point, Jesus, according to all three Synoptic Gospels, actually reassured his disciples: "If any one will not receive you or listen to your words, shake off the dust from your feet as you leave that house or town. Truly, I say to you, it shall be more tolerable on the day of judgment for the land of Sodom and Gomorrah than for that town" (Matthew 10:14 f.; cf. 11:24; Mark 6:11; Luke 10:10 ff.). Far from being an isolated dictum, the prospect of damnation is one of the central motifs of the Gospels.

Returning once more to the story of the rich man: at the end, those who heard Jesus' words ask him, understandably:

"Then who can be saved? But he said: What is impossible with men is possible with God." Here it is suggested that salvation is a gift of divine grace. Inequality is instituted by God: some are chosen, others rejected.

Indifference to the social order is expressed in Jesus' next words: "Truly, I say to you, there is no man who has left house or wife or brothers or parents or children, for the sake of the kingdom of God, who will not receive manifold more in this time, and in the world to come eternal life." If one wants a briefer formulation for this rigorous indifference to the social and political realm, there is the famous "Render to Caesar what is Caesar's" (Matthew 22:21; Mark 12:17; Luke 20:25).

This phrase should be understood in its historic context. The question is one of subordination or resistance to a foreign oppressor—a perennial issue. And the answer is: oppression is unimportant; "render to God what is God's"; the social sphere is not God's and merits no concern.

Jesus' association with the publicans illustrates this point, too. The publicans, who collected taxes for the Roman conquerors, were the quislings of their day. To Jesus, this was utterly irrelevant. The one thing needful was salvation.

Only an age in which salvation had all but lost meaning could misconstrue Jesus' moral teachings the way liberal Protestantism did. The morality of the Sermon on the Mount, too, is centered not in the neighbor but in salvation. Each of the nine Beatitudes in the beginning announces a reward, and they conclude with the promise: "Rejoice and be glad, for your reward is great in heaven." In the Sermon itself, promises and threats alternate continually: "shall be called great in the kingdom of heaven"; "will never enter the kingdom of heaven"; "judgment"; "hell fire"; "your whole body should be cast into hell"; "if you love those who love you, what reward have you?"; "will reward you"; "have their reward"; "will reward you"; "your heavenly Father also will forgive you"; "neither will your Father forgive your trespasses"; "they have their reward"; "will reward you"; and more in the same vein.

The point is clearly stated both in the middle and at the end. "Do not lay up for yourselves treasures on earth, where moth and rust consume, and where thieves break in and steal, but lay up for yourselves treasures in heaven, where neither moth nor rust consumes and where thieves do not break in and steal." At the conclusion, those who do as told are called "wise," and those who do not are called "foolish." Actually, *phronimos* might be translated as "prudent" and *moros* as "moronic."

Moses and the prophets had also often referred to the future, though categorical demands were more characteristic of their style and pathos. But the future they envisaged was a social future; for Micah and Isaiah it even involved the whole of humanity. The Jesus of the Gospels appeals to each man's self-interest.

This may strike some modern readers as paradoxical because liberal Protestantism has persuaded millions that the essence of Christianity is altruism and self-sacrifice. But our analysis may help to explain why so many people take it for granted that morality depends on the belief in God and immortality. It is not uncommon to hear people admit that if they lost their belief in a life after death, no reason would remain for them to be moral. In fact, they cannot see why anyone lacking this belief should be moral; and this accounts in large measure for the widespread horror of atheism.

In the Gospels, one is to lose oneself only to find *oneself*. Sacrifices are demanded, but only of what moth and rust consume. We are taught to give up what is of no account. In what truly matters, we are expected to see to our own interest. The "reward" is always *my* reward. Really sacrificing oneself for the sake of others, for the chance, uncertain as such matters are in this world, that our neighbor or society might benefit—or foregoing one's own salvation for the salvation of others, as Mahayana Buddhism says its saints do—the Gospels do not ask of man.

There are, therefore, no grounds for differing with the formulations of by far the best, most comprehensive, and most careful study of "The Social Teachings of the Christian Churches"—that of Ernst Troeltsch. He does not overstate the case when he calls Jesus' moral teachings, as recorded in the Gospels, "unlimited and unconditional individualism";

when he remarks that "of an ideal for humanity there is no thought"; or when he claims that "any program of social renovation is lacking" (39, 41, 48).

The relation of the Gospels to the prophets has often been presented in a false light by those lacking either Troeltsch's scrupulous scholarship or his forthright honesty. The claim that the great innovation of the Gospels lies in a reputed distillation of the older moral teachings is practically a cliché. It is nonetheless false, bars any real understanding of the history of social thought in the past 2000 years, and leads to countless further errors in historical interpretation. As we have seen, there is a crass discontinuity, best summarized in the word otherworldliness.

Much has been made of the Golden Rule; and when it was found that Hillel, the Pharisee, an older contemporary of Jesus, had condensed the morality of Moses and the prophets into the so-called negative formulation of the Golden Rule, which is also encountered, 500 years earlier, in Confucius, Protestant theologians were quick to call this the Silver Rule and to claim that Jesus' formula was far superior.[1] In reply to that, three things need to be said.

First, the negative version can be put into practice while the positive version cannot; and anyone who tried to live up to Jesus' rule would become an insufferable nuisance.

Second: no such formula should be overestimated in any case; try, for example, to derive a sexual ethic from Jesus' rule. This example also illustrates the first point.

Finally, there are the wonderful words with which Thomas Hobbes concluded Part III of his *Leviathan:* "It is not the

---

[1] "Once a pagan went to Shammai and said: Accept me as a proselyte, on condition that you teach me the whole Law [Torah] while I stand on one leg. Shammai pushed him away with a measure that he had in his hand. He went to Hillel who accepted him as a proselyte. Hillel said to him: What you don't like, don't do to others; that is the whole Law; the rest is commentary; go and learn!" (Talmud Babli, Sabbath 31a). Hillel died about A.D. 10. Other similar formulations, some of them earlier, are listed in Strack's and Billerbeck's *Kommentar,* I, 460. That in the Letter of Aristeas, which is much earlier, combines the positive and negative forms, but I find Hillel's pithy four-part formulation superlative.

bare Words, but the Scope of the writer that giveth the true light, by which any writing is to bee interpreted; and they that insist upon single Texts, without considering the main Designe, can derive no thing from them cleerly; but rather by casting atomes of Scripture, as dust before mens eyes, make every thing more obscure than it is; an ordinary artifice of those that seek not the truth, but their own advantage."

When we consider the main design, it appears that the Gospels reject all concern with social justice and reduce morality to a prudent concern for one's own salvation; indeed, that morality itself becomes equivocal. No agreement can be had on where Jesus stood on moral questions—not only on pacifism, the courts, and other concrete issues: most of his formulations do not seem to have been meant literally. Parable and hyperbole define his style. Specific contents are disparaged.

Superficially, of course, a very different view suggests itself. The Pharisees had tried to build what they themselves called "a fence around the Law"—for example, by demanding that the observation of the Sabbath should begin a little *before* sunset, to guard against trespasses. It might seem that Jesus, in the Sermon on the Mount, was similarly erecting a fence around *morality*. For he introduces his most extreme demands: "Till heaven and earth pass away, not an iota, not a dot, will pass from the law until all is accomplished. Whoever then relaxes one of the least of these commandments and teaches men so, shall be called least in the kingdom of heaven. . . . Unless your righteousness exceeds that of the scribes and Pharisees, you will never enter the kingdom of heaven." Then Jesus goes on to say that it is not enough not to kill: "Whoever says, 'You fool!' shall be liable to hell fire." It is not sufficient not to commit adultery, nor—the omission of any reference to the Tenth Commandment is surprising— not to covet one's neighbor's wife, but "every one who looks at a woman lustfully has already committed adultery with her in his heart. If your right eye causes you to sin, pluck it out and throw it away." (We shall return to this saying later in this chapter.)

On reflection, the old morality is not protected but undermined, not extended but dissolved; and no new morality is put in its place. Where murder is not considered importantly different from calling a man a fool, nor adultery from a lustful look, the very basis of morality is denied: the crucial distinction between impulse and action. If one is unfortunate enough to have the impulse, no reason is left for not acting on it.

Again, it might well be asked: "Then who can be saved? But he said: What is impossible with men is possible with God." At this point one can understand Luther's suggestion that the moral commandments in the Bible were "ordained solely that man might thus realize his incapacity for good and learn to despair of himself" (see § 31 above).

Jesus' few remarks about the Jewish ceremonial laws have to be placed in this context. He speaks not as a reform Jew or a liberal Protestant; he does not, like the prophets, unequivocally reject specific rituals to insist instead on social justice; rather, he depreciates rules and commandments as such, moral as well as ceremonial. What ultimately matters is the other world.

As was shown in Chapter VI, it is not only in time that the Gospels are closer to Ezekiel and Daniel than to the pre-exilic prophets. Jesus and the evangelists lived in an age in which apocalypses flourished, and the atmosphere was apocalyptic. In the oldest Gospel, Mark's, "he said to them: Truly, I say to you, there are some standing here who will not taste death before they see the kingdom of God come with power" (9:1; cf. 13:30; Matthew 10:23). The end is at hand, and Jesus himself is understood in the Gospels as an intrusion of the other world into this world. It was not morality or ceremonial law that became the central issue between Jesus and the Pharisees, but the person of Jesus.

Almost all scholars agree that the Sermon on the Mount is not a sermon Jesus delivered in that form, but Matthew's compilation of some of the most striking dicta. (Luke constructed all kinds of situations to frame some of the same dicta.) It is doubly revealing that Matthew should have said, right after the end of the Sermon: "The people were astonished at his teaching"—why?—"for he taught them as one who

had authority, and not as their scribes." Moral questions could
be argued; one was used to different opinions. Matters of
ceremonial law were debated too much, if anything, with a
vast variety of views. It was Jesus' conception of his own person that caused astonishment; and if he said half the things
about himself that the Gospels relate, it must have seemed
the most shocking blasphemy to the Pharisees. The three
Synoptics agree that the scribes condemned Jesus not for being too liberal but for blasphemy—for what he said about
himself. They relate that he not only called himself the
Messiah, or—to use the familiar Greek translation of that term
—the Christ—but that he went on to say, alluding to Daniel:
"You will see the Son of Man sitting at the right hand of
Power, and coming with the clouds of heaven."[2] Then, they
say, the high priest tore his mantle, said, "You have heard his
blasphemy," and they condemned him.

Whether this is how it actually happened, we have no way
of knowing for sure; but this is the Christian story, as related
in the Gospels. It was only in recent times, when salvation
had ceased to be meaningful for large numbers of liberal
Protestants, that men who did not believe any more in "the
Son of Man sitting at the right hand of Power, and coming
with the clouds of heaven" began to see Jesus as primarily a
moral teacher. The apocalyptic tradition suggested by these
words, derived from Daniel and Ezekiel, seemed dated.
Neither the Catholic church nor the Greek Orthodox church,
nor the overwhelming majority of Protestant denominations
have ever accepted this liberal view; but it is still popular with
a large public that knows what it likes—without *knowing*
what it likes.

Let us return once more to the parable of the Good Samaritan. Asked, "What shall I do to inherit eternal life?" Jesus
retorts, "What is written in the law?" and receives the reply:
"You shall love the Lord your God with all your heart, and
with all your soul, and with all your strength, and with all
your mind; and your neighbor as yourself." Although Luke

[2] For the history of this conception, see Baeck, "The Son of Man"
in *Judaism and Christianity,* translated with an introduction by
Walter Kaufmann.

has Jesus agree with this, this is not the teaching of the Gospels. On occasion we are given the impression, noted at the beginning of this chapter, that this constituted an area of agreement between Jesus and the Pharisees. But the fourth Gospel denounces this idea constantly:

"Unless one is born of water and the Spirit, he cannot enter the kingdom of God" (3:5). "He who does not believe is condemned already, because he has not believed in the name of the only Son of God" (3:18). "He who does not honor the Son does not honor the Father who sent him" (5:23). "He who believes has eternal life" (6:47). "I am the living bread which came down from heaven; if any one eats of this bread, he will live for ever" (6:51). "No one comes to the Father, but by me" (14:6).

This list could easily be lengthened. In the other Gospels these themes are not nearly so prominent; but, according to Matthew, Jesus said: "Every one who acknowledges me before men, I also will acknowledge before my Father who is in Heaven; but who ever denies me before men, I also will deny before my Father who is in heaven" (10:32 f.). Luke 12:8 f. agrees almost literally, and there is a parallel passage in Mark (8:38).

It is exceedingly doubtful that Jesus himself said all these things, especially those ascribed to him in the Gospel according to John. Enslin remarks, in *The Literature of the Christian Movement*, that the Jesus of the fourth Gospel is really not very attractive, and that if it were not for the other three Gospels and the fact that most readers create for themselves "a conflate," the Jesus of St. John would lose most of his charm. Surely, the same consideration applies to all four Gospels. Most Christians gerrymander the Gospels and carve an idealized self-portrait out of the texts: Pierre van Paassen's Jesus is a socialist, Fosdick's a liberal, while the ethic of Reinhold Niebuhr's Jesus agrees, not surprisingly, with Niebuhr's own.[3]

The problem these men confront is not of their making. The Jesus of the Gospels confronts the serious Christian less

[3] For Niebuhr, see my *Critique,* § 68.

as a challenge than as a stumbling block, to use Paul's word. It should be fruitful to consider how three of the most eminent and earnest Christians of all time have sought to solve this problem—three men of very different background and temperament, one in the first century, one in the sixteenth, and one in the twentieth: Paul, Luther, and Schweitzer.

58

Those who see Jesus as essentially a moral teacher often see Paul as the real Judas. Clearly, Paul's letters bear the stamp of his personality; and since they were written earlier than any of our Gospels, they may well have influenced the Gospels, especially that according to John.

Jesus had spoken Aramaic, to Jews; Paul wrote Greek, to Gentiles. Jesus had grown up in Nazareth and taught in Galilee and Jerusalem; Paul grew up in a town where Hellenism flourished, and he traveled widely in the Hellenistic world and became a Roman citizen. Jesus had spoken elusively and, according to the Gospels, did not mind puzzling his listeners; Paul preached a doctrine and tried to back it up with arguments—which, to be sure, have to be understood in their contemporary climate of opinion.

Paul had not known Jesus, had not listened to his stories, had not heard his commandments. Jesus appeared to him as the Lord had appeared to the ancient prophets. Paul knew that such an appearance meant a call to go and bear witness of the Lord's revelation; but the Lord now is "Jesus Christ our Lord." Is this a betrayal of Jesus of Nazareth?

To justify an affirmative reply, one must reject as apocryphal all the manifold indications in the Gospels that Jesus did not consider himself an ordinary human being. Yet we have already tried to show that this seems to have been the crucial issue between Jesus and the Sadducees and Pharisees; and presumably it was this, too, that led to the ironic inscription on the cross: King of the Jews. It is the unequivocal centrality of this idea in Paul that is new, also the doctrinal formulations.

With this further development, Christianity as a separate religion was born.

What else was Jesus' legacy? If individual salvation counts for everything and is conceived as otherworldly; if action is deprived of its significance and the distinction between deed and impulse is dissolved, what remains but faith in the person around whom the lines were drawn, faith that he was the Messiah, the Christ? Now one could wait for the kingdom to come with power, and meanwhile recall his life and his stories and sayings; or one could accept in all seriousness, with all its implications, as Paul did, the idea that the Messiah had come, and that this must be the clue to salvation.

At this point Paul transformed Jesus' preaching and assimilated the crucified and resurrected Savior to the mystery religions that were prevalent throughout the Roman world. The pagan sacraments found their way into the new religion. Around A.D. 200, when it was still obvious to many educated people where the sacraments had come from, Tertullian said boldly that Satan had counterfeited the Christian sacraments in advance. In our time, Toynbee, once again aware of scores of borrowings from Hellenistic folklore in our Gospels, concludes that God chose to reveal himself in folklore (*A Study of History*, Vol. VI, Annex).

Understandably, many Protestants feel that these Hellenistic elements were merely features of the age that are dispensable today, and that we must go back to original pre-Hellenic, pre-Pauline Christianity. Toynbee, in *An Historian's Approach to Religion*, asks in this vein: "In what sense did Christians, in those very early days before the statement of Christian beliefs began to be Hellenized, mean that Jesus was the Son of God, that He rose from the dead, that He ascended into heaven?" It is widely felt that this is the right question. In fact, however, these "very early days" are a figment of the imagination, and the question is unfair to Paul.

Even some of the later books of the Old Testament are by no means pre-Hellenistic; Jewish literature of the period between the Testaments (the *Apocrypha*, for example) shows strong Hellenistic influence; and the hopes, beliefs, and expectations of the Jews of Jesus' time owed a great deal to Hellenistic thought. Some recent studies have tried to show how deeply Jewish Paul was, notably, W. D. Davies' *Paul and Rabbinic Judaism: Some Rabbinic Elements in Pauline Theology*. And the literature about the Dead Sea scrolls has made it a commonplace that Hellenistic elements—which, it was previously supposed, Paul might have introduced into Christianity—were well established in at least some Jewish circles in the time of Jesus. Some people put this last point rather oddly, saying: These things, which we considered Hellenistic, were really Jewish. It would be more accurate to say that the Judaism of Jesus' time was no longer pre-Hellenistic.

Still, some circles had resisted syncretism more than others, and one need only read the Book of Acts in the New Testament to see that the Jerusalem group, dominated by Peter and James, was inclined to resist more than Paul was. But how could one possibly go back to the religion of this group? They lived in the expectation that they would soon see Jesus return "sitting at the right hand of Power, and coming with the clouds of heaven." They believed that Jesus had assured them that some of them would "not taste death before they [would] see the kingdom of God come with power." Meanwhile, they were willing to preach and make converts, but few Jews were converted, and practically no Gentiles. Was Jesus' legacy, then, a hope that proved vain?

A Jew might say so; a heretic might; but Paul, far from wishing to betray his Lord, refused to see it that way. Never having heard the preaching *of* Jesus, he felt free to develop a new teaching *about* Jesus; and he transformed a message of parables and hyperboles into a theological religion. What he said was clearly different from what Jesus had said; but Jesus' teaching had been so utterly elusive that neither Peter nor James, the brother of Jesus,[4] nor the other disciples who had listened to him day after day were able to point to anything clear or definite to combat Paul. That they *wanted* to fight Paul's new doctrines, the Book of Acts makes very clear; but

[4] See, e.g., Galatians 1:19, 2:11 ff.; *Harper's Bible Dictionary* (1959 ed.), 301, "James the brother of Jesus"; and *Encyclopaedia of Religion and Ethics*, VIII, 661, "The Position of James the Lord's Brother at Jerusalem."

the truly extraordinary fact is that these men, whose authority seemed clearly established because they had known Jesus and heard his teaching, had to capitulate to the strong convictions of Paul—himself a recent convert, discredited by his anti-Christian past—because they could not pit any notion of Jesus' legacy against his.

I can see no good reasons for supposing that this was their fault. Indeed, it is not at all uncommon for a teacher to exert a strange and strong fascination on his students—by the force of his personality, his way of speaking, gestures, metaphors, intensity—although they cannot say just what he taught them. It is hardly reasonable in such cases to insist: But he must have taught them something—indeed, something of crucial significance—that we, by painstaking reflection, should be able to recover. It is even less reasonable to assume this when the whole climate was thoroughly authoritarian, when the master was surrounded by an air of mystery and constant reports of miracles that could not possibly be questioned, and when there were occasional suggestions that everything would become clear soon—when the world would end. The four evangelists agree in ascribing to Jesus evasive and equivocal answers to plain questions; some of the parables are so ambiguous that different evangelists interpret them differently; and it was evidently unthinkable for a disciple to ask searching questions and persist.

Paul did not villainously overturn the purest teaching that the world had ever heard: he filled a vacuum. Had it not been for him, there would not have been far-flung churches that required Gospels, cherished, and preserved them; there would have been no large-scale conversion of Gentiles; there would have been no Christianity, only a short-lived Jewish sect.

What is ironical, though there are parallels, is that Jesus' dissatisfaction with all formulas and rules should have given way within one generation to an attempt, not yet concluded, to define the most precise dogmas. It is doubly ironical because, according to the Gospels, Jesus constantly inveighed against hypocrisy: indeed, the Gospels have made Pharisee and hypocrite synonymous. Yet the hypocrisy possible within a legalism that prominently emphasizes love and justice is as a mote compared to the beam of the hypocrisy made possible where dogma and sacraments have become central. If "he who eats me will live because of me" (John 6:57), why worry about loving one's enemies?

According to Micah, God demands "only to do justice, to love mercy, and to walk humbly with your God"; according to John, "This is the work of God, that you believe in him whom he has sent" (6:29). Since the Reformation, in spite of the Reformers who pitted their doctrine of justification by faith *alone* against the Catholic doctrine of justification by faith and works, the prophetic ethic has been so widely accepted, however far one falls short of it, that the contrast of these two quotations may strike some readers as almost black and white. But those who study the *Documents of the Christian Church,* selected and edited by Henry Bettenson for the Oxford University Press, will find that neither the church councils nor the Reformers would have been likely to question this juxtaposition. The body of Bettenson's book happily belies the misleading singular in the title; but one finds that the documents of the various Christian churches agree in rejecting the supremacy of Micah's imperatives, that there is scarcely a reference to love, justice, mercy, or humility, and that what mattered most throughout was right belief about Christ and the sacraments. To this day, it is dogma that keeps the churches apart—different beliefs, creeds, and sacraments —not morality, not the Sermon on the Mount. Only one motif from the Sermon on the Mount was echoed constantly: the threat of hell. As dogma upon dogma was carefully defined, in an effort to determine what precisely one had to believe in order to be saved, the refrain was always: if anyone believes otherwise, "let him be anathema"—let him be damned, let him go to hell!

The Rule of Saint Francis represents a notable exception. Without taking issue with the doctrines and dogmas of the Catholic church, and while fully subordinating his judgment to the church's, he tried to create an island of love in an unloving world. He lived to see corruption and hatred in his order, and soon after his death the Franciscans came to vie with the Dominicans in implementing the Inquisition.

For Paul, as for Jesus, social justice and political arrangements seemed irrelevant. He accepted the prevailing order, sometimes with contempt because it was merely secular, sometimes with respect because it was ordained by God.

Jesus' "render to Caesar what is Caesar's" is elaborated in Paul's fateful Letter to the Romans: "The powers that be are ordained by God. Whoever therefore resists these powers, resists the ordinance of God; and whoever resists shall incur damnation" (13:1 f.). That had not been the view of Elijah and the pre-exilic prophets. But now moral courage before royal thrones and despots gives way to resignation and submission—not from lack of courage (neither Paul nor Luther, who echoed Paul's injunctions, was timid), but because this world has ceased to matter.

The ancient notion of the equality and brotherhood of men is reinterpreted in a purely otherworldly sense; even coupled with a Platonizing, anti-egalitarian, organic metaphor: "As the body is one and has many members, and all the members of the body, though many, are one body, so it is with Christ. For by one Spirit we were all baptized into one body—Jews or Greeks, slaves or free—and all were made to drink of one Spirit. . . . Now you are the body of Christ and individually members of it. And God has appointed in the church first apostles, second prophets, third teachers, then workers of miracles. . . . Are all apostles? Are all prophets? Are all teachers? Do all work miracles?" (I Corinthians 12). The foundation is laid for an elaborate hierarchy and for radical inequalities even within the church, while in the social order outside it inequality and injustice are accepted as fated. "Every one should remain in the state in which he was called. Were you a slave when called? Never mind" (I Corinthians 7). If you can become a free man, fine; if not, it does not really matter.[5]

In the same spirit, Paul says in the same chapter: "But be-

[5] The New English Bible offers a footnote to verse 21: *"Or but even if a chance of liberty should come, choose rather to make good use of your servitude."* Contrast Exodus 21, discussed in § 49 above.

cause of fornication, each man should have his own wife, and each woman her own husband. . . . To the unmarried and the widows I say that it is well for them to remain single as I do. But if they cannot exercise self-control, they should marry. For it is better to marry than to burn." Later, in the same chapter, Paul explains: "I want you to be free from care. The unmarried man cares for the things of the Lord, how to please the Lord; but the married man cares about the things of this world, how to please his wife." It is the importance of the social order, it is this whole world that is rejected here. Paul, like Plato, believes that marriage would distract the elite from that other world on which they should concentrate. At least by implication, Paul, too, introduces the conception of an elite. Henceforth, there are, as it were, first- and second-class Christians. "He who marries his betrothed does well; and he who refrains from marriage will do better."

For Paul, the otherworldly equality in Christ has a vivid meaning that was soon to be lost. His advice seems to hinge on his conviction that the end is at hand: "I think that in view of the present distress it is well for a person to remain as he is. . . . I mean, brethren, the appointed time has grown very short; those who have wives shall be as though they had none, and those who mourn as though they were not mourning, and those who rejoice as though they were not rejoicing, and those who buy as though they had nothing, and those who deal with the world as though they had no dealings with it. For the form of this world is passing away."

Equality has its place only as this world passes away and all distinctions are lost. Equality is not the final triumph of love and justice, presented to man as a challenge and a task; it is what remains after the diversity of the phenomenal world drops away. But this event is for Paul not so distant that it is almost void of meaning; on the contrary, "the appointed time has grown very short."

In this context, the preceding chapter is readily understood, too: "To have lawsuits at all with one another is defeat for you. Why not rather suffer wrong? Why not rather be defrauded?" This is a significant variation on the theme, "I want you to be free from care." One should not become involved in this world and take it seriously. The end of this world is at hand, and the other world alone matters.

Even in the other world, however, inequality appears, as it does in the Gospels. Men are not equal even in the eyes of God. Not only are there first- and second-class Christians; not only are some called to be free and some to be slaves; there are the elect and the damned. Once convinced of a truth, Paul, like the rabbis, looks to Scripture, to the Old Testament, to find it there. "When Rebecca had conceived children by one man, our forefather Isaac, though they were not yet born and had done nothing either good or bad, in order that God's purpose of election might continue, not because of works but because of his call, she was told, 'The elder will serve the younger'" (Romans 9). The story is found in Genesis, as is the story of the Garden of Eden; but the doctrines Paul derives from them are alien to the mainstream of Old Testament religion and opposed to the very core of Hebrew prophecy.

The prophets do not *predict* disaster; they threaten disasters that are bound to happen if the people persist in their ways, but the hope is always that they will not persist in their ways and thus avoid the disaster. Jonah, annoyed that his prophecy will remain unfulfilled, tells God that this was why he fled in the first place to avoid making the prophecy: "Is not this what I said when I was yet in my country? That is why I made haste to flee to Tarsus; for I knew that thou art a gracious God and merciful, slow to anger, and abounding in steadfast love, and repentest of evil." But part of the point of the Book of Jonah is clearly that the prophet who has led men to repentance, who has made them change their ways to avoid imminent disaster, has done his job and should be glad when his prophecies are not fulfilled.

Paul from Tarsus is the great anti-Jonah. Like the Pharisees and millions of rabbis, ministers, and theologians ever since, he finds verses to corroborate his doctrines. Since the Old Testament is a collection of history and poetry, laws and wisdom, folklore and traditions, verses can always be found for every situation. But there is no want of central ideas, of great currents that flow through this great garden and water it—no want of backbone. And it is one of these central conceptions and the very backbone of Hebrew prophecy that Paul ignores: the idea of *t'shuvah,* return, repentance.

Paul's whole argument for the impossibility of finding salvation under "the Law" and for the necessity of Christ's redemptive death depends on this. If, as the rabbis were still teaching in Paul's day, God could at any time freely forgive repentant sinners, Paul's theology collapsed and, in his own words, "then Christ died in vain" (Galatians 2:21). If God could forgive the men of Nineveh simply because they repented of their wicked ways, though they had not been converted, circumcised, or baptized—and this is the teaching of the Book of Jonah, which is also implicit in many other books of the Old Testament—then Paul's doctrines, which have become the very core of Christianity, lose their point and plausibility and come to look bizarre.

Consider the Christian story the way it looks to an outsider. God causes a virgin, betrothed to Joseph, to conceive his own son, and this son had to be betrayed, crucified, and resurrected in order that those, and only those, might be saved who should both believe this story and be baptized and eat and drink on regular occasions what they themselves believe to be the flesh and blood of this son (or, in some denominations, merely the symbols of his flesh and blood); meanwhile, all, or most, of the rest of mankind suffer some kind of eternal torment, and according to many Christian creeds and teachers they were actually predestined for damnation by God from the very beginning.

Paul did not contribute all the elements of this story—not, for example, the virgin birth, of which most scholars find no trace in his letters. But he did contribute the central ideas of Christ's redemptive death and justification by faith. Protestants and Catholics may argue whether Paul taught justification by faith *alone* or justification by faith and works; it is plain and undisputed that he did not allow for justification by works alone. It is no longer enough "only to do justice, to love mercy, and to walk humbly with your God."

In a long note on Paul, in the third volume of his classical work on *Judaism,* George Foot Moore declared himself utterly unable to understand how a Jew of Paul's background could ignore such a central idea as that of repentance and forgiveness. But the history of religions abounds in parallels. The great religious leaders of humanity have generally been richer in passion than in justice or fairness; their standards of honesty have been far from exemplary; and with an occasionally magnificent one-sidedness, they have been so obsessed by some features of the positions they opposed that they thoroughly misunderstood and misrepresented the religion they denounced. If they deserve blame for this, how much more blameworthy are those who use them as historical authorities, turning to Luther for a portrait of Catholicism, or to the New Testament to be informed about Judaism!

When Paul turned his back on the old notion of forgiveness for the repentant sinner and embraced the doctrine of predestination, he gave up the idea of the equality and fraternity of all men. To cite Troeltsch once more: "The idea of predestination breaks the nerve of the idea of absolute and abstract equality"; and henceforth "inequalities are accepted into the basic sociological scheme of the value of personality" (64, 66).

I am rejecting two clichés: that of the Judaeo-Christian tradition as well as the claim that Western civilization is a synthesis of Greek and Christian elements. Against the former, I stress the discontinuity between Jesus and the pre-exilic prophets: one might as well speak of the Judaeo-Islamic tradition or of the Greco-Christian tradition. Against the latter, I point to the fact that Christianity itself was a child of Greek and Hebrew parents; that the Gospels are a product of Jewish Hellenism; and that Paul, though he claimed to have sat at the feet of Gamaliel, was in important respects closer to Plato and to Gnosticism than to Micah or Jonah.

Paul's decisions have occasionally been explained as highly expedient. When the Jews did not accept the Gospel, the new teaching could survive only by turning to the Gentiles, by abrogating circumcision and the dietary laws, which stood in the way of mass conversions, and by emphasizing faith and preaching obedience to the powers that be. But expediency in this case did not involve any compromise of principle or any sacrifice of Paul's convictions. His innovations make sense in the context of his profound otherworldliness: this was the meeting ground of the Gospel and the mysteries, of Jesus and Gnosticism. Jesus, who had stood in the apocalyptic tradition, was readily assimilated to Hellenistic ideas about salvation. Twelve centuries before St. Thomas wrought the so-called medieval synthesis, Paul fashioned an impressive synthesis of two great heritages. He even found a place for that curious equation of virtue, happiness, and knowledge which we find in Plato: but by knowledge Paul meant the knowledge of faith; by happiness, salvation; and his virtues were not the virtues of Plato.

Paul was not the first to attempt such a synthesis: Philo of Alexandria had fused Plato and the Hebrew Scriptures in an intricate philosophy at least a generation earlier. Nor was Paul's synthesis entirely deliberate: it grew out of the Hellenistic Judaism of that age. But its historic effect has been staggering. No doubt, it would have astonished and distressed Paul himself.

From his letters one gathers that he placed the primary emphasis on faith when he made converts, and that he was shocked when the new congregations took him by his word and did not live up to the moral standards that he had simply taken for granted. In his letters he frequently gives expression to his exasperation. It was therefore in a sense in keeping with Paul's spirit that the new church should have made the Old Testament part of its canon, along with the New. Paul, like the other early Christians who had been raised as Jews, lived in the Hebrew Scriptures, constantly citing them, understanding contemporary events in terms of them, and looking to them for guidance and truth. One cannot read the Gospels or Epistles without being aware of this. The Old Testament was the authors' canon, and much of what they said was meant to be understood against the background of the Hebrew Scriptures—or their Greek translation, the Septuagint. This was so plain that those who later canonized their works retained what they then called the Old Testament to distinguish it from the New Testament.

Eventually, the message of the prophets came to life again. For over a thousand years it slept quietly in the midst of

Christendom. Then, early in the sixteenth century, their voice was suddenly heard again, and a new era began. It is customary to date the Modern Age from 1453, when the Turks took Constantinople; or from 1492, when Columbus discovered America; or from the day in 1517 when young Martin Luther nailed his 95 Theses on the cathedral door in Wittenberg. But if a striking symbol is wanted, one could also reckon the end of the Middle Ages from the day when Michelangelo placed above the pope's most holy altar in Rome, the capital of Nero and the Inquisition, not the Mother of God, nor the Christ, nor the expulsion from Paradise, but Jonah.

59

Human history cannot boast of a more vivid, valiant, and vindictive character than Luther. He performed three apparently unrelated feats, each of which would have sufficed to make him one of the outstanding figures of all time: he smashed the unity of Western Christendom; he translated the Bible and put it into every household that his influence could reach; and he developed a new *Weltanschauung*.

With nothing to begin with but passion and the power of his language, this simple monk dealt the papacy a blow compared to which the drawn-out efforts of generations of German emperors with huge armies and vast resources seem as nothing: he surpassed the very imagination of the supple scheming of Henry IV and the refined hatred of Frederick II.

Then he put his genius at the disposal of the Bible and, translating it, created a new language: modern German. Though he found God's revelation above all in Paul, particularly in the Letters to the Romans and Galatians, his heart caught fire as he read the Hebrew Scriptures; and, far more than the King James Version almost a century later, he communicated much of their austere simplicity, laconic majesty, and the immediacy of the experience with which so much of the original is still alive. Though it was the New Testament —and really only a very small part of this—that became the center of his new religion, he not only left the Old Testament in the Protestant Bible, he helped it to a popularity it had never before had in the Western world.

Finally, the reformer and translator fashioned a new religious and political world view, based on the Bible and his break with Rome. It, too, bears the distinctive stamp of his unique personality. Luther thought he was offering a return to Paul. He felt that he was fighting corruption and re-establishing the ancient and pure doctrine. Yet his message was a reflection and projection of his own genius, not the Gospel according to Paul but a characteristically Lutheran piety.

A sincere Christian could scarcely differ more from the mild and milk-faced Jesus of Hofman's popular paintings than Luther did. Not even Calvin outdoes him in this respect. Fanatical from beginning to end, as monk, Reformer, and politician, Luther did whatever he did with all his heart, all his soul, and all his power: fiery, fierce, with the force of a bull rhinoceros— but thoroughly devoted to Christianity, which was the one constant in his life. Monk or married, preaching rebellion or obedience, it was Christianity that he had at heart. And moderation was not for him. Even apart from his doctrinal differences with the followers of Aquinas, Aristotelianism with its subtleties, its praise of wisdom and philosophy, was antithetical to Luther's vision of Christianity: radical through and through, and opposed alike to wisdom, reason, and subtlety.

He was thirty-three when he nailed his 95 Theses to the cathedral door in Wittenberg. Before this, he had tried to gain salvation through works. For salvation was still central for him as it had been for Jesus' and Paul's original audience. "Works" had not meant to Luther middle-class decency or a respectable regard for convention. Being a Christian meant something extraordinary, extreme, exalted. Works led to no conclusion; there is no end to works, no final salvation. Striving for salvation through works is like struggling against quicksand.

Luther believed in the devil and in hell, as Jesus and Paul had done. A life devoted to the quest for salvation through works became intolerable for him: one could never cease without perishing. And cease one must, if only sometimes. There are moments of weariness, discouragement, temptation, disgust. Not only moments. Hamlet's famous advice to his mother, how continence breeds more continence and virtue makes virtue ever easier, is surely one of those half-truths which owe their popularity to wishful thinking, as does much glib talk about sublimation. Luther knew through the torture of his own experience how continence bred the half-crazed desire for incontinence, and virtue like a cancer could corrode the soul with the obsession to do evil. There is a peace of mind born of transgression which is sweeter than that of good conscience: the peace that attends virtue is a guarded joy, dependent on past triumphs and continued perseverance; *relative* to these, not absolute—not extraordinary, extreme, exalted. But still finding oneself in and after evil, knowing all the joy of sin and feeling that sin is not the great power virtue thinks it, not the menace against which we must at all times be on our guard, but a foe to whom one can concede a battle and survive—this sense of peace which comes of saturation and the new experience of a deadness to desire is indeed a peace surpassing unreflective understanding. Hence, not only must salvation through works be abandoned but a place must be found for sin. It is hardly an exaggeration to say that for Luther the Gospel, the glad tidings, was that one could sin and yet be saved, and that sin need not even be rationed.

Paul and Luther notwithstanding, salvation through works never was the doctrine of the Jews or the Catholics. The Old Testament was, for the most part, not at all concerned with individual salvation in another world or life; and the Pharisees who did believe in immortality never failed to supplement their teaching of the Law with the prophetic doctrine of repentance and forgiveness. They did *not* believe that salvation required unexceptional fulfillment of all laws, moral and ceremonial, or that they, and only they, could point to perfect records and hence were entitled to salvation while the rest of mankind was less fortunate. Nor did the Catholic church, prior to Luther, teach that only the perfect ascetic could win redemption while the rest of mankind would be damned. Paul and Luther passionately, but erroneously, projected their own frantic efforts on two great religions within which they had failed to realize their self-imposed conception of salvation.

At no time had the church accepted Jesus' hyperbolic counsels. How could it? How could an institution which expects to outlast centuries take as its motto, "Take no thought for the morrow"? How could it reach men with the teaching, "Whoever then relaxes one of the least of these commandments and teaches men so, shall be called least in the kingdom of heaven"? How could it discipline men if it accepted the command, "Resist not evil"? How could it possibly accept the Sermon on the Mount and its eloquent conclusion: "Every one who hears these words of mine and does not do them will be like a foolish man who built his house upon the sand; and the rain fell, and the floods came, and the winds blew and beat against that house, and it fell; and great was the fall of it"? Organized Christianity could be defined as the ever renewed effort to get around these sayings without repudiating Jesus. This is what the Roman Catholic and the Greek Orthodox church, Luther and Calvin, Barth and Schweitzer have in common.

Luther and the church against which he rebelled agreed that there must be some dispensation from the stern demands of Jesus, and that sin must not be considered a bar to salvation.

Their difference? A joke may crystallize it. A hostess offers a guest some canapés. Says the guest: "Thank you. I have already had three." Says the hostess: "Had three? You've had five; but who counts?" What enraged Luther was that the church counted.

Lutheran children are often brought up on Luther's protests against the sale of indulgences and are appalled to learn how freely people sinned with the assurance that a small formality would soon restore them to their former state of grace—or even how a man planning a robbery might obtain indulgence in advance. They are less likely to be told how Luther, on the Wartburg, wrote his friend Melanchthon on August 1, 1521: "If you are a preacher of grace, do not preach a fictitious, but a true, grace; and if the grace is true, carry a true, and not a fictitious sin. God does not work salvation for fictitious sinners. Be a sinner and sin vigorously [*esto peccator et pecca fortiter*]; but even more vigorously believe and delight in Christ who is victor over sin, death, and the world." And later on in the same letter he writes: "It is sufficient that we recognize through the wealth of God's glory, the lamb who bears the sin of the world; from this, sin does not sever us, even if thousands, thousands of times in one day we should fornicate or murder."

Luther and the church agreed on the compatibility of sin and salvation; but Luther insisted on justification by faith alone, *sola fide*. Not by works and not through any mediator other than Christ. Works are by their nature inconclusive: even if one should persist in works, all one's accomplishments are dwarfed by what one *might* have done. If salvation involves, as both Jesus and Paul taught, an assurance even now, a conviction, a triumphant sense of ultimate redemption, it cannot be found in works. But faith is ultimate; faith is conclusive; faith is final. A verse in the Book of Habakkuk (2:4), cited in the first chapter of Paul's Letter to the Romans, becomes the cornerstone of Luther's religion: "The just shall live by faith."

Faith for Luther is not merely assent to certain propositions, though this is a necessary element of faith: it is a liberating experience which suffuses a whole life with bliss. Care is dead, also worry about sin. One is saved in spite of being a wretched and incorrigible sinner. It is like knowing that one is loved— loved unconditionally with all one's faults. And the Catholic church would still keep count of faults and impose penances or sell indulgences! As if the glad tidings were not that our sins no longer matter.

What is wrong with the indulgences is not that they make sin compatible with ultimate salvation, but that they are incompatible with the glad tidings of salvation by faith alone. What is wrong with all the preaching of pleasing God by works is that the Gospel can be understood only when we have experienced the impossibility of pleasing God by works. What is wrong with the church's assumption of the role of mediator between God and man, wrong with the hierarchy and faith in intervention by the saints, is once again that all this stands opposed to the glad tidings. Christ loves us! That means that his love need not be earned by works. In fact, we brazenly exclude ourselves from the redeeming power of his love if we insist that we deserve it or must, by some future works, still earn it.

The glad tidings that Christ loves us permeate Luther's prose; and more than 400 years later we can still experience their intoxicating power. But if, instead of trying to re-experience Luther's faith, we step back to look at it with some detachment, we find that Luther's version of Christianity falls within our previous definition: it gets around the Sermon on the Mount without repudiating Jesus.

With the radical power of his language, Luther himself expressed this again and again. "The law is fulfilled not insofar as we satisfy it, but insofar as we are forgiven for not being able to do anything" (XII, 377*). "The hearts that are filled with God's bliss do not fulfill the Ten Commandments; but Christ has brought about such a violent salvation that he deprives the Ten Commandments, too, of all their claims" (VII, 1516*). And in a letter to his young friend Jerome Weller: "You must believe that this temptation of yours is of the devil, who vexes you so because you believe in Christ. You see how contented and happy he permits the worst enemies of the gospel to be. Just think of Eck, Zwingli, and others. It is necessary for all of us who are Christians to have the devil as an adversary and enemy; as Saint Peter says, 'Your adversary, the devil, walks about' [I Peter 5:8]. . . . Whenever the devil pesters you with these thoughts, at once seek out the company of men, drink more, joke and jest, or engage in some other form of merriment. Sometimes it is necessary to drink a little more, play, jest, or even commit some sin in defiance and contempt of the devil in order not to give him an opportunity to make us scrupulous about trifles. We shall be overcome if we worry too much about falling into some sin. So, if the devil should say, 'Do not drink,' you should reply to him, 'On this very account, because you forbid it, I shall drink, and what is more, I shall drink a generous amount.' Thus one must always do the opposite of that which Satan prohibits. What do you think is my reason for drinking wine undiluted, talking freely, and eating more often, if it is not to torment and vex the devil who made up his mind to torment and vex me? . . . When the devil attacks and torments us, we must completely set aside the Ten Commandments. When the devil throws our sins up to us and declares that we deserve death and hell, we ought to speak thus: 'I admit that I deserve death and hell. What of it? Does this mean that I shall be sentenced to eternal damnation? By no means. For I know One who suffered and made satisfaction in my behalf. His name is Jesus Christ, the Son of God. Where he is, there I shall be also'" (July [?], 1530).

Many will say, no doubt: Luther was terrible, but the Sermon on the Mount shows Jesus to have been the greatest moral teacher of all time. This facile view lacks that impassioned seriousness which commands respect for Luther. It is fashionable to pay lip service to the Sermon on the Mount even if one works for, or constantly patronizes, million-dollar industries that involve systematic efforts to increase the frequency of lustful looks. Luther had tried with all his might to eradicate all lustful thoughts from his tormented mind: as a monk he had denied himself food and sleep, scourged himself, prayed, done penance—all to no avail.

He was not the kind of man that practices law while avowing belief in Jesus' ethic; not one to extol the Sermon on the Mount as the best rule of conduct, while making elaborate plans for the future; not one to hail Jesus as a moral genius while thinking nothing of calling another man a fool. When he arrived at the conclusion that one could not live by Jesus' moral teachings, he said so outright.

A number of conclusions are open to us at this point. We can say that Hillel, the Pharisee, was a greater moral genius when he said a generation earlier: "Do not judge your neighbor till you have seen yourself in his position" (Mishnah Avoth, 2:5). For this is an attainable ideal, not moral utopianism; and as one approximates it, one becomes a better man. Or one could become a Buddhist. Or, convinced of the futility of good works and the liberating force of sin, one might adopt a pagan ethic depriving "even the Ten Commandments of all their justice." But Luther had the unshakable conviction that the Bible was the word of God, that all religious and all moral truth was to be found in it, and that Christ was the Truth—if not in one sense, then in another.

The problem here, unlike the solution, was not a function of Luther's personality or outlook. As long as we do not realize this, we cannot hope to understand either Luther or Christianity. The same problem confronts everybody who takes Christianity seriously. This is perhaps best shown by considering a man whose Christianity is in some ways antithetical to Luther's: Albert Schweitzer.

60

Schweitzer, organist, Bach scholar, and New Testament scholar, who at thirty turned his back on his manifold achievements to practice medicine among the natives in Central Africa, is to many minds the one true Christian of our time—the one outstanding personality whose scholarly and thorough study of the Gospels led him to realize their ethic in his life. This view depends on ignorance of Schweitzer's writings. For Schweitzer, like Luther, takes the Sermon on the Mount too seriously to claim that he accepts it. Like Luther, he repudiates it without repudiating Jesus.

His study of the texts and his definitive work on outstanding previous interpretations led him to the conclusion that Jesus' moral teachings must be understood as a mere "interim ethic"—designed and appropriate only for the interim, which Jesus firmly believed to be quite brief, before the kingdom of God would come with power. Schweitzer's result implies not only that Jesus' ethic is inapplicable today but that it has *never* been applicable and that Jesus' most central conviction was wrong.

With this, one might expect Schweitzer to give up Christianity—unless he accepts traditional Christian solutions of this problem. He does neither. He disagrees with the early Christians and the medieval church, and repudiates Luther's belief that he was returning to the ancient teaching—and yet Schweitzer considers himself a Christian and a Protestant.

Let us concentrate on two major issues: otherworldliness and remission of sins. Far from denying the essential otherworldliness of Jesus' outlook, Schweitzer has used his vast scholarship to establish its importance against the entrenched preconceptions of liberal Protestants. Jesus' otherworldliness is, to Schweitzer's mind inseparable from Jesus' firm conviction that *this* world was about to come to an end. When this expectation was not realized, belief in the beginning of the kingdom did not all at once evaporate, but the event was moved into the future; and as generation after generation passed, it was gradually projected into an infinite distance. As this happened, otherworldliness changed its character.

Paul, according to Schweitzer, had retained the belief in the impending end of this world, even after most other Christians had become resigned to the vague prospect of an indefinite future. Paul believed that the kingdom *had* come with Christ's death and resurrection, and that this would soon become manifest through a transformation of the natural world. But Paul was wrong, and the indefinite postponement of the expectation of the kingdom became universal.

In the perspective of this infinitely distant hope, the Christian negation of this world acquired a new and, Schweitzer feels, unfortunate importance. Originally, the negation had been almost void of content: this world was depreciated as something that was about to pass away, and one concentrated on the other world because it was about to be the only one. But now *this* world is negated even though it is assumed to have duration; and—though Schweitzer himself does not sharpen the contrast in this manner—it is the affirmation that is almost void of content now: an essentially positive outlook is converted into a primarily negative one.

The triumphant conviction that the kingdom was about to come—or had come, as Paul believed—is gone beyond recall; and the conviction that the affairs of this world do not matter any more is no longer a mere corollary, but broadens out into pervasive resignation. In Schweitzer's words: "By their negation of this world as well as by the conception that the kingdom will eventually come all by itself, the believers are sentenced not to undertake anything to improve the present. Because Christianity must pursue this course, it cannot be to the Greco-Roman world in which it appears what it ought to have been to it. The ethical energies contained in Christianity cannot regenerate the world empire and its peoples. Christianity triumphs over paganism: it becomes the state religion. But in accordance with its nature, it must leave the world empire to its fate."

Thus Schweitzer stands opposed to Christian otherworldliness, both in its hopeful, eschatological form, which he associates with Jesus and Paul and considers inseparable from clearly erroneous beliefs, and in its subsequent negativistic form which he considers a moral disaster. Judged by his moral standards, which are shared by millions who do not care to press the point, Christianity did not do what it ought to have done; and Schweitzer has the rare honesty to insist that *Christianity failed morally not because Christians have not been Christian enough, but because of the very nature of Christianity.*

Discussions of Christianity and liberty are full of such phrases as the following, from a recent book by R. M. Thompson: "The Christian Ethic, which reverences personality and recognizes the individual's right to a full and free life in cooperation with his fellows, is the only hope for a world that subordinates man to collective materialism." In line with these glib generalities, it is often supposed that Christianity spread the idea of liberty in the West: the suffering of the Christian slave is stressed, the problem of the Christian slaveholders ignored; the Christian martyrs of the early pagan persecutions are emphasized; the martyrs, Christian and non-Christian, of subsequent Christian persecutions overlooked; and it is scarcely ever doubted that, in principle, Christianity was always on the "right" side, regrettable lapses notwithstanding.

In fact, neither Jesus and Paul nor the early church, nor medieval Christianity, nor Luther recognized "the individual's right to a full and free life." Nor need one think only of Jesus' saying that it is better to live "maimed" and go to heaven "than with two hands to go to hell, to the unquenchable fire" (Mark 9:43); or of Paul's view of marriage. Take the article on slavery in the Encyclopaedia of Religion and Ethics, which is written from a distinctly Christian point of view.

"The abolitionist could point to no one text in the Gospels in defence of his position." The church "tended to make slavery milder, though not to abolish it, and, owing to its excessive care for the rights of the masters, even to perpetuate what would otherwise have passed away." "Legislation forbade Christian slaves to be sold to pagans or Jews, but otherwise tended to recognize slavery as a normal institution." "The general tone of this legislation can hardly be said to favor the slave." "In Spain slavery was a prominent feature of medieval society. . . . Here, as elsewhere, the Church was a slave-owner."[6]

If Schweitzer is scrupulously correct up to this point, his transition to his own this-worldly ethic gives us pause: both for his history and for his logic. In the Renaissance he finds a turning point: the Christian negation of this world is finally opposed by a new attitude of affirmation; and this new positive outlook is blended with the ethic of late Stoicism, as we find it in the writings of Cicero, Seneca, Epictetus, and Marcus Aurelius. "From this originates, as something absolutely new in the cultural history of Europe a *Weltanschauung* characterized by an ethical affirmation of world and life. This constitutes the fundamental difference between the Europeans of classical antiquity and those of modern times. The modern European has a different spirit because he has achieved faith in progress, a will to progress, the conception of a further and higher development, and the idea of universal love of man." The similarity between the ethic of Jesus and that of late Stoicism made it possible for modern Protestantism to adopt these new attitudes. "Thus the transition of Christianity from an ethical negation of life and world to an ethical affirmation of life and world takes place in modern times, quietly and without a struggle."

Once again the faith in the kingdom of God becomes

---

[6] Cf. Troeltsch, 19; Westermarck, I, 693 ff.

central—although the kingdom is now no longer conceived as "eschatological, cosmic, and eventually coming all by itself" but as something "uneschatological, spiritual-ethical, for whose realization men, too, must work." Only after this complete transformation, "the kingdom of God can regain in our faith the importance which it had for Jesus and original Christianity. But it must have this importance if Christianity is to remain, in its inmost nature, what it was in its beginnings: a religion dominated by the idea of the kingdom of God. The role which the kingdom of God plays in the faith constitutes the essence of the faith. *The conception of the kingdom and its realization is only of secondary significance.* Although modern Protestant Christianity is modern, it is nevertheless also truly in accordance with the Gospel because it is again a religion with a living faith in the kingdom of God" (my italics).

The logical enormity of Schweitzer's argument is obvious. Few men have done more than he to demonstrate the complete incompatibility of Jesus' conception of the kingdom with any social or this-worldly aspirations. He has fought the errors of Harnack, who maintained in his famous Berlin lectures on "The Essence of Christianity" that Jesus brought a revolutionary and prophetically modern notion of the Kingdom. Schweitzer denies Jesus all originality at this point: "All evidence is lacking that Jesus had a conception of the kingdom and of the Messiah differing in any way from the late Jewish eschatological one." And he adds: "It is hard for us to resign ourselves to the fact that Jesus, who possesses the spirit of God in a unique manner and who is for us the highest revelation of religious and spiritual truth, does not stand above his time in a manner appropriate to the significance which he has for all time."

This is not a passing concession but a central motif of Schweitzer's thought. Among Jesus' ideas are some "which we can no longer experience as truth or accept. Why is Christianity sentenced to this? Is this not a wound for which there is no balm? Should it be impossible to maintain Jesus' freedom from error in religious matters? Does he not cease, then, to be an authority for us? . . . I have suffered deeply from having to maintain something out of truthfulness which must give offense to the Christian faith." And again: "All attempts to escape the admission that Jesus had a conception of the kingdom of God and its impending arrival which remained unfulfilled and cannot be taken over by us, mean trespasses against truthfulness."

Nevertheless, Schweitzer maintains that his social and ethical conception of the kingdom is "truly in accordance with the Gospel because it is again a religion with a living faith in the kingdom of God"; and "the conception of the kingdom and its realization is only of secondary significance." Here we are close to the ancient *credo quia absurdum*. Jesus' otherworldly kingdom is rejected in favor of an affirmation of *this* world; his disparagement of social problems is considered most unfortunate and countered with an ethic of social regeneration—and then we are assured that this apparently diametrical opposition "is only of secondary significance" because the new ideal can borrow the ancient name: "kingdom of God." This phrase, of course, reflects not an artful attempt to deceive, but the believer's sincere, if entirely subjective, sense of continuity.

Schweitzer's subjective logic must be seen in the light of his subjective history. The quotes given here have been taken from his important essay on "The Idea of the Kingdom of God in the Course of the Transformation of the Eschatological Faith into an Uneschatological One." In the whole careful historical account, which is full of names and dates, we find no reference whatever to either the Old Testament or John Calvin. Yet it was in Calvinism rather than in Lutheranism— to which Schweitzer devotes a large part of his essay—that the modern affirmation of this world found its expression. It was here that the idea of refashioning society took hold. And Calvinism was inspired much less by late Stoicism than by the Old Testament. Indeed, Schweitzer's own conception of the kingdom is far closer to that of the pre-exilic prophets than to that of Jesus.

Schweitzer himself knows how far he stands from traditional Christianity. Almost half of his essay is devoted to developing the proposition: "Christianity ceased to be the religion of faith in the kingdom of God and became the

religion of faith in the resurrection and the remission of sins."
Jesus, according to Schweitzer, still believed, like the Jews of
his time, that God could freely forgive a repentant sinner
without Jesus' sacrifice or any other intervening mechanism.
Schweitzer himself belongs to those "who cannot reconcile
it with their conception of God that he should have required
a sacrifice to be able to forgive sins."

Jesus did believe, Schweitzer maintains, that his atonement
would cause God not to exact the penance of a pre-messianic
time of troubles, "but to let the kingdom of God commence
soon without this frightful prelude." Schweitzer leaves no
doubt that he considers Jesus' view to have been factually
mistaken, but he does not say whether he can reconcile Jesus'
conception of God with his own.

That Schweitzer finds Paul's view of God unacceptable is
clear. "Paul creates the conception of justification solely by
faith in Jesus Christ." This faith wins complete remission of
sins. "The possibility of further sinning after the attainment of
faith is not considered by him." Only when the kingdom
failed to come, and generation after generation was born into
a sinful world, did the church become aware of a great problem—and solved it: baptism won forgiveness for all previous
sins, including original sin, and subsequent sins had to be
forgiven subsequently, by the church. "Augustine (354–430)
introduces the principle that forgiveness for all sins committed
after baptism is to be found in the church, if only an appropriate penance is performed. Outside the church there is
no pardon. And whoever does not believe in the continual
remission of sins within the church, commits the sin against
the Holy Spirit. Among the new conceptions which had in
the course of time developed in connection with the attainment of the continual remission of sins, we encounter in
Augustine the notion of purgatory and the idea that prayers,
alms, and sacrificial masses of the survivors can help the
departed souls to attain remission of sins." But Augustine
still understood the sacrifice of Christ in the mass "only in
a spiritual sense. It was under Pope Gregory I (590–604)
that the realistic conception prevailed that in the mass Jesus
is again and again sacrificed sacramentally in order that the

atonement thus provided may profit the living and the dead."

Luther, finally, breaks with these traditions and understands baptism as effecting not only the remission of sins previously incurred—it assures man of the full benefits of Christ's atoning death and of continual forgiveness. "He thinks that he is restoring the original simple doctrine from which the Catholic church has deviated. Yet it is not he but the Catholic church that maintains the original conception of baptism. His conception, however, is religiously justified."

Later, Schweitzer sums up once more: "Historically, both Luther and modern Protestant Christianity are in the wrong; but religiously they are right." In other words, Luther and modern Protestantism have not only broken with Catholic traditions; they have broken with Jesus' teaching and early Christianity, too. But they are right because all previous Christianity, including even Jesus' teaching, has been wrong. And—here comes the leap of faith beyond the bounds of rationality—if modern Protestantism and Albert Schweitzer are right, then their views must after all be "truly in accordance with the Gospel" because Christ was the Truth—if not in one sense, then in another.

Here Luther and Schweitzer face the same problem and resort to the same *salto mortale:* they not only repudiate the Sermon on the Mount and Jesus' teaching without repudiating Jesus; they claim that their own convictions are, even if not historically or empirically, in some higher sense the essence of the Gospel. Superficially it often seems that certain doctrines are held to be true because they are encountered in the Gospels; in fact, we are confronted with the postulate that certain views must represent the real meaning of the Gospel because they are so firmly held to be religious truth.

It would add little if we went on to consider some Catholic thinkers. On the whole, Catholics have concerned themselves less with the figure of Jesus than have Protestant writers: it was only after the Reformers' protest against the church's assumption of the role of mediator, after their insistence that Christ was the only mediator man required, and after their call for a return to the authority of Scripture, that Jesus was once again moved into the center from which he had disappeared after the first century. And the point of this chapter is not to cover twenty centuries of Christian thought but rather to follow up the chapter on the Old Testament by showing how I see Jesus.

Because most accounts of Jesus are highly subjective, it seemed best to relate my own reading of the Gospels to the views of some of the most eminent Christian interpreters. Whether the choice of Paul, Luther, and Schweitzer was justified depends on how fruitful it has proved to be. As for Calvin, he will be cited in the next chapter in a manner that should indicate how he fits into our picture.

Only one further view will be quoted here. Early in the nineteenth century—about 1818—William Blake said: "There is not one Moral Virtue that Jesus Inculcated but Plato & Cicero did Inculcate before him; what then did Christ Inculcate? Forgiveness of Sins. This alone is the Gospel. . . ." And again:

> If Moral Virtue was Christianity,
> Christ's Pretensions were all Vanity. . . .

61

My account of the New Testament is less positive than my analysis of the Old Testament. Even those who might concede that this makes for a wholesome antidote may feel that it is odd in a book that attacks the double standard and pleads for honesty.

Heresy and polemics inveigh against traditional views, stressing their shortcomings and points that have been widely overlooked. As a result, they rarely give a balanced picture. That is true of Jesus' and Paul's polemics as well as of Luther's.

Still, I shall not plead guilty to a charge of gerrymandering the Bible. It is essential to recognize the discontinuity between the prophets and Jesus, also the modern falsification of the New Testament idea of love. If Jesus and Paul believed that the world was about to end, and that "few are chosen" to escape eternal torment, that is not a marginal belief that can be safely ignored. And their praise of love was intimately related to this central conviction. I have tried to show this in the case of Jesus; it is no less obvious in Paul's.

Consider Paul's great hymn on love, I Corinthians 13: "If I give away all I have, and if I deliver my body to be burned, but have not love, *I gain nothing*." Or, as the King James Bible puts it: "It profiteth me nothing." Long familiarity has dulled the bite of these words. Jesus and Paul teach us to love others—for our own profit.

This analysis does not depend on partiality but on a contextual reading. It is the traditional reading that depends on ignoring what is not considered timely and attractive.

From a scholarly point of view, the fashionable picture of Jesus is fantastic. It disregards Jesus' concern with the end of the world and his appeal to every man's interest in his own salvation, and it is derived in very large measure from two sayings that are missing in most ancient manuscripts (a fact duly acknowledged not only in scholarly works but also in the Revised Standard Version of the Bible): "Let him who is without sin among you be the first to throw a stone" (John 8:7) and "Father, forgive them; for they know not what they do" (Luke 23:34).

Even so, something besides gerrymandering has been at work here. These two sayings, as well as a few others, do somehow leap out of their context and haunt the mind. Actually, they have not haunted as many minds as one might wish: historically, they have been staggeringly ineffective. But there are two levels worth distinguishing. Take Shakespeare's line, "Ripeness is all." It surely cannot mean much to most readers. But those who after the experience of a lifetime suddenly are ripe for this insight will feel hit by it and note that it says in three words what, but for that, might well have seemed ineffable. It may have taken the experience of well over eighteen centuries of history for men in some parts of the world to be struck in somewhat the same way by some verses in the Gospels and Epistles. The claim that these sayings changed the course of history is false; but a book containing words like these is obviously not merely of historic interest.

One may wonder whether the Gospels did not at least spread sympathy for suffering, if only by moving into the center of a great religion the symbol of Christ crucified. Did this not produce in literature, art, and morality a new preoccupation with man's misery, a new note of compassion? Such pleasant suggestions conflict with the historic evidence. These concerns were common in the Hellenistic world—the motif of the tormented body and anguished face of a man, for example, is encountered in the sculptured giants of the Pergamon altar and in the Laocoon group—but they vanished with Hellenism and were largely absent during the first twelve centuries of Christianity. When the Gothic developed a taste for such motifs, the crucifixion was available; but in Byzantine and Romanesque art it had not been treated in any such manner. Nor was the age of the Gothic remarkable for compassion. Neither do the Christian fathers, Augustine and Aquinas, Luther or Calvin, impress us with the importance of compassion. These things were undeniably present in the Gospels, and we may find inspiration in them. But they do not issue the unequivocal challenge that the prophets fling at us.

The place of the child in the Gospels affords a parallel example. Many verses reflect the unusual feeling of the Jewish father for his son, which is familiar to us from the Old Testament. We need only to recall David's attitude toward Absalom, Jacob's toward Joseph and Benjamin, and Abraham's toward Isaac, especially the suggestion in Genesis that Abraham made the supreme sacrifice by being willing to sacrifice his son, "the only one, whom you love." And if some other Near Eastern religion had become the state religion of the Roman empire, we might well have had just as many Madonnas in Western art. The motif of a woman nursing a baby is found in ancient Egyptian art—the Brooklyn Museum owns two examples from around 1800 B.C., one in limestone, the other in copper—and statues of Isis with her mysteriously conceived son, the god Horus, on her lap were common indeed. Some Hellenistic examples might well be taken for

Gothic Madonnas by those not familiar with Egyptian art. For all that, these motifs are present in the New Testament and move us.

Regarding social ideas, the matter has been well stated by Troeltsch: "In sum: the egalitarian-socialist-democratic conceptions of natural and divine law, and of Christian liberty founded on such law, never issue from the dialectic of the pure Christian idea, but are brought about in all instances only by political and social revolutions; and even then they are related only to those elements in Patristic ethics which are not derived from the development of Christian ideas. Wherever these ideas are to be realized by force, and a revolution is to be given a Christian basis, it is always, here also, the Old Testament that must help out" (411). For "with the New Testament alone, no social teachings at all can be generated" (254).

Similar considerations apply to Jesus' denial of the crucial distinction between impulse and action, which we have discussed. It, too, has been misrepresented. Liberals have spread the myth that Jesus protested against Jewish legalism and extolled pure morality. The Gospels do not support either claim. The Jesus of the Gospels was no liberal Protestant. But sayings like, "Every one who looks at a woman lustfully has already committed adultery with her in his heart," also leap out of the context; and the modern reader happily forgets the following words, which are not so readily assimilated to Freud's heritage: "If your right eye causes you to sin, pluck it out and throw it away; it is better that you lose one of your members than that your whole body be thrown into hell. And if your right hand causes you to sin, cut it off and throw it away; it is better that you lose one of your members than that your whole body go into hell." Indeed, if one interprets this dictum as an exhortation to purge lust from one's heart, it becomes a counsel of repression and, in practice, self-deception.

"The spirit bloweth where it listeth" (John 3:8), and one man feels addressed by one saying while another man's heart opens up for another. At different times in his life, the same person may respond to different verses, and interpret the same verses differently. It is one of the marks of the greatest books that they have this power to speak to us in moments of crisis. Unquestionably, the New Testament possesses this power to a rare degree.

Some will say, no doubt, that I am "against" it. But to adopt a simplistic stand "for" or "against" Jesus and Paul, Luther or Schweitzer, would not be in keeping with the aims of this book. According to Matthew and Luke, Jesus said: "He that is not for me is against me." By that token, I should indeed be against Jesus. But according to the oldest Gospel, that of Mark, Jesus said: "He that is not against us is for us."

I have tried to determine honestly what the Jesus of the Gospels, Paul, Luther, and Schweitzer say to us. Some of my results are controversial, but they are not prompted by malice. My Luther is neither the democratic milksop of the celebrated motion picture sponsored by the Lutheran churches of America, nor the hateful devil of much anti-German propaganda, but one of the most impressive figures of world history. My Paul is neither the infallible saint of many believers nor the traitor to Jesus that many liberals have found in him. And my Jesus is closely related and indebted to Albert Schweitzer's.

My heresy is hardly that I go along with such highly regarded scholars as Schweitzer and Troeltsch, but that I refuse to make amends for honesty. It is pretty well known by now that scholarship may lead one to attribute to Jesus views that are not in favor today; and such honesty is forgiven, no less, if only it is coupled immediately with the protestation that facts, if inconvenient, are irrelevant, and that in a higher sense, whatever that may mean, all that was good and true and beautiful was really taught by Jesus. In such contexts, "really" means "not *really*, but—*you* know."

Perhaps it is the essence of organized religion to read current insights into ancient books and rites. But if one does this, disregarding Jesus' counsel not to do it, one should realize that one could do it with almost any religion. I am not against Jesus but against those who do this with Jesus' life and teachings, or with anyone else's. It is well to forgive them; for they know not what they do. But it is also well for us to realize what they do, lest we should do it, too. Perhaps I myself have done this in the case of the Old Testament? I do not think so, but shall return to this question once more in Section 70 in the next chapter.

IX

Organized Religion

62

Since the Second World War there has been much talk of a revival of religion. But it is not at all clear what is meant. In his fascinating study of *The Greeks and the Irrational,* E. R. Dodds gives a detailed account of the revival of religion during and after the Peloponnesian War. There is no doubt about what he means: the phenomenon that another great British classicist, Gilbert Murray, called "the failure of nerve." Athens was approaching the end of her enormous creative energies, and during the great war more and more people turned away from the rich harvest of the fifth-century enlightenment to embrace ancient as well as novel superstitions.

"The most striking evidence of the reaction against the Enlightenment is to be seen in the successful prosecutions of intellectuals on religious grounds which took place at Athens in the last third of the fifth century. About 432 B.C. or a year or two later, disbelief in the supernatural and the teaching of astronomy were made indictable offenses. The next thirty-odd years witnessed a series of heresy trials. . . . The victims included most of the leaders of progressive thought at Athens—Anaxagoras, Diagoras, Socrates, almost certainly Protagoras also, and possibly Euripides. In all these cases save the last the prosecution was successful. . . . It happened at Athens, . . . nowhere else. . . . It has been observed that 'in times of danger to the community the whole tendency to conformity is greatly strengthened: the herd huddles together and becomes more intolerant than ever of "cranky" opinions.' . . . To offend the gods by doubting their existence, or by calling the sun a stone, was risky enough in peacetime; but in war it was practically treason—it amounted to helping the enemy."

Dodds himself stresses parallels to the twentieth century throughout the chapter on "Rationalism and Reaction," long before he says: "I am inclined to conclude that one effect of the Enlightenment was to provoke in the second generation a revival of magic. That is not so paradoxical as it sounds: has not the breakdown of another Inherited Conglomerate been followed by similar manifestations in our own age?"

Dodds not only informs us that at the end of the Second World War there were over 25,000 practicing astrologers in the United States and that about 100 American newspapers provided their readers with daily divinations—phenomena that throw an interesting light on the revival of religion—he also reminds us of the rapid demise of Greek civilization.

Clearly, the great war between Athens and Sparta precipitated a revival of religion along with a revival of magic and superstition. Is a revival of religion necessarily a hopeful sign? When the phenomenon has been discussed since the Second World War, it has usually been assumed that the only question is whether there really has been a revival of religion; and it has been taken for granted that if only there has been, all is well.

63

Reading the quote within the quote from Dodds' book—the passage about "times of danger" and "conformity," which comes from R. Crawshay-Williams' *The Comforts of Unreason*—one is likely to think, first of all, of Senator Joe McCarthy. Suppose, however, we look back to an age long preceding the Peloponnesian War. It is one of the leitmotifs of the Old Testament, particularly but by no means only in the Book of Judges, that in times of prosperity the people tended to abandon their religion, while in times of danger they returned to it. But when we read the Old Testament in our childhood, or later on, provided we do not read as scholars or committed critics of religion, we are likely to put a different evaluation on this phenomenon. Is this because we approach the Bible under priestly guidance, if only indirectly? Should we put aside childish perspectives, cheer the conqueror kings of Israel and Judah, and deplore the prophets? Are we inconsistent when we thrill to Socrates as well as Jeremiah? Would it be more consistent for an admirer of Socrates to view Jeremiah with horror? Many a rationalist thinks so.

The prophets, like Socrates, were solitary individuals who criticized the inconsistencies, hypocrisies, and—as Socrates probably did not, though the indictment on which he was sentenced claimed he did—the organized religion of the time. At the time of the Hebrew prophets, there was a revival of religion in the sense that Dodds describes—in the sense in which there has been a revival of religion since the Second World War. The priests enjoyed more prestige than ever; temple attendance was up; the cult and talk about God flourished. If there had been a Congress, we need not doubt that it would have opened every session with a prayer. But the prophets did not agitate for references to trust in God on coins, for an increase of ritual in schools and public life, for still more massive or more regular attendance at worship services; nor did they conduct revival meetings and request decisions for God. What the prophets criticized, mocked, and denounced was precisely the kind of religion that has been revived since the Second World War, the kind of religion that Dodds describes.

There is a sense in which religion flourished during the Crusades, the Inquisition, and the Thirty Years' War. There was a great deal of talk about religion then, and people took it seriously, believed strongly, and acted with a will on their beliefs.

There is another sense in which religion flourished under Hitler, in an age of persecution. Those who went to hear Pastor Niemöller or Cardinal Faulhaber did not compare in numbers to those attending Billy Graham's meetings; but it was an act of daring rather than conformity to go. The preachers made demands, not promises, and few things mattered as much to those who listened as these sermons and the Biblical texts on which they were based. What was revived was the central importance of religion in the lives of many intelligent individuals—the willingness not to kill or to torture or to persecute but rather to be persecuted and even tortured and killed if it came to that.

Karl Barth is reported to have said that it is better for a Christian to live in East Germany than to live in Western Germany, and that few things could be worse for a Christian than to live in the United States. Reinhold Niebuhr took him to task for this. But Niebuhr missed the point. Kierkegaard, who informed a newspaper that praised him how thoroughly he detested it, and how he would prefer to be pilloried by it, which he promptly was, would certainly have understood. The point is not just that religion tends to become repulsive when it prospers, or that religion is at its best in times of persecution. After all, in times of danger, conformity grows, and so does intolerance. What makes the decisive difference is not whether religion is persecuted or not, but whether religion is a pious name for conformity or a fighting name for non-conformity. The men who conducted the Greek heresy trials, the Inquisition, and the witch hunts, who went on Crusades and to holy wars, were conformists, men of the crowd, true believers. The Hebrew prophets were not.

64

Revival of religion can mean three very different things. First, a mass phenomenon, accompanied by a recrudescence of superstition, increased intolerance, and even outright persecution of heretics. Second, the intensification of religiousness among non-conformist minorities who are willing to make sacrifices and even to die for their religion. Third, the appearance of such great men as the Hebrew prophets.

In the last sense, religion was revived and flourished when the Buddha appeared, or Lao-tze. In the first sense, religion flourished centuries later when both men were deified and their cult was centered in temples, permeated with magic, and attended by millions. In the age of the Hebrew prophets, religion flourished both in the first and the last sense. After the Second World War, religion flourished only in the first sense.

In the times of the Buddha and Lao-tze and the prophets, the greatest minds of the age devoted their staggering originality to the revival of religion. Since the Second World War, the greatest and most original minds have in no way whatsoever refined religion: they are men of science and literature, of the arts and perhaps politics; and if some of them, if only a few, are religious or speak of religion with approval, the spokesmen of organized religion and their flocks are very grateful. Great men who deride organized religion in the name of some religious vision of their own, like Lao-tze and many of the prophets, have disappeared with Kierkegaard and Tolstoy.

The religious thinkers of our age whose books have some prestige and influence on intellectuals are not bold innovators who, like Jeremiah, have the courage "to pluck up and to break down, to destroy and to overthrow, to build and to plant." They are professors who disdain to overthrow and do not seem to have anything to plant: they are theologians and interpret. Some interpret St. Thomas, and some interpret the New Testament, and their notion of reviving is exceedingly literal: like Elijah and Jesus, they prostrate themselves over what seems dead and breathe their own spirit into it to bring it back to life. But unlike Elijah and Jesus, they avoid conflict with the organized religion of their day. They resemble the sages of the Upanishads and the priests of Jerusalem, who were intelligent, reverent, and thoughtful guardians of fine old traditions, not the Buddha and the prophets who were heretics.

Too many critics of religion agree with the theologians that we have to choose between acceptance of the religion of the theologians and repudiation of the great religious figures. Parson Thwackum in *Tom Jones* says: "When I mention religion, I mean the Christian religion; and not only the Christian religion but the Protestant religion; and not only the Protestant religion but the Church of England." Since the Second World

War, it is no longer fashionable to be parochial in that way. Anybody reasonably up-to-date no longer cares about the differences between the Church of England and the other Protestant denominations; hardly anybody even knows what the differences are. The modern parson says: "What denomination a man belongs to makes no difference. My father was Presbyterian and my mother Episcopalian; my wife was brought up a Congregationalist; and I am a Methodist. When I mention religion, I usually mean the Protestant religion; but there are many fine Catholic and Jewish people, too. What matters is that the family that prays together, stays together; that one should belong to some church and worship together."

In another Fielding novel, *Joseph Andrews*, Parson Adams says: "The first care I always take is of a boy's morals; I had rather he should be a blockhead than an atheist or a Presbyterian." Our new respectability says: "I had rather he should be a blockhead and a Presbyterian, or even a Catholic or a Jew, than a brilliant chap who mocks the theologians. Mind you, he does not really have to believe anything; but that's no reason for not going to church and being respectful. Why, take me: I don't believe much, and I may even be a bit of a blockhead, but nobody can accuse me of atheism. I may not read the theologians, but at least I don't find fault with them, and I know they are scholars who know what it is all about. And who, anyway, is Lao-tze?"

It is all right to suppose that the Buddha was a Chinese or even some sort of Zen beatnik; it is natural never to have heard of Habakkuk; half the students at top colleges don't know in what language the New Testament was written, and some students "know" that Voltaire invented electricity, that Goethe is a style of architecture, and that Isaac was one of the prophets. They spell medieval "mid-evil" and, without irony, write "crucifiction"; but they do not criticize theologians. In fact, they aren't too sure what a theologian is. But if a man wears a round collar or has the title of Reverend, he is above criticism. What he says may be dull, but one does not question it.

65

Any criticism of organized religion ought to take into account the aims of organized religion. We cannot fairly evaluate schools, libraries, armies, or other institutions without some notion of their purposes. But while we generally have a good idea of the objectives of other institutions, the aims of organized religion in general, or of particular churches and denominations, are neither obvious nor frequently discussed.

The Nun's Story was an exceptionally moving film, well acted and beautifully photographed; but it completely avoided the question what the aim or *raison d'être* of a religious order might be, not to speak of the purpose of the church. It was clearly suggested that saving the lives of patients cannot be the ultimate aim of a nun who is a nurse, and that "the religious life" is more important; but the intention and justification of the so-called religious life and of religious orders were never considered. This lack of thoughtfulness was not merely a flaw of one sensitive and touching picture or one interesting book; what is symptomatic is rather that scarcely anyone noticed this point.

Self-control, self-denial, and self-sacrifice conjoined with courage and devotion and a more than normal sensitivity are bound to move us; but the same combination of qualities could be presented in connection with a unit of a Communist or Fascist army. Our attitude toward any such organization should not depend solely on the presence of such qualities in some, or even many, of its members, any more than on the bigotry, stupidity, or cruelty of many others.

Not all religions have the same aim: some are designed to save souls, some are not. Let us concentrate first on the first type. Not all religions that aim to save souls wish to save them from the same fate. Hinduism and Buddhism try to save souls from transmigration, Christianity from hell. In both cases it is impossible to estimate success or failure.

That there are many times as many people on the earth today as there were 2500 years ago does not establish that millions of souls may not conceivably have been redeemed from the wheel of rebirth. Since Hinduism and Buddhism teach that human beings may be reincarnated as animals, and animals as men, one would have to know, for instance, whether the earth's insect population has not possibly decreased by two billion during the past 2500 years; and we should require statistics about life in other galaxies.

The success of Christian attempts to save souls from hell is also impossible to judge. Christian ideas about hell are elusive. Most twentieth-century Christians still believe in hell—or at least say and think they do—but few have ever given any thought to the idea that they might end up there.

To make sense of the churches' mission to save souls, one must suppose that those who either are not reached by Christian preaching or reject it are not saved but left to some bad fate, traditionally named hell. To make sense of the churches' mission, one has to suppose that a man's eternal fate does not depend on his own efforts or his conduct, and that God lets our eternal bliss or torment hinge, at least in large part, on the efficiency of one or another organization. A human judge acting in analogous fashion would be said to have abdicated any effort to be just.

Mormons believe that couples joined in holy matrimony in a Mormon temple will enjoy each other's company in all eternity, while those married elsewhere are married for this life only. What strikes them as enviable would be more likely, in most cases, to be hell itself. They further believe that only the first marriage can be for eternity, while any second marriage, contracted after the death of the first spouse, is for this life only. This belief reflects the crucial influence of sociological change on otherworldly faith, for neither original Mormon doctrine nor the Bible prohibit polygamy. But what is most relevant here is the great labor of love in which hundreds of Mormons in Salt Lake City are engaged: they spend a great deal of their free time searching through old files to find records of couples who were not married in Mormon temples, although they had lived clean lives and would have been permitted to be married in a temple if they had applied. Such couples are then married in a temple retroactively, posthumously, and henceforth may enjoy each other's company in all eternity. Here is a wonderful example of religious charity coupled with thoughtlessness about the character of God. What would God have to be like if he let eternal bliss depend on the efficiency of human office workers? Protestants will readily grant that Catholic beliefs about purgatory raise exactly the same problem. But this is not a peculiarity of Mormonism or Catholicism: all Christian beliefs about the afterlife and missions raise this question.

These incriminating beliefs about God are based on a minimum of evidence. They are not forced upon us by relentless experience. The evidence for the existence of hell consists in the fact that four men, writing a generation or more after Jesus' death, reported that he voiced a firm belief in hell, along with many other beliefs shared by some of his contemporaries—for example, the conviction that the world would come to a dramatic end before some of those standing about him would die. Assuming that he quite emphatically believed both things, which seems highly probable, one may well wonder whether he might not have been wrong both times. But millions of Christians would rather attribute the most appalling cruelty and lack of charity and justice to their God than attribute another false belief to Jesus.

Although hardly any Christian ministers or theologians publicly avow a disbelief in hell, many indeed will qualify their faith in hell out of existence when they are confronted with, and pressed about, the implications for God's moral character. At first: "Our Lord said . . ." and "We know . . ." Soon: "Of course, we do not know. . . ." Neither what hell is nor whether anybody actually is there. In the end it turns out that all of us might go to heaven. *Might.* "We do not know."

Here the Christian faces a dilemma. Either he impugns God's moral character—not, like Job, compelled by inexorable evidence; not, like Job, admitting that God is not just nor merciful; not, like Job, challenging God in anguished agony, refusing every human comfort and assurance—but, quite unlike Job, insisting that God is completely just and merciful and nothing less than perfect morally. Or the Christian admits that the churches are engaged in enterprises as chimerical as Mormons searching their old files and then performing marriage ceremonies for the dead. If it is the purpose of the churches to save men from fates to which, even without the churches' labors, no man would be likely to be sentenced, we have to conclude: the churches are like clubs for the prevention of homesteading on the sun.

66

There are religions that do not aim or claim to save souls: Moses', for example, and Confucius'. These religions involve a minimum of belief and no precisely formulated dogma whatever. They do involve morality and ritual. Critics of this type of religion generally ignore the central moral emphasis and concentrate their fire on the ritual.

Ritual may be, but need not be, based on belief in magic. Critics of Moses, Confucius, and their followers usually make things easy for themselves by assuming gratuitously that all ritual is superstitious.

Confucius called himself "a transmitter and not a creator, a believer in and lover of antiquity" (*Analects*, VII.1). He found that the traditional music was not properly performed and exerted himself to have the bells and drums handled as they should be. "He would not sit on his mat unless it was straight" (X.9). But there does not seem to have been any superstition in any of this. "The Master would not discuss prodigies, prowess, lawlessness, or supernatural beings" (VII. 20). And when someone "asked about his duty to the spirits, the Master replied: When still unable to do your duty to men, how can you do your duty to the spirits? When he ventured to ask about death, Confucius answered: Not yet understanding life, how can you understand death?" (XI. 11). He evidently prized being civilized.

As Rembrandt found beauty in an old woman cutting her nails, and Haydn's and Mozart's contemporaries in a flawlessly executed minuet, Confucius found that a touch of graciousness could redeem the prose of everyday life. Ritual, if one takes a little trouble over it, can make the difference between mind-killing routine and beauty.

Among the French aristocracy before the French Revolution, refinement had become an end in itself. In the vast gardens of Versailles, style was imposed even on nature. One can view this period through the eyes of Rousseau and deplore its artificiality. But one should not forget how a generation of aristocrats went to the guillotine with exquisite manners, noble poise, and a proud lack of fear.

Their regard for ritual was emphatically not based on superstition, though they may have lacked any keen social conscience. Their lack of superstition distinguished them from most of the great Christians; their lack of a keen social conscience did not.

Confucius was not a callous man. Asked, about 500 B.C., "Is there any one word that could be adopted as a lifelong rule of conduct?" he replied: "Do not do to others what you do not like yourself" (XV. 23). Still, Mo-tze, born soon after Confucius' death considered the concern with culture evidence of callousness. We should address ourselves wholeheartedly to the reduction of human suffering instead of frivolously occupying ourselves with music. "To have music is wrong" (176 f.).

Mo-tze raised yet another objection to the Confucian preoccupation with ritual. "Mo-tze asked a Confucian: What is the reason for performing music? The reply was: Music is performed for music's sake. Mo-tze said: You have not yet answered me. Suppose I asked: Why build houses? And you answered: It is to keep off the cold in winter and the heat in summer, and to separate men from women. Then you would have told me the reason for building houses. Now I am asking: Why perform music? And you answer: Music is performed for music's sake. This is like saying: Why build houses? and answering: Houses are built for houses' sake" (237).

Precisely because the most intelligent Confucians were not superstitious, Mo-tze considered their concern with ritual sheer madness. "Kung Meng-tze said: There are no ghosts and spirits. Again he said: The Superior Man should learn sacrifice and worship. Mo-tze said: To hold that there are no spirits and hold sacrificial ceremonies is like learning the ceremonials of hospitality when there is no guest, or making fish nets when there are no fish" (236).

Confucius was no utilitarian. He was not motivated by any concern with expediency but by his devotion to what he considered decency. In the Confucian *Analects* it is said of him: "Is he not the one who knows that he cannot succeed but keeps on trying?" (XIV. 41).

Mo-tze, his critic, was a utilitarian. But, in the last analysis, his attitude was very similar to that of Confucius. On scores of details they differed, above all, on Mo-tze's central teaching of universal love. But "Wu Ma-tze said to Mo-tze: For all the righteousness that you do, men do not help you and ghosts do not bless you; yet you keep on doing it. You must be demented. Mo-tze replied: Suppose you have two employees. One of them works when he sees you, but will not work when he does not see you. The other one works whether he sees you or not. Which of the two would you value? Wu Ma-tze said that he would value the one who worked whether he saw him or not. Then Mo-tze said: Then you value him who is demented" (Chapter 46).

Could it be that the churches are like clubs for the prevention of homesteading on the sun; that Confucianism teaches rites of hospitality when there is no guest; and that Mo-tze is right that religion holds up as exemplary him who is demented? To say that there is a touch of madness in religion, a quixotic element, is not offensive. But is organized religion organized madness? Before attempting an answer, let us consider one more organized religion.

67

In the Old Testament the central concern is with a way of life, not with beliefs; and the way of life is not defended in terms of expediency. It is justified by appeals to tradition, loyalty, and, in the end, authority. God demands that thou shalt and thou shalt not.

The reproach of callousness and insufficient social conscience can hardly be raised: our social conscience comes largely from the religion of Moses, in which concern with the orphan and the widow, the stranger and the poor is central. When the organized religion of a later age came to stress the ritual at the expense of social justice, the prophets took as radical a stand as any great religious figures ever did: they found the essence of their ancestral religion in morality, denounced the fusion of careful attention to the rites with indifference to social justice as a rank abomination, and suggested that rites, unlike social justice, were dispensable.

Taken at their word, some of the Hebrew prophets "pluck up and break down, destroy and overthrow" all organized religion. That is not the way Judaism went. The Jewish religion fully accepted the prophetic protest that ritual without social justice is a hateful travesty, that love and justice and humility are absolutely central, but elected to perpetuate the ethic of the prophets and of Moses in the context of traditional rites.

Rather more than other religions, Judaism can avow its purpose and be judged by its success, if the purpose of the ritual and the organized Jewish religion is to perpetuate the Jewish people and their moral message. If the Jewish people in their Babylonian exile had abjured all ritual and clung only to Amos' ethic, if they had abandoned any wish to rebuild their old temple in Jerusalem, if they had dispensed with organized religion, there is no reason at all to think that either they or their moral message would have survived for any length of time. The same is true of the age of the Maccabees.

"It happened that seven brothers together with their mother were arrested and flogged with whips and straps, and the king tried to force them to eat pork against the law. And one of them, the first, said: What do you ask and what would you know from us? We are ready to die rather than transgress the laws of our fathers. Then the king became angry and had copper pots and pans heated, and when they were glowing ordered that he that had spoken first should have his tongue cut out, be scalped, and have his hands and feet cut off, before his mother and his other brothers. Then . . . the king ordered that he should be led to the fire and fried alive in a pan. . . . When the first had died in this way, they led up the second and mocked him. They scalped him and asked him whether he wanted to eat before his whole body should be tormented in every limb. But he answered in the language of his fathers: I will not. . . . Finally, the mother, too, was murdered after her sons" (II Maccabees 7).

By this time, only two centuries before Jesus' crucifixion, the martyrs also found comfort in the hope of heaven. But if they had eaten pork and given up their ancient and distinctive ways of life, there would have been no Judaism by the time of Jesus, and the message of the prophets would presumably have perished.

It was only through their ritual and organized religion that the Jews survived to bear perennial witness of the ethic of the prophets. That Ethical Culture or Unitarianism will survive so long is not at all likely, and to survive at all, even for a few generations, they have had to introduce some ritual. The expurgated hymns Unitarians sing are certainly dispensable; but without some communal gatherings and something more than weekly lectures there would not be anything to create a sense of identity, of loyalty. And if there has to be some ritual, why not the time-hallowed poetry of rites that have survived two or three thousand years, soaking up anguished tears and martyrs' blood and untold associations, rather than the generally thin and unsubstantial hymns of Reform congregations, Unitarians, and Ethical Culture? Once you start to expurgate, there is every presumption that all that is kept is meant literally, which makes most progressive liturgies offensive, for they cannot bear this strain. But if it is pleaded that they are not to be taken at face value, then why is the ancient poetry, that was much better, given up?

There is much more to be said for ritual than most critics of, and spokesmen for, religion think. Ritual, far from being the worst part of organized religion, is almost the least objectionable element. For ritual can bestow some beauty, dignity, and a sense of nobility on life; and even when it approximates humbug, it may still help to preserve traditions that are worth preserving.

68

No organized religion seems to be able to dispense with ritual. Some liberal groups are hostile to any great emphasis on ritual and would prefer to approximate an exclusive emphasis on morality. But their effort runs into two closely related difficulties.

First, the distinction between ritual and morality is not thought through. When is a rule not merely ceremonial but moral? The religious liberals answer in effect: whatever seems particularistic, distinctive of some denomination, is mere ritual and dispensable, and whatever is universal is part of morality; and in this context "universal" means "commonly acknowledged by decent liberal people in other denominations as well—and by liberals without religious affiliation, too." Not eating pork is a matter of ritual, not eating one's relatives after they have died a natural death is a matter of morals. Prohibitions against cremating the dead would be considered part of the ceremonial law; but if anyone followed Heraclitus' suggestion, "Corpses should be thrown away more than dung," and dealt that way with his deceased father or wife, most religious liberals would call him immoral. Marrying one's first cousin or niece would not be called immoral, but marrying one's sister, as the Pharaohs did, would be. Taking two wives, as Jacob and Moses did, would also be called immoral; and so would begetting children with one's wife's maid, as Jacob also did. Most obviously, for a man and woman to live together without first going through the marriage rite is considered immoral par excellence. The religious liberal sees himself as a bold non-conformist who rejects traditional ritual; but usually he is a conformist who rejects the traditions it is fashionable to reject while retaining those it is fashionable to retain.

Ritual, of course, also involves conformity; that is of its very essence and true even of the seven brothers and their mother who preferred torture and death to eating pork, and of Antigone, who would rather die than not perform the traditional ritual over her brother's corpse. It is only in exceptional cases that conformity with traditional ritual requires martyrdom. Still, one cannot conform with everybody, and conformity with one set of rites, traditions, and beliefs necessarily involves non-conformity with others. The conformist from a small town in the Bible Belt, or from a tightly knit Catholic or Orthodox Jewish community, may suddenly find himself in a changed environment where continued conformity would cast him in the role of a stiff-necked non-conformist. It does not follow that every non-conformist is also a conformist; but before we come to that, let us consider the second difficulty faced by the religious liberals who depreciate ritual.

As we have seen, they consider important what is accepted by decent men and women outside their own denominations; this is a prime criterion of importance. As a result, whatever distinguishes one's own denomination is not considered ultimately important. On this basis, however, no organized religion can survive—especially in a highly mobile society.

When one moves from one neighborhood or city to another, no important reason remains for not attending the nearest liberal house of worship, whether that should be Reform Jewish or Unitarian, Ethical Culture or liberal Protestant. The Reform Jews, of course, may have reintroduced some Hebrew into their service and may still, or again, feature some ancient rituals, diluted more or less, and the liberal Protestants may offer Communion and refer to Christ in their hymns; but the more liberal they are, the less importance they attach to many of their proceedings. As a result, an air of detachment, slight embarrassment, and pointlessness develops. A large part of the reason for going at all is that other people go to worship, that other people send *their* children to Sunday school, that it would be embarrassing to have to answer questions about one's religious preference or affiliation: None.

It is possible to be a non-conformist on one's own, without the benefit of the clergy. One can oppose ritual because one wants to retain in one's emotional, no less than in one's intellectual, life a high degree of openness—a readiness for the unprecedented call, experience, or demand. Throughout one's life one may seek to reduce to a minimum the deadening power of routine and regularity that threatens to distract us from the unique challenge of the moment.

This contrast between ritual and readiness cannot be rashly generalized. For many men, precisely the absence of all ritual would entail nearly total blindness to the mysteries of this world, while ritual provides occasions when one regularly tries to listen for the voice that the rest of the time one is prone to forget. The very regularity that antagonizes some liberals who prefer change and improvisation may induce a readiness by association with previous experiences of mystery; and by not introducing deliberate novelties, it minimizes distraction.

Non-conformity, moreover, that does not involve some fundamental conformity runs the risk of forsaking all continuity and thus all culture, seeing that culture requires continuity. To this, however, an answer is possible. The prophets who depreciated and denounced ritual pinned their hopes on the remnant, not on large masses of men. The heretic who is a non-conformist on his own may similarly pin what hopes he has on a new conception of the remnant—as consisting of individuals scattered over the continents and centuries, different from each other in national and religious background but related to each other in their quest, heretics all of them, each in his own way. They kindle flames across oceans, give comfort and issue a challenge, and raise the hope that in time to come there will be others like them, though never more than a remnant.

A heretic need not feel strongly about organized religions, as long as they do not persecute anyone. He can dispense with organized religions as, say, he dispenses with cigarettes, certain that they do more harm than good. Asked whether he does not require religion in emergencies, he may point out that those used to cigarettes require them when the going gets rough, while those not so habituated do not. Still, he will not expect great things from their abolition, and he will insist that adults should be allowed to make up their own minds. The harm done to children is another matter; and we shall return to that at the end of this chapter.

The man who can least afford to be resigned to the inanities and failures of the major organized religions is the man who loves their founders and reflects on their intentions. The most obvious failure of organized religions is surely that almost all of them have made a mockery of what their founders taught.

In religious ages, immorality has flourished—judging not only by the moral standards of a heretic but by the standards the founders set and millions of members of these same religions avow. As far as Christianity is concerned, one may again refer to G. G. Coulton's studies of the Middle Ages. Immorality not only flourished; a great deal of it was enjoined by organized religions, by no means only during the Crusades, the Inquisition, and the witch hunts, nor only when Joshua conquered the promised land and when Manu taught the Hindus how to treat the outcastes.

Japan during the Second World War, China since the Second World War—and also before, for that matter—the Soviet Union, and Hitler Germany stand as so many monuments to the moral failures of Buddhism, Confucianism, and Christianity. So does the treatment of the Negroes in the Union of South Africa and in the United States. The moral failures of organized religions are legion and fill libraries. Incredulous Christians may make a beginning by reading Malcolm Hay's short book on *Europe and the Jews*. Not having read such books, one does not know Christianity; one lives in a fool's paradise.

69

Where does a critique of organized religion leave morality? This odd retort is in a way irrelevant, but often gives expression to a heartfelt worry. Why irrelevant? The same retort might well be made when Santa Claus is questioned. In that case, one answers: You have to grow up and face the facts; honesty is important, too; and parents can still reward the well-behaved child while withholding presents from the naughty one, without invoking Santa Claus. In the case of

God and organized religion, the same answer will do: secular authorities remain to discourage evil.

Will that do? Suppose one can elude detection by men. Do we cling to Santa Claus because a child might do some naughty thing that his parents fail to notice? At this level, the existence of a deity or Santa Claus is really out of the picture, and what is discussed is the social usefulness of some beliefs—the effect these beliefs, even if false, will have upon the faithful. Where organized religion is defended in this manner, one of its moral failures is illustrated: the lack of respect for truthfulness and honesty.

Belief in Santa Claus is convenient and perhaps also charming and enchanting up to a point; but is such charm and convenience worth the price of lying to one's children and discouraging their intellectual curiosity and their respect for truth and honesty? It is no different with critiques of organized religion. Truth is not determined by reflections on social convenience. On the contrary, social expediency depends on whether a belief is true.

To encourage false beliefs and to protect them by discouraging, if not prohibiting, honest discussion and free inquiry may well be inexpedient in the extreme. Those who assume that some beliefs, even if false, are necessary to preserve morality have a peculiar notion of morality and imply that dishonesty and rigorous discrimination against honesty are moral.

Does this misrepresent the case? Might it not be that these beliefs are true, unlike the belief in Santa Claus? Might it not be that every criticism offered against organized religion happens to be false and therefore ought to be suppressed? In that case, it is still implied that honesty is not a virtue and must be suppressed. For there are people who believe, in all honesty, that organized religion is open to criticism—people who not only happen to believe this but care sufficiently to have devoted a good deal of time and effort to considering the evidence and arguments for and against organized religion. Millions in the modern world believe in penalizing such men and detest inconvenient honesty while being willing to reward hypocrisy; and this curious morality has been imparted to them by organized religion.

They also imply that only the belief in God, heaven, and hell keeps people from commiting murder, theft, and rape. Yet most of them abhor Freud's claim that the desire to commit such deeds is almost universal. Nor can the apologist save his position by acclaiming Freud; for although Freud lacked the beliefs of organized religion, he did not find it beyond his powers to avoid murder, rape, and theft. Nor was Freud an uncommon man in this respect: he went on to describe the reasons why most men refrain from such deeds, and he argued that morality would not collapse if religion came to be widely recognized as an illusion.

Now it might be said that most of us avoid crimes, or are not even tempted at the conscious level to commit them, because as children we have been indoctrinated with the ethic of the Bible: morally, we live on borrowed capital which will soon be exhausted. This is perhaps the best defense of organized religion, but it is not good enough.

First of all, it presupposes that men brought up in the framework of some organized religion are less likely to commit crimes. A look at our prison population shows how wrong this is. The percentage of theists in our prisons is much higher than outside. The percentage of men who believe in hell is much higher in the prisons than outside. A much higher percentage of Roman Catholics than of Unitarians or Reform Jews, agnostics or atheists, commit murder. This does not mean that Catholicism predisposes men toward murder, but that more crimes are committed by the poor, the uneducated, and the underprivileged; and a greater percentage of the members of the Catholic faith are in this category. For the same reason, Baptists have more than their share of the worst crimes.

"There are surprisingly few non-believers in prison. . . . Of 85,000 convicts . . . only 8,000 . . . were not affiliated with some faith. The avowed infidels and atheists were microscopic, some 150. . . . *The proportion of religious affiliates is at least 50 per cent higher among convicts than among the general population.* . . . A majority of our criminals—certainly our convicts—are brought up in orthodox religious surroundings. . . . A high percentage of church membership in the total population has no apparent influence in reducing criminality in the community. . . . It seems to make little difference whether children go to Sunday School or not, so far as delinquency is concerned. . . . P. R. Hightower showed definitely that the tendency to lie and cheat among 3,000 children tested, was in direct proportion—not in inverse ratio—to their knowledge of the Bible and scriptural precepts. He concluded that 'mere knowledge of the Bible is not sufficient to insure proper character attitudes.' . . . An interesting study was made of children exposed to a certain system of education in which considerable 'morality' was interwoven in a conscious effort. . . . Children who had been exposed to progressive education methods, based upon secular premises and modern psychology, appeared to have a far better record as to honesty and dependability. . . . Both young people and adults are likely to keep their religion and moral code quite separate."[1]

All this fits in very well with the preceding chapter. The attitude of the traditional Christian denominations toward morality is much more equivocal than that of Jews and liberals, whether they are secularists or not. The glad tidings of Christianity are not that you must sin no more: forbidding sin is not glad tidings. The glad tidings are that, though you sin, there is forgiveness. Even if your sin is grievous, you can confess it and be forgiven if you are sincerely sorry. This is not by any means the gospel of Catholicism only.

On August 1, 1521, soon after his famous stand at the

---

[1] Barnes and Teeters, *New Horizons in Criminology,* 184–87 (italics mine). The section on "Religion and Criminality," cited here, furnishes ample references to many different studies. The "interesting study" referred to was sponsored by the Institute of Social and Religious Research. The children in the group in which "morality" was stressed "kept a daily record of their good deeds, including truth telling. . . . 'The members of the organization cheated more on every test than the nonmembers except in the case of the athletic contest, in which there was no difference between the two groups. Furthermore, the higher the rank achieved [in the system] the greater the deception. . . .'" Cf. also Sutherland's *Principles of Criminology,* 201–3. Both of these standard texts agree that the low crime rate among Jews in the United States and in Europe is due to their close family and community ties.

Diet of Worms, which sealed his break from Catholicism, Luther wrote his friend Melanchthon the letter cited in Section 59, which contains the famous words: "Be a sinner and sin vigorously." As we have seen, this magnificent formulation does not stand alone in Luther's writings. It should therefore suffice to add one further quotation:

"St. Paul bears witness that the heart becomes so pure that one no longer makes things a matter of conscience, as he says to Titus (1:15): To the pure all things are pure. And Christ says (Matthew 5): Blessed are the pure in heart, for they shall see God. Thus, having a pure heart does not merely mean, having no impure thoughts, but rather: when conscience has been illuminated by God's word and made secure that it does not befoul itself with the law, then a Christian knows that it does him no harm whether he keeps it or not; indeed, he may do what is otherwise forbidden, or omit what is otherwise commanded—it is no sin for him, for he can commit none because his heart is pure" (Erlangen ed., LI, 284).

Luther certainly did not always speak and write in this vein. At other times he suggested that, while faith alone saves and works have no saving power whatever, faith naturally overflows into charity and good works. Luther himself, Calvin, the Crusaders, Inquisitors, and witch hunters show how false that is as a matter of empirical fact.

Still, few writers have ever depreciated morality as eloquently as Luther did. That does not mean that a higher percentage of Lutherans than Catholics have become criminals. The opposite is the case. Nor does it mean that crime is much more common in the Scandinavian countries, which are Lutheran, than it is in Italy. The opposite is the case. The connection between religious preaching and moral conduct is much less close than most men suppose, while the importance of the environment and the level of education is far greater. Nor has organized religion thrown its full weight behind a high morality. Least of all does organized religion have a monopoly on teaching morals.

In *The Social Sources of Denominationalism*, Richard Niebuhr says: "Almost always and everywhere in modern times the churches have represented the ethic of classes and nations rather than a common and Christian morality" (24 f.). He tries to show that "it is almost inevitable that the churches should adopt the . . . morale of the national, racial, and economic groups with which they are allied. Hence they usually join in the 'Hurrah' chorus of jingoism, to which they add the sanction of their own 'Hallelujah'; and through their adeptness at rationalization, they support the popular morale by persuading it of the nobility of its motives" (22). One might add that there *is* no common Christian morality.

To be sure, there have been Christian teachers and even founders of organized religions who were greatly concerned about morals—John Wesley, for example, who founded Methodism in the eighteenth century. But, as Niebuhr says, "the primary question . . . is this: . . . from what did they want to save men? Now it is evident in Wesley's case that he envisaged sin as individual vice and laxity, not as . . . oppression. . . . From Wesley the entire Methodist movement took its ethical character. Wesley was more offended by blasphemous use of the name of God than by a blasphemous use of His creatures. He was much more concerned about swearing in soldiers' camps than about the ethical problem of war or the righteousness of their cause" (67 f.). Richard Niebuhr's indictment speaks for itself. One may add that, even to reduce swearing, environment and education are infinitely more effective than the churches and preaching.

Will Herberg, in *Protestant, Catholic, Jew,* confirms Niebuhr's charges, catering heavily to the post-Second World War infatuation with statistics, polls, and phony precision. What emerges is a picture of hypocrisy, self-righteousness, and self-deception, with the benefit of the clergy.

In one postwar poll, "over 50 percent [were] asserting that they were in fact following the rule of loving one's neighbor as oneself 'all the way'!" But "when asked, 'Would you say your religious beliefs have any effect on your ideas of politics and business?', a majority of the same Americans who had testified that they regarded religion as something 'very important' answered that their religious beliefs had no real effect on their ideas or conduct in these decisive areas of everyday life" (73). One gathers that organized religion may influence to some slight extent what men profess in a general way, but that it does not mold their conscience—not to speak of conduct—in specific situations. Asked whether they "really obeyed the law of love" when the person to be loved was "a member of a different race," fully "80 per cent said yes and 12 per cent no" (76). The other 8 per cent evidently did not know that they didn't. But surely the United States would have been a very different country, in the North as well as in the South, if, in 1948, when this poll was taken, 80 per cent of the people had really loved those of different races as themselves.

Sociologically, morality does not depend on organized religion. (Philosophically, it does not depend on religion either, as will be shown in the next chapter.) Indeed, organized religion after the Second World War is still doing what it did in Jeremiah's days: it gives men a good conscience, crying "peace, peace" when there is no peace.

70

Still, the influence of the Old Testament on Western morality has been enormous. Few would care to say that it has all been to the good. In sexual morality, for example, this influence has favored high standards of cleanliness, respect for human beings, and the discouragement of many practices that most heretics, too, would discourage. But the Old Testament has also promoted unenlightened horror of practices and relationships that might at the very least deserve some calm discussion; it has inculcated lack of sympathy and Draconic punishments for people with abnormal inclinations, and, though teaching respect for women, has confirmed and sanctified their subjugation.

For all that, the Law of Moses and the teachings of the prophets have been a crucial social ferment. Most modern social theories with their anti-Platonic emphasis on freedom and equality have drawn decisive inspiration from the Hebrew Bible. In their epoch-making social treatises, Milton, Locke, and Rousseau appeal to the Old Testament.

To give at least one example, Milton declares in *The Tenure of Kings and Magistrates:* "No man, who knows aught, can be so stupid to deny that all men naturally were born free, being the image and resemblance of God himself." And he reminds his readers that the Jews "chose a king against the advice and counsel of God . . ." (cf. § 53 above).

Richard Niebuhr is certainly right when he says, speaking of a later period: "It is significant that much of the leadership of the social movement now came from a group which had been nurtured in the ideals of Old Testament prophecy, and which even when it lost its religious faith did not fail to give expression to ideals which had been derived from that religion. The leadership of the Jews in the social revolutions of the nineteenth and twentieth centuries had these religious sources; it was the only effective substitute for the Christian leadership which had . . . died out, perhaps as a result of attrition in a theological and other-worldly church" (74 f.).

By making the Old Testament available to large masses of people in a readable and powerful translation, Luther produced consequences he had not intended; and by constantly calling attention to the Old Testament, Calvin, too, precipitated long-range developments which would have horrified him. In Luther's Germany, the reaction was swift; and its gist may be gathered from Luther's response: "'It does not help the peasants,' he wrote, 'that they claim that in Genesis I and II all things were created free and common and that we have all been equally baptized. For in the New Testament Moses counts for nothing, but there stands our Master Christ and casts us with body and possessions under the Kaiser's and worldly law when he says, "Give to Caesar the things that are Caesar's."'"[2] Luther also cited Romans 13 and many other tests, but Niebuhr says rightly, after citing other appalling passages: "All of this . . . Luther justified by ample appeal not to the Old Testament but to the New" (36).

In the English-speaking world, many people are willing to believe the worst about Luther, while they assume that Calvin was politically more to their taste. Consider, then, some

[2] Weimar ed., XVIII, 358; quoted by Niebuhr, 36. Cf. my *Critique*, § 58 for further quotations and discussion.

quotations from Chapter 20 of the fourth book of Calvin's major work, the *Institutes of the Christian Religion:*

"The spiritual kingdom of Christ and civil government are things very widely separated. Seeing, therefore, it is a Jewish vanity to seek and include the kingdom of Christ under the elements of this world, let us, considering, as Scripture clearly teaches, that the blessings which we derive from Christ are spiritual, remember to confine the liberty which is promised and offered to us in him within its proper limits. For why is it that the very same apostle who bids us 'stand fast in the liberty wherewith Christ has made us free, and be not again entangled with the yoke of bondage' (Galatians 5:1), in another passage forbids slaves to be solicitious about their state (I Corinthians 7:21), unless it be that spiritual liberty is perfectly compatible with civil servitude?" (§ 1.)

After citing other New Testament passages, including Romans 13, Calvin says: "We cannot resist the magistrate without resisting God. . . . Under this obedience I comprehend . . . attempting anything at all of a public nature. If it is proper that anything in a public ordinance should be corrected, . . . let them not dare to do it without being ordered" (§ 23).

"Those who domineer unjustly and tyranically are raised up by him to punish the people for their iniquity. . . . Even an individual of the worst character, one most unworthy of all honor, if invested with public authority, receives that illustrious divine power. . . . In so far as public obedience is concerned, he is to be held in the same honor and reverence as the best of kings" (§ 25).

Partly under the stress of changed political circumstances, partly inspired by Old Testament ideas, Calvin's successors changed his teachings on these matters to the point of taking a completely opposite stand. In his monumental *Social Teaching of the Christian Churches*, Troeltsch deals with these points in admirable detail.

Popular notions about the relation of morality to organized religion are for the most part completely out of touch with fact. For all that, it would be a dreadful loss if young people were not exposed to the Old Testament, and the New Testament, too. Exposed, not indoctrinated.

71

It *would* be a dreadful loss? It *is*. Whatever organized religion in the twentieth century is doing, it certainly is not exposing the young to the Old or the New Testament. Students at our leading colleges and universities who have attended Sunday school for years and still attend church with reasonable frequency display the most appalling ignorance of Scripture. And when one assigns Genesis or a prophet to them, one of the Gospels or an Epistle, it is a new experience for almost all of them.

Herberg fully bears this out in a manner that should satisfy all pedants: "Though 83 percent of Americans affirmed the Bible to be the revealed word of God, 40 percent confessed that they read it never or hardly ever" (220); and "asked to give the 'names of the first four books of the New Testament of the Bible, that is, the first [*sic* WK] four gospels,' 53 per cent could not name even one" (2).

What statistics about the revival of religion in the twentieth century could possibly be more revealing? Between 1926 and 1950, church membership in the continental United States increased twice as much as the total population (47). Asked which group "is doing the most good for the country," Americans "placed religious leaders third, after government leaders and business leaders, in 1942, but first in 1947." By 1957, "46 per cent of the American people chose religious leaders as the group 'doing the most good' and most to be trusted," as opposed to 32.6 per cent in 1947, and 17.5 per cent in 1942. Clearly, there has been a revival of *organized* religion. Organized religion flourishes. And so do thoughtlessness, hypocrisy, and dishonesty.

The point is not merely that dishonesty permeates all walks of life from advertising and TV to income taxes and expense accounts. People profess to consider the Bible the revealed word of God but cannot be bothered to find out what it tells them to do and not to do. They assume that religion and morality are so closely related as to be almost identical; they profess not to understand how anyone who is not religious could possibly still be moral; and few statements could strike almost all Americans as safer and less controversial than Eisenhower's declaration in December 1952: "Our government makes no sense unless it is founded in a deeply felt religious faith—and I don't care what it is": or the statement of a best-selling novelist: "Although I am not a practicing religionist, I have a great respect for organized religion, no matter what shape it takes."[3]

What would Tolstoy, Luther, and Aquinas, or the Hebrew prophets have thought of these last two statements? They elevate thoughtlessness into a principle. By what magic does "a deeply felt religious faith," *no matter what it is,* make sense of our government? Tolstoy's "deeply felt religious faith," so far from making sense of the American form of government, was incompatible with it. So, in a different way, was Luther's. So was Calvin's. And why should it be so impossible without a deeply felt religious faith to make sense of our form of government—assuming that Eisenhower meant our *form* of government and not, as he said, "our government," i.e., his administration?

I do not have "a great respect for organized religion, no matter what shape it takes." While this may be a heresy in postwar America, I am at one in this with almost all Christians and Jews of former ages. But, unlike the Jews and Christians of former ages and almost all who now teach Sunday school, I think that encounters with Luther and the prophets, Tolstoy and St. Francis, Confucius and the Buddha, are immensely desirable to make men more thoughtful about life's most momentous decisions.

Living in the Soviet Union, it might be a cowardly thing to

[3] Herberg, 85 and 95. If these quotations refer only to Judaism and Christianity, as Herberg assumes, I am unsure why *he* so evidently disapproves of the former. Many of his own public utterances suggest forcibly that what is needed in our time is a deeply felt religious faith—no matter whether it be Protestant or Jewish.

detail the failures of the Greek Orthodox church, real as they are. Living in a country where the revival of religion is generally hailed and no man can be elected to high public office if he criticizes organized religion, it is a duty to speak up. What I propose is, of course, antithetical to the Soviet attitude toward religion. Few things are as important for an education as an exposure to the Bible and the Dhammapada, to the Analects and Lao-tze, the Upanishads and the Law of Manu, to Servetus and to Calvin, to the persecutors and the persecuted.

It is as serious a charge as any against organized religions that they do not provide any education of this sort. They monopolize religious education and, for the most part, make a wretched mess of it. What they offer rarely deserves the name of education.

A critic of organized religion need not oppose religious education. On the contrary, he may charge organized religion with having done its best for centuries to prevent such education.

X

Morality

72

How are we to live? By what standards should we judge ourselves? For what virtues should we strive? Speaking of nobility, a quest for honesty, and the originality of the Old Testament, while criticizing organized religion and theology and fallacies about commitment, does not settle these most urgent questions. A way of life may be implied, but morality is so important that it ought to be examined with some care.

Let us ask first whether morality can be based on religion; then, whether an absolute morality is possible. It is widely taken for granted that both questions must be answered in the affirmative. Indeed, this is presumed to be so obvious that these questions are hardly ever asked. After giving reasons for answering both in the negative, I shall proceed to submit my own ethic for the reader's consideration.

73

Can morality be based on religion? Kant, who is regarded as the greatest modern philosopher by more men than any other thinker, thought it could not. He made a point of his belief in God, but insisted that faith in God must be based on morality, not vice versa. His attempt to show that our moral sense demands belief in a judge who effects a posthumous proportion of happiness and virtue has convinced few philosophers. It is ingenious: God must be omniscient to know all men's deeds and intentions and thoughts; he must be omnipotent to be able to give each the happiness he deserves, if only after death. It is more than ingenious: not only Kant's own moral sense but that of millions of other men does indeed demand this. But the argument suffers from two fatal flaws.

First, it is inconsistent with Kant's own philosophy. One of the central claims of his greatest work, the *Critique of Pure Reason*, was that such categories as causality, unity, and substance have no valid application beyond our experience, and that any attempt to employ them in speculations about what transcends experience is completely illegitimate. Yet Kant postulates God as a single, substantial cause of that conjunction of happiness and virtue which his moral sense demands. It is noteworthy in this connection that some of the religions of the East teach a posthumous proportion of happiness and virtue in the form of transmigration, without postulating any overseer or cause of this proportion.

Secondly, what the moral sense of millions demands need not be particularly rational. In some ages, for example, the moral sense of a whole religious civilization demanded that widows be burned on their husbands' funeral pyres, or that heretics be burned on pyres of their own, or that slaves be treated as animals and not as fellow human beings. Kant's case depends on the assumption that his moral sense, when it demands the posthumous conjunction of virtue and happiness, is not merely conditioned by his education but completely rational. Kant thought it was, and spoke of a postulate of practical reason. Yet it is surely not irrational to doubt, in the absence of better evidence, that Job is happy now.

Kant himself refused to base his moral views on his religion, and he argued that morality cannot be founded on religion. Indeed, he took great pride in having shown that we can *not know* that God exists but only postulate God's existence. If we *knew* that God exists, such knowledge would make true morality impossible. For if we acted morally from fear or fright, or confident of a reward, then this would not be moral. It would be enlightened selfishness.

One of Kant's contemporaries, William Paley, tried in effect to answer this objection. In the same year in which Kant first submitted his ethics to the public, 1785, Paley published his *Principles of Moral and Political Philosophy*, which went through fifteen editions before Paley died in 1805. Paley frankly founded moral obligation on the expectation of rewards and punishments beyond the grave. But he claimed that this did not involve appeals to prudence. Prudence concerns itself with the things of this world only.

This attempt to redefine terms is much too transparent to be plausible. Of course, there is a difference between thinking about rewards in this life and expecting retribution after death. But this difference is best expressed by distinguishing short-range, unenlightened selfishness from enlightened, long-range selfishness.

What both Kant and Paley realized, and what twentieth-century Protestant theologians and those who have been taken in by them hate to admit, is that enlightened, long-range selfishness has played a central role in Christianity, beginning with the Sermon on the Mount.

Still, those who have no doubt that God exists do not *have* to be motivated by enlightened selfishness, whether by fear or by hope for rewards: their motive can be love of God. The claim that Jesus did not appeal to prudence is untenable, as I have tried to show. But for all that a believer could disregard his own advantage altogether and do God's bidding simply because he loves God.

Kant, then, is not right that complete assurance that God exists is incompatible with genuine morality. It is possible to believe without a doubt what the Christian religion teaches and still to be utterly unselfish. Kant overstated his insight. But, as the young Nietzsche remarked, "The errors of great men . . . are more fruitful than the truths of little men" (30). And what Kant calls to our attention is that acceptance of the Christian religion, and of most religions, makes genuine unselfishness difficult and improbable. Once one knows that one will be rewarded or punished in eternity, it is barely possible to disregard this altogether. And few great religious teachers even tried.

There is another difficulty about doing what God wants simply because we love him: how do we know what God wants us to do? Paley and other theologians have said that nature and Scripture tell us. When Paley argued that nature shows us that "God Almighty wills and wishes the happiness of His creatures," Voltaire had already published his famous poem on the Lisbon earthquake (1756) and *Candide* (1759); and Hume's *Dialogues Concerning Natural Religion* had appeared posthumously (1779). In the nineteenth century, Schopenhauer and Dostoevsky's Ivan Karamazov dealt with this popular fancy; and in the twentieth century it ceased to be so popular. There is no need to deal with it here, especially since the problem of suffering has been considered at length in a previous chapter.

The appeal to Scripture is still popular. Scripture, however, certainly does not make it clear that "God Almighty wills and wishes the happiness of His creatures." Nor does Scripture remove doubts about what God would have us do. A quotation from Luther may illustrate both points. The passage is taken from his celebrated *Treatise on Good Works*, which is generally acknowledged to be one of the classics of the Reformation. It appeared in 1520, the same year in which Luther publicly burned the papal bull that had been issued against him. The American editor of the *Treatise*, in the Philadelphia edition of *The Works of Martin Luther* (Vol. I, 1943), agrees with Luther's own estimate that it is "better than anything he had heretofore written." The quotation comes from Luther's discussion of the fourth commandment, sections XII–XIII:

"Even if the government does injustice, as the King of Babylon did to the people of Israel, yet God would have it obeyed, without treachery. . . . We are to regard that which St. Peter bids us regard, namely, that its power, whether it do right or wrong, cannot harm the soul, but only the body and property. . . . To suffer wrong destroys no one's soul, nay, it improves the soul; but to do wrong, that destroys the soul, although it should gain all the world's wealth. This is also the reason why there is not such great danger in the temporal power as in the spiritual, when it does wrong. For the temporal power can do no harm, since it has nothing to do with preaching and faith and the first three Commandments. But the spiritual power does harm not only when it does wrong, but also when it neglects its duty and busies itself with other things, even if they were better than the very best works of the temporal power. Therefore, we must resist it when it does not do right, and not resist the temporal power although it does wrong" (263; Weimar ed., VI, 259).

Some similar passages from Calvin, who did not think either that God "wills and wishes the happiness of His creatures," have been cited in Section 70. Most of those who are appalled by Luther and Calvin, but have, in Eisenhower's words, "a deeply felt religious faith," do not approximate Luther's and Calvin's intimate knowledge of Scripture. Still, Scripture does not teach unequivocally what *they* thought it taught; and on some points that they themselves considered of utmost importance, relevant to man's salvation, they strongly disagreed. Yet Luther and Calvin were both Protestants of the same era. When we contemplate the disagreements of students of Scripture in different denominations, times, and parts of the world, it becomes inexorably clear that any attempt to base morality on religion suffers shipwreck when confronted with the question: what is moral, what immoral? (See also the "Theology" chapter.)

74

Even Christians cannot agree on what is moral and immoral. Their disagreements include matters they deem sufficiently significant to feel sure that eternal destinies depend on them. Their disagreements also include the most burning issues of our lives, from pacifism to divorce and sexual morality in general, from the right conduct toward a government like Hitler's to capital punishment. One of the few things they agree about has no basis in Scripture: almost all of them are sure polygamy is wrong.

While all this is common knowledge, it is fashionable to say that all the great religious teachers of mankind have taught the same morality. Probably this notion is in the back of the minds of those who "have a great respect for organized religion, no matter what shape it takes," or who believe that there is some kind of a white-and-black distinction between those who have and those who do not have "a deeply felt religious faith—and I don't care what it is."

It is so obvious that the religious teachers of mankind have not taught the same morality that those who care to defend this fancy, instead of merely entertaining it and having a good time with it, are forced to distinguish somehow between good and bad religious teachers. This clearly begs the question: instead of basing morality on religion and learning from religion what is moral and immoral, one requires prior moral standards to discriminate religious teachers who were right from those who were mistaken.

This is the major point about this stratagem. There is also a minor one: there is little accord to be found. If one is content to think in labels and to refrain from examining their meaning, one may find a common opposition to "sin." But as soon as we consider more specific questions about what is sinful, the accord evaporates.

Many of the Hebrew prophets were centrally concerned with social justice. Jesus, Paul, Luther, and Calvin, Lao-tze and the Buddha and the men of the Upanishads were not. According to the Hindu Law of Manu, a Sudra slave who insults a man of higher caste "with gross invective, shall have his tongue cut out; for he is of low origin. If he mentions their names and caste with contumely, an iron nail, ten fingers long, shall be thrust red-hot into his mouth. . . . A low-caste man who tries to place himself on the same seat with a man of high caste, shall be branded on his hip and be banished. . . . If out of arrogance he spits, the king shall cause both his lips to be cut off; if he urinates, the penis; if he breaks wind, the anus" (VIII. 270 f. and 281 f.). Christians in some parts of the world would not see much, if anything, wrong in that; but most modern Christians would be quick to say that Manu, of course, was not one of the "great" moral teachers. Manu's provisions for the outcastes were, on the whole, worse than his laws about the Sudras; but Nehru's successful fight to abolish the traditional discrimination against outcastes was not based on any "deeply felt religious faith." On the contrary, the men of "deeply felt religious faith" were for the most part on the other side.

If we do not hesitate to tear some sayings from their context, we can find some similarities. Isolated dicta of Jesus resemble some remarks of Lao-tze, the Buddha, Confucius, or Manu. But when we consider such sayings out of context, we misread their over-all intention, miss their tenor, falsify their meaning. What we have to ask ourselves is not whether sufficient lack of scruple could produce some parallels that will impress the gullible. The serious questions we must face are these: How are we to live? Should we have children? If so, how should we bring them up? And how should we conduct ourselves toward our wives, or husbands? And is it all right to engage in business or in politics? And if so, how should we conduct ourselves toward our competitors? Not one of these questions is contrived: these are the moral questions that we have to face, though most men with "a deeply felt religious faith" are not perplexed by these questions and, without a scruple, take their clue from their environment. If we do confront such questions honestly, we find practically no agreement among mankind's great religious teachers. Tolstoy disagrees as much with Dostoevsky as Lao-tze did with Confucius and Calvin with Luther.

75

While morality cannot be based on religion, religion can be used to help prop it up. It may supply additional motives for being moral and for not being immoral. But to determine in the first place what is moral and immoral, we cannot settle the matter by relying on "a deeply felt religious faith." And if we turn to organized religion, it makes all the difference "what shape it takes."

Protestant, atheist, and agnostic are all in the same boat: from childhood one is endowed with a more or less consistent moral code, and as one grows up one makes a few small changes here and there, most of them gradually, many altogether without knowing it, a few more dramatically. But many a Protestant, having constructed his morality haphazardly, mostly without studying the Scriptures and agonizing over verses that seem to conflict, claims that the finished product is based on religion and deserving of such titles as "Biblical morality" or "the ethic of Jesus."

There is a close parallel between religion and the state. The state, too, can be used to prop up morality, though morality cannot be based on it. In the first place, there are many different states that do not enjoin the same moralities, just as there are many different religions. Even within the same state, morality changes over a period of time: sexual morality in England, for example, was not the same in Elizabethan and Victorian times, and is still different today. Again, the same consideration applies to religion. But the first objection most people would offer if told that, to determine what is right and wrong, one needs only to accept the morality of one's own state, "and I don't care what it is," would be: But the moralities of some states are simply hideous! Again, the same consideration applies to religion.

That morality cannot be based on religion may be just as well; and relying heavily on religion to prop up morality is incompatible with the civil liberties to which Western democracies are dedicated. This was clearly understood by Jefferson, Madison, and the other great statesmen of their generation. Where morality is based on religion, even if only psychologically, criticisms of religion, no less than public avowals of disbelief, undermine morality and threaten public order; and in such countries, therefore, opposition to free speech is powerful, and the pressure for censorship overwhelming. And where it is sincerely believed that heretics will be damned in all eternity, the argument for persecuting heretics to avoid contagion is scarcely answerable.

It is so far from true that our form of government "makes no sense unless it is founded in a deeply felt religious faith— and I don't care what it is" that one might say, on the contrary, that our form of government depends utterly on the widespread abandonment of any deeply felt faith in traditional Christianity.

Jefferson realized this; and in a letter of June 26, 1822, to

Dr. Benjamin Waterhouse, he used language that would spell any man's political death in the United States after the Second World War. After speaking of "the demoralizing dogmas of Calvin" and such "impious dogmatists, as [St.] Athanasius and Calvin," he charged them with "teaching a counter-religion made up of the *deliria* of crazy imaginations" and "blasphemies," and went on to say: "I trust that there is not a *young man* now living in the United States who will not die an Unitarian" (956). Incidentally, Jefferson, too, assumed that Jesus had, of course, agreed with him.

76

We are ready for our second major question: Is an absolute morality possible? Most people assume it is. But most people also assume that morality can and must be founded on religion. And if morality cannot be founded on religion, most people would say that it follows that there cannot be an absolute morality. While I shall try to show that there cannot be an absolute morality, it is not at all true that absolute morality must stand or fall with the attempt to base it on religion. Popular fancy notwithstanding, religion does not have any monopoly on claims to absolute morality.

Philosophers have tried to present us with absolute moralities without appealing to religion, for example, Kant as well as Plato. Plato argued that, outside the world of sense experience, there were incorporeal, unchanging, eternal "Forms," including four that corresponded to his cardinal virtues of wisdom, courage, temperance, and justice; and "above" them, in some sense, there was the Form of the Good. But how could we know these Forms and learn the secret of absolute wisdom, courage, temperance, and justice?

In his *Republic*, Plato argued that a very special course of education would be needed. Reading would have to be censored; Homer and the other poets must be expurgated; and the study of philosophy must not begin until a man is thirty-five. To qualify even at that age, a man must have completed long military training, and, though Plato does not stress this point, have been habituated to a high respect for his superiors and unquestioning obedience. Then, before commencing philosophic studies, he must first take courses in mathematics and presumably, though Plato does not emphasize this either, come to see that his teachers, who were also his commanders in the army, know what he does not know, and that they can prove what he at first quite fails to see. Only after all that, is the no longer very young man exposed to the study of Platonic dialectic. Even then he may not actually see the Forms: in the end, a leap beyond the argument is needed, and the man who does not always want to have to take his teacher's word concerning the Forms of the virtues, and the other Forms as well, must have a vision. Plato did not claim that every student would in fact rise to this point but hoped—very plausibly—that if the state outlined in his *Republic* could be realized, at least some students would.

His brightest student, Aristotle, did not, although he spent twenty years at Plato's academy and left only after his great teacher's death. Some of Plato's moral ideas, moreover, are extremely controversial, though he thought that he knew what was absolutely right and what was absolutely wrong, for all time. In Book X of the *Laws*, for example, he argued that "sun, moon, stars, and earth" are gods, although certain philosophers claimed "that they are earth and stones only, which can have no care at all of human affairs." He offered highly unsatisfactory proofs that there are gods, that they care for men, and that they cannot be swayed by sacrifice or prayer, and he proposed that anyone who denied one of these three claims ought to be tried and sentenced to prison, the minimum penalty being five years; and for second offenders the death penalty ought to be mandatory.

Many of Plato's other moral judgments are much more appealing: he was an extremely profound thinker and in many ways deeply humane. But of his conception of justice, as it is developed at great length in the *Republic*, a hostile critic has said, not without reason, that what it means in effect is that rulers ought to rule, and slaves slave. For Plato defined justice as each performing his proper function; and though he believed that no Greek should ever be reduced to slavery, he scorned the emancipation of non-Greek slaves (563, 567 f.).

Probably no other philosopher educates the mind like Plato. At every turn he challenges the reader to consider new ideas, to examine striking arguments, to be surprised at unforeseen conclusions, and to reconsider. Few, if any, writers are more worth reading. But his absolute moral convictions have commended themselves to exceedingly few readers—not even to many of those who firmly believe that morality has to be absolute. Certainly, Plato failed to show that *his* morality was absolute.

77

Kant's morality, by the Bible out of the enlightenment, is enormously impressive. If there is an absolute morality, even as there is an absolute mathematics, it must be founded on reason and plainly perceivable by all men, regardless of race, color, or creed, like mathematics. The absolute or, as Kant prefers to say, categorical imperative must be to act on maxims that can be made universal without giving rise to any contradiction.

Many critics of this Kantian suggestion have failed to get its point. If you universalize the maxim to break promises, promises themselves would disappear; for once it is understood that promises are to be broken, there would be no point in making promises. Kant's critics have for the most part concluded that he did not like this consequence because he was attached to promises. After all, this consequence does not involve a contradiction in the usual sense of that word. Promises would simply disappear. But from Kant's point of view it is quite irrelevant whether you do or do not like the institution of promises. There is something inconsistent about breaking promises: it involves making an exception in one's own behalf. If everybody did it, one could not do it. Universalizing the maxim is merely a device for bringing out the inconsistency. That is Kant's point.

Promise-breaking is Kant's own example; stealing is not. But here the same point can be made. Stealing involves appropriating someone else's property. If everybody stole, there would be no property. The concept of property, of something's being mine or yours, entails that others are not supposed to take it at will. If everybody is allowed to take whatever he likes, then there is no property. But the man who steals would make an exception in his own behalf: he takes what was yours to claim it as his property, which no one else is now supposed to take away.

These two examples, however, are exceedingly simplistic. A man's maxim is not likely to be simply "steal!" or "breaking promises is all right, at least for me." Suppose I promised to return a book to you on the first of the month, and a few days before that you unexpectedly leave town for three weeks; or I am suddenly called out of town to visit a sick relative. Let us suppose that in both cases it is possible to keep the promise, but only at staggering expense or inconvenience. Or, to take an illustration from Plato's *Republic*: "Suppose that a friend when in his right mind has deposited arms with me, and he asks for them when not in his right mind, ought I to give them back to him?" Suppose I promised.

Even if Kant was right that it is immoral to make an exception in one's own behalf, it is certainly not necessarily immoral to include some of the exceptional features of a situation in our maxim. But once we start doing that, any action whatsoever can be performed on a maxim that would stand the test of being universalized. Kant faces a dilemma at this point. *Either* he says that inclusion of specific features in a situation is incompatible with universalizing: universalizing a maxim means abstracting from specific features. The maxim may indeed be: "It is all right to break minor promises if. . . ." But when you universalize this maxim, the word "minor" and the if-clause must be dropped. In other words, it is never under any circumstances whatever defensible to break a promise. This is a possible moral view but clearly not the only rational, the one and only absolute morality. *Or*, we are permitted to include the special features of a situation in our maxim even when we universalize it; but then every action can be justified, and we are left with no guidance at all.

This last point may perhaps require illustrations. Take such maxims as: "Torturing Jews to death is perfectly all right"; or "Lynching Negroes is permissible"; or, "Leaders as glorious as Stalin should be obeyed whatever they command"; or, "Men as wise and sound as I am ought to be allowed discretion in such cases." Such maxims can be universalized without fear that any contradiction would result.

Kant also offered a second formulation of his categorical imperative: "Act in such a manner that you treat humanity, both in your own person and in others, never as a means only but always as an end also." Again, some critics have made things too easy for themselves by overlooking Kant's "only" and "also." They have pointed out that we must constantly use our fellow men as means, whether we employ them or depend on them to pay our wages, whether we buy from them or depend on them to buy from us. But what Kant called immoral was using other men as a means only.

This is surely one of the most memorable attempts ever made to formulate a single basic moral principle. One may rank it with Confucius' "Do not do to others what you do not like yourself"; with Micah's "Do justice, love mercy, and walk humbly with your God"; and with Moses' "Love your neighbor as yourself."

For all that, Kant's principle leaves difficulties. Like Confucius' rule, it would rule out killing enemy soldiers, not to speak of civilian city populations, in wars. Kant, however, was not a pacifist, although he hoped that eventually there would be a League of Nations. It may be replied that his rule was right though he was wrong in not consistently applying it: killing *is* wrong even in war. But is it immoral to shoot enemy soldiers in battle, if, say, they are trying to extend Hitler's dominion? How do we know whether it is? How do we know what is absolutely right and wrong?

It seems clear how Kant arrived at his rule. It is the morality of the Old Testament, stripped of any reference to God, love, or emotion. Every man, according to the Hebrew Bible, is made in God's image; no man is a mere thing. Moses says: "Love your neighbor as yourself: I am the Lord" (Leviticus 19:17). We are to respect God's image in ourselves and our fellow men: and that means treating "humanity, both in your person and in others, never as a means only but always as an end also." If Kant was inconsistent when it came to war, he followed Moses at that point, too. But how do we know that every man is made in God's own image and to be respected as Kant, following Moses, says?

Even if we accept the Bible, Luther says, as we have seen (§ 70), that "in the New Testament Moses counts for nothing," and he appealed to the Gospels and Paul to justify serfdom; and Calvin, too, considered it "a Jewish vanity" to argue for equality and liberty in this world. The basic document of Presbyterianism, the Westminster Confession of Faith, proclaims in Article 3 that God was pleased to pass by all but the elect, "and to ordain them to dishonor and wrath." The third Articles of the first Baptist Confession of Faith, of 1646, and of the second one, 1677, are similar.

The question is not whether we like Kant's basic moral principle—the second formulation of his categorical imperative—but whether we *know* that it is right. And the answer is that Kant was one of mankind's greatest moralists, but that he did not succeed in establishing an absolute morality.

78

Two other attempts may be dealt with more summarily. The first is utilitarianism. This is usually not considered an absolute morality, but there are many forms of utilitarian ethics. The one that might lay claim to being absolute says that whatsoever promotes the greatest possible happiness of the greatest possible number of human beings is morally good, and what does not is not. Utilitarianism may say further, as John Stuart Mill did, at least according to some interpreters, that we should not calculate in every single instance; moral rules should be subjected to this test. We ask, for example, whether promise-breaking, or promise-breaking in some fairly typical conditions, will promote the greatest possible happiness; or whether a piece of legislation will; or pacifism. Thus we find out once and for all what is moral.

Again, the question arises how we know that concern for

the greatest possible happiness of the greatest possible number should guide our conduct. Luther, as we have seen—and not only he, for that matter—taught that "to suffer wrong destroys no one's soul, nay, it improves the soul." And John Stuart Mill himself said it was better to be Socrates dissatisfied than a happy fool. If we could achieve the greatest possible happiness of the greatest possible number by instituting some such state as Aldous Huxley's in his *Brave New World* or George Orwell's in his *Nineteen Eighty-Four,* ought we to do that? Is it right to sacrifice man's moral, intellectual, artistic, cultural potential to his happiness? John Stuart Mill, to his credit, would have said unhesitatingly: No.

One could revise utilitarianism, keeping the appeal to consequences, but judge these not by the standard of pleasure or happiness but by some other standard. There always remains the question: How do we know which standard is the right one?

79

The final attempt is fashionable in the modern world. It is claimed that, human nature being what it is, certain kinds of behavior are bound to be disastrous and to bring unhappiness: for example, murder, theft, polygamy, dishonesty. Altruism, monogamy, and honesty are the best policy. This last way of putting it sounds cynical, but the vogue of this view depends on complete avoidance of all cynicism and on appeals to anthropology, sociology, and psychology, coupled with respectful bows to mankind's greatest moral teachers.

The homiletic psychologist is the eggheads' answer to the fundamentalist atomic physicist. Even as there is a readymade audience for the archaeologists who prove the Bible right, the social scientist who proves the great religious teachers right can hardly fail—as far as popularity goes.

The first thing that is wrong with this attempt is that, as we have seen, the great religious teachers did not agree about morality. And as soon as this appeal is dropped, the second fault, which is crucial, meets the eye: science may present facts, but it does not establish standards. It may conceivably show us what makes people happy and what does not; what conditions favor a great burst of poetic creativity, or excellence in sculpture, or great architecture, or impressive music —always assuming that there is agreement on artistic standards—and what patterns have promoted major scientific breakthroughs. What science cannot tell us is what goals we ought to choose.

It is popular to assume that we can have everything and religion, too; that there is no need to make choices; that a maximum of pleasure, science, art, philosophy, music, morality, comfort, religion, liberty, and poetry can be obtained if only we will learn the art of loving. "Seek ye first the kingdom of God and his righteousness, and all these things shall be added unto you." In modernese: Become mature, and all these things shall be yours as well.

The apostles of maturity who seem to base morality on science offer us a view that is the quintessence of immaturity besides being thoroughly unscientific. They see the world in black and white, with Jesus, justice, joy, love, truth, and Freud, and all the good guys ranged on one side, and guile, gloom, and guilt, tyrants and totalitarians on the other. This extremely simple-minded scheme obviates all difficult decisions. While it looks as if moral conduct had been reduced to psychological maturity, we really do not have to grow up and face the frightening complexities of life. Like children, we are saved from serious choices, quandaries, and dread responsibility; there is no need for tragedy; we can have all good things without missing anything worth having.

There are those who say that our survival is at stake and hinges on agreement on some absolute morality. What, then, is the standard? Survival at any price? Would it be better for humanity to endure for a few more thousand years under a Hitler, or in Huxley's "Brave New World," or in some antlike state with drastically reduced potential, than to have a final flowering of culture, far exceeding anything yet known, and then to perish nobly? Does survival as such constitute an absolute value? Rather each of us must decide after painstaking reflection and discussion what he is to value ultimately.

Monogamy is said to be clearly right because there are approximately equal numbers of men and women. But in Germany, at the end of the Second World War, there were far more women than men. Would it then be moral there for one man to take many wives, and in some other country for one woman to have many husbands, while in most countries monogamy should be the rule? We might also consider, as Plato did, whether the whole institution of marriage might not be abolished, at least under certain circumstances.

No appeal to science or expediency settles the central moral question which concerns ultimate standards. What is expedient depends on the goal. And science may tell us how various goals can, or cannot, be reached; but it does not tell us what goals to seek.

80

The main objection to absolute morality is that even if there were absolute moral standards we should have no way of knowing whether we had found them.

In perhaps the greatest play of the enlightenment, *Nathan der Weise* (Nathan the Sage), Lessing, who decisively influenced all subsequent German literature and also won the enthusiastic admiration of Kierkegaard, adapted the old fable of the three rings:

> In ancient times a man lived in the East
> Who had a priceless ring, a cherished gift.
> The stone, an opal gleaming in a hundred
> Enchanting colors, had the secret power
> To make agreeable to God and men
> Whoever wore it with this confidence. . . .
> He left the ring to that one of his sons
> Whom he loved best, and bade that he in turn
> Must leave the ring to that one of his sons
> Whom he should love most . . . .
> Thus came the ring from son to son at last
> Down to a father of three sons who were

One as obedient as the other, whom
The father therefore could not keep himself
From loving equally. Only from time
To time, now this one seemed, now that, and now
The third—as each enjoyed his company
Alone and did not share his outpoured heart
With his two brothers—more deserving of
The ring which in his pious weakness he
Promised to each in turn. . . .
Confronting death, the good old father was
Embarrassed, for it pained him that two of
His sons, who counted on his word, should be
Offended. What, then, could he do? He sent
In secret for an artist and commissioned
Two rings after the model of the first,
And bade him spare neither expense nor trouble
To make them like, completely like, the first.
The artist was successful. When he brought
The rings, the father could not tell himself
Which was the model ring. Rejoicing and
Delighted, he called in his sons, each one
Alone, gave each his blessing and his ring,
And died. . . .
No sooner was the father dead than each
Came with his ring and staked his claim to be
Prince of the house. One makes inquiries, fights,
And sues. In vain; the model ring was not
To be established—any more than now
The one true faith. . . .   Whose
Reliability are we inclined
To doubt the least? Is it not that of our
Own family—whose blood is in us? Those
Who from our childhood gave us proofs of love?
Who never have deceived us, save when it
Was in our interest to be deceived?
How could I trust my fathers less than you
Believe yours? Or, conversely, how could I
Demand that you should charge your ancestors
With lies to avoid contradicting mine? . . .

The sons, as mentioned, sued each other. Each
Swore to the judge he had received his ring
From his own father's hand. . . . The father,
Insisted each, could never have been false
To him; and sooner than permit such a
Suspicion about him, such a dear father,
He must accuse his brothers, much as he
Preferred to think only the best of them,
Of playing false; and he would prove their treason,
And have revenge. . . .
The judge replied: . . .

                 I hear the true ring has
The magic power to make one beloved,
Agreeable to God and men. That must
Decide the case. For the false rings will not
Possess this power. Now, then, whom do two
Of you love most? Speak up! Why are you silent?
The rings' effect is backward only? Not
Toward the outside? Each of you only loves
Himself most?—Then you are all three
Deceived deceivers! And of your three rings
Not one is genuine. The one that was
Has probably been lost. To cover up
This loss, as a replacement, did your father
Commission three for one.

Lessing was a heretics' heretic. Kierkegaard thrilled to his remark that, confronted with a choice between all the truth in God's right hand and the ever live striving for truth, coupled with eternal error, in God's left, he would choose the left. He also said, immediately preceding this: "Not the truth in whose possession any man is, or thinks he is, but the honest effort he has made to find out the truth, is what constitutes the worth of man."

For all that, Lessing's heresies, like those of other men of the enlightenment, concerned only faith, not morals. He did not take the image of the father's death in the parable as Nietzsche would, or Kafka; he probably did not even realize how the final sentence could be interpreted as a dig at the

Trinity; nor did he press the implicit indictment of the father and the irony that each of the sons would rather accuse his brothers of treachery than permit the least suspicion of the father. Above all, Lessing found the moral of the story in Nathan's suggestion that each son ought to take care of proving his ring true by living an exemplary life—and Lessing assumed that there was agreement on the character of such a life.

As soon as we extend the parable to ethics, we confront the objection that faith and morals are quite different in this respect: men of different faiths can live together in peace, provided they agree on standards of behavior; but without moral agreement, men cannot live together in peace.

This objection is half true but quite insufficient to establish any absolute morality. Where there is much traffic, there have to be traffic rules to avoid needless injuries and deaths and to ensure the attainment of the purposes of traffic. After all, one drives to reach a destination; and to get there without endless delays, there has to be agreement on what side of the road one is supposed to drive. It does not matter whether the rule is to drive on the right or on the left; what matters is that everybody should follow the same rule. As long as there is scarcely any traffic across international borders, it is perfectly all right for traffic in Germany to move on the right side of the road, and in Austria on the left. As international traffic increases, it becomes more and more convenient to reach international agreement on such matters. But it would be silly to insist that driving on the right is absolutely preferable, true, or moral, while driving on the left is absolutely false and immoral.

To live together peaceably, men need rules, and these rules may even have to be enforced, if all else fails, with penalties. It does not follow that these rules are absolutely right or that every act that conflicts with a rule, even if the rule should be important, is immoral in some absolute sense, unless, of course, we define immorality as violation of mores, of conventions—as non-conformity.

What is obvious in the case of traffic rules is by no means obvious in some other cases. The question is how far the parallel to traffic rules extends. Driving on the left side of the road is not at all wicked in itself; but when it involves breach of a rule and an utter lack of consideration for others, it may well be considered wicked. Is this also true of consideration for others? Could it be that a lack of that, too, is not wicked in itself and that only breach of a rule and the fact that men's living together peaceably depends on consideration for others lead us to call it wicked? Or is lack of consideration for others the quintessence of depravity?

How can these questions be settled? They involve the very meaning of morality and of such terms as moral and depraved, wicked and good. Before going any further, we shall have to consider these terms, if only briefly.

81

Most discussions of morality rest on the false assumption that "moral," "morally good," "evil," and "wicked" have some single central meaning, like such words as "elephant" and "ocean." Even those who make much of the fact that different individuals and groups apply these labels to different kinds of behavior usually assume that the labels themselves always mean the same thing.

On the basis of this false assumption, philosophers go on to argue whether "moral" means "approved by God" or "conducive to the greatest possible happiness of the greatest possible number"; "approved by me" or "approved by a certain group of people"; "what I prefer and would like everybody to prefer" or "what all of us should do if we had perfect wisdom and if we were not impeded by some weakness of the will." This enumeration is sufficient to show that different people, and even the same persons in different contexts, mean different things when using the same word. What is common to the different meanings is that whatever is called "moral" is approved by somebody and related to conduct; but the reference may be primarily to character and only derivatively to conduct, and the approval need not be unqualified. To illustrate the last point: in a caste system, the same action may be considered moral for one caste and the height of immorality for other castes or outcastes. It is therefore idle to speculate or argue about *the* meaning of "moral" or its synonyms and antonyms.

Agreement that stealing is immoral may be comparable to a case in which five men refuse to eat beef and warn others not to eat it either: the first does not like the taste and either does not believe that tastes differ or, admitting that they do, considers his own taste the only "true" one. The second loves the taste but wants to punish himself; and he, too, thinks that what is right for him is right for others. The third thinks the meat is poisonous or dangerous. The fourth is a Hindu. The fifth, who is not a Hindu, is a vegetarian. Their superficial agreement is not altogether unimportant. As long as they do not enter into questions of meaning, faith, or morals, they may get along; and they may even suppose erroneously that they agree on certain facts—absolutely true facts—which moral idiots who eat beef deny. But on these supposed facts, some of them actually happen to agree with men who eat beef rather than with men who don't, while others base their conduct on assumptions about facts that are demonstrably false.

Now consider a case of disagreement. Aristotle, Luther, and Tolstoy are meeting in an unspecified place to discuss what we should do when asked by someone to walk, say, one mile with him. Tolstoy might say that it would be moral to walk at least two miles with him, while admitting that he himself might conceivably get angry and not walk with him at all. Luther might suggest that we should not accede to the request since Christ's commandments were given for us to realize our utter incapacity to fulfill them, and any attempt to please God by works is immoral: perhaps morality consists in faith overflowing into works—but hardly in such a manner that a Luther would have to walk two miles to suit someone else. Aristotle might suggest that half a mile would be dignified and generous, while two miles would be excessive and likely to conflict with other obligations, and not going along at all would be ungentlemanly. They might not take exactly these positions, but that does not matter here. Suppose they did: would their disagreement be like that of three men who are arguing whether a dimly perceived shape belongs to an elephant or a tree? Clearly not. In that case, there would be agreement on the meaning of the label "elephant," and the question would be whether it applies in a given instance. Aristotle, on the other hand, as pictured here, says that a certain mode of conduct would not be in keeping with the manners of Athenian gentlemen; that it would be excessive, radical, likely to conflict with other obligations, and not very dignified. Luther and Tolstoy are not debating these claims at all: both might agree with them wholeheartedly. What they are discussing is the significance of some verses in the New Testament. They disagree with each other, but not on the question what is gentlemanly. Their disagreement involves exegesis of Greek texts and particularly the question which verses are the most crucial. For Tolstoy, Jesus' "resist not evil" is the "key" to the whole New Testament; for Luther, Paul's "by faith alone."

Philosophers are fond of asking whether, when one says something is moral, one purports to state his own attitude, the preferences of some group, the will of God, or what not. To this question no general answer is possible. When *I* say that something is moral, I may be expressing a personal attitude without the least pretension to any further fact, though I may ask you to give very serious consideration to my attitude; while *you*, when calling something moral, may believe that you inform me of the will of God.

Further, it is possible that Jones, when calling *stealing* immoral, means that it is counter to the will of God; while, when he calls eavesdropping immoral, he means, on reflection, that it is counter to the way in which he and other people whom he would call nice have been brought up; and when he calls big-game hunting immoral, he means, on reflection, that while some of his best friends are doing it, he personally has a strong feeling against it. In sum, the word "moral" is used in many different senses even by the same persons; and unless we think that we should ostracize some perfectly idiomatic uses of it that are encountered among intelligent and reasonable people who are solid citizens, we cannot define *the* meaning of the term.

Statements like "it is immoral not to be meek" are elliptical and cannot be discussed profitably until the meaning of "immoral" in this context is spelled out. The apparent difference of opinion about meekness between Aristotle and St. Francis was not due to one man's lack of a moral sense that the rest of us have. The saint was concerned with God's will and the kingdom of heaven, neither of which entered into Aristotle's thoughts. Once the elliptical statement is completed, we can examine the evidence or lack of evidence for it. We can see what evidence there is that God considers meekness moral, and lack of it immoral, or that lack of meekness bars a man from the kingdom of heaven. We can discuss whether there is conclusive evidence for God's approval of anything at all— or even for his existence. We can consider whether God's will, even if it could be made out, should decide our course of action. But to argue whether this or that is moral without specifying what we mean by "moral" is one way of generating heat without light.

Some people think moral disagreements are like disagreements about facts; others claim they are like differences of taste. Actually, moral judgments are almost invariably elliptical, and when they are spelled out they are found to involve all kinds of assumptions about facts as well as an element of taste. And moral disagreements generally involve disagreements about facts, differences in taste, or both. Spelling out the factual disagreements may at times dispel a moral disagreement; but even when it does not, it will generally lead to a drastic reduction of heat.

Men of intelligence have their moral disagreements, like everybody else, but they often fume less because they know what they disagree about. Fuming not only prevents us from seeing clearly; it is a smoke screen that covers up a lack of clarity.

Recommendation: try not to call people or actions "immoral." Most educated people do not do this anyway, any more than they call what they like "divine" or "marvelous." By demanding greater clarity and more specific judgments of oneself, one avoids utterly unprofitable arguments and stands some chance of finding out what one means. It may not be easy, but it is a step in the direction of honesty.

82

We have seen that the main objection to absolute morality is that even if there were absolute moral standards we could never know if we had found them. We are now ready to add that this is not the only objection. For one thing, it is not clear what such a phrase as "absolute moral standards" means, since the term "moral" is so far from being univocal; and "absolute" is not unambiguous either.

Justice Holmes is reported to have said that he preferred champagne to ditch water, but that he saw no reason for believing that the cosmos did. Some people who are partisans of "absolute values" have found fault with him and proclaimed that, of course, the cosmos, too, prefers champagne to ditch water. For myself, I should not think that the cosmos has preferences of any kind, not to speak of a taste for champagne. But there are surely many living organisms, far exceeding in sheer numbers people with a taste for champagne and indeed the whole of mankind, who thrive in ditch water while they would perish in champagne. It does not follow by any means that ditch water is "absolutely" preferable. The point is rather that "absolute" is one of those words that often give off heat without light.

Sometimes it is tempting to generate a little heat; and in that spirit one might transgress the recommendation only just offered and go beyond the previous two objections to speak of the immorality of absolute morality. That sounds paradoxical and may not do much harm if we proceed immediately to make amends by demanding greater clarity and spelling out in detail what is meant.

For all the talk of humility that pervades some self-styled absolute moralities, there is something arrogant about those who profess that their morality is absolute.

For all the talk of love that pervades some self-styled absolute moralities, the word "immoral" is rarely spoken without a strong charge of resentment. "She is immoral" immediately suggests the voice of a woman whose resentment shows that she, too, would have liked to do what someone else has done, but she did not permit herself this pleasure and would be aggrieved to see another person get away with it. "She is immoral" is the antithesis of "Let him who is without sin among you be the first to throw a stone at her" (John 8:7).

For all the talk of courage that pervades some self-styled absolute moralities, there is an element of fear and self-mistrust that, like resentment, is present in the overwhelming number of cases, though not in all. "Would you ever allow yourself to be blackmailed?" I don't think so. "I have made it an absolute rule for myself never to permit myself to be blackmailed. Why? Well, if I had not, there might be a situation in which I might be tempted to give in.— But, of course, in that case even the rule might not help." There is a difference between making an absolute rule for oneself and claiming that some acts are absolutely immoral. But the human reality behind both attitudes is similar.

Finally, and most important: there is an element of self-deception in the claim to have an absolute morality. One claims to know what in fact one does not know. One pretends to knowledge about matters about which one really does not have knowledge—and about which, for the most part, one prefers not even to think too carefully.

83

My own ethic is not absolute but a morality of openness. It is not a morality of rules but an ethic of virtues. It offers no security but goals.

To communicate it, one has to enumerate virtues. A long list would be ineffective; a short list would probably leave out much that I deem important. Here are four cardinal virtues.

The *first* lacks any single name but is a fusion of humility and aspiration. Humility consists in realizing one's stark limitations and remembering that one may be wrong. But humility fused with smugness, with complacency, with resignation is no virtue to my mind. What I praise is not the meekness that squats in the dust, content to be lowly, eager not to stand out, but humility winged by ambition. There is no teacher of humility like great ambition. Petty aspirations can be satisfied and may be hostile to humility. Hence, ambition and humility are not two virtues: taken separately, they are not admirable. Fused, they represent the first cardinal virtue. Since there is no name for it, we shall have to coin one—at the risk of sounding humorous: humbition.

An example might help, since popular prejudice considers ambition and humility irreconcilable. Consider news reports about the pianist Sviatoslav Richter. Often, we are told, "he has found himself so dissatisfied with his performance that he has sat down after the audience has left and played the entire program over again." When he made a recording, "the musicians were aghast when he would come to the end of a movement that seemed letter-perfect and then hold up his hand to signify that he wanted to do it over again. . . . He completed the 50-minute concerto after seven concentrated hours of recording and re-recording." When a critic asked him to explain the difference between two performances he had given in New York of the same sonata, he answered: "It's very simple. The first time I played it badly." The critic protested: "But that's not what I meant." Richter replied: "But it's what I meant."

What is at stake transcends any such example. Few things are more difficult than seeing some of one's own faults. Ours usually look quite different from the faults of others—not really like faults at all. When we realize this, meekness says: Judge not, that you be not judged! And under his breath the devil adds: That way the lot of you will go to hell. But humbition says: I can see the back of your head and the black of your soul, but not my own, and you can see what escapes me; by being frank, we can help each other. No, the devil interposes; you will hurt each other's feelings; be polite; be meek! But humbition replies: Judge, that you may be judged!

A writer like Tolstoy, for example, wants you to judge the characters in *Anna Karenina*. He all but forces you to see their many weaknesses and self-deceptions. But the reader who is not hopelessly blind must say: *ego quoque;* I, too, am guilty. Traditionally, a certain fallacy is sometimes called, for short: *Tu quoque;* you, too. Accused of a fault, whether a crime or illogic, a man turns on his accuser and charges him with the same fault. But two wrongs do not wipe out one. Similarly, the meek reader is apt to say *ego quoque,* supposing that he is in no position to pass any judgment. But the reader Tolstoy wants says: this man deceives himself; he lives in bad faith; he falls short of what he might be—and so do I. Humbition outsoars resignation.

Judgment, of course, may be prompted by envy, resentment, and hatred; and "judge not" may mark a triumph over resentment. But one should not rest content with such a triumph. Soon "judge not" becomes the counsel of timidity. Who, after all, am I to judge? If I forgive him, he may forgive me. If I am not severe with them, they may not be severe with me; and if others are not severe with me, why should I be severe with myself? We are all small people; let us stay that way. But I say: such meekness is no virtue.

It is not in the least probable that Jesus meant to encourage meekness of that sort. He also said: "Do you think that I have come to give peace on earth? No, I tell you, but rather division . . . father against son and son against father, mother against daughter and daughter against her mother." He judged—even organized religion, theologians, and men's faith and men's commitments. Nor did his disciples and the early Christians hesitate to judge religion and its spokesmen. It is only in the modern world that men who think it blasphemous of anyone to question organized religion, theologians, and men's faith invoke the name of Jesus. The early Christians, in the Greco-Roman world, were confronted with a similar respect for organized religion, "no matter what form it takes" —and opposed it.

To be sure, they did not say: Judge, that you may be judged! They judged others, confident that perfect truth was on their own side. Humbition lacks such confidence; it says: Surely, there must be faults and errors on my side, but it is difficult for me to find them. If I ignore the faults of others,

I abandon hope for them and for myself. If I had never seen your faults, and yours, and yours, I might have thought that truth was on my side. Seeing your shortcomings, I infer the likelihood of mine and actually spot dozens of faults in myself that, but for yours, I should have missed. Judging you, I judge myself.

You have been told: Love your neighbor as yourself. I add: Judge yourself as you judge your neighbor, and demand more of yourself than of him. Dissatisfied with your neighbor, tell him—and try to excel him.

The *second* cardinal virtue is love. "Love" may seem to cover a multitude of virtues, but again it is only a fusion of several things that deserves the name of a cardinal virtue. Martin Buber retells a Hasidic tale originally related by Rabbi Mosheh Leib: "How one should love men, I have learned from a peasant. He sat in an inn with some other peasants, drinking. For a long time he was silent like the others, but when his heart was moved by the wine he said to his neighbor: 'Tell me, do you love me or don't you?' And he replied: 'I love you very much.' But the first peasant answered: 'You say, I love you; and yet you do not know what hurts me. If you loved me in truth, you would know.'" That is a much higher standard of love than most men have, and yet it is clearly not enough: one might have the insight to know what hurts others and not care, not share their hurt, not love. The Hasidic rabbi concluded: "I understood: that is love of men, to sense their wants and bear their grief."

As far as "love of men" or neighbor love is concerned, that is a splendid definition. For this much we can aim in relation to all men with whom we deal, all men toward whom we must adopt some attitude: members of our family, colleagues, employees, employers, writers—even men like Hitler. It is not true that such an attitude toward men who persecute one or who have inflicted grievous suffering on millions is impossible or superhuman. Any writer of distinction has to do as much. Dostoevsky, Tolstoy, and Shakespeare excelled in the ability not only to sense the secrets of perverse souls whom most men would hate but to compel the reader to project himself into such men. Far better than generations of preachers, they teach the secret of love of men, which is an expansion of our imagination that begins as curiosity and ends with projection.

Love in the more usual sense is often held to be an altogether different experience from such love of men. In fact, ordinary love and neighbor love are neither identical nor entirely different; they are continuous. Those who speak and write judiciously do not consider the mere intensity of emotion sufficient to warrant the name of love; there must also be a strong, sustained concern with the other person's wants and grief. It is because love is not a mere emotion that the Old Testament as well as the New could command us to love; and for the same reason it makes sense to speak of love as a virtue. The continuity of the two kinds of love is reversible. The lover who is initially overcome by an intense emotion is gradually led to more and more profound concern about the loved one's feelings, thoughts, and welfare. Conversely, if we begin by thinking of other human beings as essentially like ourselves and sense their wants, we may be led to bear their griefs, too.

The paradox of love is not that love should be commanded but that there is a sense in which it is hardest to love those whom we love most. To command people to put themselves into their fellows' places, thinking about the thoughts, feelings, and interests of others, makes excellent sense. What few men have ever consciously realized is that highly intelligent people are frequently least capable of achieving such love in relation to those closest to them—those whom they, they themselves would say, love most.

The enormous impact of Sophocles' first *Oedipus* tragedy is related to this fact. Oedipus' tragedy is a common human tragedy; his condition is our condition; and his failure shakes us because it is our failure, too. In his outstanding intelligence, courage, and honesty, he is the image of nobility. But though he fathomed the riddle of the Sphinx and understood the human condition as no one else, he was blind, confronted with his father, mother, and children. This does not involve reading one's own ideas into the text: the contrast between the blind Tiresias who sees Oedipus' relations for what they are and Oedipus who, mocking Tiresias' blindness, does not see, is central in Sophocles' tragedy; and when Oedipus finally sees what, for all his intelligence and all the gradually accumulating clues, he had been blind to, he blinds himself.

When it comes to those closest to us, we ourselves are so involved; we are such interested parties, and discovery would place us in such strange positions and point to our own responsibilities and guilt that even those who usually have a keen eye typically fail at this point.

Freud realized that Oedipus' condition must somehow be ours, too; but he failed to note this aspect of the tragedy. If Ernest Jones is right in his biography of Freud, and some of the close disciples who eventually broke away were mentally quite ill, one implication quite escapes Jones. He thinks that he has shown that Freud was right and they were wrong. Unwittingly, however, he also suggests that Freud, the modern Oedipus who solved the riddle of the Sphinx and understood man's condition like no one else, was singularly blind confronted with his closest friends and followers, unable to perceive how sick they were. Let us, in the words of Deuteronomy, "hear and fear."

Love as a virtue does not end with projection and understanding. It is not content to perceive and sympathize; it involves the willingness to assume responsibility and to sacrifice. Devotion and commitment as such elicit some admiration but are no virtues—and have been considered at length in the chapter on "Commitment." Fused in love, they represent the second cardinal virtue.

Is this the Christian conception of love? There is no such thing as "the" Christian conception of love: at different times, different Christians have held many different conceptions of love. But when one offers four cardinal virtues, it is appropriate to consider Paul's celebrated paean on love in First Corinthians 13, since this is the classical exposition of the three Christian virtues. Paul couples love with faith and hope, and his conception of love involves faith and hope: "Love," he says, "believes all things, hopes all things." The love I mean does not believe all things and hope all things. It survives disillusionment and persists in despair. Love is not love that ceases without hope or faith. As long as faith and hope support it, it is hardly more than puppy love. That love is pleasant is a fashionable myth, or, to be more charitable about it, the exception. The Buddha knew that love brings "hurt and misery, suffering, grief, and despair"; and he advised detachment.[1] The love I consider a virtue is not the blind love of the lovers or the trusting, hopeful love of Paul, but the love that knows what the Buddha knew and still loves, with open eyes.

The *third* cardinal virtue is courage. It enters into each of the other three but deserves admiration in itself. To be greatly ambitious while knowing one's own limitations takes courage. The counsel of timidity is to stay low rather than to risk great failures. To love without illusions takes courage. The counsel of cowardice, prudence, and simple sense is to avoid getting hurt. Is courage, then, less basic than the first two virtues and no more than one ingredient in them? On the contrary, courage is more basic; and without courage there is no virtue.

In all life there is a thrust beyond the present. In man this thrust becomes conscious, becomes reason, becomes conscience. Fundamentally, reason is the capacity for forming general concepts—to leap beyond *this* present instance and *that* by conceiving universals. "Green" and "round" and "fast" and "reliable" are so many thrusts beyond the given, so many triumphs over the prison house of the present. General concepts can become goals and standards and reproaches: what I have drawn is not round; I want to run fast; you were not reliable. Conscience is born when reason makes aspiration self-conscious.

As soon as aspiration becomes self-conscious and conscience emerges, courage is needed. Without courage, aspiration is denied and conscience muted by inactivity, failure to try, sloth—the humility that is no virtue, meekness. Courage is vitality knowing the risks it runs.

Courage may participate in deeds that we do not admire; but even then the courage evokes admiration. Without cour-

[1] See "A Buddhist text," § 92 of my *Critique*. For Paul's conception of love, see §§ 58 and 61 above.

age, Odysseus would be sly, mean, and contemptible; because he has courage, he is one of mankind's most widely admired heroes to whom generations have looked up. Without courage, Coriolanus, Julius Caesar, Hamlet, Macbeth, and Othello would all lose what claims they have on our sympathies; it is courage that makes them heroes. There is no tragic hero without courage: every tragic poet demands sympathy and admiration for his hero by endowing him with exceptional courage. Even when allied with causes we detest, courage speaks to us, the voice of conscience, calling us from sloth and resignation, a reproach and an appeal.

The *fourth* virtue is honesty. Like courage, it enters into the other three. *Humbition* involves honestly facing our limitations and remembering what dishonesty always tempts us to forget: that we may be wrong. *Love* involves honestly facing what hurts: the sufferings of others that it would be more convenient not to notice, and the shortcomings of others that set bounds to hope and faith, shatter illusions, and invite despair. *Courage* involves honestly confronting risks: not to fear dangers of which one lacks awareness is not courage.

Is honesty, then, less basic than the other three? Or is it fundamental because without honesty there is no virtue? It would be idle to try to answer because honesty admits of so many degrees. A little honesty is so easy, so common, so unavoidable, it is hardly a virtue. But thorough honesty is the rarest and most difficult of all the virtues; and without that, each of the other three is somewhat deficient.

My conception of honesty, and of the crucial difference between honesty and sincerity, has already been explained in Chapter II. That thorough honesty is difficult and rare is the burden of this book. Lack of thorough honesty takes so many forms that it takes a book to explore even some typical ways. There is no devil; there is no need for one: dishonesty does his work.

Dishonesty says: My views are what I mean; yours are what you said.

Dishonesty says: You are doing all you can. You are better than your achievements and your conduct. You never had a chance. There is no use trying because all the cards are stacked against you. You lack the ability to make much of yourself. You are going to do great things, but not yet. You are never dishonest.

Dishonesty also says: Of course, you are an honest man, but this situation is exceptional. Of course, we do not approve of dishonesty, but when you try to clean up the government you cannot be fastidious; after all, he is doing a great job, and it serves them right, and it is good for the party, and he is one of us—and anybody who objects to his methods must have something to hide.

Dishonesty also says: Honesty in all honor, but anybody who questions the honesty of theologians must be an atheist; and atheists ought to have the decency to keep quiet. Honesty in all honor, but this is a time when positive, constructive thinking is needed more than anything else; we have had too much criticism as it is. And positive, constructive thinking is pleasant, uplifting balm for the weary soul.

On the contrary: the positive thinking of the false prophets who cry, "Peace, peace," when there is no peace, is soothing but hardly honest. As Moses and the prophets knew, one has to pluck up and break down before one can build and plant.

Whoever praises honesty will not be understood unless he explains what he means by dishonesty. Affirmations that imply no denials are meaningless. Moses and the prophets were constructive, and their moral affirmations ring through history. So do their criticisms, their negations, their impassioned condemnations.

Dishonesty approximates the mythical ubiquity of original sin. It finds expression in unnecessary complications that, even if not designed to look impressive to the gullible, help to deceive the writer, or the speaker, about his own lack of clarity and other weaknesses. It finds expression in the ostentatiously uncomplicated prose of those who oversimplify and give a false impression. It conceals itself behind a veil of false sophistication in the dictum that dishonesty is simply unavoidable. With that it returns to its favorite line: you are doing all you can.

84

These are my four cardinal virtues: humbition, love, courage, and honesty. As in Plato's four cardinal virtues, the last two enter into the other three. Wisdom, courage, and justice, as Plato conceived of them in the *Republic*, were instances of temperance, which he defined as the better element ruling the worse; and wisdom, courage, and temperance were instances of justice, which he defined as each performing his proper function. Yet only one of Plato's four appears in my list: courage. Are we justified in not including the other three?

Wisdom is a rare adornment but not properly a virtue. Moreover, what Plato, in the *Republic*, meant by wisdom was really a special kind of knowledge; it precluded the admission that one might be wrong; and it conferred the privilege—the monopoly—of deceiving men for their own good, which is a form of dishonesty. Wisdom so conceived is incompatible with my four virtues.

Temperance or moderation—what Plato calls *sophrosune*—may be understood as self-control. If so, it is implicit in my four virtues. But Plato's conception of self-discipline is relatively static: the better element rules over the worse, and the experts know once and for all what is better, what is worse. Reason, which has absolute knowledge, is better; appetite, worse. Those who lack absolute knowledge are incapable of attaining *sophrosune* unless they submit to the rule of their betters. So understood, *sophrosune* is not one of my virtues.

Justice is the crown not only of Plato's virtues but also of the ethic of the prophets. Can we omit justice? Plato understood justice as each performing his proper function. He thought each man had a proper function, and he believed it would be nothing short of a disaster if a shoemaker should try his hand at soldiering, or a lens grinder at philosophy. He did not suppose, like Manu, that a man's place in society could always be determined by heredity: experts might recognize occasional exceptions and assign a man a function that had not been that of his fathers. But each man was made for one job and must stick to that. My view of man is different, and I have no qualms about rejecting Plato's justice from my set of virtues.

There are other conceptions of justice: "You shall have one law for the stranger and for the native." With this Mosaic conception of justice I not only have no quarrel; I consider it one of the greatest advances in human history. But equality before the law is not, strictly speaking, a virtue. It is not on the same level with courage, love, and honesty.

Still, should I not try to be just as an individual in my dealings with others? Should I not treat like cases alike? No two cases are entirely alike. "That is a subterfuge: justice consists in disregarding inequalities that are irrelevant." But what is relevant? Does justice know what is and what is not? "Take desegregation: is that not an issue that calls simply for justice?" Let us see how it would fare if left to my four virtues.

Humbition would begin by admitting ignorance about many pertinent considerations, without being resigned to ignorance. Instead of pitting doctrinaire stand against doctrinaire stand, it would begin by admitting that one's preconceptions might be wrong and by inviting relevant instruction. It would not begin on the assumption that I, being white, am superior to the man whose skin is black: to assume that would hardly be humility.

Love would perceive and share the other human being's hurt and grief. It might also assume responsibility and be willing to make sacrifices to help. Without believing all things and hoping all things, without expecting the millennium from a piece of legislation and without giving up because there will be no millennium, love persists.

Courage does not shrink from danger, does not hide from risks in sloth and resignation, even if they are concealed behind the name of prudence. If lack of humbition, lack of love, and lack of courage do not fully account for the injustice inflicted on the Negro, dishonesty remains.

How much falsehood, hypocrisy, and self-deception permeate the cause of segregation! Dishonesty says: The blacks are perfectly happy. They really like to be kept in their place. There is no use trying because all the cards are stacked against you. This situation is exceptional. And when bogus science, false statistics, slander, and all else fail, it says: You are doing all you can.

There is no need here for an additional virtue of justice. In this particular case, moreover, the course of virtue is also the course of self-interest. It is clearly in the white men's most urgent interest that the colored boys and girls of Mississippi, Arkansas, and Louisiana, of the northern states, and of Africa, too, should get just as good an education as possible before it is too late. The most precious opportunities have been missed for decades. Now lack of humility, of love, of courage, and of honesty would make the worst of a dreadful situation by recourse to tyranny, suppression, and violence, thus ensuring, albeit unwittingly, that the slightly delayed explosion will be a complete disaster.

Then take another example: a teacher grading his students. Must we not introduce justice as a virtue in this case? Surely, he ought to treat like cases alike. But in this situation honesty suffices. To call excellent a paper that is not excellent, or to rank in the bottom quarter a student who deserves better, is dishonest.

There are more difficult cases. Suppose a sheriff is in charge of a prisoner, and a lynch mob approaches. Courage alone cannot tell him what to do, though chances are that if he acts dishonorably it will be from want of courage. Suppose he honestly wonders what the path of virtue might be. Could humbition, love, courage, or honesty tell him? The sacrifice of one man's happiness might make many people happy. Might not love lead him, then, to surrender the prisoner, humbly and honestly stating his reasons? And if he did that, should we not consider him anything but a model of virtue? However clear and strong our feelings in this matter may be, this is an exceptionally difficult case to analyze—a classical case adduced against utilitarianism.

It is not at all clear that including justice among our cardinal virtues would help. If justice means treating like cases alike, the sheriff might say that in all cases in which a hanging without due process made the majority of his constituents happy, he always handed over the prisoner. If we assume that this is contrary to his oath of office, his crime would be a matter of dishonesty.

Somehow, that does not get to the root of the matter. But it is difficult to say *what* virtue he would be lacking, even if he had far more than four or five to choose from. I think the objection to his conduct would be twofold. First, his view of man would be degrading. He would regard the prisoner as a mere thing that can be mutilated for pleasure, and he would look on the members of the mob as on a pack of dogs. Second —and this point is closely related to the first—he would harm both the prisoner and the members of the mob, indeed the whole community. His action would not be in their interest even though, *ex hypothesi,* they would enjoy themselves. But if these are really our two basic objections, this means that the sheriff would be lacking in humbition and love. His failure would be that he was resigned to man's being a mere beast, and that he did not know love which plainly does not mean that one gratifies every beastly whim of those one loves. It does mean, as was said before, to sense men's "wants and to bear their grief." And honesty involves facing the short-comings of those one loves. And humbition says: Judge, that you may be judged. If the sheriff had these virtues, and courage, too, he *would* deserve our admiration.

None of this is meant to depreciate justice, any more than one would depreciate love or courage by pointing out that they are individual virtues and not the business of the legis-lator. Justice, conversely, is preeminently a social virtue which must be of central concern to legislators. And the difficulty of the case just considered arises in part from the fact that we do not know what the laws in that community are sup-posed to be. *Laws* surely *can* be unjust, and this is what one criticizes them for; one does not criticize them for wanting love, courage, or honesty.

If handing over the prisoner was against the law, as is usually assumed in this example, then the sheriff would be guilty of dishonesty if he accepted the job with the intention of breaking the law, and guilty of cowardice if he merely gave in to the mob. But if there was an inhumane law that allowed the populace to do as they wished with certain kinds of prisoners, the question would arise whether the sheriff himself considered this practice inhuman. If he did but complied, he lacked courage. If he did not, he lacked love and had low standards of honesty. We can deal with this case without introducing justice as an individual virtue.

Much of what I have found in the Old Testament and in Plato has prevailed through subsequent encounters with objections and alternatives, but not the ideal of a just man. In both Hebrew and Greek, the words translated as "just" are often inclusive encomia, almost like our own "good"; and translators have therefore sometimes spoken of a "righteous man." Surely, Socrates, whom Plato at the end of the *Phaedo* calls "the wisest and justest and best" man of his time, was not outstanding in anything we today should call justice—say, in always treating like cases alike. But he did reach rare heights of humbition, honesty, and courage. And in the Old Testament the word for justice, *sedakah,* also often means merciful love and hence came to mean alms, among other things, in later times.

That justice, in English, is not a virtue on the same plane with honesty, courage, and love is also indicated by the fact that Plato's superlative goes against our grain: we should not say "juster" or "justest," though we should not hesitate to say "more honest," "most courageous," or "more loving," or to speak of "greater love."

The similarity between the Old Testament and Plato, and our difference from both, can be pinpointed. Justice was for them the sum of the virtues because it meant conformity to law, though not necessarily to the laws made by men: their conception of the just man depends on what later came to be known as "natural law." This conception depends on the belief that the universe is governed by a benign purpose. When that belief is abandoned, the ideal of the "just" man must be abandoned, too.

While the belief in a cosmic purpose is a necessary condition for the belief in natural law, it is clearly not a sufficient condition: most Protestants do not believe in natural law. My objections to any attempt to base morality on natural law have been spelled out earlier in this chapter, and Chapters V and VI are relevant to this question, too; but it should be noted that other writers have raised many additional objections against the conception of natural law.

85

My four virtues cannot be proved. Whoever claims to prove his ethic deceives others and probably also himself. Are these virtues, then, intuited? Does the appeal to specific cases mean that my virtues are based on a moral sense that all but moral idiots have? Moral intuitionism has enjoyed a vogue in England; but, characteristically, it was also a Briton who wrote the most devastating satire on it: Lord Keynes in "My Early Beliefs."

"How did we know what states of mind were good? This was a matter of direct inspection, of direct unanalysable intuition about which it was useless and impossible to argue. In that case who was right when there was a difference of opinion? . . . It might be that some people had an acuter sense of judgment, just as some people can judge a vintage port and others cannot. On the whole, so far as I remember, this explanation prevailed. In practice, victory was with those who could speak with the greatest appearance of clear, undoubting conviction and could best use the accents of infallibility. [G. E.] Moore at this time was a master of this method—greeting one's remarks with a gasp of incredulity— Do you *really* think *that,* an expression of face as if to hear such a thing said reduced him to a state of wonder verging on imbecility, with his mouth wide open and wagging his head in the negative so violently that his hair shook. *Oh!* he would say, goggling at you as if either you or he must be mad; and no reply was possible."

Such an attitude is widespread indeed in discussions of moral matters. If one finds in it a lack of humility and a pretension to knowledge in cases where one does not have knowledge, and if one also renounces any possibility of *proving* one's ethic, is one reduced to relativism? Must one agree with the intuitionist that there is no disputing of tastes, adding only that one taste is as good as another? Far from it.

Once again, as at the end of Chapter III, we are confronted with Scylla, the rock that thinks that she alone is right, and Charybdis, the whirlpool that supposes that all views are equally defensible. In morality, as in religion and philosophy and other fields, both are wrong. Both make things very easy for themselves: they avoid the hard task of examining alternatives, criticizing what is open to objections, finding gradually what prevails and stands up. Near the end of Chapter IV, Jean-Paul Sartre's "Portrait of the Anti-Semite" was quoted—a picture not merely of racial prejudice but of Scylla: "The rational man seeks the truth gropingly. . . . But there are people who are attracted by the durability of stone. They want to be massive and impenetrable, they do not want to change. . . ." Charybdis is equally slothful and timid: by admitting once and for all that all views are equally acceptable, she escapes the onus of examining either her own views or others. But what is the alternative?

An ethic cannot be proved; to be held responsibly, it has to be based on encounter upon encounter. This notion of encounter is of the utmost philosophic importance. It makes possible safe passage between the untenable claim of proof and the unwarranted charge of irrationality. A position may be rational though it cannot be deduced from universally accepted premises, and a man may be rational without claiming that his views, his ethic, or his faith are susceptible of such proof.

The pose of Socrates, always willing to subject any view to objections, was that of the rational man *par excellence*. I say, the *pose*, because in the heat of argument Socrates' procedure was by no means always a model of rationality, if Plato's early dialogues give a fair picture. At times, for example, Socrates succumbed to the delightful temptation of making fools of his opponents and took advantage of personal weaknesses. Moreover, he affected ignorance, if only ironically, and claimed to have no views of his own. But there is no reason why a man in quest of honesty, fighting irrationality, should not have his own views, or ethic, or faith, provided only he is willing to subject them to encounter on encounter.

Still, what are the reasons for the four virtues suggested here? One must begin by replying: What are the reasons for any set of virtues, whether Plato's, Paul's, yours, or those of some solid bourgeois? I do not mean that all tables of virtues are equally good. But to ask simply, "Why faith, hope, and love?" or "Why wisdom, courage, temperance, and justice?" is not to ask seriously. To ask seriously, one has to ask specifically, offering some objection to one or another virtue, and one must be willing to consider the ramifications of abandoning it. Instead of asking: Why honesty? one should ask: What can be said against honesty? and what would it be like to consider dishonesty a virtue, or at least permissible? and what would a society be like in which honesty would not be considered a virtue?

Negative thinking is essential for the reasons just indicated: it is what saves us from relativism. One has to show in what ways alternative suggestions are untenable, lest one be taken to say what the author of an influential book on *Nietzsche: Attempt at a Mythology* said succinctly: "Suffice it that the figure of Nietzsche was at least once envisaged thus." If one is not content to offer just another mythology, or a view that is at most as good as some other long-accepted views, one must show where the accepted views fail.

It is more popular, and easier, to proceed in the opposite direction: to begin by proposing one's own "philosophy" and then to judge other views from there, externally. In that case, other views are rarely taken seriously; one generally has not really exposed oneself to them; there have been no genuine encounters.

I wrote a book on Nietzsche after finding previous interpretations inadequate: as they did not do justice to the evidence, I tried to do better. In religion and morality, similarly, I did not begin with my own outlook and then repudiate whatever conflicted with it. I began by accepting old ideas, found difficulties, then developed some criticisms—and eventually asked myself: What, then, can I believe?

It does not follow that as much as possible has been done

in these pages to defend my table of virtues. But perhaps enough has been said to commend them for serious consideration and discussion, and to make clear that I do not claim to *know* that these are the true virtues.

Those who claim to base their values on direct, unanalyzable intuition are like the Protestants who claim to base theirs on the Bible after they have introduced a few haphazard changes into the morality on which they were brought up (§ 75 above). What is beheld in such a direct intuition is the result, so far, of a long process that one has not the least wish to examine. If one wants to be rational instead of rendering all argument "useless and impossible," to use Lord Keynes' phrase, one has to recapitulate the process, though not necessarily in its original sequence. One has to expose oneself—and those whom one wants to persuade rationally of the merits of one's own position—to objections and replies and to encounters with alternatives.

Humility and honesty do not dictate our saying: I am probably wrong; what is the use? That is the course of meekness, sloth, and cowardice. Honest humbition says: This is my view; I may be wrong, though I do not see in what way; but if you offer informed criticisms or objections, I am eager to consider them. Tolstoy put the matter very beautifully when he answered those who excommunicated him; and the relevant part of his answer will be found among the mottoes at the beginning of this book.

Value judgments can be informed or uninformed, responsible or irresponsible. They cannot be perfectly rational any more than a man can be perfectly honest, or an action perfectly courageous; but they can be more or less rational, and the differences may be considerable and deserve emphasis.

A man who does not consider how his actions are likely to affect other people is to that extent irresponsible, even if he acts on "principle." Moral judgments on specific actions are also irresponsible insofar as they are passed in ignorance of the background, the interests involved, and the probable consequences—even if such judgments appeal to "principle." The principles themselves may be held in a more or less informed, responsible—and in this case one might well add, rational—

manner. To be responsible and rational in such matters, one must consider what can be said against one's moral principles and standards. The man who gives no thought to objections and alternatives is, to that extent, irrational. But if one considers the codes of different religions and societies, the arguments of outstanding philosophers, relevant plays and novels, and concrete situations as well, moral judgments based on such reflection are, to that extent, informed, responsible, and rational.

Few undertakings could be more difficult, and any complete success is plainly out of the question. Hence, good philosophers, who value thoroughness, prefer solid work in well-defined fields. In those who are not scholars, on the other hand, the very understandable desire to escape exposure to so many different views sometimes has recourse to protests against annoying erudition or detail. Intuition, whether secular or sacred, is much simpler and less arduous. So is relativism, whether secular or holy.

Holy relativism has "a great respect for organized religion, no matter what shape it takes" and advocates "a deeply felt religious faith—and I don't care what it is." Like secular relativism, it exhorts us to be peaceful and agreeable and not to exert our minds: If you will lull your critical intelligence to sleep, I shall not trouble mine either. Or, to cite Eisenhower once more: "What American is entitled to criticize the accomplishment of 180,000,000 others?"[2] Imagine Socrates' or Jeremiah's reply to these comfortable words.

As a last resort, those who would rather avoid sustained exposure to the slings and arrows of diversity may raise the charge of eclecticism. But I have tried to show elsewhere why I abhor eclecticism and how what I have in mind differs from it.[3]

Is honesty dangerous? Most greatly worth-while things are —love, for example, and courage. It is also worth asking whether *opposition* to honesty is not dangerous. Once we de-

---

[2] New York *Times*, October 29, 1960, front page: In a speech, presumably not written by Eisenhower himself, "the President interpolated this question."

[3] *Critique*, § 93: "Against eclecticism."

cide to be dishonest with our children, our students, or our readers, we have a vested interest in suppressing honesty, in censorship. It would be most embarrassing if other parents, teachers, or writers should teach truths that we have tried to hide. The dangers of a low regard for honesty can also be illustrated by the phenomenal success of Senator Joe McCarthy. His influence was due primarily to the fact that honesty was widely held in such low esteem—and, next to that, to a lack of courage in high and low places, and, like almost all cruelty, to a lack of love.

Surely, many people say, one cannot be honest with children in matters of sex and religion. Why not? If honesty entailed giving people information for which they had not expressed the least desire—perhaps even giving all men all information at all times—it would not only be impossible of attainment but an absurd ideal, and the man that approximated it would hardly deserve admiration. It does not show a low regard for honesty if one does not make the rounds of the local hospital every evening, looking for old women about to die, so one can deprive them of their faith before it is too late. We need not give children lectures on subjects about which they have not asked us or give them answers that we ourselves consider untrue in answer to questions they *have* asked. When you answer your child and tell him falsehoods, you undermine your relationship, you cannot expect the child to be honest with you, and you inculcate a low regard for honesty. If on the other hand you give a truthful answer, indicating the limits of your own knowledge or points on which intelligent people do not agree, occasionally explaining, if the child remains interested, how different people might answer that question, without laboring your own view unless the child presses you for yours, this will rarely do harm.

Perhaps responsibility or rationality, as understood in this chapter, should be called a virtue and replace honesty? After all, a man might reach a decision by honestly flipping a coin! But we should not say that he was lacking in virtue or irresponsible if he chose this method for deciding, say, between two desserts. His procedure would be objectionable only in cases in which it showed a lack of love or, less frequently perhaps, a lack of humbition, courage, or honesty. He might not consider the impact of his decision on other human beings; or he might take the easy way out, showing a lack of ambition or courage, being fearful, for example, of what careful reflection might make him aware of; and he might generally prefer not to think, not to know, not to be honest. If so, my table of virtues suffices.

Virtues are habits that one can cultivate. What is less obvious is that emotions, appetites, and conscience can be cultivated—or uncultivated—too; and that what is pleasurable is also subject to education. This is often overlooked by moral philosophers who would base their ethics on emotions, appetites, conscience, or pleasure. What gives pleasure, how men feel, what they want, and what their consciences say, is morally interesting, but it can never be morally decisive. For these phenomena are all subject to training, and the question always remains how one should train oneself and one's children. Hence, the argument for a set of four virtues cannot take the form of an appeal to such spurious authorities. It must take the form of considering the ramifications both of these virtues and of alternative sets, and of seeing what can be said against each.

Might not a different set be as good or superior? Produce one, and we can consider it. My criticisms of the New Testament conception of love and of faith—and of hope, in Chapter XII—are not digs, or offered from the security of my own position; they precede my position and, autobiographically speaking, established the need for it.

Are there not other virtues more important than the four defended here? As Tolstoy said: "Should I find such a one, I shall at once accept it." What about a sense of humor? Like wisdom, it is a great gift; but a virtue? More likely than not, it is an epiphenomenon of my four virtues; particularly of humbition and honesty. While humbition consists of humility and ambition, there is also an overtone of humor in it.

86

Is this ethic existentialist? This label would be misleading. Jaspers, Heidegger, and Sartre have not developed any ethics, and on many ideas that the existentialists have developed I disagree with them, as will be shown in Chapter XII.[4] Moreover, few of Sartre's ideas are better known than some remarks he made on ethics in his celebrated lecture, "Existentialism Is a Humanism"; and these remarks strike me as patently ill considered and quite unacceptable. If they could be said to represent the ethic of existentialism, my ethic would certainly be much more radical.

Sartre said: "To choose between this or that is at the same time to affirm the value of that which is chosen; for we are unable ever to choose the worse. What we choose is always the better; and nothing can be better for us unless it is better for all." In every significant sense, we *are* able to choose the worse, and what we choose is *not* always the better. To be sure, there is a sense in which choosing something proves that we *consider* it better. Still, other people may consider it worse; we ourselves may have thought only a moment before that it was worse and may return to that view immediately after; our momentarily preferring it may have been due to patent confusion or a mistaken view of the facts. It is also possible for a man to choose something because he considers it worse. Dostoevsky's Underground man is an example of such perversity. But in such cases one could maintain that by preferring the worse, a man shows that he considers the worse as better in some sense.

All this is relatively academic. It may only go to show that the whole passage was not well thought out. Certainly, it is not a fair sample of Sartre's thought; and it is worth mentioning only because these remarks on ethics are so well known and so widely discussed.

The most objectionable part of Sartre's statement, as quoted

[4] See also *From Shakespeare to Existentialism*.

so far, is the final sentence: "Nothing can be better for us unless it is better for all." Coming from a thinker steeped in Gide and Nietzsche, who devoted so much of their work to disproving this view, this sentence is astonishing.

The lecture was designed, as Sartre declares in the opening sentence, "to offer a defence of existentialism against several reproaches that have been laid against it." Sartre's emphasis on individual choice had given rise to the charge that existentialism was irresponsible. The objectionable sentence introduces Sartre's attempt to show that "our responsibility is thus much greater than we had supposed, for it concerns mankind as a whole." But this attempt fails, as is readily seen by considering Sartre's own example: "If, to take a more personal case, I decide to marry and have children, even though this decision proceeds simply from my situation, from my passion or my desire, I am thereby committing not only myself, but humanity as a whole, to the practice of monogamy. I am thus responsible for myself and for all men, and I am creating a certain image of man as I would have him to be. In fashioning myself I fashion man."

That is fine rhetoric and a noble conclusion; but if I marry one wife I am not necessarily implying that monogamy "is better for all." It is not irrational or irresponsible to propose to make a go of it with this one wife, without any wish whatever to limit men who have more money or different desires, or who find themselves in quite a different situation or environment, "to the practice of monogamy." Just as in having two children I need not object to other couples' having either no children at all or one, or three, or more, so I might not object to other men's marrying not at all or, if they and the women concerned like it, more than one wife.

When we consider choosing a profession or writing a book, the point is still more obvious. When I elect to become a philosopher, I certainly do not imply that such a career "is better for all." I might even prefer being a great composer or a Michelangelo, but may have found that I lack the necessary talents. That does not mean that others, more fortunate than I, should become philosophers; or that others who happen to lack whatever gifts I might have ought to follow my example.

Before writing a book, should I ask myself whether I should want all men to write the book I plan to write? Of course I don't want that. In his attempt to meet the charge of irresponsibility, Sartre sought refuge in what seems to be an improvised, attenuated Kantianism, modeled on Kant's first formulation of his categorical imperative (§ 77 above). There is a literature on this question of universalizing maxims and no need to add to it here. The point is that Sartre does not consider even the most obvious objections. But this is not Sartre at his best. (Too much of Sartre is not Sartre at his best. But his best is most impressive; for example, but not only, "Portrait of the Anti-Semite" and *The Wall, No Exit,* and *The Flies.* The ethic of Orestes in *The Flies* is far superior to the better-known remarks considered here.)

Responsibility does not consist in legislating for humanity, if only in my own mind. It consists in honestly confronting objections and alternatives. Choosing an ethic without doing that is irresponsible—doubly so if we claim that "nothing can be better for us unless it is better for all."

Sartre is right, of course, that if I propose—and I do—that humanity would be the better for adopting my four virtues as goals, my responsibility is increased. But few of my choices are so prodigious. And what saves my ethic from being anarchic and irresponsible is not portentousness or the sweep of its claims but only the attention given to objections and alternatives.

The motifs my ethic shares with existentialism include emphasis on courage, on which existentialism does not have any monopoly, and the concern with honesty and self-deception. French existentialism excels in its vivisections of the latter. Above all, some existentialists have faced up to the human condition in our time.

About 1825, Hegel could still say in his lectures: "The morality of the individual consists in this, that he fulfills the duties of his station; and these are easy to know. . . . To inquire what our duties might be is useless rumination; in the tendency to consider morality something difficult we may recognize the desire to dodge one's duties. . . . Civic life constitutes the basis of duty; each individual has his occupation and the duties that go with it; and morality consists in behaving accordingly." Hegel added: "Every individual is the son of his people at a certain stage in the development of this people"; and he noted further that some ages are marked by "great collisions between the old, recognized duties, laws, and rights and, on the other hand, possibilities that stand opposed to this system, violate it, even destroy its basis," and yet also "appear good" (72–75).

Hegel lived at the end of an age when, as he himself once remarked, "a form of life has grown old." The era that followed and includes our time is one of "great collisions." F. H. Bradley (1846–1924) still wrote a remarkable essay on "My Station and Its Duties," but he also returned again and again to the theme of "collisions," long familiar to tragic poets. In the field of reflective literature, however, it is preeminently Kierkegaard and Sartre that call attention to the experience of moral quandaries.

Those, whether white or black, who live in Africa or in the American South, no longer find it "easy to know" their duties; and in many moral questions most thoughtful people are sometimes perplexed by the collision of different traditions. Neither "civic life" nor religion can tell us what to do: too many traditions would have us do different things.

Hegel wanted to raise philosophy to the level of science, which to him meant rigor, system, and knowledge. The immense advances in the sciences during the past century *have* increased knowledge; they have also spread the habit of questioning authoritative statements, of asking for evidence and reasons, and of weighing alternatives. In morality, the authority of the many conflicting traditions that confront us has become questionable and can no longer quiet our quandaries. A thoughtful individual can no longer help developing his own ethic.

One can go about this haphazardly or obstinately; irresponsibly or, as far as possible, rationally. Insofar as existentialism opposes reason and fails to understand the nature of responsibility, I stand opposed to it. But I do not propose some new orthodoxy, as if it mattered that there should be exactly four cardinal virtues. I offer *four* virtues to be precise and concise, and to facilitate reflection.

This is one way, the best I have found. It does not obviate all collisions, and I shall return to this question in the Epilogue. Conceivably, moreover, the same implications might follow from another set of virtues; or another set might have divergent implications that, upon reflection, I, too, should prefer. Mine is no absolute morality but the ethic of a heretic.

XI

Freud and the Tragic Virtues

87

Is greatness possible in our time? Are the virtues of humbition, love, courage, and honesty goals that defy all achievement, or could one point to a human being who embodied them? Preferably not the hero of a play or novel, nor a figure of the past shrouded in legend, but a man of our century whose life is fully documented. Perhaps even a heretic. Or is the belief in greatness incompatible with honesty, and especially with the youngest child of honesty: psychology?

Freud, even more than Lincoln, might well be called the Great Emancipator. Like no man before him, he lent substance to the notion that all men are brothers. Criminals and madmen are not devils in disguise but men and women who have problems similar to our own, and there, but for one experience or another, go you and I.

Without any wish to do so, Freud also confirmed many millions in the comfortable notion that the great are really no different from the small—indeed, that there are no great men. To be sure, there are great scientists and people who achieve great things. Ideas, theories, and engineering feats are readily called great; discoveries and exploits—successes, in one word—are great; but human beings are supposed to be essentially alike, and it is considered unsophisticated and undemocratic to suppose that a man, instead of merely *doing* something great, *is* great, regardless of success or failure.

A hundred and fifty years ago, Hegel, the philosopher, and Goethe, the poet, remarked that no man is a hero to his valet —not because there are no heroes, but because valets are valets. Now that few valets are left and the intimate failings of men of distinction have become the business of the psychoanalysts, one may well ask whether this quip fits them, or whether there really are no heroes.

Freud himself believed in great men. But, before considering his attitude, it may be well to lend more substance to the notion of the human being who is great apart from any success—in fact, great in failure. There is a form of literature that is specifically dedicated to such greatness: tragedy. Tragic heroes fail by definition, but the tragedy depends on the conviction that the hero in his failure is still—indeed, more than ever—nobler than the rest of us. In Shakespeare's two greatest tragedies, *Hamlet* and *Lear,* the hero neither has done nor does anything that raises him above most men; and yet there is somehow the presumption, quite unwarranted by their accomplishments, that Lear and Hamlet are superior, particularly when they are about to die.

English literature since Shakespeare represents a variety of escapes from tragedy. For 300 years after Shakespeare, not a single great tragedy was written in English. The major poets shut their eyes to the terrors of existence and took refuge in contrivance: the metaphysical poets contrived "conceits," and Milton, Blake, and Yeats, mythologies. One did not make a fuss about one's pains—not until the romantics came along and contrived a special language for such themes, worlds removed from the spontaneous power of Shakespearean outbursts of emotion.

Shakespeare had no heirs in England. His wit, which suggests the writer's emergence from the abyss rather than an escape from the brink, was taken up by Goethe and Heine, by Kierkegaard and Nietzsche, and by Gide. In British literature, wit became cleverness and part of the refusal to dwell on the tragic. One knows those things exist, but one doesn't make a point of them.

In the United States one did not have to be quite so genteel during the first hundred years, but there was no stage. Melville's Captain Ahab is a tragic hero even so, and the influence of Shakespeare is writ large all over *Moby Dick.* Again, the author's feeling for his hero is not warranted by any great accomplishment but lavished on a character that is outstanding in its uncompromising courage, its defiant obstinacy, and its proud contempt for popularity.

It is not the fault of the psychologists that many college teachers are no longer sure that Ahab is the hero of the book —he lacks love, and some teachers are not comfortable in his presence—and some critics even argue that the fact that Ishmael survives may show that he, having learned love, is the real hero. By the same token, Hamlet may yet be dismissed, and Horatio may be called the real hero.

It is partly the American infatuation with success that stands in the way of our having tragedies. It is well known that the Puritans closed the British theaters; it is less well understood that Calvin's ethos dealt tragedy a much more lasting blow by preaching success and lack of sympathy for failure.

The Puritan, as Tawney describes him in *Religion and the Rise of Capitalism,* saw "in the poverty of those who fall by the way, not a misfortune to be pitied and relieved, but a moral failing to be condemned, and in riches . . . the blessing which rewards the triumph of energy and will" (191). Tawney also points to "the suggestion of Puritan moralists, that practical success is at once the sign and the reward of ethical superiority" (221). Richard Niebuhr gives a similar picture in *The Social Sources of Denominationalism* (87).

Such ideas are a far cry from Jesus' view that "it is easier for a camel to go through the eye of a needle than for a rich man to enter the kingdom of God" (Luke 18:25). Even so, the ethic of Jesus, too, is incompatible with tragedy because the Gospels also insist that virtue will be rewarded, albeit in the other world; that suffering in this world is not tragic because it will not last long and is unimportant; and that eternal misery in the other world is not tragic because it is richly deserved and merits no compassion. Even if the matter of compassion were debatable, the crucial element of respect for the man who fails is certainly lacking: there is no possibility of considering him greater than most men who do not fail.

Traditional Christianity did not depart from these untragic, anti-tragic views and hence produced no tragedies. For the traditional Christian, failure is either an episode or eternal, and in neither case tragic, for it is sinful to admire the damned. Nor is Christ's passion a tragedy, and Bach, for example, in what may well be the two most sublime treatments of that story since the Gospels, did not misrepresent it that way. Understanding its doctrinal significance and the essential significance of the resurrection, he treated the passion story as a glorious epic.

To return to Calvin, he emphasized the anti-tragic doctrines of Christianity with simple clarity—for example, but by no means only, in his *Institutes* (III.24.17): "The reprobate are hated by God, and that most justly, because, being destitute of his Spirit, they can do nothing but what is deserving of his curse."

There is no need here to treat further of the relationship of Christianity to tragedy, as I have explored this elsewhere.[1] What matters here is that the prevalent attitude toward greatness has changed not only since Shakespeare's time but even since Freud's. This recent change is certainly not due primarily to Christian influences; it owes more to Freud's work.

This is ironical because Freud not only believed in great men but, his own modest self-estimates notwithstanding, was himself a great man. So we can contrast his own outlook with the now popular outlook that invokes his name; and I shall also juxtapose my own estimate of Freud's greatness with that of America's most popular psychoanalyst.

88

Freud had a sense for tragedy and believed that greatness was not a function of success. In a letter to Ludwig Binswanger, April 14, 1912, he wrote: "It always seemed to me that

[1] *Critique*, § 77; §§ 3–4 of the introduction to *Goethe's Faust: A New Translation* (with reference to the Faust theme); *Religion from Tolstoy to Camus* (the claim that *Anna Karenina* is a Christian tragedy); and *From Shakespeare to Existentialism*, Chapters 1–3 (Chapter 3 deals with some of the problems that psychology poses for tragedy).

self-reliance and a self-confidence that is simply taken for granted were the indispensable conditions of that which, after it has led to success, appears to us as greatness; and I think further that greatness of achievement must be distinguished from greatness of personality."

Freud always admired nobility far above success. Late in life, he wrote Arnold Zweig, the novelist, speaking of Nietzsche: "In my youth he signified a nobility which I could not attain. A friend of mine, Dr. Paneth, had got to know him . . . and he used to write me about him" (Jones, III, 459 f.). We know what Paneth wrote his fiancée about Nietzsche (the relevant passages are cited in my *From Shakespeare to Existentialism*, 324): he emphasized Nietzsche's humility, his ambition, his courage, and his honesty. When these letters were written, early in 1884, and Freud, then in his twenties, thrilled to Nietzsche's unattainable nobility, Nietzsche was in no sense whatsoever a success. Pleading his ill health, he had resigned his professorship at Basel while still in his thirties, and he was publishing a book a year without creating any stir at all. But the image of Nietzsche evoked in Paneth's letters evidently exerted a formative influence on the young Freud, who soon developed the same qualities.

Freud, like Nietzsche, defied the indifference, hostility, and smug complacency of those who ridiculed him or ignored him without reading him. Both also defied a rarely rivaled crescendo of agonies, devoting themselves to their work as long as any strength at all was left them. They prized courage above pleasure, honesty above popularity, and integrity above success. Neither of them expected or desired the least reward. There was something Stoic about both of them, especially about their attitude toward pain; but on occasion both displayed the passion of the prophets, and Nietzsche's modesty and never failing kindness in his personal relations with the simple people among whom he lived in Switzerland and Italy while writing, and his vitriolic wit, and Freud's usually less acid humor and his warm affection for his children and grandchildren are remote from Stoicism.

There are several biographies of Freud. Even if it were only on account of its massive documentation, Ernest Jones' three-volume *The Life and Work of Sigmund Freud* would dominate the field. Moreover, Jones was the dean of British psychoanalysts and very close to Freud for over thirty years before he saved Freud's life in 1938, by getting him out of Austria soon after the Nazis entered Vienna. Based on intimate knowledge of Freud's personality, his works, his letters, unpublished material, and the whole literature about him, Jones' work is unquestionably our best source for Freud's life and character.

Jones' psychoanalytic interpretations of Freud's character are, ironically, the feeblest part of his work. When he tries to explain Freud's genius, he becomes ridiculous:

"There was his half-brother Philipp . . . whom he suspected of being his mother's mate and whom he tearfully begged not to make his mother again pregnant. Could one trust such a man, who evidently knew all the secrets, to tell the truth about them? It would be a curious trick of fate if this insignificant little man—he is said to have ended up as a peddler—has through his mere existence proved to have fortuitously struck the spark that lit the future Freud's determination to trust himself alone, to resist the impulse to believe in others more than in himself, and in that way to make imperishable the name of Freud."

Thus ends Volume 2. But when Jones forgets about such attempts at explanation and records the story of Freud's sixteen years of cancer, how he suffered thirty-three facial operations, was in almost constant pain, but worked, remaining dedicated and humane until the end, and when Jones quotes Freud's own remarks and letters, then we feel that we are face to face with greatness. No success could possibly command as much respect as the old seeker's fortitude and honesty, his mixture of humility and pride, his contempt for "the hubbub on all sides of a popularity that I find repellent," and the unique way in which he blended heroism and nobility with warmth and humor. If all his theories were wrong, one feels, he would still be one of the great men of all time, one of the few who made themselves into enduring images of humanity.

Oddly perhaps, Freud's greatness emerges most clearly when the attitude of his biographer is, as it were, pre-

Freudian. Surely, the most obvious way to communicate greatness is to let a man's life, actions, and words speak for themselves, resisting any impulse to explain.

A fine example of an effort of this sort is Norman Malcolm's *Ludwig Wittgenstein: A Memoir*. Wittgenstein's pupil and first successor to his chair at Cambridge, Georg Henrik von Wright, says in his "Biographical Sketch," which prefaces Malcolm's memoir: "It is probably true that he lived on the border of mental illness. A fear of being driven across it followed him throughout his life." But neither he nor Malcolm tries his hand at amateur psychology. Both consider Wittgenstein a hero and let the facts and some of his remarks in conversation and some of his letters speak for themselves. There is no effort to omit what might put Wittgenstein into a dubious light. Malcolm tells of the man whom he remembers—a man who was not comfortable company, a man much too intense for comfort, a man sometimes clearly in the wrong—a man who struck the writer as more memorable, noble, haunting than the other men and women he has met. Without any attempt at explanation, he allows us to encounter a great man.

This, it may be objected, is a pre-Freudian approach, now dated and no longer honest. We today, it may be said, cannot in candor stop short with a mere description. Freud himself, to be sure, might not have agreed with this objection. In the very letter in which he told Arnold Zweig how Nietzsche had once signified for him "a nobility which I could not attain," Freud expresses serious doubts about Zweig's plan to write a book on Nietzsche and, in general, about the possibility of reconstructing and unraveling his psychical processes and motives. But perhaps we must at this point go beyond Freud, taking full advantage of his work and that of his successors.

89

That is the aim of Erich Fromm, America's most popular psychoanalyst, both in his earlier, more scholarly books and in his recent tracts on *The Art of Loving* and *Sigmund Freud's Mission*. Fromm is a master of titles, but these two are a bit misleading, and the central aim of the second book is really to explain Freud by laying bare, as Fromm says on the first page, "the driving forces in him which made him act, think and feel in the particular way he did." In ten chapters of about ten pages each, Fromm, with confident assurance, reveals all—or all that fits his theses.

Like many another critic of Freud, Fromm argues that the master was a little simple-minded, that he tried mistakenly to explain everything in terms of sex, and that he overlooked the vast importance of cultural differences. We gather that in our time and culture, sex and other such unedifying matters are not so important as the master thought, and that what we need today is some good, old-fashioned preaching—for example, on *The Art of Loving*.

Nietzsche, to whom the early Fromm owed a good deal, said in his *Genealogy of Morals*—and Freud would surely have agreed wholeheartedly:

"Why stroke the hypersensitive ears of our modern weaklings? Why yield even a single step . . . to the Tartuffery of words? For us psychologists that would involve a Tartuffery of *action* . . . For a psychologist today shows his good taste (others may say his integrity) in this, if in anything, that he resists the shamefully *moralized* manner of speaking which makes all modern judgments about men and things slimy."

This quotation throws much more light on Freud's attitude toward Jung and Adler and some other men who broke with him, and toward Breuer, with whom he broke, than does Fromm's claim that Freud's "pride made him repress the awareness of dependency and negate it completely by breaking off the friendship when the friend failed in the complete fulfillment of the motherly role." In this context, Fromm, who had been harsh on Jung to the point of unfairness in a previous book (*Psychoanalysis and Religion*), soft-pedals his own objections to Jung. On Breuer, Fromm quotes from Jones what he likes but stops quoting before Jones adds, on the very same page, that Breuer "had certain characteristics which were particularly antipathetic to Freud's nature. One was a weakness in his personality that made it hard for him ever to take a definite stand on any question. The other was a pettifogging kind of censoriousness which would induce him to mar any appreciation or praise by searching out a small point open to criticism—an attitude very alien to Freud's open-hearted and generous spirit" (I, 255).

"Freud's Passion for Truth and his Courage" are acknowledged in Fromm's first chapter—and explained: "He was a very insecure person, easily feeling threatened, persecuted, betrayed, and hence . . . with a great desire for certainty." Indeed, "he had to conquer the world intellectually if he wanted to be relieved of doubt and the feeling of failure." It was really a weakness "related to his position as the undisputed favorite son of his mother." Yes, he was really a mother's boy and never outgrew "the deep-seated receptive wish to be nursed." And "to account for his passion for truth, we must point to a negative element in his character, his lack of emotional warmth, closeness, love, and beyond that, enjoyment of life."

Freud certainly lacked many things, but *this* "negative element" is Fromm's invention, based on utter disregard for ample evidence. Nor is there any place in Fromm's portrait for Freud's heart-warming sense of humor, evident both in his writings and in scores of letters and remarks quoted by Jones. Fromm quotes only one mildly humorous remark—and fails to recognize its humor. He informs us that Freud once frankly admitted his "lack of understanding of women . . . when he said in a conversation: 'The great question that has never been answered, and which I have not been able to answer, despite my thirty years of research into the feminine soul, is what does a woman want? [*Was will das Weib?*]'" Fromm does not mention that Freud said this to a woman who was also one of his most devoted friends and followers.

With *one* of Freud's closest disciples, Ferenczi, who toward the end of his life developed a non-Freudian approach, Fromm sides passionately against Freud, but simply ignores all the evidence that does not fit his claims; for example, Freud's humane and humorous letter to Ferenczi about their differences (Jones, III, 163–65). Many other letters, too, show clearly that Freud was not as stubborn and authoritarian as Fromm pictures him; but some degree of obstinacy is, no doubt, a necessary element of greatness. Fromm sees the steel but not the velvet, the sternness but none of the humor, and offers us a caricature. In the Freud chapter of my *From Shakespeare to Existentialism* (Section 4 of the Anchor edition), I have documented the traits at issue here.

Surely, Freud did underestimate the importance of cultural differences, though not as much as Fromm and other critics overestimate it. But Freud certainly did not try to explain all things in terms of sex, and in a crucial sense he was less simple-minded than most of his critics. In his first major work, *The Interpretation of Dreams*, Freud proposed a new interpretation of *Hamlet* in a celebrated footnote, which was later expanded into a whole book by Ernest Jones. By now the psychoanalytic interpretation of *Hamlet* is unfortunately better known than the conclusion of Freud's footnote:

"Just as, incidentally, all neurotic symptoms—just as even dreams are capable of overinterpretation, and indeed demand nothing less than this before they can be fully understood, thus every genuine poetic creation, too, has presumably issued from *more than one motive*. . . . and *permits more than one interpretation*. What I have attempted here is merely an interpretation of the deepest layer of impulses in the soul of the creative poet."

By "deepest," Freud, no doubt, meant that which was least accessible, most hidden, and most unexpected. And he had a way of generally emphasizing that which was in this sense deepest, most ignored, and most offensive. But he did not claim, his critics notwithstanding, that the deepest layer is the only one and sufficient for an explanation.

Fromm, on the other hand, usually concentrates on what is not deep in this sense, but tells us again and again that he has given us *the* explanation. After relating one of Freud's dreams, which has been variously interpreted by Freud and by several critics, Fromm, ignoring the literature, says with his customary confidence: "The meaning of the dream is quite clear. . . ." In an earlier book, *The Forgotten Language*, he furnishes us in the same vein with *the* explanations of three Sophoclean tragedies, Kafka's *Trial*, and *Little Red*

Ridinghood.[2] Under his psychoanalytic wand, all tragedy and mystery evaporate: if Creon (in Sophocles' *Antigone*) and K. (in Kafka's *Trial*) had only read a little Fromm, everything could have had a happy ending. Since Fromm published *Man for Himself*, tragedy has become unnecessary, if not inexcusable.

In 1696, John Toland published a book entitled *Christianity not Mysterious.* Fromm's lifework, but not Freud's, might well be superscribed: Everything Unmysterious. But is it not simple-minded in the extreme to suppose that Sophocles' and Shakespeare's tragedies and Kafka's novels, quite deliberately fraught with ambiguity, or a dream that has elicited a literature, or the character and work of men like Freud, Nietzsche, or Wittgenstein, could be reduced to one simple and unmysterious explanation?

A little honesty inclines a man to give an explanation, but depth in honesty brings his mind to realize the limitations of any one explanation and confronts him with a renewed sense of mystery. To convey human greatness, one must either refrain from explanation or show how no single explanation is sufficient. Psychology is not incompatible with the belief that there are great men; only a simple-minded psychology is.

Fromm ends his book by calling Freud a great man, but throughout the book we are made to feel that he was really far less great than we had supposed. Without being as calculated as Mark Antony's great speech in Shakespeare's *Julius Caesar,* Fromm's tributes to Freud's courage and his stature invite comparison with Antony's refrain that "Brutus is an honorable man." The leveling tendency that permeates the book and leaves its mark on the reader shows the extent of those cultural influences upon Fromm that have led millions to disbelieve in great men altogether. But the insistence on cultural influences is not something that we owe to Fromm and other heterodox psychoanalysts, but merely a fancy name for something Freud well knew, no less than Nietzsche and generations before him: conformity.

[2] For a detailed discussion, also of Fromm's views on religion, see my *Critique,* § 77; for some criticisms of Freud's views, §§ 42 and 97 f.

At all times men are subject to insidious pressures to accept the prejudices of their age and to rationalize them, whether theologically or scientifically. Nietzsche and Freud found that the best, if not the only, way to resist this danger is not to humor the hypersensitive ears of one's contemporaries by choosing comfortable words but to emphasize precisely that which is not fashionable, not heard gladly—that which gives offense.

Fromm says of Freud: "Like Marx, he found a certain satisfaction in saying things *pour épater le bourgeois* (to shock the bourgeois)." Surely, that is to miss the point. Perhaps no writer ever wrote of sex more unsensationally than did Sigmund Freud, whose pure and simple prose is never cheap and always informed by a deep humanity. But he did insist on calling sex sex; he did not like words like erotic; and it is easy to imagine what he would have thought of a psychoanalyst who entitled one of his books *The Art of Loving*.

90

Kierkegaard was a Christian who insisted that Christianity must give offense; but his twentieth-century heirs, at least in the United States, speak comfortable words. They speak more of courage than he did but, if we listen closely, ask no more than that we take the risk of having faith although we might be wrong—the risk, specifically, to be Protestants. But does it take such a great deal of courage to be a Protestant in the United States today? The whole tenor of American theology today is not to give offense but to show that one can well be religious and quite up-to-date, too. One can combine Christianity with Freud and Nietzsche, with Marx (in the thirties when he was fashionable) and with existentialism (after the Second World War, now that Marx is out of fashion). Whatever you have, Christianity has, too. The theologians offer everything and heaven, too.

When the salt has lost its savor and Christianity its sting, when a culture has successfully assimilated even a religion which, as Kierkegaard insisted, is quite plainly incompatible with it, is it strange that Freud's new teaching, too, should have been made wholesome and inoffensive? Fromm's small tract on Freud is a mere symptom of the tendencies of our time—almost a parable about cultural influence. Fromm is but one of scores who started out as radicals and later came to savor popularity and, not deliberately, to be sure, came more and more to write what their large audience likes to hear.

The men who come before us as the heirs of Kierkegaard and Freud join in the common cry that courage is a good thing while conformity is bad. But Kierkegaard's successors, unlike Kierkegaard, confirm the no less popular demand that we should join some church, and Fromm, unlike Freud, looks with suspicion, if not moralistic condescension, upon obstinacy, hardness, and the willingness to pit one's own integrity against the judgment of the world. Today's prophets are like headmasters who denounce conformity in their commencement speeches but, during the year, refer boys who are indifferent to popularity to the psychiatrist. No sooner has Freud's moral courage been mentioned than it is treated like a disease. But not the least value of Freud is that he shows us that in our time, too, true nobility is possible.

To return to tragedy, Fromm's book is a symptom of those attitudes that go far toward accounting for the lack of tragedies on our stages. We like to tell ourselves that those whose suffering is great are like ourselves: we sympathize with them but don't look up to them as, in spite of ourselves, we do look up to Shakespeare's tragic heroes or to Sophocles'. The hero of *Death of a Salesman,* for example, is no hero but the un-hero *par excellence:* he is pathetic, not tragic. And the only victim of the Nazis who has touched the hearts of millions is a little girl, Anne Frank. An occasional motion picture glorifies the tragic virtue of nobility, of courage that holds out after success appears to be out of the question: *Bad Day at Black Rock,* for example, *Twelve Angry Men,* and *High Noon.* But on the screen the hero's obstinate integrity is in the end crowned with success: how else could you sell these virtues to the public?

It is often said that the confident faith of communism

must be met by us with a no less firm faith that the future belongs to us. What we truly need is not such foolishness but more intelligence, integrity, and moral courage. Also some of the stubbornness that refuses to surrender when no reasonable chance of victory remains. Sometimes it prevails over stupendous odds, as Freud did after standing quite alone for many years, or as England did in the Second World War. Sometimes it does not, as the Jews in the Warsaw ghetto did not, and as Freud in his fight with cancer did not. In the end, against death, none of us prevail, but there is a difference between death and death.

It is easy to see why a democratic society would be skeptical about great men and suspicious of the tragic virtues. Democracy depends on compromise. But democracy can ill afford to dispense with moral courage. Under certain circumstances, it may require moral courage to advocate compromise. What matters is that the decision is not influenced by the desire for acclaim. And there are few better representatives in our time of the rare combination of humbition, love, courage, and honesty than Sigmund Freud.

91

Still, the concept of tragedy remains unclear. As long as ordinary usage is accepted, this cannot be helped. Originally, the word was attached to certain Greek plays which therefore have a primary claim to the label; but some of these plays have no tragic end. Aeschylus' *Oresteia* trilogy and Sophocles' *Oedipus Coloneus* end untragically, on a note of elation and conciliation, Goethe subtitled the two parts of his *Faust,* "The First Part of the Tragedy" and "The Second Part of the Tragedy"; but few critics consider it a tragedy, especially not the Second Part. In ordinary discourse, moreover, "tragic" and "tragedy" are used freely in a way of which most literary people violently disapprove.

Unable to agree with all the common uses of the word, and unwilling to give it up, I should say that tragedy requires that at the very least two, if not three, conditions are satisfied.

First, the hero must be a great human being. Traditionally, it was supposed that he must be of noble birth; but this strikes me as clearly unnecessary and irrelevant. Second, he (or she) must fail, and still be great and admirable in failure—usually, more so than ever before. Third, and this may be more doubtful, the failure must be inevitable because the hero is in a situation in which he cannot possibly satisfy all legitimate claims and is therefore bound to incur some great guilt, whatever he does.

Confronted with Aeschylus' *Eumenides* or Sophocles' *Oedipus Coloneus,* I should say that neither play is tragic and that it would hardly occur to anyone to call them tragedies if they had been written in recent times. Etymologically, tragedy means goat song, and the Greeks obviously had every right to call these plays tragedies because they had developed out of a certain ritual. But in later times it became less and less customary to call every play that was not a comedy a tragedy—we can speak of sublime plays or dramas—and it would be perverse to take our clue for the modern use of "tragedy" from such plays as these.

That the hero is confronted with a choice that leads him into guilt, whatever he does, is not a feature of all great tragedies, but of many of the greatest. If Oedipus stops his inquiries as he is advised to do, he fails in his duty as king and is responsible for the continuation of the plague; if he presses his questions as he does, he incurs responsibility for his mother's death and wrecks the lives of his children. It was the genius of Sophocles that found *this* situation tragic instead of trying to construct the play around the hero's murder of his father.

If Antigone obeys Creon, as her sister does, she fails in her duty to her brother; if she disobeys, as she chooses to do, she breaks the law and bears some responsibility for deaths other than her own. Again, it is striking that Sophocles bases his tragedy on this situation. And again it is not inevitable that the central figure should become a tragic hero or heroine: by refraining from action, as Ismene does, one incurs guilt, too; but one does not rise to heroic stature.

Aeschylus placed Orestes in a similarly tragic situation. If

avenge his father, he fails in his filial duty and
grave guilt; if he does avenge his father, he must
his own mother. Again, he becomes the tragic hero
by choosing the guilt of action, by electing the path of courage. Hamlet's predicament is essentially the same, but more
complicated because Shakespeare introduces many more characters, subplots, and deaths.

Shakespeare's Coriolanus eventually finds himself in a situation in which he must either destroy Rome, his own and his
mother's city, or betray the trust placed in him by the Vol-
scians. Brutus, as Shakespeare sees him, must betray either
Caesar, whom he loves, or Rome. *Macbeth* and *Othello* do not
fit this pattern so readily, though the witches' prophecy at
the beginning of *Macbeth* suggests some inevitability.

Lear, unquestionably one of the greatest tragedies of all
time, does not seem to be based on any such tragic choice at
all. But if Lear were simply a silly old man who, quite
gratuitously, made a terribly stupid decision in the beginning and then reaped the consequences, would the play be a
great tragedy? Perhaps it is only because the initial decision
is presented as a fairy tale or a myth, as a prologue or presupposition of what follows, that the play becomes a tragedy.
Certainly, it would not be a tragedy, and Lear would not
be one of the greatest of tragic heroes, if he continued to be a
pathetic, pitiable, wretched old man, persecuted past endurance. He is that, he is a brother to Ophelia and Gretchen and
many a modern un-hero; but he not only retains the mythical
stature of the stylized prologue, he grows to titanic dimensions
until Brutus and Orestes seem small by comparison. *Lear*
would not be such a great tragedy if Lear in his failure did
not become the titan *par excellence*.

92

If I called my own view of the world tragic, I should mean
mainly four things. First, failure is compatible with greatness.
The same point can be put negatively, and has been discussed

in that form earlier in this chapter: human greatness is not a function of success.

Second, while the meaning of greatness can be spelled out in terms of virtues, greatness—indeed, the universe—remains mysterious. Where psychological explanations are attempted, belief in greatness is diminished and may even evaporate unless one insists, as Freud did, that no one interpretation is adequate, and that no conjunction of interpretations is exhaustive. At that point, one can claim either that an indefinite number of interpretations would be required or that mutually incompatible interpretations increase our understanding.

That is how the ancient rabbis understood the greatness of Scripture, and how Kafka, in *The Trial,* communicates the mystery of a short parable—"Before the Law"—and at the same time furnishes his readers with a hint about the nature of *The Trial* itself, and *The Castle,* too. I am suggesting that what is true of the greatness of books is also true of human greatness. Mysteriousness is certainly not a sufficient condition of greatness, but it is a necessary condition.

Where I speak of mystery, others have sometimes spoken, *more* mysteriously, of freedom. Freedom is a positive word, seemingly clear but actually charged with ambiguities and puzzles. For a belief in greatness it is not necessary to sort out these puzzles and to develop a theory of freedom; what is required is merely a sense of mystery, a humble feeling that one does not know it all.

Does the belief in human greatness require the conviction that no adequate explanation of the hero's actions could ever be given, as a matter of principle? It is certainly not necessary to believe that great men differ in this respect from other men. Nor do I mean that we should impose limits on honesty, curbing it to leave mystery untouched. On the contrary, a little honesty accepts one explanation as *the* explanation which removes all mystery, while depth in honesty leads to humility. It is for this reason that one might call not only courage but also humility and honesty tragic virtues: they are essential ingredients of that tragic world view which involves a central sense of human limitation. And love? The difference between tragedy and comedy is surely not, as was once assumed, that the former deals with royal personages and the latter with common people. The very same story, with the same characters in it, will strike us as comic or tragic depending on our attitude. If that attitude is one of callousness, it may strike us as comic; if it is one of love, as tragic in the ordinary, non-literary sense of the word; and if it is one of admiration and awe, as tragic in the narrower, literary sense. The traditional distinction depends on the assumption that the misfortunes of ordinary people are comic, and that only those of noble birth can be noble. Whether one finds *The Merchant of Venice* comic depends on whether one feels like laughing at Shylock. A sufficiently callous person might find Auschwitz comic; most people find it tragic; but to make of it a literary tragedy, one would have to center attention on a figure that inspired awe and admiration and made us feel humble in comparison, and his greatness in meeting disaster would have to be a challenge.

Still, all this does not fully answer the question whether a tragic world view, as I use that term, involves the claim that no complete explanation of a man's character, actions, and work can ever be given, no matter how far science might advance. The obvious way to answer would be to analyze the concept of explanation. But it is not necessary here to proceed at all far along that line. A tragic world view need not conflict with science, philosophy of science, or the ethos of scientists. What is ruled out is the simplistic claim that *the* explanation can be given in a few pages of unmysterious prose —or for that matter in a great many pages of mysterious prose.

Explanations answer questions. In answer to a specific question, a certain explanation may be adequate without therefore being entitled to be considered *the* explanation of the event under consideration.

Two examples may help. Why did two ships crash into each other? Because the captain of one was drunk. Under certain circumstances, that might be a perfectly adequate and sufficient answer. Yet it leaves thousands of questions unanswered, and the event might well be made the subject of immensely tangled legal proceedings or of a novel that stressed absurdity or the punishment of pride or any number of other themes, such as the problem of suffering.

As another example, consider a letter Freud wrote the novelist Stefan Zweig, after reading Zweig's essay on Dostoevsky. "I believe you should not have left Dostoevsky with his alleged epilepsy. It is highly improbable that he was an epileptic. . . . Only a single example is known of the occurrence of this disease in a man of outstanding spiritual gifts, and that was a giant of the intellect of whose emotional life little is known (Helmholtz). All the other great men to whom epilepsy has been ascribed were pure hysterics. . . . I think the whole Dostoevsky could have been constructed on the basis of this hysteria. . . . Somewhere in a biography of Dostoevsky I was shown a passage that related the later affliction of the man to a punishment of the boy by his father under very serious circumstances—the word tragic comes to my mind; I am not sure if justifiably. . . . It was this childhood scene—I need not persuade the author of *First Experiences* of this probability—that bestowed on the later scene when he was about to be executed the traumatic power to repeat itself as an attack. . . . Almost all the peculiarities of his fiction, of which you have missed scarcely one, are to be traced back to his psychic disposition, abnormal for us, more usual among Russians—really, more accurately, his sexual constitution; and this might be shown very beautifully in detail. Everything tormented and strange, above all. He cannot be understood without psychoanalysis: i.e., he does not require it because with every character and every sentence he himself provides a commentary on it. . . . With you I need not worry about the misunderstanding that this emphasis on the so-called pathological side might be intended to belittle or clear up [*verkleinern oder aufklären*] the magnificence of Dostoevsky's creative poetic power" (October 19, 1920).

Here Freud suggests that any claim to "clear up" would automatically "belittle." His use of *aufklären* is striking. In German the two most obvious associations with this word are that it is the term for telling children the facts of life, and that *Die Aufklärung* is the enlightenment. Freud here dissociates himself from the overconfidence and the buoyantly optimistic rationalism that are widely, though unjustly, associated with the enlightenment. Actually, of course, few great philosophers had ever been more keenly aware of the limits of reason than the two greatest philosophers of the enlightenment, Hume and Kant. The central point, however, can be put quite simply: when we tell a child the so-called facts of life with the most scrupulous scientific honesty, disdaining all fig leaves, this surely does not entail any claim that no mysteries remain. Some questions have been answered, others not.

In introducing this second tenet of the tragic outlook, I said that not only greatness but the universe must remain mysterious. This, too, involves no conflict with science. Freud formulated this beautifully when he insisted in *The Future of an Illusion* (Section VI) that it is not the feeling of dependence "that constitutes the essence of religiousness, but only the next step, the reaction to it, which seeks a remedy against this feeling. He who goes no further, he who humbly resigns himself to the insignificant part man plays in the universe, is, on the contrary, irreligious in the truest sense of the word."

The third feature I have in mind when speaking of a tragic world view can be put as briefly as the first. A tragic world view is incompatible with the belief that human failure is merely an episode, compensated by subsequent rewards. Failure must be final. The end must be tragic.

Fourth, failure must be inevitable. Suppose it were not; suppose success and failure were both within reach, and it were a matter of accident or choice which we reaped. Accidents are not usually considered tragic by people who weigh their words; nor should I call them tragic. But if failure is the outcome of a choice in a situation in which a man might have achieved success if only he had chosen differently, we can ask whether he himself was aware of this at the time. If he was not, his choice approximates an accident. It was unfortunate, too bad, a pity—not tragic.

Suppose, then, the failure is the outcome of a deliberate choice, made with full knowledge of its dire consequences. There are still two possibilities. Either the alternative course of action would have led to dire consequences, too—in which case failure was inevitable—or the agent deliberately spurned success. The second possibility forms part of the traditional Christian picture of the damned. In some passages in the Gospels they are said to be simply foolish; and quite generally they are not considered at all great or admirable in the Gospels. In Paul's Letters and in later Christian writers, God hardens the heart of those whom he wishes to damn, and they emphatically deserve no admiration, nor even compassion. Far from being greater in their failure than most men who succeed, they are horrible examples and a lesson to the rest of us, teaching us how grateful we should be to God for having treated our brothers in this way, not us.

If we changed the Christian view and imagined a man who deliberately chose damnation either to comfort the damned or, if that should prove impossible, at least to retain his integrity—because he would rather be in hell than near God in heaven, watching the torments of the damned—such a man might well be considered as a tragic hero. But that is precisely because he would be greater than most who succeed, because he would deserve respect and admiration, and because in this context failure *would* be inevitable. *Ex hypothesi,* this man would have to sacrifice either his eternal happiness or his humanity, his love and courage, his humbition and his honesty. He would rather be honest with his God and go to hell than be a hypocrite and go to heaven.

The idea of inevitable failure is not particularly enigmatic and can be clarified in two ways. First, we cannot satisfy all claims we ought to meet. Instead of illustrating this point with some intimate personal relationships, it will suffice to recall Sartre's eloquent remarks about "The Responsibility of the Writer," cited at the end of Chapter III. "If a writer has chosen to be silent on one aspect of the world, we have the right to ask him: Why . . . ?" But every writer has to remain silent on most aspects of the world. "Why do you want to change this rather than that?" In one lifetime one can press for relatively few changes. If a man presses for many, we may ask him why he scatters his energies. Is it not purity of heart to will one thing? But if he concentrates on one point, we may ask why he neglects others. This is the situation Luther understood when he discovered that in a life devoted to works failure was inevitable. Here Luther came close to a tragic world view; but he believed in salvation through faith in Christ—in rewards after death for Christ's vicarious atonement.

Inevitable failure may also be found in another aspect of the human situation. If death is the end and there is no life after death, and humanity will perish utterly, then all our efforts will eventually come to nothing. Honesty and humility admit this futility, but ambition, courage, and love spur us nevertheless into attempts that we know must in the end fail inevitably. To explore this further, we must deal with death at some length.

XII

Death

93

When a student interrupted one of Whitehead's seminars at Harvard, asking, "What has all this to do with death?" most of those present immediately assumed that he was under the influence of Heidegger. The concern with extreme situations had been one of the characteristic features of Kierkegaard's work, as even the titles of some of his books show: *Fear and Trembling* (1843), *The Concept of Dread* (1844), and *The Sickness unto Death,* which is despair, (1849). But Kierkegaard was, and considered himself, a religious writer, and such themes had long been prominent in religious writing. Nietzsche, too, had dealt with some of the most intense experiences, though at least as much with joy as with despair; and when he had written of death, he had celebrated "death freely chosen, death at the right time, brightly and cheerfully accomplished amid children and witnesses" (536 f.). Neither Kierkegaard nor this aspect of Nietzsche's work was widely noted until Jaspers and Heidegger renewed these concerns after the First World War. In his *Psychologie of Weltanschauungen* (1919), Jaspers devoted a central section to extreme situations (*Grenzsituationen*), among which he included guilt and death. Eight years later, Heidegger, in *Being and Time,* moved death into the center of discussion.

During the Second World War, Sartre included a section on death in his major philosophic work, *Being and Nothingness* (1943), and criticized Heidegger. Camus devoted his two would-be philosophic books to suicide (*The Myth of Sisyphus,* 1942) and murder (*The Rebel,* 1951). Sartre also dealt with men's attitudes toward their own death in his story, "The Wall," and in his play, *The Victors* (*Morts sans sépulture*); with murder, in *The Flies* and in *Dirty Hands;* and with the meaning of death in *No Exit*. Camus, in *The Stranger*, dealt both with murder and with a man's reactions to his own impending death; and his major effort, *The Plague*, is a study of attitudes toward death, one's own as well as that of others.

This list is far from exhaustive but sufficient to suggest why the concern with death is so widely associated with existentialism. If now one simply offers one's own ideas about death, they are likely to be met with the response: why should we accept these rather than those? One might even be taken for an existentialist, because one deals with death. I shall therefore begin by considering briefly, but critically, some of Heidegger's, Sartre's, and Camus's claims.

94

Heidegger's discussion of death bears the uninviting title, "The possible Being-whole of Being-there and Being-toward-death" (*Das mögliche Ganzsein des Daseins und das Sein zum Tode*). At great length, Heidegger argues to establish this conclusion: "Death does reveal itself as a loss, but rather as a loss experienced by the survivors. The suffering of this loss, however, does not furnish an approach to the loss of Being as such that is 'suffered' by the person who died. We do not experience in a genuine sense the dying of the others but are at most always only 'present'" (239). "The public interpretation of Being-there says, 'one dies,' because in this way everybody else as well as oneself can be deceived into thinking: not, to be sure, just I myself; for this One is *Nobody. . . .* In this way the One brings about a *continual putting at ease about death*" (253). A footnote on the following page adds: "L. N. Tolstoy, in his story, *The Death of Ivan Ilyitch*, has presented the phenomenon of the shattering and the collapse of this 'one dies.'"

Without doubt Tolstoy's story was one of the central

inspirations of Heidegger's discussion. *The Death of Ivan Ilyitch* is a superb book—with an emphatic moral. It is a sustained attack on society in the form of a story about a member of society whose life is utterly empty, futile, pointless —but no more so than the life of all the other members of society who surround him, notably his colleagues and his wife. They all live to no point and tell themselves and each other that "one dies" without ever seriously confronting the certainty that they themselves must die. The only appealing person in the book is a poor muzhik who, realizing that he, too, will have to die one day, patiently and lovingly does all he can to help Ivan. In the final pages of the book, Ivan becomes aware of the futility of his own life and overcomes it, realizing that his malady is not merely a matter of a diseased kidney or appendix but of leaving behind a pointless life to die. He ceases pretending, and "From that moment began that shriek that did not cease for three days"; but during these three days he learns to care for others, feels sorry for his wife, and, for the first time, loves. Now, "In place of death was light! 'Here is something like!' he suddenly said aloud. 'What joy!'" Death had lost its terror.

Heidegger on death is for the most part an unacknowledged commentary on *The Death of Ivan Ilyitch.* "Even 'thinking of death' is publicly considered cowardly fear. . . . *The One does not allow the courage for anxiety of death to rise.*" Propriety does not permit Ivan to shriek. He must always pretend that he will soon get better. It would be offensive for him to admit that he is dying. But in the end he has the courage to defy propriety and shriek. "The development of such a 'superior' indifference alienates Being-there from its own-most, unrelated Being-able-to-be" (254). It is only when he casts aside his self-deceiving indifference that Ivan returns to himself, to his capacity for love, and leaves behind the self-betrayal of his alienated inauthentic life. "Being-toward-death is essentially anxiety" (266)—in Tolstoy's story, if not elsewhere.

It is no criticism of Tolstoy to note that not all men are like Ivan Ilyitch. I might suppose that I myself am possibly exceptional in frankly living with the vivid certainty that I must die, were it not for the fact that in a recent World War my whole generation—millions of young men—lived with this thought. Many got married, saying to themselves: I do not have much time left, but I want to live just once, if only for one week or possibly a few months. And Heidegger's generation (he was born in 1889) had the same experience in the First World War. Tolstoy's indictment of an un-Christian, un-loving, hypocritical world cannot be read as a fair characterization of humanity. Nor is it true that "Being-toward-death is essentially anxiety," and that all illustrations to the contrary can be explained as instances of self-deception and the lack of "courage for anxiety of death."

At this point, one begins to wonder whether, under the impact of the First World War, some other thinker did not possibly consider death a little earlier than Heidegger, without basing himself so largely on a single story. Indeed, in 1915, Freud published two essays under the title, "Timely Thoughts on War and Death." I shall quote from the first two pages of the second essay, which he called "Our Relation to Death." Heidegger did not refer to Freud and did not even list Freud's later discussions of conscience in his footnote bibliography on conscience (272). But while Heidegger's discussion of conscience is the worse for ignoring Freud's analyses, Heidegger's pages upon pages about death are in large part long-winded repetitions of what Freud had said briefly at the outset of his paper:

The war, according to Freud, disturbed "our previous relation to death. This relation was not sincere. If one listened to us, we were, of course, ready to declare that death is the necessary end of all life, that every one of us owed nature his own death and must be prepared to pay this debt—in short, that death is natural, undeniable, and unavoidable. In reality, however, we used to behave as if it were different. We have shown the unmistakable tendency to push death aside, to eliminate it from life. We have tried to keep a deadly silence about death: after all, we even have a proverb to the effect that one thinks about something as one thinks about death. One's own, of course. After all, one's own death is beyond imagining, and whenever we try to imagine it we can see that we really survive as spectators. Thus the dictum could be dared in the psychoanalytic school: at bottom, nobody believes in his own death. Or, and this is the same: in his unconscious, every one of us is convinced of his immortality. As for the death of others, a cultured man will carefully avoid speaking of this possibility if the person fated to die can hear him. Only children ignore this rule. . . . We regularly emphasize the accidental cause of death, the mishap, the disease, the infection, the advanced age, and thus betray our eagerness to demote death from a necessity to a mere accident. Toward the deceased himself we behave in a special way, almost as if we were full of admiration for someone who has accomplished something very difficult. We suspend criticism of him, forgive him any injustice, pronounce the motto, *de mortuis nil nisi bene,* and consider it justified that in the funeral sermon and on the gravestone the most advantageous things are said about him. Consideration for the dead, who no longer needs it, we place higher than truth —and most of us certainly also higher than consideration for the living."

The simple, unpretentious clarity of these remarks, their unoracular humanity and humor, and their straight appeal to experience could hardly furnish a more striking contrast to Heidegger's verbiage. It is said sometimes that Heidegger more than anyone else has provoked discussion of phenomena which, in spite of Kierkegaard and Nietzsche, were ignored by the professors and their students. But in the wake of Heidegger discussion concentrated not on these phenomena but on his terms and weird locutions. Death, anxiety, conscience, and care became part of the jargon tossed about by thousands, along with Being-there, to-hand-ness, thrown-ness, Being-with, and all the rest. But he did not present definite claims for discussion, not to speak of hypotheses.

His remarks about death culminate in the italicized assertion: "The running-ahead reveals to Being-there the lostness into One-self and brings it before the possibility . . . of being itself—itself, however, in the passionate *freedom for death* which has rid itself of the illusions of the One, become factual, certain of itself, and full of anxiety" (266). (The words italicized here are printed in bold type in the original.) Un-questionably, the acceptance of the fact that I must die (my running-ahead to my death in thought) may forcibly remind me of the limited amount of time at my disposal, of the waste involved in spending it in awe of the anonymous One, and thus become a powerful incentive to make the most of my own being here and now. But Heidegger's habit of gluing his thought to words, or of squeezing thoughts out of words, or of piling up such weird locutions that, as he himself insists, not one of his disciples of the days when he wrote, taught, and talked *Being and Time* seems to have got the point, has not encouraged questions like this one: Is it necessary that the resolute acceptance of my own death must still be accompanied by a feeling of anxiety, as Heidegger insists?

At this point Heidegger relies too heavily on the Christian writers who have influenced him most: above all, in this case Kierkegaard and Tolstoy, and perhaps also Jacob Böhme (*Of the Incarnation of Jesus Christ* II, 4.1, and *Six Theosophic Points* I) and Schelling, who claimed in *Die Weltalter* that anxiety is "the basic feeling of every living creature." In Heidegger, Schelling's *Grundempfindung* becomes *Grundbefindlichkeit.*

Consider the letter which President Vargas of Brazil wrote to his people before committing suicide. It ends: "I fought against the looting of Brazil. I fought against the looting of the people. I have fought barebreasted. The hatred, infamy, and calumny did not beat down my spirit. I gave you my life. Now I offer my death. Nothing remains. Serenely I take the first step on the road to eternity and I leave life to enter history."[1] Or consider this letter which a Japanese flier trained for a suicide mission, Isao Matsuo, wrote to his parents: "Please congratulate me. I have been given a splendid opportunity to die. . . . I shall fall like a blossom from a radiant cherry tree. . . . How I appreciate this chance to die like a man! . . . Thank you, my parents, for the 23 years during which you have cared for me and inspired me.

[1] *New York Herald Tribune,* August 25, 1955.

I hope that my present deed will in some small way repay what you have done for me."[2] Or consider David Hume's complete lack of anxiety which so annoyed his Christian "friends" who hoped for a deathbed conversion. Or Socrates' calm in the face of death. Or the Stoic sages who, admiring Socrates, committed tranquil suicide when in their nineties. Or the ancient Romans.

Heidegger's talk about anxiety should be read as a document of the German nineteen-twenties when it suddenly became fashionable to admit one was afraid. In Remarque's *All Quiet on the Western Front* (1929) it was obvious that this new honesty was aimed against militarism and of a piece with Arnold Zweig's noting that when "the Sergeant Grischa" at the end of Zweig's great novel (1928) was shot, "his bowels discharged excrement." But while it took some courage to disregard propriety and to admit that some men, when confronting death, are scared and that some, when shot, fill their pants, it remained for Heidegger to blow up observations of this sort into general truths about Being.

He was not quickly refuted with a list of fatal counter-instances because he put things into such outrageous language that reactions to his prose have in the main belonged to one of four types: either one did not read him at all and ignored him, as the majority of mankind did; or one read him a little, found him extremely difficult, and took it for granted that the fault was one's own and that, of course, there must be more to his assertions than they seemed to say—especially since he himself says frequently that they are not anthropological but ontological—truths not about man but about Being; or, thirdly, one read him, found him difficult, persevered, spent years studying him,—and what else could one do after years of study of that sort?—became a teacher of philosophy, protecting one's investment by "explaining" Heidegger to students, warding off objections by some such remark as: "There is much that I, too, don't understand as yet, but I shall give my life to trying to understand a little more." The fourth type, now gaining ground among

2 Inoguchi, 200. The whole last chapter, "Last Letters Home," 196–208, is supremely relevant.

American intellectuals, has not read Heidegger at all but heard about him and his influence and assumes that there must be a great deal to him. Perhaps one has penetrated to the point of recognizing that he alludes to some genuine experiences—such as the sense of our utter loneliness in this world—and this is taken to show that there is more to Heidegger than those admit who shrug him off as writing merely "nonsense." But not everybody who does not write bare nonsense is original, illuminating, or deep.

It is widely taken for granted that Heidegger is a far more profound thinker than Sartre, and that his philosophy is related to French existentialism as Goethe's *Faust* is to Gounod's. If I had skipped Heidegger, in keeping with the resolve to criticize only men I admire, and begun straightaway with Sartre and Camus, many a reader might have concluded that these Frenchmen are, of course, easy prey, while the one great philosopher in the existentialist camp is Heidegger. This myth is also accepted and spread by the spokesmen for existential psychotherapy, though no evidence is offered to back it up. For the most part, they merely use some of Heidegger's quaint expressions, without even asking whether the same points could not be made in plain English, or had not actually been made earlier in excellent German by Freud; and they simply ignore Sartre. But Sartre is far from inferior to Heidegger.[3]

95

Sartre has offered one crucial criticism of Heidegger in his own discussion of death in *Being and Nothingness*. Heidegger argues that only the running-ahead to my own death can lead me to my own-most, authentic Being because "*Dying*

[3] Cf. my *Existentialism from Dostoevsky to Sartre*, Chapter I; for a detailed critique of the later Heidegger, *From Shakespeare to Existentialism*, Chapters 17–18; and for a fuller treatment of *Being and Time*, my essay "Existentialism and Death" in *The Meaning of Death*, ed. Herman Feifel. I have made liberal use of that essay in the present chapter, but omitted entirely the first section, which deals with *Being and Time*.

is something which nobody can do for another. . . . Dying shows that death is constituted ontologically by always-mine-ness and existence." And more of the same sort (240). As Sartre rightly points out, this in no way distinguishes dying (533 ff.). Nobody can love for me or sleep or breathe for me. Every experience, taken as *my* experience, is "something which nobody can do for" me. I can live a lot of my life in the mode of inauthenticity in which it makes no decisive difference that it is I who am doing this or that; but in that mode it makes no difference either whether the bullet hits me or someone else, whether I die first or another. If I adopt the attitude that it does matter, that it makes all the difference in the world to me, then I can adopt that attitude toward the experience of my loving this particular woman, toward my writing this particular book, toward my seeing, hearing, feeling, or bearing witness, no less than I can adopt it toward death. As Sartre says: "In short there is no personalizing virtue which is peculiar to *my* death. Quite the contrary, it becomes *my* death only if I place myself already in the perspective of subjectivity" (535).

Sartre goes on to criticize Heidegger's whole conception of "Being-toward-death." Although we may anticipate that we ourselves must die, we never know when we shall die; but it is the timing of one's death that makes all the difference when it comes to the meaning of one's life. "We have, in fact, every chance of dying before we have accomplished our task, or, on the other hand, of outliving it. There is therefore a very slim chance that our death will be presented to us as that of Sophocles was, for example, in the manner of a re-solved chord. And if it is only *chance* which decides the character of our death and therefore of our life, then even the death which most resembles the end of a melody cannot be waited for as such; luck by determining it for me removes from it any character as a harmonious end. . . . A death like that of Sophocles will therefore *resemble* a resolved chord but will not *be* one, just as the group of letters formed by the falling of alphabet blocks will perhaps resemble a word but will not be one. Thus this perpetual appearance of chance at the heart of my projects cannot be apprehended as *my* possibility but, on the contrary, as the nihilation of all my possibilities, a nihilation which *itself is no longer a part of my possibilities*" (537). "Suppose that Balzac had died before *Les Chouans;* he would remain the author of some execrable novels of intrigue. But suddenly the very expectation which this young man was, this expectation of being a great man, loses any kind of meaning; it is neither an obstinate and egotistical blindness nor the true sense of his own value since nothing shall ever decide it. . . . The final value of this conduct remains forever in suspense; or if you prefer, the ensemble (particular kinds of conduct, expectations, values) falls suddenly into the absurd. Thus death is never that which gives life its meaning; it is, on the contrary, that which on principle removes all meaning from life" (539). "The unique characteristic of a dead life is that it is a life of which the Other makes himself the guardian" (541).

Suicide is no way out, says Sartre. Its meaning depends on the future. "If I 'misfire,' shall I not judge later that my suicide was cowardice? Will the outcome not show me that other solutions were possible? . . . Suicide is an absurdity which causes my life to be submerged in the absurd" (540).

Finally, Sartre asks: "In renouncing Heidegger's Being-toward-death, have we abandoned forever the possibility of freely giving to our being a meaning for which we are responsible? Quite the contrary." Sartre repudiates Heidegger's "strict identification of death and finitude" and says: "human reality would remain finite even if it were immortal, because it *makes* itself finite by choosing itself as human. To be finite, in fact, is to choose oneself—that is, to make known to oneself what one is by projecting oneself toward one possible to the exclusion of others. The very act of freedom is therefore the assumption and creation of finitude. If I make myself, I make myself finite and hence my life is unique" (545 f.).

Before evaluating these ideas, let us consider Camus.

96

Although Camus's politics were more acceptable to the Nobel committee and are surely more attractive than those of Sartre, and although few writers have ever equalled Camus's charming pose of decency and honesty and a determination to be lucid, Henri Peyre is surely right when, in a review of Camus's books and of several books about him, he charges *The Myth of Sisyphus* and *The Rebel* with being "not only contradictory, but confused and probably shallow and immature."[4]

With the utmost portentousness, Camus begins the first of his two philosophic works, *The Myth of Sisyphus:* "There is but one truly serious philosophic problem, and that is suicide." Soon we are told that the world is "absurd." A little later: "I said that the world is absurd, but I was too hasty. This world in itself is not reasonable, that is all that can be said. But what is absurd is the confrontation of this irrational and the wild longing for clarity whose call echoes in the human heart. The absurd depends as much on man as on the world" (21).

This point could be put more idiomatically and accurately by saying that the hunger to gain clarity about all things is quixotic. But Camus prefers to rhapsodize about absurdity, although he says: "I want to know whether I can live with what I know and with that alone" (40). He speaks of "this absurd logic" (31), evidently meaning the special logic of talk about the absurd, as if such talk had any special logic. Then he speaks of the "absurd mind," meaning a believer in the absurdity of the world—or rather of the absurdity, or quixotism, of man's endeavors—as when he says: "To Chestov reason is useless but there is something beyond reason. To an absurd mind [i.e., Camus] reason is useless and there is nothing beyond reason" (35). The word "useless,"

[4] What Peyre says is, to be precise, that Philip Thody, in *Albert Camus,* "is forced to confess when he comes to those two volumes that they are not only . . ."

too, is used without precision; what is meant is something
like "limited" or "not omnipotent." A little later still: "The
absurd . . . does not lead to God. Perhaps this notion will
become clearer if I risk this shocking statement: the absurd
is sin without God" (40). Without being shocked, one may
note the looseness of the style and thinking: no attempt is
made to explain what is meant by "sin," and Camus is evidently satisfied that his vague statement, even if it does not
succeed in shocking us, is at least evocative. But from a
writer who quotes Nietzsche as often as Camus does in this
book—and in *The Rebel*, too—one might expect the question to
be raised whether, by not including God in our picture of
the world, we don't restore to being its "innocence," as
Nietzsche claimed, and leave sin behind.

As far as Kierkegaard, Jaspers, and Chestov are concerned,
Camus is surely right that "The theme of the irrational, as
it is conceived by the existentials [*sic*], is reason becoming
confused and escaping by negating itself." But when he adds,
"The absurd is lucid reason noting its limits," it becomes
apparent that all the oracular discussions of absurdity are
quite dispensable and that Camus has not added clarification
but only confusion to the two sentences from Freud's *The
Future of an Illusion*, cited in section 92. Like Freud in 1927,
fifteen years before *The Myth of Sisyphus*, Camus spurns the
claims of religion and, in Freud's words, "humbly resigns
himself to the insignificant part man plays in the universe."
The same thought permeates the books of Nietzsche.

Nietzsche, however, had gone on to celebrate "Free
Death," both in *Zarathustra* (183 ff.) and in *The Twilight
of the Idols:* "usually it is death under the most contemptible
conditions, an unfree death, death *not* at the right time, a
coward's death. From love of *life*, one should desire a different
death: free, conscious, without accident, without ambush"
(536 f.). Nietzsche's thought is clear, though he collapsed,
but did not die, in his boots, as it were—and his relatives
then dragged out his life for another eleven years.

Camus writes against suicide: "Suicide, like the leap, is
acceptance at its extreme. Everything is over and man returns
to his essential history. . . . In its way, suicide settles the

absurd. It engulfs the absurd in the same death. . . . It is essential to die unreconciled and not of one's own free will. Suicide is a repudiation." Camus wants "defiance" (54 f.).

Now suicide is "acceptance," now it is "repudiation." Surely, sometimes it is one and sometimes the other, and occasionally both—acceptance of defeat and repudiation of hope. Nietzsche's "free death" was meant as an affirmation of sorts, an acceptance of one's own life and of all the world with it, a festive realization of fulfilment, coupled with the thought that this life, as lived up to this point and now consummated, was so acceptable that it did not stand in need of any further deeds or days but could be gladly relived over and over in the course of an eternal recurrence of the same events at gigantic intervals.

No less than in his later work, *The Rebel*, in which "the rebel" replaces the editorial we, exhortations are presented in the form of literally false generalizations. "The rebel does x" means "I do x and wish you would." In *The Myth of Sisyphus*, Camus hides similarly behind "an absurd mind" and "an absurd logic."

The first part of Camus's *Myth of Sisyphus* is ambiguously and appropriately entitled "An Absurd Reasoning." Portentousness thickens toward the end. "The absurd enlightens me on this point: there is no future" (58). "Knowing whether or not one can live *without appeal* is all that interests me" (60). "Now, the conditions of modern life impose on the majority of men the same quantity of experiences and consequently the same profound experience. To be sure, there must also be taken into consideration the individual's spontaneous contribution, the 'given' element in him. But I cannot judge of that, and let me repeat that my rule here is to get along with the immediate evidence" (61). In sum: men don't, of course, have the same quantity of experiences, and least of all the same profound experiences, but in the name of simple honesty we must pretend they do.

This paraphrase may seem excessively unsympathetic; but consider what Camus himself says on the next page: "Here we have to be over-simple. To two men living the same number of years, the world always provides the same sum of experiences. It is up to us to be conscious of them. Being aware of one's life, one's revolt, one's freedom, and to the maximum, is living, and to the maximum.[5] Where lucidity dominates, the scale of values becomes useless. Let's be even more simple."

Why in heaven's name must we be so "over-simple" and then "even more simple?" Two men who live the same number of years do *not* always have the same number of experiences, with the sole difference that one is more aware of them, while the other is partly blind. Life is not like a film that rolls by while we either watch or sleep. Some suffer sicknesses, have visions, love, despair, work, and experience failures and successes; others toil in the unbroken twilight of mute misery, their minds uneducated, chained to deadening routine. Moreover, a man can avoid or involve himself in experiences; he can seek security or elect to live dangerously, to use Nietzsche's phrase. Finally Camus writes as if experiences were like drops that fall into the bucket of the mind at a steady rate—say, one a second—and as if the sequence made no difference at all; as if seeing *Lear* at the age of one, ten, or thirty were the same.

Let us resume our quotation where we broke off: "Let us say that the sole obstacle, the sole deficiency to be made good, is constituted by premature death. Thus it is that no depth, no emotion, no passion, and no sacrifice could render equal in the eyes of the absurd man (even if he wished it so) a conscious life of forty years and a lucidity spread over sixty years. Madness and death are his irreparables. . . . There will never be any substitute for twenty years of life and experience. . . . The present and the succession of presents before a constantly conscious soul is the ideal of the absurd man."

Camus is welcome to his absurd man, who is indeed absurd, wishing to imbibe, collect, and hoard experiences, any experiences, as long as they add up to some huge quantity —the more the better. If only Camus did not deceive himself so utterly about the quality of his own thinking—as when he

[5] This sentence is not so bad in the original, and might be rendered: "The more fully one is aware of one's life, . . . the more fully one lives."

concludes the second essay of the book by counting himself among those "who think clearly and have ceased to hope." Of course, Camus's novels are far superior to the arguments discussed here. He was a fine writer and a profoundly humane man, but not a philosopher. Why, then, discuss his attempts at philosophy at all? For at least three reasons.

First, his was a kindred effort; our agreements far outweigh our differences; so it seems right to relate my own attempts at answers to his. Then, he illustrates the shortcomings of that now popular philosophy which is at the opposite pole from analytic or linguistic philosophy. The so-called existentialists have not only advanced few problems toward a solution; they have often impeded fruitful discussion of important and fascinating problems by the eccentricity of their prose. Finally, this analysis of Camus should help to set the stage for some of my ideas.

97

Camus's confusions bring to mind a poem by Hölderlin: *"Nur einen Sommer . . ."* Heidegger has devoted essay after essay to this poet and eventually collected the lot in a book, but has not written about this poem, which is both clearer and better than the ones Heidegger likes—to read his own thoughts into.

> A single summer grant me, great powers, and
>   A single autumn for fully ripened song
>   That, sated with the sweetness of my
>   Playing, my heart may more willingly die.
>
> The soul that, living, did not attain its divine
>   Right cannot repose in the netherworld.
>   But once what I am bent on, what is
>   Holy, my poetry, is accomplished,
>
> Be welcome then, stillness of the shadows' world!
>   I shall be satisfied though my lyre will not
>   Accompany me down there. Once I
>   Lived like the gods, and more is not needed.

Of the "absurd man" Camus says, as we have seen: "Madness and death are his irreparables." Hölderlin did become mad soon after writing this poem, but the point of the poem is surely that still he should not have preferred to be Edgar Guest or even Methuselah. Not only *is* there a "substitute for twenty years of life," there is something more desirable by far: "Once I lived like the gods, and more is not needed."

This is overlooked by Sartre, too. Rightly, he recognizes that death can cut off a man before he had a chance to give his life a meaning, that death may be—but he falsely thinks it always is—"the nihilation of all my possibilities." Not only in childhood but long after that one may retain the feeling that one is in this sense still at the mercy of death. "But once what I am bent on, what is holy, my poetry, is accomplished," once I have succeeded in achieving—in the face of death, in a race with death—a project that is truly mine and not something that anybody else might have done as well, if not better, then the picture changes: I have won the race and in a sense have triumphed over death. Death and madness come too late.

We see the poet's later madness in the light of his own poem. Nor does it greatly matter that Nietzsche, like Hölderlin, vegetated for a few more years before death took him: his work was done. To be sure, others make themselves the guardians of the dead life and interpret it according to their lights; but we have no defense if they begin to do the same while we are still alive. Nor can we say that this is the price of finitude, of finite works no less than finite lives. Men say that God is infinite but can hardly deny that theologians and believers make themselves the guardians of the infinite and offer their interpretations, if not behind his back then in his face.

A common fault of Heidegger, Sartre, and Camus is that they overgeneralize instead of taking into account different attitudes toward death. The later part of *The Myth of Sisyphus* represents a somewhat arbitrary and portentous attempt at a study of types: three ways are open to "The Absurd Man"—to become a Don Juan, an actor, or a conqueror. Surely, one learns more from Malraux's novel, *La*

Condition Humaine (*Man's Fate*), which offers almost a catalogue of different ways of meeting death. Nor did either these
men or Tolstoy initiate the concern with death.

Heinrich von Kleist (1777–1811) was a Prussian officer
more than a century before World War I. His *Prinz Friedrich
von Homburg* is one of the most celebrated German plays;
and here Kleist had the courage to bring to life on the stage
the Prince's dread after he, a general who has disobeyed
orders, is sentenced to death. Then Kleist went on to depict
his hero's conquest of anxiety, to the point where in the final
scene he is ready to be shot without the slightest remnant of
anxiety. Indeed, he welcomes death, is blindfolded, and—
one thinks of Dostoevsky and of Sartre's story, "The Wall"—
pardoned. Kleist himself committed suicide.

Georg Büchner (1813–37), best known as the author of
Woyzek, dealt with death in an even more strikingly modern
way in another play, *Danton's Death*. But these playwrights
do not claim to offer any general theory of death, any more
than Shakespeare did. I tried to show in the first chapter of
From Shakespeare to Existentialism how many supposedly
existentialist themes are encountered, and important, in
Shakespeare. Surely, he also offers an imposing variety of
deaths and suicides.

Among the points understood by Shakespeare but neglected
by the existentialists are these. Much dread of death is due
to Christian teaching, and pre-Christian Roman attitudes
were often very different. So, we might add, was the Buddha's: after his enlightenment experience he transcended all
anxiety, and the stories of his death represent an outright
antithesis to the Gospels' account of Jesus' dreadful death.

Vitality influences one's reaction to impending death: a
soldier in a duel does not die like patients in their beds. And
attitudes toward death may be changed, too, by the confidence that there is absolutely nothing one will miss—either
because the world will end for all when we die or because life
"is a tale told by an idiot, full of sound and fury, signifying
nothing," and it is well to be rid of "tomorrow, and tomorrow,
and tomorrow."

Finally, not one of the existentialists has grasped the most crucial distinction that makes all the difference in facing death. Nietzsche stated it in *The Gay Science:* "For one thing is needful: that a human being attain his satisfaction with himself—whether it be by this or by that poetry and art; only then is a human being at all tolerable to behold. Whoever is dissatisfied with himself is always ready to revenge himself therefor; we others will be his victims, if only by always having to stand his ugly sight. For the sight of the ugly makes men bad and gloomy" (98 f.). Or, as Hölderin says: "The soul that, living, did not attain its divine right cannot repose in the netherworld." But he that has made something of his life can face death without anxiety: "Once I lived like the gods, and more is not needed."

98

Our attitude toward death is influenced by hope as much as it is by fear. If fear is the mother of cowardice, hope is the father.

Men accept indignities without end, and a life not worth living, in the hope that their miseries *will* end and that eventually life may be worth living again. They renounce love, courage and honesty, pride and humanity, hoping. Hope is as great an enemy of courage as is fear.

The early Romans and Spartans faced death not only fearlessly but also void of mean hopes. There was nothing for the surviving coward to hope.

In the Israel of Moses and the prophets, religion did not hold out hope for individuals. There was hope for the people as long as men and women lived and died with courage and without hope for themselves.

Paul made of hope one of the three great virtues. Doing this, he did not betray Jesus, whose glad tidings had been a message of hope for the individual. Neither of them abetted cowardice or fear of death as such; for their hope was not of this world. Men who accepted the faith of Paul died fearlessly, hopefully, and joyously when the Romans made martyrs of them.

Indeed, "the desire for martyrdom became at times a form of absolute madness, a kind of epidemic of suicide, and the leading minds of the Church found it necessary to exert all their authority to prevent their followers thrusting themselves into the hands of the persecutors. Tertullian mentions how, in a little Asiatic town, the entire population once flocked to the proconsul, declaring themselves to be Christians, and imploring him to execute the decree of the emperor and grant them the privilege of martyrdom. . . . 'These wretches,' said Lucian, speaking of the Christians, 'persuade themselves that they are going to be altogether immortal, and to live for ever, wherefore they despise death, and many of their own accord give themselves up to be slain.'"

"Believing, with St. Ignatius, that they were 'the wheat of God,' they panted for the day when they should be 'ground by the teeth of wild beasts into the pure bread of Christ!'" (Lecky, I, 415 ff.)

As the otherworldliness of Jesus and Paul gave way to a renewed interest in this world, as Christianity became the state religion, hope reverted from the other world to this. The temporary bond of hope and courage was broken. The age of the martyrs was over. Now Christianity became the great teacher of fear of death, and dread of purgatory and damnation became fused with hope for a few more years in *this* world.

The Greeks had considered hope the final evil in Pandora's box. They also gave us an image of perfect nobility: a human being lovingly doing her duty to another human being despite all threats, and going to her death with pride and courage, not deterred by any hope—Antigone.

Hopelessness is despair. Yet life without hope is worth living. As Sartre's Orestes says: "Life begins on the other side of despair." But is hope perhaps resumed on the other side? It need not be. In honesty, what is there to hope for? Small hopes remain but do not truly matter. I may hope that the sunset will be clear, that the night will be cool and still, that my work will turn out well, and yet know that nine hopes out of ten are not even remembered a year later. How many are recalled a century hence? A billion years hence?

> The cloud-capp'd towers, the gorgeous palaces,
> The solemn temples, the great globe itself,
> Yea, all which it inherit, shall dissolve;
> And, like this insubstantial pageant faded,
> Leave not a rack behind. We are such stuff
> As dreams are made on, and our little life
> Is rounded with a sleep.
>
> *(Tempest,* IV, i.)

It is possible that this is wrong. There may be surprises in store for us, however improbable it seems and however little evidence suggests it. But I do not hope for that. Let people who do not know what to do with themselves in this life, but fritter away their time reading magazines and watching television, hope for eternal life. If one lives intensely, the time comes when sleep seems bliss. If one loves intensely, the time comes when death seems bliss.

Those who loved with all their heart and mind and might have always thought of death, and those who knew the endless nights of harrowing concern for others have longed for it.

The life I want is a life I could not endure in eternity. It is a life of love and intensity, suffering and creation, that makes life worth while and death welcome. There is no other life I should prefer. Neither should I like not to die.

If I ask myself who in history I might like to have been, I find that all the men I most admire were by most standards deeply unhappy. They knew despair. But their lives were worth while—I only wish mine equaled theirs in this respect—and I have no doubt that they were glad to die.

As one deserves a good night's sleep, one also deserves to die. Why should I hope to wake again? To do what I have not done in the time I've had? All of us have so much more time than we use well. How many hours in a life are spent in a way of which one might be proud, looking back?

For most of us death does not come soon enough. Lives are spoiled and made rotten by the sense that death is distant and irrelevant. One lives better when one expects to die, say, at forty, when one says to oneself long before one is twenty: whatever I may be able to accomplish, I should be able to do by then; and what I have not done by then, I am not likely to do ever. One cannot count on living until one is forty—or thirty—but it makes for a better life if one has a rendezvous with death.

Not only love can be deepened and made more intense and impassioned by the expectation of impending death; all of life is enriched by it. Why deceive myself to the last moment, and hungrily devour sights, sounds, and smells only when it is almost too late? In our treatment of others, too, it is well to remember that they will die: it makes for greater humanity.

There is nothing morbid about thinking and speaking of death. Those who disparge honesty do not know its joys. The apostles of hope do not know the liberation of emergence from hope.

It may seem that a man without hope is inhuman. How can one appeal to him if he does not share our hopes? He has pulled up his stakes in the future—and the future is the common ground of humanity. Such rhetoric may sound persuasive, but Antigone gives it the lie. Nobility holds to a purpose when hope is gone. Purpose and hope are as little identical as humility and meekness, or honesty and sincerity. Hope seeks redemption in time to come and depends on the future. A purposive act may be its own reward and redeem the agent, regardless of what the future may bring. Antigone is not at the mercy of any future. Humanity, love, and courage survive hope.

Occasionally, to be sure, they may not persist in despair; but that does not prove that they depend on hope. Much more often, humanity has been sacrificed to some hope; love has been betrayed for some hope; and courage has been destroyed by some hope.

Humbition, love, courage, and honesty can make life meaningful, and small hopes can embellish it. For a few decades one may be able to love and create enough to make suffering worth while. If that becomes impossible:

> I will despair, and be at enmity
> With cozening hope: he is a flatterer,

> A parasite, a keeper-back of death,
> Who gently would dissolve the bands of life,
> Which false hope lingers in extremity.
>
> (*Richard II*, II, ii.)

We do not all have the same breaking point; each man has to discover his. When Freud heard of Franz Rosenzweig's unusual exertions to work to the end (described in § 20, above), he said, "What else could he do?" But a man unable to emulate Rosenzweig or Freud need not resign himself to becoming a vegetable. It is better to die with courage than to live as a coward.

Of course, there are deaths that one views with horror: slow, painful deaths; deaths that destroy us by degrees; deaths that, instead of taking us in our prime, demean us first. But, fearing such deaths, I do not fear death, but what precedes it: pointless suffering, disability, and helplessness. Death in a crash might be exhilarating; death in sleep, peace; death by poison, dignified.

When Hannibal, who had humiliated the Romans like no man before him, could not escape from their vengeance and had nothing to look forward to but being led in triumph through the streets of Rome, and then imprisonment, and finally a miserable death, why should he not have taken poison as he did? Suicide can be cowardice; it need not be. In *Antony and Cleopatra*, Shakespeare contrasts suicides: Antony botches his, while Cleopatra's death has enviable dignity and beauty.

The Greeks have often been held up as models of humanity. There are few respects in which their humanity compares more favorably with that of most modern nations than the way in which death sentences were carried out. They did not grab men unawares in the middle of the night to drag them to the guillotine and chop their heads off, as the French did until recently; they did not hang them, British fashion; burn them, Christian fashion; or strap them, the American way, into an electric chair or a gas chamber—depriving a human being of his dignity and humanity as far as possible: Socrates was given hemlock and could raise the cup to his own lips and die a man.

Is it possible that the fear of death and the prohibition of suicide have been as deliberately imposed on men as laws against incest—not owing to any innate horror, but because dying, like incest, is so easy? Culture depends on men's attempting to do what is difficult. We are naturally endowed with aspirations but also with a tendency toward sloth; and when ambition meets obstacles we are always tempted to take the easy way out.

Even if there is a natural instinct of self-preservation and an innate aversion to death, culture depends both on reinforcing this aversion and on teaching men to overcome it under certain circumstances. Culture requires that men should not seek death too easily, but also that they should sometimes consider it the lesser evil. A life worth living depends on an ambivalence toward death.

My own death is no tragedy. But may I deny that the death of others is unjust, unfair, and irremediably tragic? We like to blame death rather than those who died, if we loved them; hence we deceive ourselves as they might have deceived themselves. We do not say, "How many months did they waste!" but, "If only they had had a few more weeks!" Not, "How sad that they did not do more!" but, "How unfair that they died so soon!" Still, not every death allows for this response. There are deaths that reproach us, deaths that are enviable.

Often we mourn the death of others because it leaves us lonely. But we do not hate sleep because we are sometimes lonely when others have gone to sleep and we lie awake. Death, like sleep, can mean separation; it usually does. We rarely have the honesty to remember how alone we are. The death of those we loved reminds us of what dishonesty had concealed from us: our profound solitude and our impending death. In the quest for honesty, death is a cruel but excellent teacher.

Our attitudes toward death are profoundly influenced by religion. From the Old Testament we have learned to think of every single human being as crucially important. Buddhism and other Oriental religions spread a very different view. To men brought up on the idea of the transmigration of souls, the teaching of Darwin could not have come as a shock: they assumed all along that a generation or two ago I, or any man, might well have been an animal, and that after death I might become one again. To men who had read in their scriptures of millions of myriads of ten million cycles, of thousands of worlds and vast numbers of Buddhas who had appeared in these worlds in different ages, the Copernican revolution would not have involved any blow to man's pride. That there are about a hundred million galaxies within range of our telescopes, and that our own galaxy alone contains hundreds of thousands of planets which may well support life and beings like ourselves seems strange to those brought up on the Bible, but not necessarily strange to Oriental believers.

For those not familiar with the sacred books of the East, the contrast may come to life as they compare Renaissance and Chinese paintings: here the human figures dominate the picture, and the landscape serves as a background; there the landscape is the picture, and the human beings in it have to be sought out. Here man seems all-important; there his cosmic insignificance is beautifully represented.

Modern science suggests that in important respects the Oriental religions were probably closer to the facts than the Old Testament or the New. It does not follow that we ought to accept the Buddha's counsel of resignation and detachment, falling out of love with the world. Nor need we emulate Lao-tze's wonderful whimsey and his wise mockery of reason, culture, and human effort. There are many possibilities: I say with Shakespeare, "All the world's a stage." Man seems to play a very insignificant part in the universe, and my part is negligible. The question confronting me is not, except perhaps in idle moments, what part might be more amusing, but what I wish to make of my part. And what I want to do and would advise others to do is to make the most of it: put into it all you have got, and live, and, if possible, die with some measure of nobility.

XIII

Trilogue on Heaven, Love, and Peace

99

IRENE: Have you found peace, Bruno?

CHRISTOPHER: What matters is not finding peace on earth but to attain the peace that passeth understanding, after death.

BRUNO: I don't want either.

CHRISTOPHER: What, then, do you want after death?

BRUNO: Nothing.

CHRISTOPHER: But if there were nothing after death, life would be altogether meaningless. Why go on living if there is no aim, no goal, no final bliss?

BRUNO: There are aims and goals enough in this life.

CHRISTOPHER: But they don't give life meaning; they can't.

IRENE: Hypocrite!

CHRISTOPHER: What do you mean?

IRENE: You talk as if the only thing that gave your life some meaning were your hope to enter heaven after death; but in fact your life is full of projects, purposes, and expectations that bear absolutely no relation to such hopes. It is surely these this-worldly aims and goals on which you count to give your life some meaning—at the very least, six and a half days of the week. At most you hedge your bet by making a minute investment that requires nothing but a few hours a week; but to say that this marginal speculation alone gives your life meaning is hypocrisy.

CHRISTOPHER: Your name calling depends on the slanderous assumption that I don't believe what I profess. But I do believe, and without faith, life makes no sense.

BRUNO: It wasn't nice of her to charge you with hypocrisy; but she is right, you know.

CHRISTOPHER: I know nothing of the sort and find your supercilious tone still more annoying than her lack of manners.

BRUNO: You claim your hope for bliss gives your life meaning.

CHRISTOPHER: I don't just claim that: it does. And I dare say that if you do not have a hope like that, you, no doubt, find life meaningless, whether you care to admit it or not.

BRUNO: There is a sense in which life *is* meaningless and another in which it is not.

CHRISTOPHER: Before you drown in evasions, sophistries, and plain equivocation, I wish you would withdraw your insult.

BRUNO: But you *are* hypocritical when you profess to care so much about what happens to you after death. A man who is seriously involved in his speculation investigates the company before investing. In the field with which you claim to be so seriously concerned there are a multitude of companies, and you know hardly anything about the lot, have not compared their merits and their weaknesses, but simply acted on a tip without checking on it.

IRENE: Bruno, you have no principles; you stole my metaphor.

CHRISTOPHER: I have the utmost confidence in the man who gave me what you call, disgustingly, a tip. In fact, it was not just one man but several men and women of the very highest quality. Moreover, they are associated with an old firm that is thoroughly respectable. Even if I gave the matter three whole days a week, I could not possibly come up with anything half as reliable as this fine team of specialists. I simply lack their expert qualifications. There are other things of which I have a firsthand knowledge. In this case I need none because my case could hardly be in better hands.

IRENE: So you admit that you do not put very much time into this little speculation.

BRUNO: Your metaphor does not stand up, Christopher.

CHRISTOPHER: *My* metaphor? *Mine?* What will you say next? It's yours, Bruno, not mine.

IRENE: *His?* It is *mine.*

BRUNO: All right, all right! Irene started it all, and all of us have used it now. But the way she and I employed it, it stood up, while your use of it doesn't. Suppose you were thinking of getting married.

CHRISTOPHER: Now you are changing the metaphor.

IRENE: He wants one of his own.

BRUNO: I am getting sick of all this talk about metaphor and which is whose. If you contemplated marriage you would not go to an old, established firm and seek advice; you would pick your own girl.

IRENE: What makes you so sure he would?

CHRISTOPHER: What does that prove?

BRUNO: In matters that are really important to you, you don't pass the buck.

CHRISTOPHER: Another vulgarism—designed, I suppose, to cover up your want of logic. When it comes to marriage, I know better whom I love, with whom I get along——

IRENE: Where the shoe pinches, or will pinch, if you don't mind the vulgarism——

CHRISTOPHER: I do mind; but I trust you get the point. There is no need to defer to experts. In this matter every one of us is the best expert there could be. Or, if not every one of us, most of us. I, at any rate, am satisfied with my own qualifications.

IRENE: He's got you there.

BRUNO: If you don't start to argue which metaphor is whose, you are sure to get off on another tangent. Perhaps my example of marriage was unfortunate; yes, I am sure it was.

IRENE: You see, you'd better stick to my examples.

BRUNO: Suppose you had to make a really important choice between several alternatives. Now you knew of an old, highly respected firm and of several good people who served it with pride. And they gave you some straightforward advice.

IRENE: Bruno is leaning over backward to be fair to you. As if the kind of outfit that he has in mind were in the habit of giving straightforward advice!

BRUNO: Now suppose that someone pointed out to you

that some of your best friends were dealing with a great variety of other firms, some possibly not quite as old as yours, others considerably older—all widely respected. Suppose you were also shown that in your own firm there had been, and still were, some unscrupulous and even some downright dishonest characters, occasionally even in positions of responsibility and influence. And that in some of the other firms there had been, and were even now, people in no way inferior to the best in yours. For the moment, let's not weigh their merits closely, but suppose that they were rather even.

CHRISTOPHER:	But that supposition begs the question.

IRENE:	On the contrary. I should have said that he is still leaning over backward to be fair. Your firm has a reputation for intolerance and for waging wars and crusades while it talks of peace.

BRUNO:	If my supposition begged the question, if the issue really depended on the merits of the firms and of the men associated with them, especially at the policy-making level——

CHRISTOPHER:	Of course, it does; that's what I said before.

BRUNO:	Then nothing, absolutely nothing, could excuse you from a careful study of the various firms, their members past and present, and the way their policies were formulated centuries ago.

IRENE:	You would find that the policies were, as often as not, the result of cutthroat competition, wars, wily diplomacy, and very earthy compromises.

CHRISTOPHER:	She is rude, rude, rude; and you say constantly: suppose, suppose, suppose. Suppose I don't suppose. Suppose I do not care to play your little game. Suppose I'd rather stick to facts.

BRUNO:	The fact is that Irene called you a hypocrite; and I admitted that was rude of her, though she was right. What I have tried to show you, without being rude, is how she is right. You do not do what you would clearly do if you considered what you claim to be so terribly important one tenth as important as you say you do.

CHRISTOPHER:	You are every bit as rude as she is. I only pray that both of you may find forgiveness. But I am hardly

surprised. Without faith there is no charity, but only nastiness
and——

IRENE: Honesty. When honesty is not particularly flatter-
ing, you call it rudeness. But I'll admit there is another kind
of rudeness: the rudeness of faith lacking honesty—that kills,
charitably, of course, to prevent the disastrous effects of honesty. And when no longer able to kill, it imposes censorship;
and deprived of that weapon too, one *tries* to prevent the
truth from being stated—for example, by appealing to good
manners and discrediting devotion to the truth as rudeness. I
only wish you might admit that what you really mind is not
rudeness: you are as rude as anybody when you say, for example, that all other firms are far inferior to your own; that
their executives lack the fine qualities of yours; and, in short,
that it so happens you are right and everybody who does not
agree with you is wrong. And that our lives are meaningless,
while yours is meaningful. No, what you mind is not rudeness;
what you mind is honesty. You may call it insulting, uncivil,
or say it is in bad taste. All those are subterfuges. What you
cannot stand is honesty—except, of course, in trivial matters,
where it does not hurt.

CHRISTOPHER: There is nothing greater than charity; and
in the name of charity I oppose hurting people.

IRENE: You see, it is not rudeness that you mind. You
even said yourself a while ago that you found Bruno's polite
superciliousness much worse than my straightforward rudeness.

CHRISTOPHER: I don't make a fetish of manners. What I
object to is hurting people. Surely that makes sense.

IRENE: Not altogether. When a man named Bruno was
burned as a heretic in 1600, I suppose that did not hurt.

CHRISTOPHER: In the first place, he was burned to save
his soul from eternal fire after death. In the second place, he
was burned lest his heretic teachings should infect his fellow
men and lead them to endure eternal fire. So a little hurt
was inflicted to prevent a bigger, *far* bigger one.

IRENE: I like that: "a little hurt."

CHRISTOPHER: It is like a vaccination.

IRENE: And you are so squeamish about rudeness, because it hurts. Poor dear! If torturing and burning heretics alive is like a vaccination, rudeness should not even itch.

CHRISTOPHER: I have no desire whatsoever to defend the Catholics for their cruel persecutions of heretics.

IRENE: Of course not. Only the Protestants. Only Calvin's burning of Servetus—and, after all, Calvin only burned the man himself after first betraying him to the Inquisition, hoping that the Catholics would take care of him. And the Salem witch-hunters. They were Protestant and clean and full of charity.

BRUNO: You are really unfair to Christopher. He has no wish to defend that sort of thing.

IRENE: Doesn't he? Didn't he defend it only a moment ago?

CHRISTOPHER: I did not defend it. I merely mentioned the reasons these deluded people had for doing what they did.

IRENE: Now I am more confused than ever. Then you don't think that heretics and those "infected" by their doctrines suffer in eternity?

CHRISTOPHER: I never said I did.

IRENE: Then our beliefs do not affect what happens to us after death.

CHRISTOPHER: I didn't say that.

BRUNO: Of course you didn't. But it would be interesting to find out what you do think about this.

CHRISTOPHER: The fact is that I don't know what happens after death. I don't know if our beliefs make a difference.

BRUNO: If you don't know what happens after death, nor what makes and what does not make a difference, your initial statement has become almost empty of meaning.

CHRISTOPHER: What initial statement?

BRUNO: That your belief in some bliss after death gave your life meaning, and that this alone gave your life meaning.

CHRISTOPHER: So? I believe in bliss, or heaven, or whatever you prefer to call it.

IRENE: Do you think we all go there?

CHRISTOPHER: I don't know.

BRUNO: Do you think it likely?

CHRISTOPHER: I should not be surprised if, in the end, we

should all find ourselves where some of us will be surprised to find ourselves.

IRENE: How clear! How neat! How unambiguously stated!

BRUNO: You mean, I suppose, in heaven.

CHRISTOPHER: If you want to put it that way.

BRUNO: I don't, particularly. I am just trying to find out what precisely you were saying.

CHRISTOPHER: Say, near God.

IRENE: He has jumped from the mist into the fog. That's what the theologians call "the leap."

BRUNO: You seem to be saying, Christopher, that you would not be surprised if all that we believed and did during out lives turned out to make no difference whatsoever after death.

IRENE: He put on his broad-minded hat. He is being charitable. He would not be surprised if the heretics rubbed elbows in eternity with those who burned them. Anyway, it's an improvement over the old Christian idea that the burners would divert themselves in heaven with the spectacle of seeing all the unregenerate broiling in hell.

CHRISTOPHER: Why—would *you* reverse that dreadful notion and allow the heretics to look upon the tortures of their persecutors?

BRUNO: Of course not. Why should consciousness survive death? Let them all find peace—but not peace surpassing understanding. Simply peace and quiet and uninterrupted sleep. Or call it disintegration, or extinction. But the odd thing, Christopher, is that we two agree.

CHRISTOPHER: We certainly do not.

BRUNO: You agree with me that our lives are meaningless in an important sense. They make no difference whatsoever to what happens to us after death. Their significance is strictly limited to *this* life, allowing for some small effect on the lives of others after our death.

CHRISTOPHER: I am not so sure about that.

IRENE: But you only just said it.

CHRISTOPHER: I said it was possible. I should not be surprised.

BRUNO: You see, we do agree. I don't expect to be surprised either.

CHRISTOPHER: But I think *you* will be.

IRENE: I see it all now. According to Christopher, what happens to people after death is the same for all of them. Everybody finds himself in the unutterable vicinity, in close company with everybody else. But those who are charitable, sociable, and not demanding intellectually enjoy this endless occasion and find it nothing less than heavenly. Those, on the other hand, who have enough intelligence and sensitivity to appreciate the frightful boredom of this party find it hell. Going to church suddenly assumes a vast importance: there is no better way of training oneself to find boredom heavenly, not to let on what one thinks, and eventually to stop thinking. It is all so clear and so ingenious: by cultivating honesty we deprive ourselves of eternal bliss; while dishonesty pays, forever and ever.

CHRISTOPHER: How nasty can you be?

BRUNO: Now you have hurt his feelings. Why are you always so sarcastic?

IRENE: Poor, poor dear! I've hurt his darling feelings. And he told us that he doesn't like to get hurt. He doesn't think honesty is worth getting hurt for. Poor, poor dear! I am so terribly, terribly sorry.

CHRISTOPHER: You aren't content to be nasty. You misrepresent me constantly. I didn't say any of those dreadful things.

IRENE: Of course not, poor dear. You lack the wit.

CHRISTOPHER: Honesty is one thing, and hurting people another.

IRENE: Yes, dear. And courage is one thing, and getting hurt another. And endurance is one thing, and getting tired another. And loving is one thing, and suffering another.

CHRISTOPHER: What on earth does she mean?

IRENE: Poor, poor dear! He doesn't get the point. I am so terribly, terribly sorry.

BRUNO: She obviously means that you have to pay a price for virtue: no price, no virtue.

IRENE: Our poor dear is all for courage, as long as he

does not get hurt. Running the risk of getting hurt is carrying courage too far. And he likes endurance. He merely hates getting tired. Poor dear! And he loves to love; there is nothing he likes better. He merely hates suffering.

BRUNO: Nasty, nasty, nasty.

IRENE: That's me.

BRUNO: Up to a point, I see your point. Honesty involves hurt so often that anyone who says he prizes honesty—but not to the point of hurting people—is rather like a man who claims to prize courage, short of getting hurt. I not only see that, I agree. But is your point that anyone who prizes love ought to accept suffering too—and that we ought to prize both?

IRENE: Yes and no.

CHRISTOPHER: Now *you* are equivocating. Not that I am blaming you. When Bruno begins to cross-question, one simply can't always give straightforward answers.

IRENE: He asked me two questions, and I answered yes to the first and no to the second.

CHRISTOPHER: Now you have lost me.

IRENE: Poor dear! I do think that anyone who prizes love ought to realize that it entails suffering; and if he really considers love as wonderful as many people claim to find it, he ought to be willing to pay that price. But as for myself, I'm not.

CHRISTOPHER: You mean you admit openly and callously that you are against love? Your nastiness is not just weakness of the quarter-pound of flesh that wiggles wickedly in your foul mouth; your spirit isn't even willing. You are evil through and through. Serpent! May you find forgiveness!

BRUNO: If you are right, she needs no special dispensation: we'll all be forgiven. Prayer is pointless. Love does not pay.

CHRISTOPHER: Must it pay to be worth while?

BRUNO: *I* don't think so, but I thought you did. I am willing to love without rewards after death. But you said that without some such reward, life was meaningless.

IRENE: The point to grasp is that love involves suffering, not just occasionally, accidentally, avoidably. Love is not a happy feeling, a form of euphoria: those are epiphenomena. Love means assuming responsibility for another human being. Love involves a decision: not to be indifferent to the sufferings, sicknesses, and failures, to the false hopes, the mistakes, the disappointments, to the terrifying limitations and the final death of someone else. Love is not infatuation, not attraction, and not lust, though all these may precede love and at times accompany it. At other times, love is free of them. There is no need to call one kind of love better, one worse, praising love of a son above love of a husband, or vice versa. Love of its very nature involves suffering: sharing the sufferings of the loved one and, besides, suffering over the limitations of the other human being, not excluding those of which the loved one is not even conscious. Love is the antithesis of peace.

CHRISTOPHER: Up to that last remark, what you said was beautiful. I even thought you might change your mind and become a preacher. Really, it was a very fine sermon. But that final diatribe, of course, is something that no preacher would say.

IRENE: They are such hypocrites and favor everything that is really popular. If it is popular, trust them to say that it was *their* idea. Imagine a preacher saying something against such "okay" ideas as peace or love. Of course, they are for both, and we are lucky if they do not claim to have a monopoly on both. And honesty is held in such low esteem, partly owing to their influence, that nobody tells them, at least publicly, what any lover knows: that love entails unprecedented suffering. Also joy, of course. But by no means only that.

CHRISTOPHER: Now you are speaking of the love of the flesh. That is not the sort of love the preachers mean.

BRUNO: That's not fair, Christopher. Remember her analysis of love? She did show how love, even in the highest sense —especially in that—involves suffering.

IRENE: So you have to decide for either peace or love, not both. I have found peace by renouncing love.

CHRISTOPHER: Poor dear, yourself! You poor unloving heart! What wretchedness! I am so sorry for you, truly sorry— not just in the mocking sense in which you say that you are sorry.

IRENE: I have found peace. Have you?

CHRISTOPHER: No, I don't expect peace in this life. I expect it beyond.

IRENE: There, if you are right, we shall both enjoy peace. And if Bruno is right, we shall also both enjoy peace, if of a different sort. But here and now I enjoy peace, and you do not. And *you* profess to be sorry for *me!*

CHRISTOPHER: If you had really found peace, you would not be so nasty. Your serpent's tongue mocks your smooth claims. You delight in hurting people. You need to assert your superiority by shamelessly humiliating others. I am sure that you are deeply insecure and restless, that you have no peace.

IRENE: Poor gullible Christopher! He is taken in not only by the preachers but also, like so many modern preachers, by the cant of social psychology.

BRUNO: What sort of a potlatch is this? Each of you trying to shame the other by feeling sorrier for him than he for her. One has found peace, the other not; but both behave alike.

CHRISTOPHER: I am not nasty as she is.

IRENE: Of course not: you are holier than I am.

CHRISTOPHER: Nasty again! And I still say, your nastiness betrays a profound insecurity and lack of peace.

BRUNO: I associate peace in this life with the Buddha—seated, smiling, permeated with serenity. He was not sarcastic but compassionate. You, Irene, puzzle me.

CHRISTOPHER: The Buddha, of course, was a sham too. He claimed to be detached and compassionate. He was deeply inconsistent.

IRENE: Similar statements about—shall we say, his colleagues?—you'd call rude, if not blasphemous. But when it comes to other people's feelings you are free and easy on the draw.

BRUNO: The Buddha was not inconsistent. He was as detached and as compassionate as you might be when you see children playing, and one falls and cries. You would not take the hurt as seriously as the little boy does: you would realize that in three minutes he will not even remember it. For all that, you would feel some compassion—not enough to suffer yourself, not enough to keep you from smiling gently. To the

Buddha, the girl disappointed in her lover is not very different from that little boy: she too thinks she will never smile again, and it takes her more than three minutes to get over it, but almost certainly much less than three years; maybe not even three months. His detachment and compassion are born of maturity, and he smiles at the immaturity of most men.

IRENE: So you think that if I had really found peace, I should smile with serene compassion at people like Christopher instead of mocking him and taking pleasure in that.

BRUNO: I am not saying you should. I am merely surprised.

IRENE: Because I am not a field, meadow, and woods variety like Christopher, the likes of whom are a nickel a dozen, but a little more unusual, you are surprised. Blessed be those who are surprising, for at least they are not dull.

CHRISTOPHER: "Surprising" is a euphemism for you. Neither are you blessed. What you are is damned annoying.

IRENE: That is just what Socrates' contemporaries thought of him.

CHRISTOPHER: At least you don't pretend to be modest.

IRENE: I don't claim to be like Socrates. But you have to admit that he was nasty, and that he had a reputation for it too. He was ironical, sarcastic, enjoyed making fools of people, and took great delight in making people squirm in argument.

CHRISTOPHER: Yes, and he also sometimes slept; and so do you; and that makes you like Socrates.

IRENE: Poor dear! He never gets the point.

CHRISTOPHER: She wants to excuse her bad manners by finding a great man who shared some of her failings. One can always do that. But it proves nothing. What you ought to imitate is the fine qualities of great men, not their shortcomings.

BRUNO: Her point is that Socrates is also famed for his serenity. In his *Apology* he was as sarcastic as ever, but few would say that he betrayed a basic insecurity or want of peace. When Socrates talked his judges into sentencing him to death, and in the way in which he subsequently faced his death, he seemed, and still seems, a marvel of peace and security.

IRENE: Thank you, scholar. Where would I be without you? Beyond Christopher.

CHRISTOPHER: Then you think that the social psychologists are wrong?

IRENE: Some social psychologists are preachers *manqués*. They picture love as a panacea rather than a source of suffering, and peace as the twin of insipidity. But peace is really delightful.

CHRISTOPHER: Nonsense. Nastiness is rooted in frustration, and you cannot attain peace without developing the art of loving.

IRENE: See what I mean, Bruno! As soon as anyone affects a homiletic tone, he believes the message.

CHRISTOPHER: It's not the tone that matters, but psychology.

IRENE: People who like preachers accept only what those psychologists say who agree with preachers. Then they make a great fuss about the authority of psychology. But as soon as a psychologist says something that does not fit their conviction—"It's only psychology, which isn't really a science yet, you know."

BRUNO: Still I am wondering if Socrates is the only example on your side. That one example would suffice to make one think. And yet, is he the only one?

IRENE: The trouble is that there are so few famous people —men whose characters are well known to us—of whom one could say that they had found peace.

CHRISTOPHER: Jesus above all men.

IRENE: There you have another illustration of my point.

CHRISTOPHER: What *do* you mean?

IRENE: Was Jesus gentle, or did He
       Give any marks of gentility?

CHRISTOPHER: Can't we stop short of blasphemy?

BRUNO: She is quoting William Blake, you know: *The Everlasting Gospel.*

IRENE: Was Jesus humble? or did He
       Give any proofs of humility?

CHRISTOPHER: Blake or no, it's blasphemy.

IRENE: The Vision of Christ that thou dost see
          Is my vision's greatest enemy.
          Thine has a great hook nose like thine;
          Mine has a snub nose like to mine.
          Thine is the Friend of all Mankind;
          Mine speaks in parables to the blind.

CHRISTOPHER: Well now, this Blake, he was a famous poet; and this, of course, is poetry.

IRENE: Sure, sure, poor dear! It's only poetry. And it was written around 1810. And that, of course, makes it all right. In any case, it would be foolish not to be broad-minded about famous poets, wouldn't it? Blake is all right; or, if he isn't, at least we do not make a point of that. And Socrates is also far too much admired to condemn him outright. What matters is that we don't want to have people like Socrates and Blake around today. Because they are nasty. Or, if anybody has got to be nasty, at least it should be in poetry, because nobody reads that. Or anyway, the people who read it are probably past corrupting.

CHRISTOPHER: You are so wrong. There have been great religious poets.

IRENE: Like Dante, for example, and like Milton. And we all know that there was not a drop of nastiness in either of them. They oozed charity.

BRUNO: I'd still like to return to the point about peace. You are right that qualities resented in contemporaries are forgiven, and not even seen, in great men of the past.

IRENE: They *should* be forgiven, as you say so archly; even admired. What is damnable is the hypocrisy of being so broad-minded about men safely enshrined in history when the same traits are denounced today and held against the people who possess them. Still, that happens all the time. There is no surer way of finding out if a broad mind is truly broad, or merely supposed to be, because it offers no resistance to the wind and follows fashion, than to see how it reacts to its contemporaries; especially to younger people who are not yet fashionable and, with luck, never will be.

BRUNO: Socrates was a fine illustration of the fusion of peace and—all right—nastiness. Jesus I am not so sure about, because we do not know enough about the historical Jesus.

IRENE: It should count for something that the literary portrait in the Gospels is a prime example of both qualities. Naturally, here we do not speak of nastiness but of prophetic wrath, impassioned honesty——

CHRISTOPHER: He was not witty. I mean—I mean—he did not try to be.

IRENE: You mean, you mean, he did not have a sense of humor. I mean, I mean, he did not try to have one.

CHRISTOPHER: He was not glib and playful and superficial.

IRENE: Yes, dear, it wasn't nastiness; only prophetic wrath and honesty. He called people vipers, and blind fools, and, according to John, said the devil was the father of the Jews, but he was very careful about hurting people; and when *he* called people hypocrites, it did not hurt.

CHRISTOPHER: But he was right: they were.

IRENE: While I am wrong, and you are not. Oh, my poor self-righteous friend!

BRUNO: Couldn't you forget about Jesus for a moment——

CHRISTOPHER: Forget about Jesus?

BRUNO: Irene, you understand me, don't you? Let us at least forget about Christopher for a moment. I am still wondering whether there are other examples besides Socrates and possibly Jesus.

IRENE: As I said before, it is so difficult to agree who found peace. Take St. John Chrysostom, whose byname means the Golden-Mouthed. A contemporary Catholic historian, Malcolm Hay, in *Europe and the Jews,* calls him "one of the greatest of the Church Fathers." He quotes a Protestant divine who called this saint "one of the most eloquent of the preachers who, ever since apostolic times, have brought to men the Divine tidings of truth and love." Cardinal Newman called him, "A bright cheerful gentle soul, a sensitive heart . . . elevated, refined, transformed by the touch of heaven." But, says Hay, "The violence of the language used by St. John Chrysostom in his homilies against the Jews has never been exceeded by any preacher whose sermons have been recorded." By quoting a great many other saints, Hay leaves no doubt about how much this means. These homilies, he tells us, "filled the minds of Christian congregations with a hatred which was transmitted to their children, and to their children's children." The homilies "were used for centuries, in schools and seminaries where priests were taught to preach, with St. John Chrysostom as their model—where priests were taught to hate, with St. John Chrysostom as their model." He called the synagogue, "worse than a brothel . . . the den of scoundrels and the repair of wild beasts . . . the temple of demons devoted to idolatrous cults . . . and the cavern of devils." Hay quotes more than that, not only from this saint. St. Ambrose preached that the synagogue was "a house of impiety, a receptacle of folly, which God himself has condemned." When his listeners set fire to a synagogue, he said, "I declare that I set fire to the synagogue, or at least that I ordered those who did it, that there might not be a place where Christ was denied." St. Simeon Stylites, an "ascetic who achieved distinction by living for thirty-six years on top of a pillar fifty feet high, had given up . . . 'all worldly luxuries except Jew-hatred.'"

CHRISTOPHER: I don't think social psychologists would consider a man who lived on top of a pillar so long a really healthy person. He was, no doubt, sick and needed help.

IRENE: My quotations come from a mere three or four pages of a long book that shows how many saints and other great Christians resembled the three I mentioned. I very much doubt that they all needed an analyst to find peace. I consider it entirely possible that they had found peace.

BRUNO: A frightening thought.

CHRISTOPHER: It would be so much more pleasant to believe the psychologists.

IRENE: You talk all the time as if psychologists were agreed on what you find so pleasant. Actually your pleasant doctrine represents a minority view. Freud did not agree with it; he did not think that all aggression came out of frustration.

CHRISTOPHER: He was an atheist, I think.

IRENE: So much for him. Chrysostom, Ambrose, and Stylites were not. And what we need is more men of strong faith like these blessed souls, and fewer men like Freud.

BRUNO: What you have shown is not quite what you

meant to show. You wanted to defend peace without love. But your examples only show how terrible a thing peace without love can be. Freud may not have found peace. He surely suffered. But he was not without love.

IRENE: Dreadful people are found in all camps. Mine is not immune. Needless to say, I loathe some of my bedfellows as much as you do.

BRUNO: There is something selfish—frankly selfish—about disavowing love to escape suffering and find peace.

CHRISTOPHER: I have been thinking——

IRENE: That's a pleasant change.

CHRISTOPHER: I do not even think it works.

IRENE: If you mean that thinking does not work, speak for yourself.

CHRISTOPHER: I mean——

IRENE: Yes, poor dear, you mean. We know, you mean.

BRUNO: *You're* mean, really mean.

CHRISTOPHER: I don't think that disavowing love makes you immune to suffering. Even if the Buddha said it did.

IRENE: Yes, yes, we know, the Buddha was a heathen; in fact, he was an atheist. So we need not listen to him.

CHRISTOPHER: The point is, he was wrong. Even if you do not love anyone, hunger and thirst, torture and sickness still cause pain.

BRUNO: Of course, the Buddha did not just teach men to fall out of love with each other, but to detach themselves from everything. You can reach the point where thirst and hunger do not hurt much any more. But have you, Irene?

CHRISTOPHER: And if I hit you, that would hurt. Not that I would. And cancer would still hurt. And lack of love itself hurts. You must feel so pitifully empty.

IRENE: Like your poor head. Of course, some things still hurt a little even after you have found peace; but those little hurts, even painful diseases, do not matter so much any more. And as for lack of love, that does not hurt. I don't feel empty. Socrates did not feel empty. The Stoics did not. There is just a feeling of freedom.

BRUNO: But Socrates loved philosophy. He cared. He was not completely detached. And whether Socrates did or not, and whatever the Buddha said, I do not want the kind of peace where I am altogether past caring. I often feel ashamed at caring about this or that and try to rise above humiliating concerns. There are many things I do not want to care about. Still, I do not want your peace. I want to love. I like your analysis of love. It does involve suffering, even a deliberate choice to accept suffering. But I make that choice with open eyes.

IRENE: Is it worth it?

BRUNO: You talk as if there were scales somewhere to measure that. There is no way of telling if it's worth it. The question makes no sense. I choose to love.

CHRISTOPHER: That sounds fantastic. Love is the gift of heaven. You cannot choose to love. And if you did, it would be irresponsible.

BRUNO: I do choose to love. I have searched my heart more than once whether to love or not to love. I have pondered Irene's alternative, felt its attraction, and resisted it. After deliberation, after exposing myself to the rival prospects, after considering what can be said for each and what against each, I made my choice. And if going about it that way is not responsible, then I don't know what it means to be responsible. What's more, to decide to love is to resolve to accept responsibility.

IRENE: Poor dear Bruno, I feel sorry for you too.

BRUNO: Your potlatch bores me utterly. I do not feel sorry for you. You have made your choice, I mine.

IRENE: But you can't help feeling sorry for Christopher. Poor, poor Christopher. He is so sweet.

BRUNO: That is one thing you are not. And your nastiness is rather tiresome, you know. Sometimes your wit redeems it, sometimes not. In any case, I can't always agree with you.

CHRISTOPHER: There is more hope for you, Bruno, than for that damnable woman. I feel sorry for both of you, but you may yet see the light.

BRUNO: That is the worst of it. Unless one is as nasty as she is, people like you will say that sort of thing. One really has to be nasty in self-defense.

XIV

Epilogue

100

I should like to write *Eine kleine Nachtphilosophie,* a little philosophy for the night, out of the night—little, unpretentious, but adequate for the night. How unpretentious he was, even in *Don Giovanni* and *The Magic Flute,* how light and humorous even at his grandest, how free of pompousness, how gay, with his eyes open to the night. There is no Mozart in philosophy.

Philosophy has to be analytic and must explore the themes it takes up to the bitter end. It must not merely entertain; it must elaborate. Must it be tedious? Music analyzes its figures, explores, elaborates, and employs the intellect.

Not *Lear,* not *Agamemnon.* Something little—without venom.

He said: How was the funeral? His father: All right. When can I go and see the grave? I'll take you tomorrow. They had a horse, not much of a horse, but I rode it. And I walked through cow manure. Does she still wear the pink corsage? Yes, she does. Does she still look as she looked yesterday? Yes. Can I go to the farm again tomorrow?

The minister had quoted more than he had said. Death was not the end. In my father's house are many mansions. Twice. What distinguishes the Christian is this comfort. Christ prepared a place for her. Nothing about the brevity of her life. Barely over thirty. Nothing about want of meaning or about accomplishment. Nothing I should have said or thought about. Nothing that I believed. Does he himself believe what he is saying? Does anyone believe it? Quotations that must have had a wealth of associations. A poem she seems to have sung sometimes. Why bring it up now? Is he trying to make the poor man cry?

When my father died, I was three thousand miles away. By the time I got the letter he was buried. He had wanted to be burned because that would eliminate all ceremony. No one was to speak. But he died so far from any city that it seemed in keeping with his will to bury him in a small cemetery in the woods nearby. And where I was, nothing was different. No change except the knowledge that three thousand miles away he was not there.

Was the meaning of the ceremony to make people cry, so the pain would not eat quite so deep into their souls? Would they feel better afterward for that? Or was it just an obligation? Did it seem *mean* not to have a splendid coffin? But the quotations! She had not been close to me, but I had been somber, seeing him and her parents; absorbed, not just a spectator. The quotations had not bothered me. They were a puzzle. Wouldn't they bother him? I had identified myself with him and her parents.

Nothing of Mozart. No music. Two short books. In the former the speaker viewed everything from beneath, from "underground." Everybody knew that. The title called attention to it. Still, when the speaker in *The Fall*, almost a hundred years later, made a point of seeing everything from a height, the deliberate contrast had been overlooked. In its own way, the earlier book is as perfect as Mozart. Little, unpompous, venomous—venomous against everything pompous. A new way. No novel, dialogue, or play. A medium rarely tried.

Not to view things from beneath or above. A speaker who viewed things from *inside*. An honest search for identity with various views. One could still bring out their limitations. But discover them first. Honestly, from inside. Without prejudging. Something little—without venom, and at least light if not gay. Not sublime. But to do justice by not sitting in judgment, by not being high and mighty or base and nasty. To

do justice by being oneself, not an insect and not a giant;
without pretensions; human, thinking and feeling and wondering without much knowledge.

He had said afterward that the minister was a great guy.
So he had not been offended. And the minister was no Swede,
though he looked like one. He has been here nine years, he
said, and is a few years younger than myself. And I had
thought: Anybody younger than you would be very young.
But I had not said it. She had been younger, of course.

Her mother had said, just before leaving the grave: Let me
touch it once more—and had stepped forward to put the fin-
gertips of one hand on the coffin, where the wood could be
seen under the flowers. That was all. She kept her control.
Like everybody else. If it had been my daughter, I shouldn't
have been so serene. I should not have placed myself in that
position. No ceremony, no last look at the coffin before so
many witnesses. No publicly spoken quotations. No crowd.
Solitude.

Afterward there was talk about recipes. How she and a
friend had swapped recipes, and which other ones had been
swapped on the afternoon when she gave out that one. And
her mother, hardly older than myself, said *she* had given her
daughter this recipe. And there was more of that, and some
talk about buying shoes, and shoe sizes. Small talk. But it
was not a matter of keeping up a front. They were really
interested. That was a large part of their lives. They were
eating as they talked. Food and clothes. They were not callous. I liked the mother.

He was cheerful and strong almost the whole time. He had
greeted us with a friendly smile. When we left, he thanked
us for coming from so far away. And then he got mixed up for
the first time and ended by saying—those were his last words—
I am very happy. He did not mean it that way. But he must
have believed the quotations.

How else could he have endured the little boy's boisterous
talk? Endured? The boy's untroubled mood was his father's
creation. One word, one gesture, one burst of tears would
have shattered it.

I had thought that talk of heaven was largely hypocrisy. If people believed what they said, they would not mind death so much. But nobody feared death more than the people who talked most of heaven. And now? I had been wrong.

One of the women in the kitchen, washing dishes to help, the director of a women's organization at the church, had told a story of someone's going to heaven. He had found the faithful in groups, but no Methodist women. Asking at last, he was told that the Methodist women were in the kitchen. Then there was talk, just a few remarks, about different denominations, how little sense it made to have lots of small churches, and how much better it was for all the Protestant groups to attend a single big church.

The ascetic strain of their religion seems forgotten, along with the doctrines that distinguish their denomination. They do not even know their creeds. How, then, could they please me? By refusing to worship together? By being ascetic? What would I have them do?

There are other alternatives. They might repudiate the doctrines, or decide what they really believe, what not; what seems probable, what not; what seems important, what not. But they feel edified by asceticism and denunciations of the things of this world, with their heart in the kitchen, in food, in clothes. And the men talk of machines and cars, of techniques and elaborate projects, while admiring the counsel to have no thought of the morrow.

It adds up to a tolerable way of life. One knows how to deal with death. And the best help their neighbors. One brings food after a death in the family, mows the lawn, cleans the house, does the dishes, is kind. Not all are that way, but a good many. Some are even inspired to fight injustice with courage. One values food and clothes and cleanliness, but admits, in principle, that there is more to life and that things of the spirit are more important. One has no clear notion of things of the spirit, but by giving praise to unselfishness, helpfulness, sacrifice, one becomes better rather than worse; and a few become very good indeed.

What is so ironical is that in the Gospels and the Epistles there is such a radical streak, while Christianity is, and has been for centuries, a religion of compromise. If Jesus came back today. We talked about that in college. The other boy is a minister now, and I have not seem him for over twenty years. He laughed when I said: If anyone turned on the electric light, He would faint. It is the obvious story to write, without venom; also with: it has endless possibilities.

If there are people whom the Christian religion helps to live kindly lives, why upset them? But who is upsetting them? Jesus would have, and most of the major Christians would have. They did not consider living kindly lives sufficient. According to John's Gospel, Jesus said that only those born of water and the Spirit could enter the kingdom of God, and that whoever does not believe the Son must bear the penalty of God's wrath. But these people are baptized and do believe the Son, and they take the sacraments, mindful of the counsel that "He who eats me will live because of me." They simply do not trouble their heads over my ilk and our fate after death.

It is not lack of charity. They do not think I shall be tormented. It is lack of thoughtfulness. And who is upsetting them? Nobody. The spirit of the great Christians is largely gone. Upsetting people is the one thing that religious people most nearly agree is bad. But the great Christians, like their Old Testament forebears, believed that just this was their task.

Where is Mozart now? Where is music? The gaiety that never offends suffering; the courage that is never obtrusive; the gentleness that is indomitable. To delight without flattery. To arrange sounds that comfort without compromise, without arousing any false hopes, without condescension. He helps by having been through all of it and showing it without making a point of it. Indirect communication. The antithesis of my soliloquy. Even a dialogue would be more indirect. Certainly, a play, a novel, a story. Is a philosophical Mozart an impossibility? Or would he tell stories? Not moral tales. But then they would be inconclusive. As music is. Must philosophy be conclusive? Yes. It need not force any final conclusion upon the reader or listener; but surely it must consider the merits of some conclusions, and, in the process, as Socrates did, discredit a few. And what does Mozart discredit? Most of us. His successors more than his predecessors. What could better symbolize ineffectiveness? Almost all who came after him stand discredited by his work. In that at least he resembles the prophets. Perhaps futility belongs to nobility. To be guided by effectiveness and by expediency is an objection to nobility. And does nobility upset—especially nice people? One cannot generalize about that. Certainly, it is not its primary aim to upset anyone. It does what it considers right, and lets the effect take care of itself. Is it, then, imprudent? Yes, probably. Nobility squanders itself.

When I die, I do not want them to say: Think of all he still might have done. There is cowardice in wanting to have that said. Let them say—let me live so they can say: There was nothing left in him; he did not spare himself; he put everything he had into his work, his life.

Oh, you want to be a vegetable during the last years? An idiot with no mind left? Or a retired writer who, demonstrably, had nothing more to say? How hideous!

No, I did not mean that. The point is to hold nothing back. Mozart, like Van Gogh, died in his thirties. One does not feel: If only he had known that he was to die soon and had worked just a little harder, driven himself just a little more, what might he have done! They gave their all, held nothing back, squandered themselves. The same is true of Goethe dying in his eighties, working till the end—and of Shakespeare, who died in retirement, not working till the end. What matters is giving what one has to give, spending oneself utterly.

Rabbi Zusya said that on the Day of Judgment God would ask him, not why he had not been Moses, but why he had not been Zusya. Neither need I make an ass of myself transposing Mozart into philosophic prose. But there is sense in asking myself whether what I write transposes *me*. Or whether it creates a false picture. Then, for heaven's sake, keep Mozart out of this! But writing as if one were trying to transpose the *Götterdämmerung* would give a false picture. And some people actually think one has to choose between the *Twilight of*

Gods and *Parsifal*. It is well to remind them of *Eine kleine Nachtmusik*.

If it does not upset, it is not philosophy. Unless it deals only with problems that are too remote from people's lives to upset them. Beyond that, it is largely a matter of explicitness. To avoid upsetting anyone, one can refrain from spelling out implications. There is much that *Eine kleine Nachtmusik* discredits, but Mozart did not spell that out. In *Don Giovanni* and *The Magic Flute* he came closer to stating what was implied, closer to polemic—closer, but, happily, did not go all the way. Music does not have to. Music should not. But philosophy?

Just this is the job of philosophy. The poets go a little further than the composers, but usually not all the way either. When we start wondering about the implications of *Antigone*, we turn to philosophy. Much can be left unstated. But if nothing is discredited, it is not philosophy.

Philosophy is always academic or upsetting. There is no middle ground. But it can rationalize, give reasons for what the audience wants to believe. It can give pleasure instead of upsetting. Are false prophets, prophets?

False prophets, said Jeremiah, cry peace, peace, when there is no peace. The philosopher who tells his audience what they want to hear, and proves to them in startling ways that they are right, cries peace, peace, when there is no peace. For most people aren't right. Most people are confused.

One does not have to upset them, though. One could write lyrically, musically, pleasingly. Why not? But if one pretends that in doing this one is still a philosopher, one is a false philosopher.

Eine kleine Nachtphilosophie is a chimera, like an Egyptian pyramid in music. Then give up philosophy! Why? Perhaps being pleasant is not that important after all. One can be grateful for Mozart without wishing that everybody were like him. One may find comfort in Mozart after listening to Jeremiah. But for Jeremiah to try to be like Mozart would have been senseless.

Mr. Jeremiah, sir, don't you realize you are upsetting people? Many of them are nice people, too, sir. But his problem was that too few were disturbed too little.

A philosopher is no prophet: a philosopher only tries to disturb a few people a little. He does not scream in the market place or disrupt religious services. He speaks softly, not to large masses. But why does he speak? You cannot generalize. Some may see something that many others do not see, something most people would not care to see—something that will make little difference even to many who are somewhat interested. There are always some who want only to be entertained. They won't be upset. Blessed are they, for they shall be contented. But if a few are disturbed, must one apologize? Sorry, old chap, about my last tragedy if it upset you. I'll have to rewrite a few scenes and change some of the speeches to make it more pleasing.

The story of the cross is really too upsetting. Not at all nice, like the bit about the manger. My God, my God, why hast thou forsaken me? That should come out. Luke and John took it out. And Luke introduced the manger, which none of the others have. Blessed Luke! But why did he leave in the cross? Really, that should come out, too. Luke had Jesus on the cross speak of paradise, and then of committing his spirit into the hands of the Father. That way, it is hardly upsetting. Blessed Luke! He was no Grünewald. But he did leave in the cross. What is upsetting is such a concession to the facts, to truth, to honesty. Still, something can be done about that. The facts can be presented as a mere episode. One can add a happy ending. And if the story begins and ends happily, what comes in between will fall into place; or at least one can try.

Now I no longer know whether the apostles tried to upset or not. Perhaps some did, some not. And there were some prophets, at least a few, who did not. And philosophers who did, and others who did not. So you cannot plead your vocation in extenuation. Can't I? Not as a genus, a business, a *métier*. But as *my* vocation. Some see comfort where others despair. Some see confusion where others find peace and respectability, and honesty where others assume depravity. And "he that sees but does not bear witness, be accursed."

You see her monstrous hat. Must you tell her that it is dreadful? Of course not. But suppose she asks you: How do you like my new hat? If that is the truth, why not say something like: You look as lovely as ever. Or: I like you even better without a hat.

Wasn't that a wonderful sermon? Why say it was? The more important the issue, the less silly and pedantic is truthfulness. I did not like it so much. And if you are asked why, tell him briefly, without becoming a bore. Or do become a bore, so you won't be asked again. In cases of hats and sermons, the tone of voice and a touch of humor carry more weight than whatever one says. A smiling, "Frankly, I don't like this one so much" will be resented less than a bored "Marvelous." Are such cases even worth mentioning? Yes, to discredit the insidious assumption that lies are of necessity the fabric of speech, and that honesty is for boors only.

Where did he go? It is the Gestapo. You lie. The issue is important, but you do not tell the truth. Yet you do not lie to avoid upsetting the questioner. It takes more courage to lie than to tell the truth. Is that the criterion? Hardly. The point is to be honest unless there are overruling considerations. Being honest is important. To overrule that, something has to be still more important. And, in case of doubt, tell the truth. Why? Because it is so easy to be in doubt, so easy to justify dishonesty, that once you decide to tell lies in case of doubt, you have really abandoned honesty as an important standard.

When in doubt, hurt people? Is it not important not to hurt people? Again, there are overruling considerations. To preserve from hurt at all costs is the recipe for inanity, immaturity, lack of strength, of courage and love, devotion, loyalty, backbone, wisdom, accomplishment. If so much that is worth while depends on being hurt again and again, should there be any rule against hurting people? Yes, one should not hurt people for no good reason. And what is a good reason? To make them better men and women. That this is a sufficient reason, we all agree. Most, perhaps all, civilizations agree on this, but they do not agree on the meaning of "better."

When in doubt if you should be honest because honesty

would hurt, ask yourself if there is a reasonable chance that the truth will make the person to whom you are speaking better. To hurt deeply where there isn't, is cruel.

That minister is a great guy. Should I have said: I am not so sure? Or: It all depends on what you mean by a great guy? Or: You really should not believe the things he said? Those quotations are not conclusive. There is the question whether Jesus really said all those things. And what is the evidence that those claims are true? And even assuming that they are, there remains the enormous problem just what they mean.

Does she still wear the pink corsage? Does she still look as she looked yesterday? Yes, son, *now*. But how will she look next year? And do you know what it means that you will never see her again? *Never*. And it is very possible that nobody will ever love you as she did. Do you understand? If not, let me try to explain.

Speaking like that to the boy does not even occur to one till one deliberately thinks about cases. One would not dream of doing that. Why not? Might it not make him a better man? It is too unlikely. Something like this might be said to him fifteen years hence, and then not about his mother, but more impersonally. Leave it to him to make the application. Let him decide when he is ready. Then, would you lie to him till he is ready? No, I should not. I should not have told him whatever he must have been told. No, I should not have lied to him. I should answer his questions truthfully, though without needless gore. But I should not answer questions he did not ask. When not face to face with popular idols, honesty should be gentle and unobtrusive.

The father is more than fifteen years older; more than twenty-five years older. Why not tell him the truth? Because he did not ask. It would be obtrusive, gratuitous. That is an arbitrary code. It is not at all obvious that his asking should make the difference. True. It is not obvious. There are no conclusive reasons. But there are reasons for it, and no equally good reasons against it.

Asking *is* relevant. You cannot tell all the truths you know to all men you meet. Excuse me, I am eight years old. Pardon me, I have read *Hamlet*. I believe that Shakespeare's plays were written by Shakespeare, not by Bacon. Bacon was born in 1561. Two plus two is four. I don't believe everything that is said in the Bible. The evidence for a life after death is far from overwhelming, and that for an eventual resurrection of the dead is even poorer. Surely, asking is relevant.

Also, this moment would be particularly bad. If at all, not now. It would not make him better just now. He needs the strength, the courage he has. Why endanger that? If you wait, of course, he might die before having considered that he might be wrong. So what? No eternal harm will have been done. Then why tell him, ever? I should not, unless he asked. But if he did, I should tell him what I think. Gently. *Eine kleine Nachtphilosophie.*

So many never ask. What about them? So many, though far less, do. Why not try to answer those who ask, which is more than there is time for, instead of seeking out those who don't? There are so many ways of asking. Taking a course, going to lectures, reading a book. Assuming the courses, lectures, and books are clearly labeled, and the author's, speaker's, or teacher's name gives some clue. Then those who come or read are asking a question; and to be less than truthful would be deception.

This does not mean preaching to the converted only. It makes so much more sense to answer those who truly ask, who do not want merely to be reassured. Some who ask feel sure that you are wrong, but still want to know what one as wrong as you might have to say. Tell them. When asked, do not lie.

Sometimes one waits long to be asked, wishes one were asked, minds that one isn't asked. Why should one be gentle and unobtrusive? Because one has heard Mozart? Seen pictures, read books, met people who were and others who were not?

So you want to be gentle but not genteel, honest but not obtrusive. Why not rather hard and relentless and, at all costs, uncompromising? How could one answer that question? In an age in which hardness is so out of fashion, one can respect it, perhaps even wish for a little more of it. But imagine an age, a society, in which it is the rule. Picture Sparta. Is that really what you want? Suppose he said, I do; precisely. What could you say then? Let us really look at Sparta, closely; and let us have a good look at Athens, too; and at Confucius, and at the Buddha, and the Law of Manu, with its ruthless treatment of outcastes; at Auschwitz; at Tolstoy; at Dostoevsky and Shakespeare. What more could one say? Only: read what I have read, with an open heart if possible; look and listen as I have; encounter what I have encountered, and think about it. I want to be gentle but not genteel, honest but not obtrusive. And you?

So you want to brainwash me? Not at all. The whole point is not to subject you to a torrent of indoctrination, not to drown criticism but to make you more thoughtful. To put my cards on the table. To say, Thinking about all these encounters is what has really led me to my code. See if it is lack of thoughtfulness that accounts for our disagreement. And if there are experiences I have not had, books I have not read that have helped to form you, tell me about them so I can read them and think about them. What more could I say?

More? Less, rather! Say no more. Quiet. I prefer Mozart. Who doesn't? But one cannot live all the time in lovely music. And one cannot savor its loveliness to the full unless one has suffered much. And one cannot endure it in perpetuity. Can one endure philosophy all the time? Of course not. Even less. Can one endure prophecy all the time? Still less. That is no reason why Jeremiah ought to have kept quiet. When the false prophets cry peace, peace, one should say firmly: There is no peace.

Bibliographical Index

The numbers in parenthesis refer to the sections in which the titles are cited.

Where German titles are listed, the translations in the text are my own, even if English versions are listed too, for the reader's convenience. Otherwise, where several editions are listed, the last one is the one cited in the text.

When no page references are given in the text and many editions are available, no edition is specified.

Austin, J. L., "A Plea for Excuses" in *Proceedings of the Aristotelian Society, New Series*, vol. LVII (1956–57). (14)
—— "Pretending," in *The Aristotelian Society Supplementary Volume*, XXXII (1958). (14) Both items are reprinted in Austin's *Philosophical Papers*, Oxford University Press, London, 1961.
Baeck, Leo, *Judaism and Christianity*, trans. with an introd. by Walter Kaufmann, Jewish Publication Society, Philadelphia, 1958; paperback edition, Meridian Books, N.Y., 1961. (57)
Barnes, H. E., and N. Teeters, *New Horizons in Criminology*, 2nd ed., Prentice-Hall, N.Y., 1951. (69)
Bible: I have followed the Revised Standard Version, except where I found good reasons for departing from it, after consulting other versions and the original Hebrew or Greek.
Billerbeck, Paul, and Hermann L. Strack, *Kommentar zum Neuen Testament aus Talmud und Midrasch*, 4 vols. in 5, C. H. Beck, München 1922–28, 2nd ed., unchanged but with Rabbinical Index vol., 1954–56. (37, 57)
Blake, William, *Poetry and Prose of*, ed. Geoffrey Keynes, complete in 1 vol., Nonesuch Press, London, and Random House, N.Y., 1927, 1946. This volume contains portions of "The Everlasting

Gospel: Written about 1818," not published previously. (60, 99)

Browning, Robert, *Andrea del Sarto*. (15)

Buber, Martin, *Die Erzählungen der Chassidim*, Manesse Verlag, Zürich, 1949, trans. by Olga Marx, *Tales of the Hassidim*, 2 vols., Schocken Books, N.Y., 1947–48; paperback edition, Schocken Books, 1961. (18, 83, 100)

Büchner, Georg, "Danton's Death," trans. by J. Holstrom in *The Modern Theatre*, ed. E. Bentley, vol. 5, Doubleday Anchor Books, N.Y., 1957. (97)

Bultmann, Rudolf, *Die Erforschung der synoptischen Evangelien*, Töpelmann, Giessen, 1925. Trans. by Frederick C. Grant, in *Form Criticism: A New Method of New Testament Research*, Willet, Clark & Co., Chicago and N.Y., 1934. (39)

—— and Karl Jaspers, *Die Frage der Entmythologisierung*; Piper, Munich, 1954; trans., *Myth and Christianity*; Noonday Press, N.Y., 1958. (27, 34)

—— *Theologie des Neuen Testaments*, Mohr, Tübingen, 1953, trans. by K. Grobel, *Theology of the New Testament*, 2 vols., Scribner, N.Y., 1951–55. (27, 39)

Calvin, John, *Institutes of the Christian Religion*; 2 vols., trans. by John Allen; 7th American ed., rev. and ed. by Benjamin B. War- field; Presbyterian Board of Christian Education, Philadelphia, 1936. (1, 70, 73, 77, 87)

Camus, Albert, *The Myth of Sisyphus and Other Essays*, trans. by J. O'Brien, Knopf, N.Y., 1955. (93, 96, 97)

—— "Reflections on the Guillotine," in *Evergreen Review*, 1957, reprinted, vol. IV.12, 1960. Reprinted in part in Kaufmann, *Religion from Tolstoy to Camus*. The complete text, in a different translation, is included in Camus, *Resistance, Rebellion, and Death*, Knopf, N.Y., 1961. (49)

Cassirer, Ernst, *Leibniz' System in seinen wissenschaftlichen Grundlagen*, Elwertsche Verlagsbuchhandlung, Marburg, 1902. (44)

Confucius, *The Analects of*, in *The Chinese Classics*, trans. by James Legge, Oxford University Press, 1865–95. There are several other good translations. (35, 57, 66)

Coulton, G. G., *Five Centuries of Religion*, vol. I, Cambridge University Press, 1923. (28)

—— *Infant Perdition in the Middle Ages: Medieval Studies No. 16*, Simpkin, London, 1922. (28)

Crawshay-Williams, R., *The Comforts of Unreason*, Kegan Paul, Trench, Trubner & Co., Ltd., London, 1947. (63)

Dodds, E. R., *The Greeks and the Irrational*, University of California Press, 1951, Beacon Press paperback, Boston, 1957. (9, 62, 63)

Enslin, Morton Scott, *Christian Beginnings,* Harper, N.Y., 1938, reprinted in 2 paperback vols., the 2nd (Part III) under the title *The Literature of the Christian Movement,* Harper Torchbooks, 1956. Selections in Kaufmann, *Religion from Tolstoy to Camus.* (30, 37, 57)

Farrar, Frederic W., *History of Interpretation,* E. P. Dutton, N.Y., 1886. (30)

Feifel, Herman, ed., *The Meaning of Death,* McGraw-Hill, N.Y., 1959. (94)

Fremantle, Anne, ed., *The Papal Encyclicals in Their Historical Context,* with introd. by Gustave Weigle, Mentor Books, N.Y., 1956. (28)

Freud, Sigmund; *Briefe 1873–1939,* ed. by Ernst L. Freud, S. Fischer, Frankfurt a. M., 1960. (88, 92)

—— *Gesammelte Schriften,* 12 vols., Internationaler Psychoanalytischer Verlag, 1925 ff. (24, 48, 69, 89, 92, 94, 96)

Fromm, Erich, *The Art of Loving,* Harper, N.Y., 1956. (89, 90)

—— *Sigmund Freud's Mission;* Harper, N.Y., 1959. (89, 90)

Gilson, Etienne, *The Christian Philosophy of St. Thomas Aquinas,* Random House, N.Y., 1956. (28)

—— ed., *The Church Speaks to the Modern World: The Social Teachings of Leo XIII,* Doubleday Image Books, N.Y., 1954. (28)

Goethe, J. W. v., *Faust: A New Translation and Introduction by Walter Kaufmann,* Doubleday, N.Y., 1961. (6, 10, 87, 91)

Grant, Frederick C., *Ancient Judaism and the New Testament,* Macmillan, N.Y., 1959. (17)

Hammurabi, Code of, in *Ancient Near Eastern Texts Relating to the Old Testament,* ed. by James B. Pritchard, 2nd rev. ed., Princeton University Press, 1955. (49, 50)

Harper's Bible Dictionary, by Madeleine S. Miller and J. Lane Miller, 6th ed., Harper, N.Y., 1959. (58)

Hay, Malcolm, *Europe and the Jews,* paperback ed. of *The Foot of Pride* (1950), Beacon Press, Boston, 1960. The first chapter is reprinted in Kaufmann, *Religion from Tolstoy to Camus.* (18, 68, 99)

Hegel, G. W. F., *Die Vernunft in der Geschichte,* ed. by Georg Lasson, 2nd rev. ed., Felix Meiner, Leipzig, 1920. (86)

Heidegger, Martin, *Sein und Zeit: Erste Hälfte,* Niemeyer, Halle, 1927. (93–95)

Heraclitus, in Kaufmann, *Philosophic Classics.* (5, 68)

Herberg, Will, *Protestant, Catholic, Jew*, rev. ed., Doubleday Anchor Books, N.Y., 1960. (69, 71)

Hesse, Hermann, *Die Morgenlandfahrt: eine Erzählung*, Fischer, Berlin, 1932, trans. by Hilda Rosner as *Journey to the East*, Noonday Press paperback, N.Y., 1957. (18)

Hillel. (30, 57, 59)

Hobbes, Thomas, *Leviathan.* (57)

Hölderlin, Friedrich, *"Nur einen Sommer."* (97)

Huxley, Aldous, *Brave New World.* (56, 78, 79)

Ikhnaton. *See* Hammurabi. (48)

Inoguchi, R., T. Nakajima, and Roger Pineau, *The Divine Wind: Japan's Kamikaze Force in World War II*, U. S. Naval Institute, 1958. (94)

James, William, "The Dilemma of Determinism," in *The Will to Believe and Other Essays in Popular Philosophy.* (2)

Jaspers, Karl, "Der Prophet Ezechiel," in *Rechenschaft und Ausblick: Reden und Aufsätze*, Piper, München, 1951. (39)

Jefferson, Thomas, *The Complete Jefferson*, ed. by Saul K. Padover, Duell, Sloan & Pearce, N.Y., 1943. (75)

Jones, Ernest, *The Life and Work of Sigmund Freud*, 3 vols., Basic Books, N.Y., 1953–57. (83, 87–89)

Kafka, Franz, "Von den Gleichnissen," in *Beschreibung eines Kampfes*, S. Fischer, Lizenzausgabe von Schooken Books, N.Y., 1946. (32)

Kant, Immanuel. (25, 73, 77)

Kaufmann, Walter, *Critique of Religion and Philosophy*, Harper, N.Y., 1958, Doubleday Anchor Books, N.Y., 1961.

—— ed., *Existentialism from Dostoevsky to Sartre*, Meridian Books, N.Y., 1956.

—— "The Faith of a Heretic," in *Harper's Magazine*, Feb. 1959, reprinted in *Essays of Our Time*, ed. by Hamalian and Volpe, McGraw-Hill, N.Y., 1960.

—— *From Shakespeare to Existentialism*, Beacon Press, Boston, 1959, rev. ed., Doubleday Anchor Books, N.Y., 1960.

—— *Nietzsche*, Princeton University Press, 1950, rev. ed., Meridian Books, N.Y., 1956.

—— ed., *Philosophic Classics*, 2 vols., 1st, *Thales to St. Thomas*, 2nd, *Bacon to Kant*, Prentice-Hall, N.Y., 1961.

—— ed., *Religion from Tolstoy to Camus*, Harper, N.Y., 1961.

—— *See also* Baeck, Feifel, Goethe, Hay, Nietzsche.

Keynes, Lord John M., "My Early Beliefs," in *Essays and Sketches in Biography*, Meridian Books, N.Y., 1956. (85)

Kierkegaard, Søren, *On Authority and Revelation: The Book on*

Adler, trans. by Walter Lowrie, Princeton University Press, 1955. (19)

—— *Fear and Trembling,* trans. by Walter Lowrie, Princeton University Press, 1941, 1954, rev. ed., Doubleday Anchor Books, N.Y., 1954. (19)

—— *The Journals,* ed. and trans. by Alexander Dru, Oxford University Press, 1938. (19)

Kleist, Heinrich von, *The Prince of Homburg,* trans. by J. Kirkup, *The Classic Theatre,* ed. by E. Bentley, vol. 2, Doubleday Anchor Books, N.Y., 1959. (97)

Lecky, William Edward Hartpole, *History of European Morals from Augustus to Charlemagne,* 2 vols., Longmans, Green, London, 1869. (98)

Leibniz, G. W. F., *Theodicy.* (44, 45)

Leo XIII, Pope, *Aeterni Patris,* reprinted complete in Kaufmann, *Religion from Tolstoy to Camus.* (28)

Lessing, G. E., *Nathan der Weise.* (80)

—— *Duplik.* (80)

Luther, Martin (19, 30, 36, 52, 57–60, 69–70, 73, 78). Where no edition is specified, references are to *Sämtliche Schriften,* ed. J. G. Walch, 24 vols., Halle, 1740–53. An asterisk (*) indicates references to the St. Louis reprint of this edition, with different pagination, 1881–1910. Erlangen edition means *Sämtliche Werke,* 67 vols., Erlangen 1826–57, plus 23 vols. of *Exegetica Opera Latina,* Erlangen, 1829–41. Weimar edition means *Werke,* over 80 vols. (not yet completed), including *Tischreden* and *Briefwechsel,* Weimar, 1883 ff. The letter cited in § 59 appears in *Briefwechsel,* vol. 5 (1934), in the original Latin; I have used the translation in *Luther: Letters of Spiritual Counsel,* ed. and trans. by T. G. Tappert, Westminster Press, Philadelphia, 1955. The other translations are my own.

Malcolm, Norman, *Ludwig Wittgenstein: A Memoir,* with a biographical sketch by George Henrik von Wright, Oxford University Press, 1958. (10, 88)

Manu, The Laws of, trans. by G. Bühler, *The Sacred Books of the East,* vol. XXV, Oxford University Press, 1886. (74)

Mill, John Stuart, *Examination of Sir William Hamilton's Philosophy.* (5, 43)

Milton, John, *Areopagitica.* (1)

—— *The Tenure of Kings and Magistrates.* (70)

Moore, George Foot, *History of Religions,* 2 vols., Scribner, N.Y., 1913–19, 1946–47. (42)

—— *Judaism in the First Centuries of the Christian Era, The Age of the Tannaim,* 3 vols., Harvard University Press, 1927–30. (58)

Mo-tze, *The Ethical and Political Works of Motse,* trans. by Yi-pao Mei, *Probsthain's Oriental Series,* vol. XIX, A. Probsthain, London, 1929. (66)

Murray, Gilbert, *Five Stages of Greek Religion,* Columbia University Press, N.Y., 1925; Beacon Press, Boston, 1951; Doubleday Anchor Books, N.Y., n.d. (62)

Niebuhr, H. Richard, *The Social Sources of Denominationalism,* Holt, N.Y., 1929; Living Age Books, Meridian Books, N.Y., 1957. (36, 37, 69, 70, 87)

Niemöller, Martin, *The Gestapo Defied,* William Hodge, Edinburgh, 1941. The sermon cited in the text is reprinted, along with two others, in Kaufmann, *Religion from Tolstoy to Camus.* (52)

Nietzsche, Friedrich, *The Portable Nietzsche,* selected and trans., with an introd., prefaces, and notes, by Walter Kaufmann, Viking, N.Y., 1954, paperback edition, 1958. (1, 13, 14, 16, 20, 24, 42, 49, 73, 89, 96, 97)

Orwell, George, *Nineteen Eighty-Four.* (20, 78)

Paley, William, *Principles of Moral and Political Philosophy.* (73)

Peyre, Henri, "Comment on Camus," in *The Virginia Quarterly Review,* vol. 34.4, Autumn 1958. (96)

Pius XII, Pope, "International Penal Law: Address to the Sixth International Congress of Penal Law, October 3, 1953," in *The Catholic Mind,* Feb. 1954. (49)

Plato, *Republic.* (14, 15, 76, 77, 79, 84; other works: 11, 44, 99)

Rosenzweig, Franz, *F. R.: His Life and Thought,* ed. N. N. Glatzer, Farrar, Straus, and Young, N.Y., 1953. (20)

Royce, Josiah, "The Problem of Job," in *Studies in Good and Evil;* reprinted complete in Kaufmann, *Religion from Tolstoy to Camus.* (45)

Ryle, Gilbert, *The Revolution in Philosophy,* by A. J. Ayer, W. C. Kneale, and others, with introd. by Gilbert T. Ryle, Macmillan, London, 1956. (12)

—— "Systematically Misleading Expressions," 1931–32, reprinted in *Logic and Language: First Series,* ed. by Anthony Flew, Basil Blackwell, Oxford, 1951. (12)

Sartre, Jean-Paul, *Being and Nothingness,* trans. by Hazel Barnes, Philosophical Library, N.Y., 1956. (1, 95, 97)

—— "Existentialism Is a Humanism" (86) and "Portrait of the Anti-Semite" (20, 85) in *Existentialism from Dostoevsky to Sartre,* ed. Walter Kaufmann, Meridian Books, N.Y., 1956.

—— "The Flies," in *No Exit and Three Other Plays,* Knopf, Vintage Books, 1955. (86, 93, 98)

—— "The Responsibility of the Writer," in *The Creative Vision: Modern European Writers on Their Art,* ed. by Haskell M. Block and Herman Salinger, Grove Press, N.Y., 1960. (16, 92)

Schweitzer, Albert, "Die Idee des Reiches Gottes im Verlaufe der Umbildung des eschatologischen Glaubens in den uneschatologischen," in *Schweizerische Theologische Umschau* (23. 1–2), Feb. 1953, trans. in E. N. Mozley, *The Theology of Albert Schweitzer,* Macmillan, N.Y., 1951. According to the British publisher, A. & C. Black, London, Schweitzer "put an enormous amount of work and time into the writing of this piece" and attaches considerable importance to it. Reprinted complete in Kaufmann, *Religion from Tolstoy to Camus.* (60)

Shakespeare, William. (15, 61, 87–92, 98)

Sutherland, Edwin H., *Principles of Criminology,* rev. by Donald R. Cressey, 5th ed., Lippincott, Chicago, Philadelphia, N.Y., 1955. (69)

Tawney, R. H., *Religion and the Rise of Capitalism,* Harcourt, Brace, N.Y., 1926, Mentor Books, N.Y., 1947. (87)

Thompson, R. Motson, *Nietzsche and Christian Ethics,* Philosophical Library, N.Y., 1951. (60)

Tillich, Paul, *Dynamics of Faith,* Harper, N.Y., 1957, Torchbooks, 1958. Reprinted in part in Kaufmann, *Religion from Tolstoy to Camus.* (32–34)

Tolstoy, Leo N., *The Death of Ivan Ilyitch.* Reprinted frequently; e.g., in Kaufmann, *Religion from Tolstoy to Camus.* (94)

—— *On Life and Essays on Religion,* trans., and with an introd. by Aylmer Maude, Oxford University Press, World Classics, 1943, 1950. (3, 37)

Toynbee, Arnold Joseph, *An Historian's Approach to Religion,* Oxford University Press, 1956. (58)

—— "Christus Patiens," in *A Study of History,* Vol. VI, 376–539, Oxford University Press, 1939. (58)

Troeltsch, Ernst, *Die Soziallehren der christlichen Kirchen und Gruppen,* Mohr, Tübingen, 1912, trans. by O. Wyon, *The Social Teaching* [singular] *of the Christian Churches,* 2 vols., Macmillan, N.Y., 1931, Harper Torchbooks, N.Y., 1960. (37, 57–61, 70)

Urmson, J. O., ed., *The Concise Encyclopedia of Western Philosophy and Philosophers,* Hawthorn Books, N.Y., 1960. (14)

Walsh, John, S.J., *This Is Catholicism,* Doubleday Image Books, N.Y., 1959. (28)

Warnock, Geoffrey, *English Philosophy Since 1900,* Oxford University Press, 1958. (12, 13)

West, Nathanael, *Miss Lonelyhearts,* in *The Complete Works of*

Nathanael West, Farrar, Straus, and Cudahy, N.Y., 1957. (43)

Westermarck, Edward, *The Origin and Development of the Moral Ideas,* 2 vols., Macmillan, London, 1906–8. (60)

White, William S., *The Taft Story,* Harper, N.Y., 1954. (49)

Whitehead, Alfred North, *Modes of Thought,* Macmillan, N.Y., 1938. (15)

Wilde, Oscar, Letter to the Editor of the *Daily Chronicle,* May 28, 1897, in the Modern Library ed. of *The Picture of Dorian Gray.* Reprinted in Kaufmann, *Religion from Tolstoy to Camus.* (19)

Wilson, John. *See* Hammurabi. (48)

Wittgenstein, Ludwig, *Philosophische Untersuchungen; Philosophical Investigations,* trans. by G. E. M. Anscombe on facing pages, Macmillan, N.Y., 1953. (10)

—— *Logisch-Philosophische Abhandlung; Tractatus Logico-Philosophicus,* Kegan Paul, London, 1922, 1933, with C. K. Ogden's English version on facing pages. (24)

Wright, Georg Henrik von. *See* Malcolm. (88)

Xenophanes, in Kaufmann, *Philosophic Classics.* (5)

Acknowledgments

This book owes much to philosophers, ministers, theologians, and students who graciously invited me to present some of my ideas in lectures, and to the long discussions that followed. They helped me to see my views in different perspectives and to relate them to the concerns of others.

Anne Freedgood has been, and is, an ideal editor. She has answered every question, giving helpful advice. To cite Paul, her faith in a heretic and in *The Faith of a Heretic* has been "patient and kind . . . not arrogant or rude . . . [and did] not insist on its own way." But happily, she did not believe all things.

W. K.

ANCHOR BOOKS

* Modern Studies in Philosophy Series

* Modern Studies in Philosophy Series

Philosophy (continued)

* Modern Studies in Philosophy Series

ANCHOR BOOKS

RELIGION

ANCHOR BOOKS

PSYCHOLOGY

Psychology (continued)